GROW

Discipleship Course

Liberty Church
Reaching Out & Raising Up

PO Box 274
300 1st Ave NW
Arab, AL 35016
256-931-4673

*Unless otherwise noted, all biblical quotations were taken
from the New Living Translation version of the Bible.

*Create interest, teaching comments, answer keys, and suggested
resources, for the presentation of the Grow lessons are notated in the Appendix.

"Every time I think of you, I give thanks to my God.
Whenever I pray, I make my request for all of you with joy,
for you have been my partners in spreading the Good News about Christ
from the time you first heard it until now.
And I am certain that God, who began the good work within you,
will continue his work until it is finally finished on the day when Christ Jesus returns.
(Phil 1:3-6).

Thank you to the following team members that developed this study guide:

Kevin & Jackie Wade + Larry & Teresa Ward - Grow I
Daryl & Donna Price + John & Pam Youngblood - Grow II
Rodney & Diana Harris + Micah Coker - Grow III
Nicholas Belpasso - Graphics

Curtis Snider – Editor
Nick Westenhofer – Editorial Updates @ Revision 7 & 8
Curtis & Diane Snider - Discipleship Elders
Keith & Kellie Hodges, Sr. Pastors

Revision 9
May 2, 2024

TABLE OF CONTENTS

INTRODUCTION TO GROW

The Discipleship Grow workbook is designed to take you on a 28-week journey to develop and be discipled into your full potential to fulfill God's plan for your life.

Grow I "Journey to Freedom" establishes six core values, after your salvation and baptism decision to follow Christ, that will be the foundation for you:

1. Stay in the Word
2. Stay in Prayer & Worship
3. Stay Filled with the Holy Spirit
4. Stay Connected & Submitted
5. Stay Humble
6. Stay Free - Moving Forward

The six core values are the fundamental basics of what it means to be a believer.

Grow II "Laying Foundations" and Grow III "Equipping and Developing Leaders" follows Grow I.

We hope that this workbook kindles a desire to continue spiritual growth, and in turn provide a disciplined path to discover your gifts and callings to be a disciple of Christ.

Discipleship begins with a life-changing Encounter Weekend. Followed by the

Additional information can be obtained by contacting Liberty Church via our web site www.libertychurchcampuses.com or calling 256-931-4673.

Grow I
Lessons

"Journey to Freedom"

GROW I
Journey to Freedom
Lesson 1

SALVATION, BAPTISM & FREEDOM

PURPOSE OF THIS LESSON:

To share the Good News of salvation through Jesus Christ, as the only way to Heaven. To understand what "being saved" means and give you the opportunity to accept the Gift of Salvation.

"Jesus told him, "I am the way, the truth, and the life. No one can come to the Father except through me" (John 14:6). "For by grace you have been saved through faith, and that not of yourselves; it is the gift of God," (Eph. 2:8). "If you openly declare that Jesus is Lord and believe in your heart that God raised him from the dead, you will be saved. For it is by believing in your heart that you are made right with God, and it is by openly declaring your faith that you are saved. For "Everyone who calls on the name of the Lord will be saved" (Rom. 10:9-10, 13).

Also, to understand the importance of water baptism to your deliverance, your new life and identity in Christ and how obedience relates to baptism. "So, beginning with this same Scripture, Philip told him the Good News about Jesus. As they rode along, they came to some water, and the eunuch said, "Look! There's some water! Why can't I be baptized" (Acts 8:35-36)? Notice in the former verse Philip shared the Good News about Jesus. Then in the latter verse the eunuch sees water and right away asks to be baptized. Although, scripture does not reveal the exact words Philip spoke while sharing the gospel of Christ it is apparent, he shared the importance of water Baptism in the name of the Father, Son, and Holy Spirit. "Therefore, go and make disciples of all the nations, baptizing them in the name of the Father and the Son and the Holy Spirit" (Matt. 28:19).

In addition, this lesson will show the power of deliverance, the role it plays in being set free and to identify ways Satan seeks to retain control in our lives. "The righteous cry out, and the Lord hears, And delivers them out of all their troubles" (Ps. 34:17 NKJV). "Jesus said to the people who believed in him, "You are truly my disciples if you remain faithful to my teachings. And you will know the truth, and the truth will set you free" (John 8:31-32).

INTRODUCTION:

At salvation, you applied the blood of Jesus, the Lamb of God to your heart, and you left your Egypt (sin) behind.

"And this is the testimony: that God has given us eternal life, and this life is in His Son. He who has the Son has life; he who does not have the Son of God does not have life" (1 John 5:11-12 NKJV). Now, like the children of Israel, you will have to walk to your promised land. But first, you must cross the Red Sea. There is no other way to get to your promised land God has waiting for you. Pharaoh, who is symbolic of Satan, did not give up because the people left Egypt. He decided to go after them. He planned to enslave the Israelites again, but God had an even bigger plan. "Then the waters returned and covered all the chariots and charioteers-the entire army of Pharaoh. Of all the Egyptians who had chased the Israelites into the sea, not a single one survived" (Exod. 14:28).

Water baptism is, therefore, quite necessary-not for your salvation (the blood of the Lamb did that), but for your freedom. Baptism is the death and burial of ourselves and Resurrection of Christ in Us.

"For you are all children of God through faith in Christ Jesus. And all who have been united with Christ in baptism have put on Christ, like putting on new clothes" (Gal. 3:26-27). Crossing the Red Sea symbolizes water baptism, providing your deliverance from the devil, his oppression and deception. "The thief's purpose is to steal and kill and destroy. My purpose is to give them a rich and satisfying life" (John 10:10). You must cross your Red Sea to be truly free of your enemies and walk in your new identity in Christ to your promised land. "I am crucified with Christ: nevertheless, I live; yet not I, but Christ liveth in me: and the life which I now live in the flesh I live by the faith of the Son of God, who loved me, and gave himself for me" (Gal. 2:20 KJV).

Jesus has done everything necessary for your deliverance. He is our deliverer! "Call upon Me in the day of trouble; I will deliver you, and you shall glorify Me" (Ps. 50:15 NKJV). "The righteous cry out, and the Lord hears, And delivers them out of all their troubles" (Ps. 34:17 NKJV). "But when people keep on sinning, it shows that they belong to the devil, who has been sinning since the beginning. But the Son of God came to destroy the works of the devil" (1 John 3:8). "For the wages of sin is death, but the free gift of God is eternal life through Christ Jesus our Lord" (Rom. 6:23). "For all who are led by the Spirit of God are children of God. So, you have not received a spirit that makes you fearful slaves. Instead, you received God's Spirit when he adopted you as his own children. Now we call him, "Abba, Father" (Rom. 8:14-15).

WHY IS THIS LESSON IMPORTANT TO YOUR LIFE?

This is the most important lesson because whether you choose to receive Jesus Christ as your Lord and Savior determines where you will spend eternity ~ Heaven or Hell. No one lives forever here on earth, so what you choose determines where you will spend eternity.

"That is the way it will be at the end of the world. The angels will come and separate the wicked people from the righteous, throwing the wicked into the fiery furnace, where there will be weeping and gnashing of teeth" (Matt. 13:49-50). "And they will go away into eternal punishment, but the righteous will go into eternal life" (Matt. 25:46). "You can enter God's Kingdom only through the narrow gate. The highway to hell is broad, and its gate is wide for the many who choose that way. But the gateway to life is very narrow and the road is difficult, and only a few ever find it" (Matt. 7:13-14). "Yes, I am the gate. Those who come in through me will be saved. They will come and go freely and will find good pastures" (John 10:9)."I have written this to you who believe in the name of the Son of God, so that you may know you have eternal life" (1 John 5:13). Based on these scriptures and what you know so far, where do   you believe you will spend eternity?

ABCs OF SALVATION: What must I do to be saved?
"Then he brought them out and asked, "Sirs, what must I do to be saved?" (Acts 16:30).

Admit you have sinned.
"For all have sinned and fall short of the glory of God" (Rom. 3:23 NKJV).

Believe in Jesus Christ.
"For God so loved the world that He gave His only begotten Son, that whoever believes in Him should not perish but have everlasting life. For God did not send His Son into the world to condemn the world, but that the world through Him might be saved" (John 3:16-17 NKJV).
Confess your sins and your salvation.
"If we confess our sins, He is faithful and just to forgive us our sins and to cleanse us from all unrighteousness" (1 John 1:9 NKJV). "If you confess with your mouth, the Lord Jesus and believe in

your heart that God raised Him from the dead, you will be saved. For with the heart one believes unto righteousness, and with the mouth, confession is made unto salvation" (Rom. 10:9-10 NKJV).

We invite you now to make the best decision you have ever made and receive Christ as your Lord and Savior. It is as simple as ABC.

PRAYER FOR SALVATION:

God, I confess to You that I have sinned.
Your Word says that You are faithful, and You will forgive me and cleanse me from all my sins.
Jesus, I believe You died on the cross for my sins and that You rose again.
I accept You right now, as my personal Lord and Savior.
I give You my heart, and I give You, my life.
I turn away from the things in my life that are not right.
Change me and make me the person You want me to be.
Thank You, Jesus! By faith in Your Word, I am saved.
I am born again. I am a Child of God. I am a Christian.
In Jesus' name. Amen.

CELEBRATE SALVATIONS:

"In the same way, there is joy in the presence of God's angels when even one sinner repents" (Luke 15:10).

THE POWER OF WATER BAPTISM:

You must understand your old enemies have been defeated by the work on the cross. Jesus has done everything necessary for your deliverance. He is our deliverer! You must learn how to "declare" your freedom from Satan and forcefully evict him from your life. The Red Sea is important to our lives because it is a picture of water baptism. "In the cloud and in the sea, all of them were baptized as followers of Moses" (1 Cor. 10:2). You need to be baptized at the beginning of your Christian journey as followers of Christ. Jesus replied, "I assure you no one can enter the Kingdom of God without being born of water and the Spirit" (John 3:5). "Therefore, go and make disciples of all the nations, [all peoples] baptizing them in the name of the Father and the Son and the Holy Spirit" (Matt. 28:19). "Anyone who believes and is baptized will be saved. But anyone who refuses to believe will be condemned" (Mark 16:16).

Peter replied, "Each of you must repent of your sins and turn to God and be baptized in the name of Jesus Christ for the forgiveness of your sins. Then you will receive the gift of the Holy Spirit. This promise is to you, to your children, and to those far away [to people far in the future]—all who have been called by the Lord our God" (Acts 2:38-39).

Being baptized is symbolic of the death, burial, and resurrection of our Lord Jesus Christ. Jesus died for all our sins on the cross. We die to sin when we turn to him as our Savior. After his death, Jesus' body was taken down from the cross and placed in a grave. Our bodies are "buried" in the waters of baptism to represent this. After three days, Jesus rose from the dead in victory. When we come out of the waters of baptism, we rise to a new life of victory and power in Christ.

Let's examine four important aspects of baptism.

1. Baptism symbolizes the death and burial of your old life.

"I am crucified with Christ: nevertheless, I live; yet not I, but Christ liveth in me: and the life which I now live in the flesh I live by the faith of the Son of God, who loved me, and gave himself for me" (Gal. 2:20 KJV).

"Well then, should we keep on sinning so that God can show us more and more of his wonderful grace? Of course not! Since we have died to sin, how can we continue to live in it? Or have you forgotten that when we were joined with Christ Jesus in baptism, we joined him in his death? For we died and were buried with Christ by baptism. And just as Christ was raised from the dead by the glorious power of the Father, now we also may live new lives. Since we have been united with him in his death, we will also be raised to life as he was. We know that our old sinful selves were crucified with Christ so that sin might lose its power in our lives. We are no longer slaves to sin. 7 For when we died with Christ, we were set free from the power of sin. And since we died with Christ, we know we will also live with him. We are sure of this because Christ was raised from the dead, and he will never die again. Death no longer has any power over him. When he died, he died once to break the power of sin. But now that he lives, he lives for the glory of God. So, you also should consider yourselves to be dead to the power of sin and alive to God through Christ Jesus" (Rom 6:1-11).

Baptism is for individuals who have already trusted in Jesus as savior. When you repent of your sins (change the way you think, line up the way you think and live your life with the Word of God) and ask Jesus to be the Lord of your life, you die to your old life of sin. When you are water baptized, you are immersed in the water, just like Jesus was when John baptized Him in the Jordan River. "One day Jesus came from Nazareth in Galilee, and John baptized him in the Jordan River. 10 As Jesus came up out of the water, he saw the heavens splitting apart and the Holy Spirit descending on him like a dove. 11 And a voice from heaven said, "You are my dearly loved Son, and you bring me great joy" (Mark 1:9-11). This going down into the water is like a burial. It symbolizes that your old life has ended and that you are starting a brand-new life. Paul said, "Therefore we are buried with Him through baptism into death, so that as Christ was raised from the dead through the glory of the Father, so we too might walk in newness of life" (Rom. 6:4 NASB).

2. Baptism is a celebration of your new life.

"This means that anyone who belongs to Christ has become a new person. The old life is gone; a new life has begun!" (1 Cor. 5:17).

So, Moses said to the people, "This is a day to remember forever-the day you left Egypt, the place of your slavery. Today the Lord has brought you out by the power of his mighty hand. (Remember, eat no food containing yeast.) On this day in early spring, in the month of Abib, you have been set free. You must celebrate this event in this month each year after the Lord brings you into the land of the Canaanites, Hittites, Amorites, Hivites, and Jebusites. (He swore to your ancestors that he would give you this land-a land flowing with milk and honey.)" (Exod. 13:3-5).

God commanded Moses and the children of Israel to remember the day they left Egypt, the place of their slavery, and to celebrate this event. Baptism is a celebration of the day you left your slavery to sin. Your old sinful self was nailed to the cross and buried with Jesus, and now through his resurrection, you have come alive to a brand-new reality. In baptism, we celebrate this repentance and faith in Christ. When you are baptized in the name of the Father, and the Son, and the Holy Spirit, we celebrate the involvement of the whole Godhead in this conversion and the new relationship to each person in the Trinity. When you are immersed in the water, we celebrate the death and burial of Jesus for our sins. When you are raised out of the water, we celebrate the resurrection of Jesus and your resurrection to a new life in Christ. When you walk out of the baptismal water, we celebrate the newness of life in love and joy that Jesus gives.

3. Baptism is important for your cleanse your conscience.

Your conscience is that part of your soul that either condemns you or assures you of who you are in Christ. "And that water is a picture of baptism, which now saves you, not by removing dirt from your body, but as a response to God from a clean conscience. It is effective because of the resurrection of Jesus Christ" (1 Pet.3:21). Your conscience needs to feel clean, like it has had a bath and that's what water baptism does for you. It's a point in time when you publicly declare before a group of witnesses that you have buried the past and are moving on in your journey with the Lord. "let us go right into the presence of God with sincere hearts fully trusting him. For our guilty consciences have been sprinkled with Christ's blood to make us clean, and our bodies have been washed with pure water" (Heb. 10:22). This is just what water baptism does for you!

4. Baptism is the immersion of a believer in water.

"After his baptism, as Jesus came up out of the water, the heavens were opened, and he saw the Spirit of God descending like a dove and settling on him" (Matt. 3:16).

The Greek word for baptism is "baptizo," which means washing or being immersed in water. This immersion is the outward expression (symbol) of an inward change (grace). Symbolically you are buried in a watery grave, covered from head to toe with God's love, and washed clean by the blood of Jesus. New Testament baptism by immersion follows Jesus' example. Matthew writes that "Jesus came up out of the water." Therefore, baptism is by immersion and only practiced after one's profession of faith in Christ. It should be done as soon as possible after salvation.

THE POWER OF DELIVERANCE:

Understanding the power of deliverance is important for two reasons:

1. You must understand that just as Pharaoh had an army that pursued the children of Israel, so does Satan. He and his armies of demons and powers pursue you and seek to retain control in your life even after you are saved. You must identify his schemes, the ways he tries to keep you in bondage. What is one area of your life where Satan is seeking control?

_____

_____

_____

_____

2. You must understand your old enemies have been defeated by the work on the cross. Just as God used Moses to deliver the Israelites, Jesus has done everything necessary for your deliverance. He is our deliverer! You must learn how to "declare" your freedom from Satan and forcefully evict him from your life.

What does it mean to "declare" your freedom?

_____

_____

_____

_____

SATAN SEEKS TO RETAIN CONTROL IN YOUR LIFE:
Many new Christians do not stay free because they have not completely renounced and removed Satan as an illegal resident in their lives. They opened a door and let him in, thus giving him a legal foothold from which he can operate. He then will try to control your body, mind, and heart.
There are four main ways Satan seeks to retain control in your life.

Generational Sins
Generational sin is an open door in your life that you did not open. Your ancestors gave a place to the enemy through sin. These sins are patterns of addiction, habits, criminal activity, divorce, poverty, anger, perfection, etc. that have moved through your family line for years. Generational sins take a stronghold because this way of life seems normal to you. There is a demonic pressure on you to follow their pattern of sin even if you do not want to. "You must not bow down to them or worship them, for I, the Lord your God, am a jealous God who will not tolerate your affection for any other gods. I lay the sins of the parents upon their children; the entire family is affected—even children in the third and fourth generations of those who reject me" (Exod. 20:5). "Then the Lord came down in a cloud and stood there with him; and he called out his own name, Yahweh. The Lord passed in front of Moses, calling out, "Yahweh! The Lord! The God of compassion and mercy! I am slow to anger and filled with unfailing love and faithfulness. I lavish unfailing love to a thousand generations. I forgive iniquity, rebellion, and sin. But I do not excuse the guilt. I lay the sins of the parents upon their children and grandchildren; the entire family is affected-even children in the third and fourth generations" (Exod. 34:5-9). "Don't you realize that you become the slave of whatever you choose to obey? You can be a slave to sin, which leads to death, or you can choose to obey God, which leads to righteous living" (Rom. 6:16).

Curses
Curses are a second way Satan tries to control you. Curses come when you willingly sin and open a door and let Satan in. God told Israel if they broke the commands of the law, a curse would come on them in every aspect of their lives. When you live in violation of God's word, Satan has a legal right to enforce the curse of the law. "But Christ has rescued us from the curse pronounced by the law. When he was hung on the cross, he took upon himself the curse for our wrongdoing. For it is written in the Scriptures, "Cursed is everyone who is hung on a tree." Through Christ Jesus, God has blessed the Gentiles with the same blessing he promised to Abraham, so that we who are believers might receive the promised Holy Spirit through faith" (Gal. 3:13-14).

Blessings for Obedience:
"If you fully obey the Lord your God and carefully keep all his commands that I am giving you today, the Lord your God will set you high above all the nations of the world. You will experience all these blessings if you obey the Lord your God: Your towns and your fields will be blessed. Your children and your crops will be blessed. The offspring of your herds and flocks will be blessed. Your fruit baskets and breadboards will be blessed. Wherever you go and whatever you do, you will be blessed. "The Lord will conquer your enemies when they attack you. They will attack you from one direction, but they will scatter from you in seven! "The Lord will guarantee a blessing on everything you do and will fill your storehouses with grain. The Lord your God will bless you in the land he is giving you. "If you obey the commands of the Lord your God and walk in his ways, the Lord will establish you as his holy people as he swore, he would do. Then all the nations of the world will see that you are a people claimed by the Lord, and they will stand in awe of you. "The Lord will give you prosperity in the land he swore to your ancestors to give you, blessing you with many children, numerous livestock, and abundant crops. The Lord will send rain at the proper time from his rich treasury in the heavens and

will bless all the work you do. You will lend to many nations, but you will never need to borrow from them. If you listen to these commands of the Lord your God that I am giving you today, and if you carefully obey them, the Lord will make you the head and not the tail, and you will always be on top and never at the bottom. You must not turn away from any of the commands I am giving you today, nor follow after other gods and worship them. (Deut. 28:1-14).

Curses for Disobedience:
15 "But if you refuse to listen to the Lord your God and do not obey all the commands and decrees, I am giving you today, all these curses will come and overwhelm you: 16 Your towns and your fields will be cursed. 17 Your fruit baskets and breadboards will be cursed. 18 Your children and your crops will be cursed. The offspring of your herds and flocks will be cursed. 19 Wherever you go and whatever you do, you will be cursed. 20 "The Lord himself will send on you curses, confusion, and frustration in everything you do, until at last you are completely destroyed for doing evil and abandoning me. 21 The Lord will afflict you with diseases until none of you are left in the land you are about to enter and occupy. 22 The Lord will strike you with wasting diseases, fever, and inflammation, with scorching heat and drought, and with blight and mildew. These disasters will pursue you until you die. 23 The skies above will be as unyielding as bronze, and the earth beneath will be as hard as iron. 24 The Lord will change the rain that falls on your land into powder, and dust will pour down from the sky until you are destroyed. 25 "The Lord will cause you to be defeated by your enemies. You will attack your enemies from one direction, but you will scatter from them in seven! You will be an object of horror to all the kingdoms of the earth. 26 Your corpses will be food for all the scavenging birds and wild animals, and no one will be there to chase them away. 27 "The Lord will afflict you with the boils of Egypt and with tumors, scurvy, and the itch, from which you cannot be cured. 28 The Lord will strike you with madness, blindness, and panic. 29 You will grope around in broad daylight like a blind person groping in the darkness, but you will not find your way. You will be oppressed and robbed continually, and no one will come to save you. 30 "You will be engaged to a woman, but another man will sleep with her. You will build a house, but someone else will live in it. You will plant a vineyard, but you will never enjoy its fruit. 31 Your ox will be butchered before your eyes, but you will not eat a single bite of the meat. Your donkey will be taken from you, never to be returned. Your sheep and goats will be given to your enemies, and no one will be there to help you. 32 You will watch as your sons and daughters are taken away as slaves. Your heart will break for them, but you won't be able to help them. 33 A foreign nation you have never heard about will eat the crops you worked so hard to grow. You will suffer under constant oppression and harsh treatment. 34 You will go mad because of all the tragedy you see around you. 35 The Lord will cover your knees and legs with incurable boils. In fact, you will be covered from head to foot. 36 "The Lord will exile you and your king to a nation unknown to you and your ancestors. There in exile you will worship gods of wood and stone! 37 You will become an object of horror, ridicule, and mockery among all the nations to which the Lord sends you. 38 "You will plant much but harvest little, for locusts will eat your crops. 39 You will plant vineyards and care for them, but you will not drink the wine or eat the grapes, for worms will destroy the vines. 40 You will grow olive trees throughout your land, but you will never use the olive oil, for the fruit will drop before it ripens. 41 You will have sons and daughters, but you will lose them, for they will be led away into captivity. 42 Swarms of insects will destroy your trees and crops. 43 "The foreigners living among you will become stronger and stronger, while you become weaker and weaker. 44 They will lend money to you, but you will not lend to them. They will be the head, and you will be the tail! 45 "If you refuse to listen to the Lord your God and to obey the commands and decrees, he has given you, all these curses will pursue and overtake you until you are destroyed. 46 These horrors will serve as a sign and warning among you and your descendants forever. 47 If you do not serve the Lord your God with joy and enthusiasm for the abundant benefits you have

received, 48 you will serve your enemies whom the Lord will send against you. You will be left hungry, thirsty, naked, and lacking in everything. The Lord will put an iron yoke on your neck, oppressing you harshly until he has destroyed you. 49 "The Lord will bring a distant nation against you from the end of the earth, and it will swoop down on you like a vulture. It is a nation whose language you do not understand, 50 a fierce and heartless nation that shows no respect for the old and no pity for the young. 51 Its armies will devour your livestock and crops, and you will be destroyed. They will leave you no grain, new wine, olive oil, calves, or lambs, and you will starve to death. 52 They will attack your cities until all the fortified walls in your land—the walls you trusted to protect you—are knocked down. They will attack all the towns in the land the Lord your God has given you. 53 "The siege and terrible distress of the enemy's attack will be so severe that you will eat the flesh of your own sons and daughters, whom the Lord your God has given you. 54 The most tenderhearted man among you will have no compassion for his own brother, his beloved wife, and his surviving children. 55 He will refuse to share with them the flesh he is devouring—the flesh of one of his own children—because he has nothing else to eat during the siege and terrible distress that your enemy will inflict on all your towns. 56 The most tender and delicate woman among you—so delicate she would not so much as touch the ground with her foot—will be selfish toward the husband she loves and toward her own son or daughter. 57 She will hide from them the afterbirth and the new baby she has borne, so that she herself can secretly eat them. She will have nothing else to eat during the siege and terrible distress that your enemy will inflict on all your towns. 58 "If you refuse to obey all the words of instruction that are written in this book, and if you do not fear the glorious and awesome name of the Lord your God, 59 then the Lord will overwhelm you and your children with indescribable plagues. These plagues will be intense and without relief, making you miserable and unbearably sick. 60 He will afflict you with all the diseases of Egypt that you feared so much, and you will have no relief. 61 The Lord will afflict you with every sickness and plague there is, even those not mentioned in this Book of Instruction, until you are destroyed. 62 Though you become as numerous as the stars in the sky, few of you will be left because you would not listen to the Lord your God. 63 "Just as the Lord has found great pleasure in causing you to prosper and multiply, the Lord will find pleasure in destroying you. You will be torn from the land you are about to enter and occupy. 64 For the Lord will scatter you among all the nations from one end of the earth to the other. There you will worship foreign gods that neither you nor your ancestors have known, gods made of wood and stone! 65 There among those nations you will find no peace or place to rest. And the Lord will cause your heart to tremble, your eyesight to fail, and your soul to despair. 66 Your life will constantly hang in the balance. You will live night and day in fear, unsure if you will survive. 67 In the morning you will say, 'If only it were night!' And in the evening, you will say, 'If only it were morning!' For you will be terrified by the awful horrors you see around you. 68 Then the Lord will send you back to Egypt in ships, to a destination I promised you would never see again. There you will offer to sell yourselves to your enemies as slaves, but no one will buy you" (Deut. 28:15-68).

Soul Ties
Soul ties are a third tactic Satan uses against you. A soul tie is an open door for Satan to enter your life through ungodly relationships. It is a covenant with another person based on an unhealthy emotional and /or sexual relationship. You form an ungodly soul tie when you join yourself sexually to another person. The Bible is clear that sex is only between a man and woman and only in marriage. "Give honor to marriage and remain faithful to one another in marriage. God will surely judge people who are immoral and those who commit adultery" (Heb. 13:4). We also can form ungodly soul ties with people when we allow them to have ungodly control over us. They use guilt, fear, or manipulation to control us and get us to do things we would not otherwise do. "God's will is for you to be holy, so stay away from all sexual sin. Then each of you will control his own body and live in holiness and honor-

not in lustful passion like the pagans who do not know God and his ways. Never harm or cheat a fellow believer in this matter by violating his wife, for the Lord avenges all such sins, as we have solemnly warned you before. God has called us to live holy lives, not impure lives. Therefore, anyone who refuses to live by these rules is not disobeying human teaching but is rejecting God, who gives his Holy Spirit to you" (1 Thess. 4:3-8). God forbids us to participate in ungodly relationships just as he forbade Israel in the Old Testament. " But if you fail to drive out the people who live in the land, those who remain will be like splinters in your eyes and thorns in your sides. They will harass you in the land where you live" (Num. 33:55). "Let there be no sexual immorality, impurity, or greed among you. Such sins have no place among God's people" (Eph. 5:3). "He is especially hard on those who follow their own twisted sexual desire, and who despise authority. These people are proud and arrogant, daring even to scoff at supernatural beings without so much as trembling. But the angels, who are far greater in power and strength, do not dare to bring from the Lord a charge of blasphemy against those supernatural beings. These false teachers are like unthinking animals, creatures of instinct, born to be caught and destroyed. They scoff at things they do not understand, and like animals, they will be destroyed. Their destruction is their reward for the harm they have done. They love to indulge in evil pleasures in broad daylight. They are a disgrace and a stain among you. They delight in deception even as they eat with you in your fellowship meals. They commit adultery with their eyes, and their desire for sin is never satisfied. They lure unstable people into sin, and they are well trained in greed. They live under God's curse. They have wandered off the right road and followed the footsteps of Balaam son of Beor, who loved to earn money by doing wrong. But Balaam was stopped from his mad course when his donkey rebuked him with a human voice. These people are as useless as dried-up springs or as mist blown away by the wind. They are doomed to blackest darkness. They brag about themselves with empty, foolish boasting. With an appeal to twisted sexual desires, they lure back into sin those who have barely escaped from a lifestyle of deception. They promise freedom, but they themselves are slaves of sin and corruption. For you are a slave to whatever controls you. And when people escape from the wickedness of the world by knowing our Lord and Savior Jesus Christ and then get tangled up and enslaved by sin again, they are worse off than before. It would be better if they had never known the way to righteousness than to know it and then reject the command, they were given to live a holy life. They prove the truth of this proverb: "A dog returns to its vomit." And another says, "A washed pig returns to the mud" (2 Peter 2:10-22). "Run from sexual sin! No other sin so clearly affects the body as this one does. For sexual immorality is a sin against your own body. Don't you realize that your body is the temple of the Holy Spirit, who lives in you and was given to you by God? You do not belong to yourself, for God bought you with a high price. So, you must honor God with your body" (1 Cor. 6:18-20).

Mental and Emotional Bondage

A fourth way Satan seeks to control is to attack your thoughts and emotions. When the Israelites came out of Egypt, the greatest challenge for them was coming out of a bondage mentality. Satan will do everything he can to drag you back to your Egypt (sin). He will try to get you to look back and long for the "good old days" instead of keeping your focus on your journey ahead. He will try to keep you in the grip of bitterness, unforgiveness, fear, anxiety, etc. He wants to make sin look good and living for God hard. "As Pharaoh approached, the people of Israel looked up and panicked when they saw the Egyptians overtaking them. They cried out to the Lord, and they said to Moses, "Why did you bring us out here to die in the wilderness? Weren't there enough graves for us in Egypt? What have you done to us? Why did you make us leave Egypt? Didn't we tell you this would happen while we were still in Egypt? We said, 'Leave us alone! Let us be slaves to the Egyptians. It's better to be a slave in Egypt than a corpse in the wilderness!" But Moses told the people, "Don't be afraid. Just stand still and watch the Lord rescue you today. The Egyptians you see today will never be seen again. The Lord himself will fight for you. Just stay calm" (Exod. 14:10-14). "If only the Lord had killed us back in Egypt," they moaned. "There we sat around pots filled with meat and ate all the bread we wanted. But now you have brought us into this wilderness to starve us all to death" (Exod. 16:3).

LESSON SUMMARY:

- "Jesus told him, "I am the way, the truth, and the life. No one can come to the Father except through me" (John 14:6).

- "If you openly declare that Jesus is Lord and believe in your heart that God raised him from the dead, you will be saved. For it is by believing in your heart that you are made right with God, and it is by openly declaring your faith that you are saved" (Rom. 10:9-10).

- "For by grace, you have been saved through faith, and that not of yourselves; it is the gift of God," (Eph. 2:8 NKJV).

- "If we confess our sins, He is faithful and just to forgive us our sins and to cleanse us from all unrighteousness" (1 John 1:9 NKJV).

- "I am crucified with Christ: nevertheless, I live; yet not I, but Christ liveth in me: and the life which I now live in the flesh I live by the faith of the Son of God, who loved me, and gave himself for me" (Gal. 2:20 KJV).

- "Jesus said to the people who believed in him, "You are truly my disciples if you remain faithful to my teachings. And you will know the truth, and the truth will set you free" (John 8:31-32).

*Note: Lesson Slides end at this point.

OBEDIENCE PRECEDES BLESSING:

Tell someone that you got saved.
"If you openly declare that Jesus is Lord and believe in your heart that God raised him from the dead, you will be saved. For it is by believing in your heart that you are made right with God, and it is by openly declaring your faith that you are saved. For "Everyone who calls on the name of the Lord will be saved" (Rom. 10:9-10, 13).

Tell someone else about Jesus.
"Andrew, Simon Peter's brother, was one of these men who heard what John said and then followed Jesus. Andrew went to find his brother, Simon, and told him, "We have found the Messiah" (which means "Christ"). Then Andrew brought Simon to meet Jesus. Looking intently at Simon, Jesus said, "Your name is Simon, son of John—but you will be called Cephas" (which means "Peter")." (John 1:40-42). "For I am not ashamed of this Good News about Christ. It is the power of God at work, saving everyone who believes—the Jew first and also the Gentile" (Rom. 1:16).

There is a story about an old man, walking the beach at dawn, who noticed a boy ahead of him picking up starfish and flinging them into the sea. Catching up with the boy, he asked what he was doing. The answer was that the stranded starfish would die if left in the morning sun. "But the beach goes on for miles and miles, and there are millions of starfish," asked the old man. "How can your effort make any difference?" The young man looked at the starfish in his hand and then threw it safely into the ocean. "It makes a difference to this one," the boy said.
Be a Difference Maker!   Each one, reach one!   And then one more.   And one more.

Water baptism is the first step of obedience after receiving our salvation.
Obedience demonstrates the surrender of the human will to the sovereignty of God expressed in his word and through the Holy Spirit. Jesus himself stated that we must lose our lives to find them, meaning that we must take up our cross and follow him. "Then he said to the crowd, "If any of you wants to be my follower, you must give up your own way, take up your cross daily, and follow me. If you try to hang on to your life, you will lose it. But if you give up your life for my sake, you will save it" (Luke 9:23-24). By water baptism, we are following Jesus' example. "Then Jesus went from Galilee to the Jordan River to be baptized by John. But John tried to talk him out of it. "I am the one who needs to be baptized by you," he said, "so why are you coming to me?" But Jesus said, "It should be done, for we must carry out all that God requires." So, John agreed to baptize him" (Matt.3:13-15). Jesus was sinless and needed no baptism, for He was God himself, but he did this anyway to leave us an example to follow. By being baptized, we are also following His command. "Therefore, go and make disciples of all the nations, baptizing them in the name of the Father and the Son and the Holy Spirit" (Matt. 28:19). So important is this step that, as far as we know, every single convert in the New Testament was baptized. Except for the thief on the cross there is no example of an unbaptized believer. "One of the criminals hanging beside him scoffed, "So you're the Messiah, are you? Prove it by saving yourself-and us, too, while you're at it!" But the other criminal protested, "Don't you fear God even when you have been sentenced to die? We deserve to die for our crimes, but this man hasn't done anything wrong." Then he said, "Jesus, remember me when you come into your Kingdom." And Jesus replied, "I assure you, today you will be with me in paradise" (Luke 23:39-43). If you have not yet taken this step of obedience, sign up for the next Water Baptism at your church.
Jesus says, "So why do you keep calling me Lord, Lord! when you don't do what I say?" (Luke 6:46). Why is it important to be obedient to Jesus' command concerning baptism?

_____

_____

_____

_____

DELIVERANCE FROM STRONGHOLDS:
You can break Satan's strongholds. Generational sins, curses, soul ties, and mental bondages have all been broken by the blood of Jesus on the cross. However, you must declare your total freedom from Satan's demonic powers, destructive habits, addictions, emotions, thoughts, and relationships.

Let's examine four ways we can break Satan's strongholds.

1. Learn to rely only on God.
God is our way maker and bondage breaker. He makes a way of escape where there seems to be no way. The children of Israel thought they were trapped between Pharaoh and the Red Sea, but God had a miracle for them. "The Lord himself will fight for you. Just stay calm" (Exod. 14:14). He stands with you and gives you strength. "But the Lord stood with me and gave me strength so that I might preach the Good News in its entirety for all the Gentiles to hear. And he rescued me from certain death" (2 Tim. 4:17). and He will continue to deliver us. "And he did rescue us from mortal danger, and he will rescue us again. We have placed our confidence in him, and he will continue to rescue us" (2 Cor. 1:10).
"As Pharaoh approached, the people of Israel looked up and panicked when they saw the Egyptians overtaking them. They cried out to the Lord, and they said to Moses, "Why did you bring us out here to die in the wilderness? Weren't there enough graves for us in Egypt? What have you done to us?

Why did you make us leave Egypt? Didn't we tell you this would happen while we were still in Egypt? We said, 'Leave us alone! Let us be slaves to the Egyptians. It's better to be a slave in Egypt than a corpse in the wilderness!'" But Moses told the people, "Don't be afraid. Just stand still and watch the Lord rescue you today. The Egyptians you see today will never be seen again. The Lord himself will fight for you. Just stay calm" (Exod. 14:10-14). "We think you ought to know, dear brothers and sisters, about the trouble we went through in the province of Asia. We were crushed and overwhelmed beyond our ability to endure, and we thought we would never live through it. In fact, we expected to die. But as a result, we stopped relying on ourselves and learned to rely only on God, who raises the dead. And he did rescue us from mortal danger, and he will rescue us again. We have placed our confidence in him, and he will continue to rescue us" (2 Cor. 1:8-10).

"The first time I was brought before the judge, no one came with me. Everyone abandoned me. May it not be counted against them. But the Lord stood with me and gave me strength so that I might preach the Good News in its entirety for all the Gentiles to hear. And he rescued me from certain death. Yes, and the Lord will deliver me from every evil attack and will bring me safely into his heavenly Kingdom. All glory to God forever and ever! Amen" (2 Tim. 4:16-18).

2.   Learn to stand in the authority given to you by Jesus.
"Look, I have given you authority over all the power of the enemy, and you can walk among snakes and scorpions and crush them. Nothing will injure you" (Luke 10:19). Jesus gave you authority over ALL the power of the enemy. You must exercise this authority by shutting all open doors. You must use your voice to declare your freedom and to demand Satan to leave.

3. Learn to rejoice in your freedom.
Like the children of Israel rejoiced on the Red Sea shore after their mighty deliverance we must rejoice in our freedom. "Then Miriam the prophet, Aaron's sister, took a tambourine and led all the women as they played their tambourines and danced" (Exod. 15:20). A proper response to deliverance is to praise, worship, and give thanks to God for his mighty intervention in our lives.

4. Learn to be Obedient.
Obedience is the key for you to stay free. God's commands in His word are clear concerning generational sins, curses, soul ties, and mental bondages. Only when we are obedient in how we live our lives will blessings come, and the strongholds of the enemy are broken. "But afterward Jesus found him in the Temple and told him, "Now you are well; so, stop sinning, or something even worse may happen to you" (John 5:14). "Then Jesus stood up again and said to the woman, "Where are your accusers? Didn't even one of them condemn you?" "No, Lord," she said. And Jesus said, "Neither do I. Go and sin no more" (John 8:10-11).
Re-read Deut. 28 to learn what makes the difference between blessings and curses.
Please describe what you have discovered in reading this passage.

_____
_____
_____
_____

MEMORY VERSE:
"If you confess with your mouth the Lord Jesus and believe in your heart that God raised Him from the dead, you will be saved" (Rom. 10:9 NKJV).

"Jesus said to the people who believed in him, "You are truly my disciples if you remain faithful to my teachings. And you will know the truth, and the truth will set you free" (John 8:31-32).
"Let us draw near with a sincere heart in full assurance of faith, having our hearts sprinkled clean from an evil conscience, and our bodies washed with pure water" (Heb. 10:22).

GROW DEEPER:
To understand each point better, the following are some additional scriptures you can read.

Admit you have sinned. "For everyone has sinned; we all fall short of God's glorious standard" (Rom. 3:23). "For the person who keeps all of the laws except one is as guilty as a person who has broken all of God's laws" (James 2:10). "As the Scriptures say, "No one is righteous-not even one" (Rom. 3:10). "For the wages of sin is death, but the free gift of God is eternal life through Christ Jesus our Lord" (Rom. 6:23). But if we confess our sins to him, he is faithful and just to forgive us our sins and to cleanse us from all wickedness. (1 John 1:9).

Believe in Jesus Christ. "For this is how God loved the world: He gave his one and only Son, so that everyone who believes in him will not perish but have eternal life. God sent his Son into the world not to judge the world, but to save the world through him. "There is no judgment against anyone who believes in him. But anyone who does not believe in him has already been judged for not believing in God's one and only Son. And the judgment is based on this fact: God's light came into the world, but people loved the darkness more than the light, for their actions were evil. All who do evil hate the light and refuse to go near it for fear their sins will be exposed. But those who do what is right come to the light so others can see that they are doing what God wants" (John 3:16-21). "The time promised by God has come at last!" he announced. "The Kingdom of God is near! Repent of your sins and believe the Good News!" (Mark 1:15). "Paul said, "John's baptism called for repentance from sin. But John himself told the people to believe in the one who would come later, meaning Jesus" (Acts 19:4). "They replied, "Believe in the Lord Jesus and you will be saved, along with everyone in your household" (Acts 16:31). "And this is his commandment: We must believe in the name of his Son, Jesus Christ, and love one another, just as he commanded us" (1 John 3:23). "God saved you by his grace when you believed. And you can't take credit for this; it is a gift from God. Salvation is not a reward for the good things we have done, so none of us can boast about it" (Eph. 2:8-9).

Confess your sins. The word "confess" means two things: agree with God that what He says is true, and to declare, to acknowledge, to admit, or to speak it. Most times, this is done with your mouth! Sometimes scripture tells us to confess to God, sometimes to others, and sometimes publicly. Ask the Holy Spirit for the discernment to know when to do which, but through these scriptures, we see benefits associated with "confessing sins." List some different benefits according to these scriptures: "But if we confess our sins to him, he is faithful and just to forgive us our sins and to cleanse us from all wickedness" (1 John 1:9). "Confess your sins to each other and pray for each other so that you may be healed. The earnest prayer of a righteous person has great power and produces wonderful results" (James 5:16). "People who conceal their sins will not prosper, but if they confess and turn from them, they will receive mercy" (Prov. 28:13). "When I refused to confess my sin, my body wasted away, and I groaned all day long. Day and night your hand of discipline was heavy on me. My strength evaporated like water in the summer heat. Interlude Finally, I confessed all my sins to you and stopped trying to hide my guilt. I said to myself, "I will confess my rebellion to the Lord." And you forgave me! All my guilt is gone" (Psalms 32:3-5). "If you openly declare that Jesus is Lord and believe in your heart that God raised him from the dead, you will be saved. For it is by believing in your heart that you are made right with God, and it is by openly declaring your faith that you are saved. For

"Everyone who calls on the name of the Lord will be saved" (Rom. 10:9-10, 13). "Many who became believers confessed their sinful practices. A number of them who had been practicing sorcery brought their incantation books and burned them at a public bonfire. The value of the books was several million dollars. So, the message about the Lord spread widely and had a powerful effect" (Acts 19:18-20).

Write your confession:

_____
_____
_____

Celebrate with all of Heaven.
"There is joy in the presence of the angels of God over one sinner who repents" (Luke 15:10).
This scripture says there is joy "in the presence of the angels of God." Who will be doing the rejoicing?

_____
_____
_____

Tell someone that you got saved.
"If you openly declare that Jesus is Lord and believe in your heart that God raised him from the dead, you will be saved. For it is by believing in your heart that you are made right with God, and it is by openly declaring your faith that you are saved" (Rom. 10:9-10).
Have you told someone yet that you got saved? If not, do it now. Who can you tell?

_____
_____
_____

Tell someone else about Jesus.
"Andrew, Simon Peter's brother, was one of these men who heard what John said and then followed Jesus. Andrew went to find his brother, Simon, and told him, "We have found the Messiah" (which means "Christ"). Then Andrew brought Simon to meet Jesus. Looking intently at Simon, Jesus said, "Your name is Simon, son of John—but you will be called Cephas" (which means "Peter")."
(John 1:40-42).
As soon as Andrew met Jesus and realized He was the Messiah, "Christ," what did he do next?

_____
_____
_____

Before you tell someone about Jesus, build your faith by reading "For I am not ashamed of this Good News about Christ. It is the power of God at work, saving everyone who believes—the Jew first and also the Gentile. This Good News tells us how God makes us right in his sight. This is accomplished from start to finish by faith. As the Scriptures say, "It is through faith that a righteous person has life" (Rom. 1:16-17). and reminding yourself that this is not dependent on your power, but God's power. A good idea would be to memorize this verse, and until you can memorize it, write it on a card and carry it with you to remind you of His power. Hide God's Word in your heart and be a Difference Maker. "I have hidden your word in my heart, that I might not sin against you" (Psalms 119:11).

Aspects of Deliverance.

The following aspects of deliverance can be studied to help you grow deeper.

The description of temporal deliverance in the Old Testament is a symbolic representation of the spiritual deliverance from sin, which is available only through Christ. Believers are delivered not because they deserve to be, but as an expression of God's mercy and love.

Sources of Deliverance:

1. Come from God:

"Victory comes from you, O Lord. May you bless your people" (Ps.3:8). "Then the Lord told him, "I have certainly seen the oppression of my people in Egypt. I have heard their cries of distress because of their harsh slave drivers. Yes, I am aware of their suffering. 8 So I have come down to rescue them from the power of the Egyptians and lead them out of Egypt into their own fertile and spacious land. It is a land flowing with milk and honey—the land where the Canaanites, Hittites, Amorites, Perizzites, Hivites, and Jebusites now live" (Exod. 3:7-8). "The Lord is my rock, my fortress, and my savior; my God is my rock, in whom I find protection. He is my shield, the power that saves me, and my place of safety" (Ps. 18:2).

2. None from other gods:

"Have the gods of any other nations ever saved their people from the king of Assyria" (2 Kings 18:33)?

3. No escape from God:

"Lord, your discipline is good, for it leads to life and health. You restore my health and allow me to live" (Isa. 38:16)!

4. Maybe declined:

"Don't you realize that I could ask my Father for thousands of angels to protect us, and he would send them instantly? But if I did, how would the Scriptures be fulfilled that describe what must happen now" (Matt. 26:53-54)? "Jesus answered, "My Kingdom is not an earthly kingdom. If it were, my followers would fight to keep me from being handed over to the Jewish leaders. But my Kingdom is not of this world" (John 18:36). "Women received their loved ones back again from death. But others were tortured, refusing to turn from God in order to be set free. They placed their hope in a better life after the resurrection" (Heb. 11:35).

Kinds of Deliverance:

1. Danger

"The Lord who rescued me from the claws of the lion and the bear will rescue me from this Philistine!" Saul finally consented. "All right, go ahead," he said. "And may the Lord be with you" (1 Sam.17:37)! "As they sailed across, Jesus settled down for a nap. But soon a fierce storm came down on the lake. The boat was filling with water, and they were in real danger. The disciples went and woke him up, shouting, "Master, Master, we're going to drown!" When Jesus woke up, he rebuked the wind and the raging waves. Suddenly the storm stopped, and all was calm" (Luke 8:23-24). "In fact, we expected to die. But as a result, we stopped relying on ourselves and learned to rely only on God, who raises the dead. And he rescued us from mortal danger, and he will rescue us again. We have placed our confidence in him, and he will continue to rescue us" (2 Cor. 1:9-10).

2. Illness
"He forgives all my sins and heals all my diseases" (Ps. 103:3). "Lord, your discipline is good, for it leads to life and health. You restore my health and allow me to live" (Isa. 38:16)!

3. Trouble
"The Lord hears his people when they call to him for help. He rescues them from all their troubles. The Lord is close to the brokenhearted; he rescues those whose spirits are crushed. The righteous person faces many troubles, but the Lord comes to the rescue each time" (Ps 34:17-19). "For you have rescued me from my troubles and helped me to triumph over my enemies" (Ps. 54:7).

4. Slavery
"I am the Lord your God, who rescued you from the land of Egypt, the place of your slavery" (Exod. 20:2).

5. Enemies
"So the king told Ebed-melech, "Take thirty of my men with you, and pull Jeremiah out of the cistern before he dies." So Ebed-melech took the men with him and went to a room in the palace beneath the treasury, where he found some old rags and discarded clothing. He carried these to the cistern and lowered them to Jeremiah on a rope. Ebed-melech called down to Jeremiah, "Put these rags under your armpits to protect you from the ropes." Then when Jeremiah was ready, they pulled him out. So Jeremiah was returned to the courtyard of the guard—the palace prison—where he remained" (Jer. 38:10-13). "We have been rescued from our enemies so we can serve God without fear" (Luke 1:74). "Pray, too, that we will be rescued from wicked and evil people, for not everyone is a believer" (2 Thess. 3:2).

6. Satan
"This dear woman, a daughter of Abraham, has been held in bondage by Satan for eighteen years. Isn't it right that she be released, even on the Sabbath" (Luke 13:16)? "Simon, Simon, Satan has asked to sift each of you like wheat" (Luke 22:31).

7. Fear
"I prayed to the Lord, and he answered me. He freed me from all my fears" (Ps. 34:4). "When I saw him, I fell at his feet as if I were dead. But he laid his right hand on me and said, "Don't be afraid! I am the First and the Last" (Rev. 1:17).

8. Sin
"Jesus gave his life for our sins, just as God our Father planned, in order to rescue us from this evil world in which we live" (Gal 1:4). "As for us, we can't help but thank God for you, dear brothers and sisters loved by the Lord. We are always thankful that God chose you to be among the first to experience salvation—a salvation that came through the Spirit who makes you holy and through your belief in the truth" (2 Thess. 2:13).

9. Coming Wrath
"When the crowds came to John for baptism, he said, "You brood of snakes! Who warned you to flee the coming wrath" (Luke 3:7)? "And they speak of how you are looking forward to the coming of God's Son from heaven—Jesus, whom God raised from the dead. He is the one who has rescued us from the terrors of the coming judgment" (1 Thess. 1:10).

10. People are to pray for deliverance.
"And don't let us yield to temptation but rescue us from the evil one" (Matt. 6:13).

11. Believers are delivered by God's power from:
This present evil age.
"Jesus gave his life for our sins, just as God our Father planned, in order to rescue us from this evil world in which we live" (Gal. 1:4).

12. Satan's reign
"We always pray for you, and we give thanks to God, the Father of our Lord Jesus Christ" (Col.1:3).

13. Trials of this life
"So, you see, the Lord knows how to rescue godly people from their trials, even while keeping the wicked under punishment until the day of final judgment" (2 Pet. 2:9).

SPIRIT, SOUL & BODY

PURPOSE OF THIS LESSON:

To understand that we were created in the image of God. What understanding the Spirit, Soul & Body principles means in walking out our freedom; likewise, that we are a trinity; we are a spirit that has a soul, and we live in a body. Have you ever considered this reality or is this a new idea?

"Then the Lord God formed the man from the dust of the ground" (body). "He breathed the breath of life" (Hebrew translation – pneuma - the spirit) "into the man's nostrils and man became a living person" (Hebrew translation neh-fesh - Soul) (Gen. 2:7). "Now may the God of peace make you holy in every way and may your whole spirit and soul and body be kept blameless until our Lord Jesus Christ comes again" (1 Thess. 5:23).

INTRODUCTION:

You are a spirit; this is the eternal part of who you are. Your spirit man will live forever; everybody is going to live forever somewhere, either in heaven or hell.

- "But when the Son of Man comes in his glory, and all the angels with him, then he will sit upon his glorious throne. All the nations will be gathered in his presence, and he will separate the people as a shepherd separates the sheep from the goats. He will place the sheep at his right hand and the goats at his left. "Then the King will say to those on his right, 'Come, you who are blessed by my Father, inherit the Kingdom prepared for you from the creation of the world" (Mat. 25:31-34).
- "Then the King will turn to those on the left and say, 'Away with you, you cursed ones, into the eternal fire prepared for the devil and his demons" (Mat. 25:41).
- "And they will go away into eternal punishment, but the righteous will go into eternal life." (Mat. 25:46).

WHY IS THIS LESSON IMPORTANT TO YOUR LIFE?

When Adam & Eve sinned, we all died spiritually, which means we were separated from God because of our sin. This is why we must be born again.

- "The serpent was the shrewdest of all the wild animals the LORD God had made. One day he asked the woman, "Did God really say you must not eat the fruit from any of the trees in the garden?" "Of course, we may eat fruit from the trees in the garden," the woman replied. "It's only the fruit from the tree in the middle of the garden that we are not allowed to eat. God said, 'You must not eat it or even touch it; if you do, you will die.' "You won't die!" the serpent replied to the woman. The woman was convinced. She saw that the tree was beautiful, and its fruit looked delicious, and she wanted the wisdom it would give her. So, she took some of the fruit and ate it. Then she gave some to her husband, who was with her, and he ate it, too" (Gen. 3:1-4, 6).
- "Jesus replied, "I tell you the truth, unless you are born again, you cannot see the Kingdom of God." "What do you mean?" exclaimed Nicodemus. "How can an old man go back into his mother's womb and be born again?" Jesus replied, "I assure you no one can enter the Kingdom of God without being born of water and the Spirit. Humans can reproduce only human life, but the Holy Spirit gives birth to spiritual life. So don't be surprised when I say, 'You must be born again" (John 3:3-7).

When you got born again.

Your spirit man was born again, literally reconnected to the Father. Your spirit man is now incapable of sin. Because we have received the righteousness of God through faith in Jesus and have been sealed with the Holy Spirit.

- "Father, I want these whom you have given me to be with me where I am. Then they can see all the glory you gave me because you loved me even before the world began" (John 17:24)!
- "Now He who has prepared us for this very thing is God, who also has given us the Spirit as a guarantee" (2 Cor. 5:5 NKJV).
- "For his Spirit joins with our spirit to affirm that we are God's children" (Rom. 8:16).
- "But when people keep on sinning, it shows that they belong to the devil, who has been sinning since the beginning. But the Son of God came to destroy the works of the devil. Those who have been born into God's family do not make a practice of sinning, because God's life [seed] is in them. So, they can't keep on sinning, because they are children of God" (1 John 3:8-9).
- "He came to His own, and His own did not receive Him. But as many as received Him, to them He gave the right to become children of God, to those who believe in His name: who were born, not of blood, nor of the will of the flesh, nor of the will of man, but of God" (John 1:11-13 NKJV).
- "We know that whoever is born of God does not sin; but he who has been born of God keeps himself, and the wicked one does not touch him" (1 John 5:18 NKJV).
- "And if Christ [is] in you, the body [is] dead because of sin, but the Spirit [is] life because of righteousness" (Rom. 8:10 NKJV).
- "For He made Him who knew no sin [to be] sin for us, that we might become the righteousness of God in Him" (2 Cor. 5:21 NKJV).
- "I do not set aside the grace of God; for if righteousness [comes] through the law, then Christ died in vain" (Gal. 2:21 NKJV).
- "In Him you also [trusted,] after you heard the word of truth, the gospel of your salvation; in whom also, having believed, you were sealed with the Holy Spirit of promise" (Eph. 1:13 NKJV).

You are a spirit, and your spirit has a soul.

- This is your mind, literally the soul, the residence of our will and emotions.
- This is the unique part of who you are.
- Your soul connects your spirit to your body.
- Your soul is not your brain; your soul is eternal, but your brain is temporal.
- Your brain is the control center for your body.
- Your soul is the control center for your brain.
- Scripture uses the words mind and heart to describe your soul.
- (Book - Switch On Your Brain by Dr. Caroline Leaf)
- "Keep your heart with all diligence, For out of it [spring] the issues of life"   (Prov. 4:23 NKJV).
- "A sound heart [is] life to the body, but envy [is] rottenness to the bones." (Prov. 14:30 NKJV).
- "A merry heart makes a cheerful countenance, but by sorrow of the heart the spirit is broken" (Prov. 15:13 NKJV).

Our thoughts and choices can grieve the Spirit.

- "For to be carnally minded [is] death, but to be spiritually minded [is] life and peace" (Rom. 8:6 NKJV).
- "that if you confess with your mouth the Lord Jesus and believe in your heart that God has raised Him from the dead, you will be saved" (Rom. 10:9 NKJV).

- "And do not grieve the Holy Spirit of God, by whom you were sealed for the day of redemption. Let all bitterness, wrath, anger, clamor, and evil speaking be put away from you, with all malice. And be kind to one another, tenderhearted, forgiving one another, even as God in Christ forgave you" (Eph. 4:30-32 NKJV).

Your flesh (body) and the Spirit war with one another.
- Your Soul (mind, will, emotions) is the battlefield.
- Whoever wins the battle for your soul wins the war for your daily life.
- What we think truly matters. It affects everything.
- You are rich or poor, healthy, or unhealthy, joyful or depressed, relationally fulfilled or dysfunctional, victorious or defeated, spiritual or carnal based on your thoughts.
- You are a spirit, you have a soul, and you live in a body.
- "I say then: Walk in the Spirit, and you shall not fulfill the lust of the flesh. For the flesh lusts against the Spirit, and the Spirit against the flesh; and these are contrary to one another, so that you do not do the things that you wish" (Gal. 5:16-17 NKJV).
- "And do not be conformed to this world, but be transformed by the renewing of your mind, that you may prove what [is] that good and acceptable and perfect will of God" (Rom. 12:2 NKJV).

Your body is your earth suit.
- It gives you authority to function on planet earth.
- This is why Jesus had to become a man and why God searches for men/women to intercede and act on behalf of His kingdom.
- "So, you see, just as death came into the world through a man, now the resurrection from the dead has begun through another man. Just as everyone dies because we all belong to Adam, everyone who belongs to Christ will be given new life" (1 Cor. 15:21-22).
- "Even common people oppress the poor, rob the needy, and deprive foreigners of justice. "I looked for someone who might rebuild the wall of righteousness that guards the land. I searched for someone to stand in the gap in the wall so I wouldn't have to destroy the land, but I found no one. So now I will pour out my fury on them, consuming them with the fire of my anger. I will heap on their heads the full penalty for all their sins. I, the Sovereign LORD, have spoken!" (Ezek. 22:29-31).

Your body allows you to see, hear, touch, smell and taste.
- Your body then sends all that information to your brain. Then your soul (mind, will and emotions) processes this information and qualifies the information with a thought. That thought then has the power to rewire your brain, change your DNA and control choices and decisions you make.
- "We destroy every proud obstacle that keeps people from knowing God. We capture their rebellious thoughts and teach them to obey Christ" (2 Cor. 10:5).
- "For to be carnally minded [is] death, but to be spiritually minded [is] life and peace" (Rom. 8:6 NKJV).
- "Guard your heart above all else, for it determines the course of your life" (Prov. 4:23).

LESSON SUMMARY:

- You are a spirit, you have a soul (mind, will, emotions) and you live in a body.
- "For his Spirit joins with our spirit to affirm that we are God's children" (Rom 8:16).
- "Jesus replied, "'You must love the Lord your God with all your heart, all your soul, and all your mind.' This is the first and greatest commandment" (Matthew 22:37-38).
- "Those who are victorious will sit with me on my throne, just as I was victorious and sat with my Father on his throne" (Rev. 3:21 NLT).

*Note: Lesson Slides end at this point.

OBEDIENCE PRECEDES BLESSING:

- "Therefore, if anyone is in Christ, he is a new creation; old things have passed away; behold, all things have become new" (2 Cor. 5:17 NKJV).

- "For his Spirit joins with our spirit to affirm that we are God's children" (Rom 8:16).

- "There is therefore now no condemnation to those who are in Christ Jesus, who do not walk according to the flesh, but according to the Spirit" (Rom. 8:1 NKJV).

- "For we through the Spirit eagerly wait for the hope of righteousness by faith" (Gal. 5:5 NKJV).

- "And everyone who has this hope in Him purifies himself, just as He is pure" (1 John 3:3 NKJV).

- "Now hope does not disappoint, because the love of God has been poured out in our hearts by the Holy Spirit who was given to us" (Rom. 5:5 NKJV).

MEMORY VERSE:
"Now may the God of peace make you holy in every way and may your whole spirit and soul and body be kept blameless until our Lord Jesus Christ comes again" (1 Thess. 5:23).

GROW DEEPER:
"I am the true vine, and My Father is the vinedresser. Every branch in Me that does not bear fruit He [lifts up] takes away; and every branch that bears fruit He prunes, that it may bear more fruit. You are already clean because of the word which I have spoken to you. Abide in Me, and I in you. As the branch cannot bear fruit of itself, unless it abides in the vine, neither can you, unless you abide in Me. "I am the vine, you are the branches. He who abides in Me, and I in him, bears much fruit; for without Me you can do nothing" (John 15:1-5 NKJV).

"The Lord is my shepherd; I have all that I need. He lets me rest in green meadows; he leads me beside peaceful streams. He renews my strength. He guides me along the right path, bringing honor to his name" (Ps. 23:1-3).

GROW I
Journey to Freedom
Lesson 3

STAY IN THE WORD

PURPOSE OF THIS LESSON:
To create a daily hunger in you for the living Word of God and teach you to apply it to your life.

"As the deer longs for streams of water, so I long for you, O God. 2 I thirst for God, the living God. When can I go and stand before him" (Ps. 42:1-2)?

What had the Psalmist discovered about his need for time with God?

_____
_____
_____
_____

"Oh, taste and see that the Lord is good; Blessed is the man who trusts in Him" (Ps. 34:8 NKJV)!

"Blessed are those who hunger and thirst for righteousness, For they shall be filled" (Mat. 5:6 NKJV). "Yes, he humbled you by letting you go hungry and then feeding you with manna, a food previously unknown to you and your ancestors. He did it to teach you that people do not live by bread alone; rather, we live by every word that comes from the mouth of the Lord" (Deut. 8:3).

What if you are not hungry or thirsty for time with the Lord in His Word?

In our physical life, we need to eat healthy food that will make our bodies strong and help us to stay in good health, but when we eat junk food, it dulls our hunger for fruits and vegetables. Do you desire to be like the Psalmist and be hungry and thirsty for the Word of God? Take a moment and think about your life.-Is it possible that there is some "junk food" in your life that is dulling your hunger for the Word of God?

The more you seek God and spend time in His Word, the more you will crave the Word of God.

"Like newborn babies, you must crave pure spiritual milk so that you will grow into a full experience of salvation. Cry out for this nourishment, now that you have had a taste of the Lord's kindness" (1 Peter 2:2-3).

Ask the Lord to give you a craving for His Word and time with Him.

"For the word of God is living and powerful, and sharper than any two-edged sword, piercing even to the division of soul and spirit, and of joints and marrow, and is a discerner of the thoughts and intents of the heart" (Heb. 4:12 NKJV).

"He sends his orders to the world—how swiftly his word flies" (Ps. 147:15)!

What do these two verses tell me about the Word of God, and what does this mean in my life each day?

_____

_____

_____

_____

INTRODUCTION:

It Is Written. This lesson and the next five lessons are about how to stay free. This lesson will be important to you for the rest of your life. God has already written down everything we need to know to STAY FREE. It is written in the Bible.

"But he answered, "It is written, "'Man shall not live by bread alone, but by every word that comes from the mouth of God'"" (Matt. 4:4 ESV).

"All Scripture is inspired by God and is useful to teach us what is true and to make us realize what is wrong in our lives. It corrects us when we are wrong and teaches us to do what is right. God uses it to prepare and equip his people to do every good work" (2 Tim. 3:16-17).

Based on 2 Tim. 3:16-17, list four things Scripture is useful for:

_____

_____

_____

_____

Notice scripture teaches us the truth, exposes lies and renews our minds!
Truth of God's Word prepares and equips us to do what is right!
Truth of who we are in Christ and how to walk in His righteousness!

When you buy a lawnmower, microwave, or any piece of equipment, you are given an owner's manual to learn how to use it properly or to troubleshoot when there is a problem. Look at it like this: God created us, and He gave us an owner's manual to show us how to live this life in the best and most fulfilling way possible. He is preparing us through the Word to do the good works He designed us to do.

If you want to know what God thinks about anything, it is written in the Bible. The Bible is God's Word that He gave to man, and it is written for us. It must be written because important documents are written. Name some important documents that people place great value on:

_____

_____

_____

_____

The fact it is written should be important to us because it was important to Jesus. He was quoted as saying, "It is written" on more than one occasion. One of the most important times was when He was tempted by Satan. Matt. 4:1-11 is the account of the temptations Jesus experienced.

The Temptation of Jesus:
"Then Jesus was led by the Spirit into the wilderness to be tempted there by the devil. For forty days and forty nights he fasted and became very hungry. During that time the devil came and said to him, "If you are the Son of God, tell these stones to become loaves of bread." But Jesus told him, "No! The Scriptures say, 'People do not live by bread alone, but by every word that comes from the mouth of God.'" Then the devil took him to the holy city, Jerusalem, to the highest point of the Temple, and said, "If you are the Son of God, jump off! For the Scriptures say, 'He will order his angels to protect you. And they will hold you up with their hands, so you won't even hurt your foot on a stone.'" Jesus responded, "The Scriptures also say, 'You must not test the Lord your God.'" Next the devil took him to the peak of a very high mountain and showed him all the kingdoms of the world and their glory. "I will give it all to you," he said, "if you will kneel down and worship me." "Get out of here, Satan," Jesus told him. "For the Scriptures say, 'You must worship the Lord your God and serve only him.'" Then the devil went away, and angels came and took care of Jesus" (Matt. 4:1-11).

Write the three temptations and Jesus' response to each temptation.

_____
_____
_____
_____

You would think Jesus could just flick Satan off like a flea, but He spoke the Word to fight Satan. If Jesus used the Word as a weapon, so should we! It is written!

WHY IS THIS LESSON IMPORTANT TO YOUR LIFE?
Because the Bible says we are destroyed for lack of knowledge.

"My people are being destroyed because they don't know me. Since you priests refuse to know me, I refuse to recognize you as my priests. Since you have forgotten the laws of your God, I will forget to bless your children" (Hosea 4:6).

The lack of knowledge is a case of what we don't know that can hurt us.
In a day with so many lies and false religions, the Bible can teach us what and who Truth is. It can also point out and convict us when we are doing wrong. The Word can correct us when we are wrong and get us back on the right path. It can teach us what is right and how to do the next right thing. Through all these things, God uses the Word to prepare us to do the right things He designed us to do.

Knowing the Word can bring prosperity and success.

"Study this Book of Instruction continually. Meditate on it day and night so you will be sure to obey everything written in it. Only then will you prosper and succeed in all you do" (Josh. 1:8).

Not knowing the Word can destroy us.

HOW CAN I STAY IN THE WORD?
When someone gets saved, many well-meaning older Christians have advised new Christians to "Get in the Word." That is excellent advice, but the question is, how?

Let's look at ways to get in the Word.

Hear – "Faith comes by hearing, and hearing by the Word of God" (Rom.10:17).
What are some ways you can "hear" the Word?

_____

_____

_____

Many people will say, "I need more faith." God has made it clear that the way to get faith is to hear the Word of God. Make yourself available to hear it and hearing the Pastor preach on Sunday is not enough. Look for other opportunities during the Lesson to increase your faith. Even reading it out loud allows you to hear it, so read it and speak it! Reading the Word out loud releases truth into your life and environment.

Examine – "Now these people were more noble-minded than those in Thessalonica, for they received the word with great eagerness, examining the Scriptures daily to see whether these things were so" (Acts 17:11 NASB).

"They read from the Book of the Law of God and clearly explained the meaning of what was being read, helping the people understand each passage" (Neh. 8:8).

Bibles in different translations are so easily available these days. There are Bible apps on your phone or computer where you can easily see any version you want to read. Choose a version that you can easily understand. If you are confused about what version to read, ask your Pastor, elders, or teachers and get their help.

Analyze – "Study this Book of Instruction continually. Meditate on it day and night so you will be sure to obey everything written in it. Only then will you prosper and succeed in all you do" (Josh. 1:8).

As you read the Word, there may be times when you do not know what a word means. Instead of passing it by, look up the word in the dictionary, get the meaning, and then read it again. You can easily look up passages online and see other people's thoughts and opinions but remember to always ask the Holy Spirit to teach you as you read. He is your teacher.

"But when the Father sends the Advocate as my representative—that is, the Holy Spirit—he will teach you everything and will remind you of everything I have told you" (John 14:26).

Remember – "I have hidden Your Word in my heart that I might not sin against you" (Ps. 119:11).

"How can a young person stay pure? By obeying your word. I have tried hard to find you—don't let me wander from your commands. I have hidden your word in my heart, that I might not sin against you. I praise you, O Lord; teach me your decrees. I have recited aloud all the regulations you have given us. I have rejoiced in your laws as much as in riches. I will study your commandments and reflect on your ways. I will delight in your decrees and not forget your word" (Psalms 119:9-16).

Memorizing scriptures is one of the most powerful ways you can win in this battle because you do not always have your Bible in your hand when you need it. Get other people involved with you in this effort: your family, your friends, your co-workers, etc. It is a great way to witness to someone, and they do not even realize what you are doing. They might resent you opening your Bible and reading it to them, but you can tell them you are trying to memorize a verse and ask them to see if you get it right. Write verses down on 3x5 index cards and carry them around with you. Study them when you are waiting on appointments or stopped in traffic, anytime you have a free moment.

Think – "Think about the things of heaven, not the things of earth" (Col. 3:2).

"Trust in the Lord with all your heart; do not depend on your own understanding" (Prov. 3:5).

"We destroy every proud obstacle that keeps people from knowing God. We capture their rebellious thoughts and teach them to obey Christ" (2 Cor. 10:5).

"And now, dear brothers and sisters, one final thing. Fix your thoughts on what is true, and honorable, and right, and pure, and lovely, and admirable. Think about things that are excellent and worthy of praise" (Phil. 4:8).

"Study this Book of Instruction continually. Meditate on it day and night so you will be sure to obey everything written in it. Only then will you prosper and succeed in all you do" (Josh. 1:8).

There are so many things you can think about in a day. How much better to think on the Word! This will improve your life! Take a verse that stood out to you in your time with the Lord that morning and think about it off and on all day. Ask others what they know or think about that verse. Ask questions and learn.

Talk – "Repeat God's Word again and again to your children. Talk about them when you are at home and when you are on the road, when you are going to bed and when you are getting up" (Deut. 6:7).

"The Lord merely spoke, and the heavens were created. He breathed the word, and all the stars were born" (Ps. 33:6).

There is power in speaking the Word of God out loud.

What happened when God spoke the Word?

_____

_____

_____

"But we continue to preach because we have the same kind of faith the psalmist had when he said, "I believed in God, so I spoke." (2 Cor. 4:13).

"The tongue can bring death or life; those who love to talk will reap the consequences" (Prov. 18:21).

That is what the Scriptures mean when God told him, "I have made you the father of many nations." This happened because Abraham believed in the God who brings the dead back to life and who creates new things out of nothing. (Rom. 4:17).

What happens when you speak?

_____

_____

_____

_____

We want to SEE something before we say it. God wants us to SAY something before we see it.

Apply your HEART to the WORD

"Listen to the words of the wise; apply your heart to my instruction" (Prov. 22:17).

"But don't just listen to God's word. You must do what it says. Otherwise, you are only fooling yourselves" (James 1:22).

This is where it all comes together. Be doers of the Word, and not hearers only.

"Then said Jesus to those Jews which believed on him, If ye continue in my word, then are ye my disciples indeed; And ye shall know the truth, and the truth shall make you free" (John 8:31-32).

This is where you move your head knowledge into heart knowledge. This is where you start applying what you have heard, examined, analyzed, remembered, and thought about.

Instead of just knowing you should forgive others, this is where you start forgiving others.
Instead of just knowing you should give cheerfully, you start giving cheerfully.
Instead of just knowing you should spend time in prayer, you start praying.
Instead of just knowing you should tell others about Jesus, you start telling others in your path about Jesus and become a Soul-Winner!
This is where you become a doer instead of just a hearer and you become a threat to the enemy!

TAKE THE WORD OF GOD AND PRAY:
The Sword of the Spirit is the only offensive weapon. It is the Word of God, the Bible.

How does the Bible become a weapon that enables you to win?

"Put on salvation as your helmet, and take the sword of the Spirit, which is the word of God. Pray in the Spirit at all times and on every occasion. Stay alert and be persistent in your prayers for all believers everywhere" (Eph. 6:17-18).

Tells us to take the Word and PRAY!

The Bible was not written in English and sometimes we can understand what it means by understanding what the original language meant. There are two words for "The Word" in the Bible in the Greek Language.

"Logos" translates "written Word of God"
"Rhema" translates "specific" or "instant" (Spoken Word of God).

When we read Eph. 6:17-18 it instructs us to take the sword of the Spirit, which is the Word of God, and pray in this passage. Word is the Greek word, "rhema," so it could be translated, "Take the sword of the Spirit, which is the "specific Word" of God, and PRAY…" What this means to us is that we should pray the specific Word of God over our circumstances.

Example: "For God has not given us a spirit of fear, but of power and of love and of a sound mind" (2 Tim. 1:7 NKJV).

HOW DO WE PRAY THE SPECIFIC WORD?

When you have a need, ask the Holy Spirit to give you a "specific Word" regarding your need. You might ask, "How does God give me a Word?" He can do it in many ways, but the main way is through His Word. The more you read the Bible, the more opportunity there is for the Holy Spirit to speak a specific Word to you.

When He does, make that Word into a personal prayer.

Instead of worrying over that need, begin to pray the Word over that need. Think of a need you have and write it down.

_____

_____

_____

_____

Ask God to give you a specific Word regarding this need, and when He does write it down.

_____

_____

_____

_____

Rewrite the specific (or rhema word) Word into a personal prayer and begin praying it, instead of worrying about the need. "Don't worry about anything; instead, pray about everything. Tell God what you need and thank him for all he has done" (Phil. 4:6).

_____

_____

_____

_____

LESSON SUMMARY:
- If we remain in God's word, we will expose the lies of the devil and be set free in the truth of who we are in Christ.
- "Then Jesus said to those Jews who believed Him, "If you abide in My word, you are My disciples indeed. And you shall know the truth, and the truth shall make you free." (John 8:31-32 NKJV).

*Note: Lesson slides end at this point.

OBEDIENCE PRECEDES BLESSING:
Don't just listen to God's Word. You must do what it says (James 1:22). One of the secrets of staying free is to do what Jesus did, and He made it a priority to spend time with His Father daily. He also

spent time in the scriptures because He quoted them often. The following are some ideas of how you can implement this daily time with the Lord into your life:

DAILY TIME WITH THE LORD:
Secret Place:
Decide on your place to spend time with the Lord, then be prepared with your Bible, notebook, and a pen.
- "Those who live in the shelter of the Most High will find rest in the shadow of the Almighty" (Ps. 91:1).
- "Then no one will notice that you are fasting, except your Father, who knows what you do in private. And your Father, who sees everything, will reward you" (Matt. 6:18).

Set Time:
Set an appointment time to meet with God.
"Then the Lord told Moses, "Go down and prepare the people for my arrival. Consecrate them today and tomorrow and have them wash their clothing. Be sure they are ready on the third day, for on that day the Lord will come down on Mount Sinai as all the people watch" (Exod. 19:10-11).

We set appointments with everyone, even people we don't like.
Make this appointment with God your highest priority. Put it on your daily calendar. The time needs to be when you are at your best and when you have the least interruption.
- "I rise early, before the sun is up; I cry out for help and put my hope in your words" (Ps. 119:147).
- "Before daybreak the next morning, Jesus got up and went out to an isolated place to pray" (Mark 1:35).

Strategic Plan:
Be still and worship.
- "Be still and know that I am God! I will be honored by every nation. I will be honored throughout the world"(Ps. 46:10).
- "But you will not even need to fight. Take your positions; then stand still and watch the Lord's victory. He is with you, O people of Judah and Jerusalem. Do not be afraid or discouraged. Go out against them tomorrow, for the Lord is with you!" 21 After consulting the people, the king appointed singers to walk ahead of the army, singing to the Lord and praising him for his holy splendor. This is what they sang: "Give thanks to the Lord; his faithful love endures forever" (2 Chron. 20:17, 21)!
- "One day as these men were worshiping the Lord and fasting, the Holy Spirit said, "Appoint Barnabas and Saul for the special work to which I have called them" (Acts 13:2).

Worship in your own way.
Plugin your iPod, tablet, or CD player. Use earphones or don't use earphones. Sing out loud. Sing in your head. Whatever works for you, just do it. Just be still and worship. Worshiping will usher you into His presence.
- "Enter his gates with thanksgiving; go into his courts with praise. Give thanks to him and praise his name" (Ps. 100:4). "Commit your actions to the Lord, and your plans will succeed"(Prov. 16:3).
- "Make the most of every opportunity in these evil days. 17 Don't act thoughtlessly but understand what the Lord wants you to do. 18 Don't be drunk with wine, because that will ruin your life. Instead, be filled with the Holy Spirit, 19 singing psalms and hymns and spiritual songs among

yourselves and making music to the Lord in your hearts. 20 And give thanks for everything to God the Father in the name of our Lord Jesus Christ" (Eph. 5:16-20).

Pray and read:
Pray for whatever is on your heart. If the President is on your heart, pray. If your child is on your heart, pray. Whatever is on your heart as you read, pray. The Holy Spirit will trigger things as you read, so pray.
- "Before daybreak the next morning, Jesus got up and went out to an isolated place to pray" (Mark 1:35).
- "I rise early, before the sun is up; I cry out for help and put my hope in your words" (Ps. 119:147).

Read the Word:
Get yourself a plan and pick up tomorrow where you left off today. Read the Bible in a year.
Read a Proverb a day. Read some Old Testament and some New Testament each day.
Read one book of the Bible at a time. Just do it. Read the Word in whatever works for you.
- "Jesus said to the people who believed in him, "You are truly my disciples if you remain faithful to my teachings. And you will know the truth, and the truth will set you free" (John 8:31-32).

Listen and write:
Don't just talk to God. Listen to God. As He speaks, write it down. Write your prayers.
Write what you think God is saying in answer to your prayers. Write what you think God is saying in the Word that you read. "For the choir director: A love song to be sung to the tune "Lilies." A psalm of the descendants of Korah. Beautiful words stir my heart. will recite a lovely poem about the king, for my tongue is like the pen of a skillful poet" (Ps. 45:1). "Every part of this plan," David told Solomon, "was given to me in writing from the hand of the Lord" (1 Chron. 28:19). Then the Lord said to me, "Write my answer plainly on tablets, so that a runner can carry the correct message to others" (Hab. 2:2).

As you write it down, understanding will come. "Meanwhile, the boy Samuel served the Lord by assisting Eli. Now in those days messages from the Lord were very rare, and visions were quite uncommon" (1 Sam. 3:1). In that day, the word of the Lord was rare, Rare – This means valuable and precious. Learn to value the Word of God, and it will change your life.

MEMORY VERSE:
"Study to shew thyself approved unto God, a workman that need not be ashamed, rightly dividing the word of truth" (2 Tim 2:15 KJV).

ROW DEEPER:
"Then Christ will make His home in your hearts as you trust in Him. Your roots will GROW down into God's love and keep you strong" (Eph. 3:17).
Read Ps. 119 - List some benefits you receive from being in the Word:

_____

_____

_____

_____

TOOLS THAT MIGHT HELP YOU HAVE A GOOD QUIET TIME WITH THE LORD:

Men - Bible, notebook, and pen.

Women - Basket, Bible, Journal, pen, candle, music, tissue, notecards, highlighter, notebook, devotional, and coffee mug.

SUGGESTIONS ON WHAT TO READ IN YOUR TIME WITH THE LORD:

- Your bible. The Sovereign Lord has given me His words of wisdom so that I know how to comfort the weary. Morning by morning He wakens me and opens my understanding to His will" (Isa. 50:4).
- Other books may be helpful but are not meant to replace reading the Word of God. It is first and foremost.
- Devotional, read chapters in the Bible, One Year Bible, a bible app for your phone
- Recommended Books:
    - Secrets of the Secret Place by Bob Sorge
    - Praying God's Word by Beth Moore

GROW I
Journey to Freedom
Lesson 4

STAY IN PRAYER AND WORSHIP

PURPOSE OF THIS LESSON:
This lesson is to lead you into a closer, personal relationship with God, your Father, Jesus His Son, and the Holy Spirit through prayer and worship.

The two main ways to have a closer relationship with someone is through communication and showing your love to them. Prayer is the way to communicate with God, and worship is the way to show your love to Him.

"Never stop praying. Be thankful in all circumstances, for this is God's will for you who belong to Christ Jesus" (1Thes. 5:17-18).

INTRODUCTION:
The disciples walked closely with Jesus for three years. They watched Him turn water into wine, heal the sick, cast out demons, and even raise the dead. The one thing they asked Him to teach them was how to pray.

"Once Jesus was in a certain place praying. As he finished, one of his disciples came to him and said, "Lord, teach us to pray, just as John taught his disciples" (Luke 11:1).

"My child, pay attention to what I say. Listen carefully to my words. Don't lose sight of them. Let them penetrate deep into your heart, for they bring life to those who find them, and healing to their whole body" (Prov. 4:20-22).

Why do you think they asked Jesus to teach them to pray instead of how to do miracles?

_____
_____
_____
_____

WHY IS THIS LESSON IMPORTANT TO YOUR LIFE?
In scripture that prayer and worship were a priority to Jesus. If He, being the Son of God, needed to pray and worship, how much more do we need to pray and worship? The disciples walked with Jesus for about three years, and during that time, they saw Him do amazing miracles, but they also saw the secret behind the miracles: His prayer time with His Father.

The Bible records many references to Jesus getting up early in the morning to pray. "Before daybreak the next morning, Jesus got up and went out to an isolated place to pray" (Mark 1:35). "But Jesus often withdrew to the wilderness for prayer" (Luke 5:16). Jesus Himself teaches us about prayer, so let's see what He says to do when you pray.

WHEN YOU PRAY:

"When you pray, don't be like the hypocrites who love to pray publicly on street corners and in the synagogues where everyone can see them. I tell you the truth, that is all the reward they will ever get. But when you pray, go away by yourself, shut the door behind you, and pray to your Father in private. Then your Father, who sees everything, will reward you. "When you pray, don't babble on and on as the Gentiles do. They think their prayers are answered merely by repeating their words again and again. Don't be like them, for your Father knows exactly what you need even before you ask him" (Matt. 6:5-8)!

"In this manner, therefore, pray: Our Father in heaven, Hallowed be Your name. Your kingdom come. Your will be done On earth as it is in heaven. Give us this day our daily bread. And forgive us our debts, As we forgive our debtors. And do not lead us into temptation, But deliver us from the evil one. For Yours is the kingdom and the power and the glory forever. Amen" (Mat. 6:9-13 NKJV).

CLOSER LOOK AT THE DIFFERENT ELEMENTS OF PRAYER:

In this manner, therefore, pray:

Praise: Our Father in heaven, Hallowed be Your name.
Purpose: Your kingdom come. Your will be done On earth as it is in heaven.
Provision: Give us this day our daily bread.
Pardon: And forgive us our debts,
People: As we forgive our debtors.
Protection: And do not lead us into temptation But deliver us from the evil one. For Yours is the kingdom and the power and the glory, for ever. Amen. (Matt. 6:9-13 NKJV).

When we break down the Lord's prayer, we find there are six parts of the prayer.

Praise: Ver 9 In this manner, therefore, pray: Our Father in heaven, Hallowed be Your name.
Adoration: For Whom God Is.
Acknowledge that the Lord is God! He made us, and we are his. We are his people, the sheep of his pasture. (Ps. 100:3).
Thanksgiving: For What God Has done.
Enter his gates with thanksgiving; go into his courts with praise. Give thanks to him and praise his name. 5 For the Lord is good. His unfailing love continues forever, and his faithfulness continues to each generation. (Ps. 100:4-5).

Purpose: Ver 10 Your kingdom come. Your will be done On earth as it is in heaven.
The Will of God.
"For he has rescued us from the kingdom of darkness and transferred us into the Kingdom of his dear Son," (Col. 1:13).
"The Lord isn't really being slow about his promise, as some people think. No, he is being patient for your sake. He does not want anyone to be destroyed but wants everyone to repent" (2 Peter 3:9).

Provision: Ver 11 Give us this day our daily bread.
Specific Needs.
"And in that day you will ask Me nothing. Most assuredly, I say to you, whatever you ask the Father in My name He will give you" (John 16:23 NKJV).

Pardon: Ver 12 And forgive us our debts,
Forgiveness of Sins.
"Search me, O God, and know my heart; test me and know my anxious thoughts. Point out anything in me that offends you and lead me along the path of everlasting life" (Ps. 139:23-24).
"But if we confess our sins to him, he is faithful and just to forgive us our sins and to cleanse us from all wickedness" (1 Jn. 1:9).
"leave your sacrifice there at the altar. Go and be reconciled to that person. Then come and offer your sacrifice to God" (Matt. 5:24).
"But if you refuse to forgive others, your Father will not forgive your sins" (Matt. 6:15).

People: Ver 12 As we forgive our debtors.
Needs of Others.
"I urge you, first of all, to pray for all people. Ask God to help them; intercede on their behalf and give thanks for them" (1 Tim. 2:1).

Protection: Ver 13 And do not lead us into temptation But deliver us from the evil one. For Yours is the kingdom and the power and the glory, for ever. Amen.

During Our Daily Spiritual Battle of Temptation. "Take my yoke upon you. Let me teach you, because I am humble and gentle at heart, and you will find rest for your souls. 30 For my yoke is easy to bear, and the burden I give you is light" (Matt. 11:29-30). "Therefore, put on every piece of God's armor so you will be able to resist the enemy in the time of evil. Then after the battle you will still be standing firm. Stand your ground, putting on the belt of truth and the body armor of God's righteousness. For shoes, put on the peace that comes from the Good News so that you will be fully prepared. In addition to all of these, hold up the shield of faith to stop the fiery arrows of the devil. Put on salvation as your helmet, and take the sword of the Spirit, which is the word of God. Pray in the Spirit at all times and on every occasion. Stay alert and be persistent in your prayers for all believers everywhere" (Eph. 6:13-18).

WORSHIP IS A WAY OF LIFE:
From sunrise in our morning prayer and devotion time in the Word with the Holy Spirit. To our sunset bedtime prayers, scripture readings as we go to sleep. In our earnest commitment and desire for a more intimate personal relationship with the Lord. We will remain in His presence throughout the day. Being led by the Holy Spirit as we grow spiritually and fulfill our holy calling. The Lord will even minister to us in our dreams of things to come.

"Never stop praying. Be thankful in all circumstances, for this is God's will for you who belong to Christ Jesus" (1Thes. 5:17-18).

"And you must love the Lord your God with all your heart, all your soul, all your mind, and all your strength. The second is equally important: 'Love your neighbor as yourself.' No other commandment is greater than these" (Mark 12:30-31).

"So, you see, faith by itself isn't enough. Unless it produces good deeds, it is dead and useless" (James 2:17).

"Since we are living by the Spirit, let us follow the Spirit's leading in every part of our lives" (Gal. 5:25).

A total life of self – giving and sacrifice.
"And so, dear brothers and sisters, I plead with you to give your bodies to God because of all he has done for you. Let them be a living and holy sacrifice—the kind he will find acceptable. This is truly the way to worship him" (Rom. 12:1)

"Don't copy the behavior and customs of this world, but let God transform you into a new person by changing the way you think. Then you will learn to know God's will for you, which is good and pleasing and perfect" (Rom. 12:2).

"And don't forget to do good and to share with those in need. These are the sacrifices that please God" (Heb. 13:16).

"Give, and you will receive. Your gift will return to you in full—pressed down, shaken together to make room for more, running over, and poured into your lap. The amount you give will determine the amount you get back" (Luke 6:38).

An earnest desire to remain in God's presence, in wholehearted devotion.
"But the time is coming—indeed it's here now—when true worshipers will worship the Father in spirit and in truth. The Father is looking for those who will worship him that way" (John 4:23).

"For God is Spirit, so those who worship him must worship in spirit and in truth" (John 4:24).

"For the Lord is the Spirit, and wherever the Spirit of the Lord is, there is freedom" (2 Cor. 3:17).

"When the Spirit of truth comes, he will guide you into all truth. He will not speak on his own but will tell you what he has heard. He will tell you about the future" (John 16:13).

"Therefore, let us offer through Jesus a continual sacrifice of praise to God, proclaiming our allegiance to his name" (Heb. 13:15).

Quiet Time Devotion:
Being in the Word with the Holy Spirit is critical to our spiritual growth and a personal intimate relationship with the Lord.

"For the word of God is alive and powerful. It is sharper than the sharpest two-edged sword, cutting between soul and spirit, between joint and marrow. It exposes our innermost thoughts and desires" (Heb. 4:12).

"Put on salvation as your helmet, and take the sword of the Spirit, which is the word of God" (Eph. 6:17).

"Jesus said to the people who believed in him, "You are truly my disciples if you remain faithful to my teachings. 32 And you will know the truth, and the truth will set you free" (John 8:31-32).

"And in that day you will ask Me nothing. Most assuredly, I say to you, whatever you ask the Father in My name He will give you" (John 16:23 NKJV).

Daily Worship to the Lord in Praise and Thanksgiving.
"Obedience is better than sacrifice, and submission is better than offering the fat of rams" (1 Sam. 22b).

"So let us come boldly to the throne of our gracious God. There we will receive his mercy, and we will find grace to help us when we need it most" (Heb. 4:16).

"Keep on asking, and you will receive what you ask for. Keep on seeking, and you will find. Keep on knocking, and the door will be opened to you" (Matt. 7:7).

"Sing a new song to the Lord! Let the whole earth sing to the Lord" (Ps. 96:1)!

"Pray in the Spirit at all times and on every occasion. Stay alert and be persistent in your prayers for all believers everywhere" (Eph. 6:18).

LESSON SUMMARY:

- Prayer is the way to communicate with God, and worship is the way to show your love to Him.

- "Enter his gates with thanksgiving; go into his courts with praise. Give thanks to him and praise his name. For the Lord is good. His unfailing love continues forever, and his faithfulness continues to each generation" (Ps. 100:4-5).

- "And in that day, you will ask Me nothing. Most assuredly, I say to you, whatever you ask the Father in My name He will give you" (John 16:23 NKJV).

- "Search me, O God, and know my heart; test me and know my anxious thoughts. Point out anything in me that offends you and lead me along the path of everlasting life" (Ps. 139:23-24).

- "Never stop praying. Be thankful in all circumstances, for this is God's will for you who belong to Christ Jesus" (1 Thes. 5:17-18).

*Note: Lesson Slides end at this point.

OBEDIENCE PRECEDES BLESSING:
"Don't just listen to God's Word. You must do what it says" (James 1:22).

When you are first learning to pray or even recommitting to making prayer a priority, you may feel distracted or overwhelmed about what to pray about. Just take a deep breath, maybe, play a worship song to get your mind focused and ask the Holy Spirit to help you pray. The Bible tells us many times to "pray in the Spirit" "And the Holy Spirit helps us in our weakness. For example, we don't know what God wants us to pray for. But the Holy Spirit prays for us with groanings that cannot be expressed in words. And the Father who knows all hearts knows what the Spirit is saying, for the Spirit pleads for us believers in harmony with God's own will" (Rom. 8:26-27).

Remember praying is having a conversation with God. You can be honest and share your deepest feelings with God. He wants to hear what you have to say. The pattern above does not have to be done every time. It is a pattern to teach you how to pray. You can talk to Him all day long, anytime, anywhere, but make a habit of beginning your day with some alone time to pray. Scripture records many times that Jesus got away by himself to pray. Let's look at how Jesus prayed: (move to grow deeper).

MEMORY VERSE:
"Lord, teach us to pray, as John also taught his disciples" (Luke 11:1 KJV).

GROW DEEPER:
"Then Christ will make His home in your hearts as you trust in Him. Your roots will grow down into God's love and keep you strong" (Eph. 3:17).

"Jesus said, "This is how you should pray: "Father, may your name be kept holy. May your Kingdom come soon. Give us each day the food we need, and forgive us our sins, as we forgive those who sin against us. And don't let us yield to temptation" (Luke 11:2-4).

JESUS HAS GIVEN US A PRAYER PATTERN TO FOLLOW:

Jesus Said:
1. Go into your room and close the door.
Nothing explains this better than The Message version "Here's what I want you to do: Find a quiet, secluded place so you won't be tempted to role-play before God. Just be there as simply and honestly as you can manage. The focus will shift from you to God, and you will begin to sense his grace" (Matt. 6:6 Message). Prayer is a personal thing between you and God, so you need a quiet, secluded place. If you have not found that place yet, stop and think about where that could be for you.

_____
_____
_____
_____

2. Do not babble.
When you pray, be yourself. God knows you; don't try to be someone else. Do not try to impress God with fancy words or speech. Speak from your heart.

"The Sovereign Lord has given me his words of wisdom, so that I know how to comfort the weary. Morning by morning he wakens me and opens my understanding to his will. The Sovereign Lord has spoken to me, and I have listened. I have not rebelled or turned away" (Isa. 50:4-5).

3. God knows what you need before you ask Him.
You do not have to catch God up with what is going on in your life. He already knows! You are praying to get close to God.

"Come close to God, and God will come close to you. Wash your hands, you sinners; purify your hearts, for your loyalty is divided between God and the world" (James 4:8).

You are opening the door and inviting your Father into the home of your heart and giving Him permission to intervene in your life.

"But if you remain in me and my words remain in you, you may ask for anything you want, and it will be granted" (John 15:7)!

What need do you have right now that you could take a moment and talk to God about it?

_____

_____

_____

_____

4. Our Father

Notice: Jesus did not say, God. He begins by calling God, Father. This implies a relationship; we are His children. Only those with the Holy Spirit can call God Father. "For all who are led by the Spirit of God are children of God. So you have not received a spirit that makes you fearful slaves. Instead, you received God's Spirit when he adopted you as his own children. Now we call him, "Abba, Father." For his Spirit joins with our spirit to affirm that we are God's children" (Rom. 8:14-16). Talking to Him as a child would talk to his loving Papa. There is no fear in asking in this kind of relationship. His love removes all fear. "We know how much God loves us, and we have put our trust in his love. God is love, and all who live in love live in God, and God lives in them. And as we live in God, our love grows more perfect. So, we will not be afraid on the day of judgment, but we can face him with confidence because we live like Jesus here in this world. Such love has no fear, because perfect love expels all fear. If we are afraid, it is for fear of punishment, and this shows that we have not fully experienced his perfect love" (1 John 4:16-18).

5. In Heaven

God is in Heaven. He is on the throne. He is eternal and is above all things. When you become aware of how great and awesome God is, your problems become small in comparison. It is like looking at a skyscraper. From the ground, the skyscraper seems huge, but from a tall mountain, the skyscraper looks like a speck of dust. Your problems may seem big, but your God is bigger.

"He heals the brokenhearted and bandages their wounds. He counts the stars and calls them all by name" (Ps. 147:3-4). Why do you think these two verses are together in the Bible?

_____

_____

_____

_____

What (is a) problem do you have that seems big to you?

_____

_____

_____

_____

Write out a prayer of praise acknowledging our God is bigger than your problem.

_____

_____

_____

_____

6. Hallowed be your name (consider adding the names of God)
Define hallowed.

_____

_____

_____

_____

Acknowledge that God is Holy. He is holy, holy, holy! When God says something twice in scripture, you should pay attention; but when He says it three times, stand up and salute. This is important! He is holy, holy, holy. Even His names are Holy. His names are sacred and set apart. His names deserve respect. He is good. He does not have any evil in Him. Trust in His goodness and praise Him with your words. Know and believe that He is for you and not against you. He wants the best for you. You praise Him for who He is and thank Him for what He has done for you. This part of the prayer is where you worship Him. When asked what worship is, most people would mention music, but music is only a channel for words. The words are what makes it worship. Let's think outside the box for a moment. How would you worship God without music?

_____

_____

_____

_____

"Enter his gates with thanksgiving; go into his courts with praise. Give thanks to him and praise his name" (Ps. 100:4). Thanksgiving is having an attitude of gratitude for what God has done. He has saved me. He has healed me. He has set me free. He let me wake up this morning. He gave me food to eat and air to breathe. Write something you are thankful for:

_____

_____

_____

_____

Praise is acknowledging God for who He is. He is my Savior, my Healer, my Deliverer, my Provider, let's stop right here and let you take a praise break! He is worthy of our praise! Write out a prayer of praise.

_____

_____

_____

_____

He is Holy, Holy, Holy! His name is Holy. If you are a Christian, you wear His name. Wear it well. Make your Daddy God proud!

7. Your kingdom come; your will be done on earth as it is in Heaven.
This is God's will for the earth. He wants heaven on earth. He wants heaven on the earth.

"Then the Lord God formed the man from the dust of the ground. He breathed the breath of life into the man's nostrils, and the man became a living person" (Gen. 2:7). What was man-made from?

_____

_____

_____

_____

Some versions say, "Your will be done IN earth." Man is made from the earth, so it is significant that we are praying, "Your will be done in earth…Your will be done in me." Jesus gave us a great example of this submitting, His will to His Father in the Garden of Gethsemane as He was facing the cross.

"Then, accompanied by the disciples, Jesus left the upstairs room and went as usual to the Mount of Olives. There he told them, "Pray that you will not give in to temptation." He walked away, about a stone's throw, and knelt down and prayed, "Father, if you are willing, please take this cup of suffering away from me. Yet I want your will to be done, not mine." Then an angel from heaven appeared and strengthened him. He prayed more fervently, and he was in such agony of spirit that his sweat fell to the ground like great drops of blood. At last, he stood up again and returned to the disciples, only to find them asleep, exhausted from grief. "Why are you sleeping?" he asked them. "Get up and pray, so that you will not give in to temptation." (Luke 22:39-46).

Do you think Jesus wanted to go to the cross?

_____

_____

_____

What did He do while He was in prayer?

_____

_____

_____

As it is in Heaven, God wants you to submit your will to Him. As it is in Heaven; God desires for everyone to know Him. As it is in Heaven, God desires for you to do good and not evil, to love Him, to love your neighbors, and to love yourself. When you pray, ask Him to let your desires align with His desires. "Take delight in the Lord, and he will give you your heart's desires" (Ps. 37:4) What do you think, "Delight yourself in the Lord" means?

_____

_____

_____

What does God promise to do after you do your part?

_____

_____

_____

How can you know what His will is? Simple, His will is His Word. When you have a need, ask God for a word. As you are reading His Word, listen for an answer to your need. When a verse speaks to your heart, you pray that Word. When you begin to pray the Word, your life will be radically changed. "And the Lord said, "That's right, and it means that I am watching, and I will certainly carry out all my plans" (Jer. 1:12). He wants to fulfill His Word in you. He wants His will to be done on earth and in earth as it is in Heaven. This is His desire because He is a very good Father.

8. Give us today our daily bread.

Now you ask for your daily necessities. Notice: Jesus said, "Give us today our daily bread." He did not say, "Give me the bread for this Lesson, this month, or even next year." This implies that prayer should be done daily. "So don't worry about tomorrow, for tomorrow will bring its own worries. Today's trouble is enough for today." (Matt. 6:34). He wants you to live a worry-free life by living a life of dependent prayer. "Don't worry about anything; instead, pray about everything. Tell God what you need and thank him for all he has done" (Phil. 4:6). The Bible also says, "Pray without ceasing" (1 Thess. 5:17). We should strive to maintain a close relationship with God throughout the day, in prayer, in our minds, and our hearts. Begin to make a habit of daily telling God what you need today and thanking Him for what He did yesterday.

9. Forgive us our debts as we have forgiven our debtors.

"Great is His faithfulness; His mercies begin afresh each morning" (Lam. 3:23). Every morning is like a new, fresh notebook. Start over. Write a new story today. Forgive anyone who wronged you yesterday and then ask God to forgive you for anything you did yesterday. Keep your forgiveness account up to date daily because you know you will need forgiveness at some point, and you want to forgive so you can be forgiven.

"Then Peter came to him and asked, "Lord, how often should I forgive someone who sins against me? Seven times?" "No, not seven times," Jesus replied, "but seventy times seven! "Therefore, the Kingdom of Heaven can be compared to a king who decided to bring his accounts up to date with servants who had borrowed money from him. In the process, one of his debtors was brought in who owed him millions of dollars. He couldn't pay, so his master ordered that he be sold—along with his wife, his children, and everything he owned—to pay the debt. "But the man fell down before his master and begged him, 'Please, be patient with me, and I will pay it all.' Then his master was filled with pity for him, and he released him and forgave his debt. "But when the man left the king, he went to a fellow servant who owed him a few thousand dollars. He grabbed him by the throat and demanded instant payment. "His fellow servant fell down before him and begged for a little more time. 'Be patient with me, and I will pay it,' he pleaded. But his creditor wouldn't wait. He had the man arrested and put in prison until the debt could be paid in full. "When some of the other servants saw this, they were very upset. They went to the king and told him everything that had happened. Then the king called in the man he had forgiven and said, 'You evil servant! I forgave you that tremendous debt because you pleaded with me. Shouldn't you have mercy on your fellow servant, just as I had mercy on you?' Then the angry king sent the man to prison to be tortured until he had paid his entire debt. "That's what my heavenly Father will do to you if you refuse to forgive your brothers and sisters from your heart" (Matt. 18:21-35).

Is there a limit to how many times you should forgive someone?

_____

_____

_____

_____

Is there ever a reason that you do not have to forgive?

_____

_____

_____

This is when you should dig down into your hearts and choose to forgive anyone who has sinned against you. You are asking God to forgive you in the same manner that you have forgiven others. If you have not forgiven someone, how do you expect God to forgive you? Forgiveness is not only for the other person but for yourself as well. It gives you a clear conscience before God and helps release any bitterness or anger which might be inside your heart. This is good for your health and your overall well-being. So, if there is anything to forgive, dig down, and forgive. How? Just choose to forgive. You probably will not feel it but choose to forgive. How can you choose to forgive? Just do it.

Forgive others, that includes yourself!

There are three levels of forgiveness:
Verbal: Start by speaking it out loud. Speak it to God, to the person, or a trusted friend. Say it! If the thought comes back, say it again. Choose to let it go. It is not saying that what they did is right. It is saying that you release the debt they owe you for what they did to you. Forgiveness is for you, not for them. Let it go.

I choose to forgive for (write out the verbal reason)

_____

_____

_____

Emotional: You will begin to feel better. You may think of that person and not feel angry or sick at your stomach. If any bad feelings come back up, say it out loud again. Let it go. Keep walking it out.

Heartfelt: At this point, you truly feel that forgiveness. You can think of that person and have no bad feelings. You can even pray God blesses that person. You have forgiven them, and God has manifested supernatural forgiveness and freedom in you.

Ask for Forgiveness:
If you have done anything wrong, you need to ask God to forgive you. Take a moment and ask God if there is anything in you that needs to be forgiven. "Search me, O God, and know my heart; test me and know my anxious thoughts. Point out anything in me that offends You and lead me along the path of everlasting life" (Ps. 139:23-24).

Take a moment to be still and see if God points out anything.

If He does, quickly ask Him to forgive you and then line up with His will for you. Forgive and be forgiven. "If you forgive those who sin against you, your heavenly Father will forgive you. But if you refuse to forgive others, your Father will not forgive your sins" (Matt. 6:14-15). "If we confess our sins to Him, what does He promise to do? 'But if we confess our sins to him, he is faithful and just to forgive us our sins and to cleanse us from all wickedness" (1 John 1:9).

_____

_____

_____

10. Lead us not into temptation but deliver us from the evil one.
Now, you are asking for God's protection during the day. First, ask for protection from the desires of the flesh and anything which might lead you to temptation. You need to ask God to help you overcome the desire to sin, and the strength to overcome any temptation you might face during the day. Second, ask for protection from the evil one. This is both supernatural and natural. Satan can use anyone and anything to hurt us, but the Bible says, "No weapon formed against you will prosper" (Isa. 54:17). Ask God to protect you from Satan's schemes and to protect you from people who wish to harm you. This way we can live in peace in the middle of a corrupt and evil world. Lord, keep me safe from myself and keep me safe from the enemy.

HOW DID JESUS PRAY?
Jesus had a Time.
Set a time. Make an appointment with God.
"Before daybreak the next morning, Jesus got up and went out to an isolated place to pray" (Mark 1:35).
"But Jesus often withdrew to the wilderness for prayer" (Luke 5:16).

He got alone in His Place.
Get alone with God, and as much as possible, get rid of noise and distractions.
"Before daybreak the next morning, Jesus got up and went out to an isolated place to pray" (Mark 1:35).
He prayed out loud.
When you pray, SAY it aloud!
"He went on a little farther and bowed with his face to the ground, praying, "My Father! If it is possible, let this cup of suffering be taken away from me. Yet I want your will to be done, not mine" (Matt. 26:39).
 "Jesus said, "This is how you should pray: "Father, may your name be kept holy. May your Kingdom come soon" (Luke 11:2).

He prayed by name.
Call your family out by name with the confidence that if He hears. He will answer what we have asked according to His will. "Simon, Simon, Satan has asked to sift each of you like wheat. 32 But I have pleaded in prayer for you, Simon, that your faith should not fail. So when you have repented and turned to me again, strengthen your brothers" (Luke 22:31-32). "And we are confident that he hears us whenever we ask for anything that pleases him" (1 John 5:14).

He prayed with others.

Find opportunities to pray with other believers.

Find a prayer partner and pray often and in agreement.

"About eight days later Jesus took Peter, John, and James up on a mountain to pray" (Luke 9:28).

"I tell you the truth, whatever you forbid on earth will be forbidden in heaven, and whatever you permit on earth will be permitted in heaven. "I also tell you this: If two of you agree here on earth concerning anything you ask, my Father in heaven will do it for you. For where two or three gather together as my followers, I am there among them" (Matt. 18:18-20).

WHEN YOU FAST:

Jesus practiced the discipline of fasting and praying, and we want to follow His example, but He also said, "When you fast…", not if you fast. "And when you fast, don't make it obvious, as the hypocrites do, for they try to look miserable and disheveled so people will admire them for their fasting. I tell you the truth, that is the only reward they will ever get. But when you fast, comb your hair and wash your face. Then no one will notice that you are fasting, except your Father, who knows what you do in private. And your Father, who sees everything, will reward you" (Matt. 6:16-18).

Fasting is giving up food and/or drink for a period as an element of private or public devotion. The fact that Jesus and the disciples practiced it by their example is one reason we should practice fasting and prayer. Another reason is He expected us to fast and pray when He said, "When you fast…" "For forty days and forty nights he fasted and became very hungry" (Matt. 4:2).

" So I turned to the Lord God and pleaded with him in prayer and fasting. I also wore rough burlap and sprinkled myself with ashes" (Dan. 9:3).

"Then she lived as a widow to the age of eighty-four. She never left the Temple but stayed there day and night, worshiping God with fasting and prayer" (Luke 2:37).

"One day as these men were worshiping the Lord and fasting, the Holy Spirit said, "Appoint Barnabas and Saul for the special work to which I have called them" (Acts 13:2).

"They called for a fast and put Naboth at a prominent place before the people" (1 Kings 21:12).

""Shout with the voice of a trumpet blast. Shout aloud! Don't be timid. Tell my people Israel of their sins! Yet they act so pious! They come to the Temple every day and seem delighted to learn all about me. They act like a righteous nation that would never abandon the laws of its God. They ask me to take action on their behalf, pretending they want to be near me. 'We have fasted before you!' they say. "Why aren't you impressed? We have been very hard on ourselves, and you don't even notice it!' "I will tell you why!" I respond. "It's because you are fasting to please yourselves. Even while you fast, you keep oppressing your workers. What good is fasting when you keep on fighting and quarreling? This kind of fasting will never get you anywhere with me. You humble yourselves by going through the motions of penance, bowing your heads like reeds bending in the wind. You dress in burlap and cover yourselves with ashes. Is this what you call fasting? Do you really think this will please the Lord? "No, this is the kind of fasting I want: Free those who are wrongly imprisoned; lighten the burden of those who work for you. Let the oppressed go free and remove the chains that bind people. Share your food with the hungry and give shelter to the homeless. Give clothes to those who need them, and do not hide from relatives who need your help. "Then your salvation will come like the dawn, and your wounds will quickly heal. Your godliness will lead you forward, and the glory of the

Lord will protect you from behind. Then when you call, the Lord will answer. 'Yes, I am here,' he will quickly reply. "Remove the heavy yoke of oppression. Stop pointing your finger and spreading vicious rumors! Feed the hungry and help those in trouble. Then your light will shine out from the darkness, and the darkness around you will be as bright as noon. The Lord will guide you continually, giving you water when you are dry and restoring your strength. You will be like a well-watered garden, like an ever-flowing spring. Some of you will rebuild the desrtcd ruins of your cities. Then you will be known as a rebuilder of walls and a restorer of homes. "Keep the Sabbath day holy. Don't pursue your own interests on that day but enjoy the Sabbath and speak of it with delight as the Lord's holy day. Honor the Sabbath in everything you do on that day, and don't follow your own desires or talk idly. Then the Lord will be your delight. I will give you great honor and satisfy you with the inheritance I promised to your ancestor Jacob. I, the Lord, have spoken!" (Isa. 58:1-14).

TYPES OF PRAYER:
The prayer of faith:
"Such a prayer offered in faith will heal the sick, and the Lord will make you well. And if you have committed any sins, you will be forgiven" (James 5:15). "What do you mean, 'If I can'?" Jesus asked. "Anything is possible if a person believes." (Mark 9:23).

The prayer of agreement:
"They all met together and were constantly united in prayer, along with Mary the mother of Jesus, several other women, and the brothers of Jesus" (Acts 1:14).
"All the believers devoted themselves to the apostles' teaching, and to fellowship, and to sharing in meals (including the Lord's Supper), and to prayer" (Acts 2:42).

The prayer of request (or supplication):
"Don't worry about anything; instead, pray about everything. Tell God what you need and thank him for all he has done" (Phil. 4:6). "Pray in the Spirit at all times and on every occasion. Stay alert and be persistent in your prayers for all believers everywhere" (Eph. 6:18).

The prayer of thanksgiving:
"Let everyone see that you are considerate in all you do. Remember, the Lord is coming soon" (Phil. 4:5).

The prayer of worship:
"One day as these men were worshiping the Lord and fasting, the Holy Spirit said, "Appoint Barnabas and Saul for the special work to which I have called them." So, after more fasting and prayer, the men laid their hands on them and sent them on their way" (Acts 13:2-3).

The prayer of consecration:
"He went on a little farther and bowed with his face to the ground, praying, "My Father! If it is possible, let this cup of suffering be taken away from me. Yet I want your will to be done, not mine" (Matt. 26:39).

The prayer of intercession:
"I urge you, first of all, to pray for all people. Ask God to help them; intercede on their behalf and give thanks for them" (1 Tim. 2:1). Read (John 17) below.

Praying in the Spirit:

"For if I pray in tongues, my spirit is praying, but I don't understand what I am saying. Well then, what shall I do? I will pray in the spirit, and I will also pray in words I understand. I will sing in the spirit, and I will also sing in words I understand" (1 Cor. 14:14-15).

"And the Holy Spirit helps us in our weakness. For example, we don't know what God wants us to pray for. But the Holy Spirit prays for us with groanings that cannot be expressed in words. And the Father who knows all hearts knows what the Spirit is saying, for the Spirit pleads for us believers in harmony with God's own will" (Rom. 8:26-27).

"After saying all these things, Jesus looked up to heaven and said, "Father, the hour has come. Glorify your Son so he can give glory back to you. For you have given him authority over everyone. He gives eternal life to each one you have given him. And this is the way to have eternal life—to know you, the only true God, and Jesus Christ, the one you sent to earth. I brought glory to you here on earth by completing the work you gave me to do. Now, Father, bring me into the glory we shared before the world began. "I have revealed you to the ones you gave me from this world. They were always yours. You gave them to me, and they have kept your word. Now they know that everything I have is a gift from you, for I have passed on to them the message you gave me. They accepted it and know that I came from you, and they believe you sent me. "My prayer is not for the world, but for those you have given me, because they belong to you. All who are mine belong to you, and you have given them to me, so they bring me glory. Now I am departing from the world; they are staying in this world, but I am coming to you. Holy Father, you have given me your name; now protect them by the power of your name so that they will be united just as we are. During my time here, I protected them by the power of the name you gave me. I guarded them so that not one was lost, except the one headed for destruction, as the Scriptures foretold. "Now I am coming to you. I told them many things while I was with them in this world so they would be filled with my joy. I have given them your word. And the world hates them because they do not belong to the world, just as I do not belong to the world. I'm not asking you to take them out of the world, but to keep them safe from the evil one. They do not belong to this world any more than I do. Make them holy by your truth; teach them your word, which is truth. Just as you sent me into the world, I am sending them into the world. And I give myself as a holy sacrifice for them so they can be made holy by your truth. "I am praying not only for these disciples but also for all who will ever believe in me through their message. I pray that they will all be one, just as you and I are one-as you are in me, Father, and I am in you. And may they be in us so that the world will believe you sent me. "I have given them the glory you gave me, so they may be one as we are one. I am in them, and you are in me. May they experience such perfect unity that the world will know that you sent me and that you love them as much as you love me. Father, I want these whom you have given me to be with me where I am. Then they can see all the glory you gave me because you loved me even before the world began! "O righteous Father, the world doesn't know you, but I do; and these disciples know you sent me. I have revealed you to them, and I will continue to do so. Then your love for me will be in them, and I will be in them" (John 17).

PUT ON YOUR ARMOR OF GOD:

"A final word: Be strong in the Lord and in his mighty power. Put on all of God's armor so that you will be able to stand firm against all strategies of the devil. For we are not fighting against flesh-and-blood enemies, but against evil rulers and authorities of the unseen world, against mighty powers in this dark world, and against evil spirits in the heavenly places. Therefore, put on every piece of God's armor so you will be able to resist the enemy in the time of evil. Then after the battle you will still be standing firm. Stand your ground, putting on the belt of truth and the body armor of God's righteousness. For shoes, put on the peace that comes from the Good News so that you will be fully prepared. In addition to all of these, hold up the shield of faith to stop the fiery arrows of the devil. Put on salvation as your helmet, and take the sword of the Spirit, which is the word of God" (Eph. 6:10-18).

Helmet of Salvation – Help me to think right and protect my mind.

Breastplate of Righteousness – Help me to choose to do the next right thing.

Belt of Truth – Help me to believe the truth and to speak the truth in love.

Shoes of the Gospel of Peace – Help me to walk in peace and be ready to share Jesus at all times!

Shield of Faith – I believe:
You are who You say You are!
You can do what You say You can do!
I am who You say I am!
I can do all things through Christ!

Sword of the Spirit, which is the Word of God – Help me to win by praying Your Word. Your Word is alive and active in me!

"Pray in the Spirit at all times and on every occasion. Stay alert and be persistent in your prayers for all believers everywhere. And pray for me, too. Ask God to give me the right words so I can boldly explain God's mysterious plan that the Good News is for Jews and Gentiles alike. I am in chains now, still preaching this message as God's ambassador. So, pray that I will keep on speaking boldly for him, as I should. (Eph. 6:18-20).

STAY FILLED WITH THE HOLY SPIRIT

PURPOSE OF THIS LESSON:

To help you actively be in a daily intimate relationship with the Holy Spirit and mature in Christ. To let Him guide you into all truth and allow Him to lead you in grace and truth.

"When the Spirit of truth comes, he will guide you into all truth" (John 16:13a). "For all who are led by the Spirit of God are children of God" (Romans 8:14). "But it was to us that God revealed these things by his Spirit. For his Spirit searches out everything and shows us God's deep secrets" (1 Cor. 2:10). This lesson will also show you the purpose and importance of the Gifts of the Holy Spirit to the Body of Christ. "A spiritual gift is given to each of us so we can help each other" (1 Cor. 12:7). "It is the one and only Spirit who distributes all these gifts. He alone decides which gift each person should have" (1 Cor. 12:11).

INTRODUCTION:

The Holy Spirit lives within you and will produce the Fruit of the Spirit in your life, transforming you to become more like Jesus.

"Don't you realize that your body is the temple of the Holy Spirit, who lives in you and was given to you by God? You do not belong to yourself, for God bought you with a high price. So you must honor God with your body" (1 Cor. 6:19-20). "The Spirit is God's guarantee that he will give us the inheritance he promised and that he has purchased us to be his own people. He did this so we would praise and glorify him" (Eph. 1:14). "But the Holy Spirit produces this kind of fruit in our lives: love, joy, peace, patience, kindness, goodness, faithfulness, gentleness, and self-control. There is no law against these things" (Gal. 5:22-23)! "Therefore, if anyone is in Christ, he is a new creation; old things have passed away; behold, all things have become new" (2 Cor. 5:17 NKJV).

The Holy Spirit has been part of the Trinity (Father, Son, and Holy Spirit) since the beginning of time as we know it. "The earth was formless and empty, and darkness covered the deep waters. And the Spirit of God was hovering over the surface of the waters" (Gen. 1:2). From the creation of man in the Old Testament through Jesus walking on the earth, the Holy Spirit was actively involved in people's lives, but this involvement was selective and temporary. For example, Saul, for whom the Spirit of God came upon, "At that time the Spirit of the Lord will come powerfully upon you, and you will prophesy with them. You will be changed into a different person" (1 Sam. 10:6). and then, the Spirit left him. "Now the Spirit of the Lord had left Saul, and the Lord sent a tormenting spirit that filled him with depression and fear" (1 Sam. 16:14). In the book of John, chapters 14-16, Jesus was preparing the disciples that He would be leaving them. He was also telling them that Father God would send the Holy Spirit, our Comforter, Encourager, Counselor, and Advocate, to not just be with the Believers, but will begin to live IN each Believer. "He is the Holy Spirit, who leads into all truth. The world cannot receive him, because it isn't looking for him and doesn't recognize him. But you know him, because he lives with you now and later will be in you" (John 14:17). "And God has given us his Spirit as proof that we live in him and he in us" (1 John 4:13). "And now you Gentiles have also heard the truth, the Good News that God saves you. And when you believed in Christ, he identified you as his own by giving you the Holy Spirit, whom he promised long ago. The Spirit is God's guarantee that he will give us the inheritance he promised and that he has purchased us to be his own people. He did this so we would praise and glorify him" (Eph. 1:13-14).

What does God giving you the Holy Spirit prove and promise to you personally?

_____

_____

_____

_____

WHY IS THIS LESSON IMPORTANT IN YOUR LIFE?
Because without the in-dwelling presence and power of the Holy Spirit, you are trying to live the Christian life in your own strength, not in Christ.

"And being assembled with them, He commanded them not to depart from Jerusalem, but to wait for the Promise of the Father, "which," He said, "you have heard from Me; for John truly baptized with water, but you shall be baptized with the Holy Spirit not many days from now" (Acts 1:4-5 NKJV). "But you will receive power when the Holy Spirit comes upon you. And you will be my witnesses, telling people about me everywhere—in Jerusalem, throughout Judea, in Samaria, and to the ends of the earth" (Acts 1:8). "John answered their questions by saying, "I baptize you with water; but someone is coming soon who is greater than I am—so much greater that I'm not even worthy to be his slave and untie the straps of his sandals. He will baptize you with the Holy Spirit and with fire" (Luke 3:16).

"Then he said to me, "This is what the Lord says to Zerubbabel: It is not by force nor by strength, but by my Spirit, says the Lord of Heaven's Armies" (Zechariah 4:6). Basically, according to God Himself, you cannot do it alone. Jesus will baptize us with the Holy Spirit and with fire. In Acts 2, the Holy Spirit exploded on the scene with dynamite power, wind, fire, tongues, miracles, joy, praise, worship, and ministry. When a Christian is baptized with the Holy Spirit, they receive the power and anointing to live a life of victory. Let's look at an example of someone in the Bible before and after the Holy Spirit. Let's look at Peter. Read about Peter before the Holy Spirit.

"From then on Jesus began to tell his disciples plainly that it was necessary for him to go to Jerusalem, and that he would suffer many terrible things at the hands of the elders, the leading priests, and the teachers of religious law. He would be killed, but on the third day he would be raised from the dead. But Peter took him aside and began to reprimand him for saying such things. "Heaven forbids, Lord," he said. "This will never happen to you!" Jesus turned to Peter and said, "Get away from me, Satan! You are a dangerous trap to me. You are seeing things merely from a human point of view, not from God's" (Matt. 16:21-23). "Then Simon Peter drew a sword and slashed off the right ear of Malchus, the high priest's slave"(John 18:10). "Simon Peter asked, "Lord, where are you going?" And Jesus replied, "You can't go with me now, but you will follow me later." "But why can't I come now, Lord?" he asked. "I'm ready to die for you." Jesus answered, "Die for me? I tell you the truth, Peter—before the rooster crows tomorrow morning, you will deny three times that you even know me" (John 13:36-38).

"Simon Peter followed Jesus, as did another of the disciples. That other disciple was acquainted with the high priest, so he was allowed to enter the high priest's courtyard with Jesus. Peter had to stay outside the gate. Then the disciple who knew the high priest spoke to the woman watching at the gate, and she let Peter in. The woman asked Peter, "You're not one of that man's disciples, are you?" "No," he said, "I am not." Because it was cold, the household servants and the guards had made a charcoal fire. They stood around it, warming themselves, and Peter stood with them, warming himself" (John 18:15-18).

Read: (John Chapters 25-27).
Name some things Peter did before he was baptized in the Holy Spirit.

_____
_____
_____
_____

"Then Peter stepped forward with the eleven other apostles and shouted to the crowd, "Listen carefully, all of you, fellow Jews and residents of Jerusalem! Make no mistake about this. These people are not drunk, as some of you assume. Nine o'clock in the morning is much too early for that. No, what you see was predicted long ago by the prophet Joel: 'In the last days,' God says, 'I will pour out my Spirit upon all people. Your sons and daughters will prophesy. Your young men will see visions, and your old men will dream dreams. In those days I will pour out my Spirit even on my servants—men and women alike—and they will prophesy. And I will cause wonders in the heavens above and signs on the earth below— blood and fire and clouds of smoke. The sun will become dark, and the moon will turn blood red before that great and glorious day of the Lord arrives. But everyone who calls on the name of the Lord will be saved.' "People of Israel, listen! God publicly endorsed Jesus the Nazarene by doing powerful miracles, wonders, and signs through him, as you well know. But God knew what would happen, and his prearranged plan was carried out when Jesus was betrayed. With the help of lawless Gentiles, you nailed him to a cross and killed him. But God released him from the horrors of death and raised him back to life, for death could not keep him in its grip. King David said this about him: 'I see that the Lord is always with me. I will not be shaken, for he is right beside me. No wonder my heart is glad, and my tongue shouts his praises! My body rests in hope. For you will not leave my soul among the dead or allow your Holy One to rot in the grave. You have shown me the way of life, and you will fill me with the joy of your presence.' "Dear brothers, think about this! You can be sure that the patriarch David wasn't referring to himself, for he died and was buried, and his tomb is still here among us. But he was a prophet, and he knew God had promised with an oath that one of David's own descendants would sit on his throne. David was looking into the future and speaking of the Messiah's resurrection. He was saying that God would not leave him among the dead or allow his body to rot in the grave. "God raised Jesus from the dead, and we are all witnesses of this. Now he is exalted to the place of highest honor in heaven, at God's right hand. And the Father, as he had promised, gave him the Holy Spirit to pour out upon us, just as you see and hear today. For David himself never ascended into heaven, yet he said, 'The Lord said to my Lord, "Sit in the place of honor at my right hand until I humble your enemies, making them a footstool under your feet."' "So let everyone in Israel know for certain that God has made this Jesus, whom you crucified, to be both Lord and Messiah!" Peter's words pierced their hearts, and they said to him and to the other apostles, "Brothers, what should we do?" Peter replied, "Each of you must repent of your sins and turn to God and be baptized in the name of Jesus Christ for the forgiveness of your sins. Then you will receive the gift of the Holy Spirit. This promise is to you, to your children, and to those far away-all who have been called by the Lord our God." Then Peter continued preaching for a long time, strongly urging all his listeners, "Save yourselves from this crooked generation!" Those who believed what Peter said were baptized and added to the church that day—about 3,000 in all" (Acts 2:14-41).

What did Peter do after he was baptized in the Holy Spirit?

_____

_____

_____

Another reason this lesson is important is because of a very important principle found in "When an evil spirit leaves a person, it goes into the desert, seeking rest but finding none. Then it says, 'I will return to the person I came from.' So, it returns and finds its former home empty, swept, and in order. Then the spirit finds seven other spirits more evil than itself, and they all enter the person and live there. And so that person is worse off than before. That will be the experience of this evil generation" (Matt. 12:43-45). When you get rid of an evil spirit, it will come back. If you have not filled your temple with the Holy Spirit (after all, it is His temple) and the Word of God, that evil spirit will find seven other spirits, more evil than itself, and they all enter the person and live there. "Don't you realize that your body is the temple of the Holy Spirit, who lives in you and was given to you by God? You do not belong to yourself" (1 Cor. 6:19). The bottom line to this is: leave no room for the enemy and keep the doors locked! This is the only way to STAY FREE! "But you belong to God, my dear children. You have already won a victory over those people because the Spirit who lives in you is greater than the spirit who lives in the world" (1 John 4:4).

WHAT DOES THE BIBLE SAY THE HOLY SPIRIT WILL DO IN YOU?
It is always very important that you base what you believe on what the Bible says vs. what man or tradition says. Some people have made the Holy Spirit out to be weird, spooky, and odd. The truth is He is God, the third person in the Trinity. Read each one of these statements and the scripture that it is based on. After reading these thirteen statements, write a Declaration of Faith (a Godly Belief based on the Word of God) about the Holy Spirit.

1. He enables you to be born again.
"Jesus replied, "I assure you, no one can enter the Kingdom of God without being born of water and the Spirit. Humans can reproduce only human life, but the Holy Spirit gives birth to spiritual life. So don't be surprised when I say, 'You must be born again.' The wind blows wherever it wants. Just as you can hear the wind but can't tell where it comes from or where it is going, so you can't explain how people are born of the Spirit." (John 3:5-8).

2. He enables you to speak as God would have you speak.
"But when you are arrested and stand trial, don't worry in advance about what to say. Just say what God tells you at that time, for it is not you who will be speaking, but the Holy Spirit" (Mark 13:11).

3. He will be your Counselor forever.
"And I will ask the Father, and he will give you another Advocate, who will never leave you" (John 14:16).

4. He lives in you.
"He is the Holy Spirit, who leads into all truth. The world cannot receive him, because it isn't looking for him and doesn't recognize him. But you know him, because he lives with you now and later will be in you" (John 14:17).

5. He teaches you and guides you into all truth.

"But when the Father sends the Advocate as my representative—that is, the Holy Spirit—he will teach you everything and will remind you of everything I have told you" (John 14:26). "When the Spirit of truth comes, he will guide you into all truth. He will not speak on his own but will tell you what he has heard. He will tell you about the future. 14 He will bring me glory by telling you whatever he receives from me. 15 All that belongs to the Father is mine; this is why I said, 'The Spirit will tell you whatever he receives from me" (John 16:13-15).

6. He reveals deep secrets.

"But it was to us that God revealed these things by his Spirit. For his Spirit searches out everything and shows us God's deep secrets" (1 Cor. 2:10).

7. He gives you the power to be a witness.

"But you will receive power when the Holy Spirit comes upon you. And you will be my witnesses, telling people about me everywhere—in Jerusalem, throughout Judea, in Samaria, and to the ends of the earth." (Acts 1:8).

8. He empowers you to drive out demons.

But if I am casting out demons by the Spirit of God, then the Kingdom of God has arrived among you." (Matt. 12:28). "These miraculous signs will accompany those who believe: They will cast out demons in my name, and they will speak in new languages" (Mark 16:17). "One day as we were going down to the place of prayer, we met a slave girl who had a spirit that enabled her to tell the future. She earned a lot of money for her masters by telling fortunes. She followed Paul and the rest of us, shouting, "These men are servants of the Most High God, and they have come to tell you how to be saved." This went on day after day until Paul got so exasperated that he turned and said to the demon within her, "I command you in the name of Jesus Christ to come out of her." And instantly it left her" (Acts 16:16-18).

9. He causes God's love to be poured into your heart.

"And this hope will not lead to disappointment. For we know how dearly God loves us, because he has given us the Holy Spirit to fill our hearts with his love" (Rom. 5:5).

10. He helps you in your weakness.

"And the Holy Spirit helps us in our weakness. For example, we don't know what God wants us to pray for. But the Holy Spirit prays for us with groanings that cannot be expressed in words. And the Father who knows all hearts knows what the Spirit is saying, for the Spirit pleads for us believers in harmony with God's own will" (Rom. 8:26-27).

11. He causes righteousness, peace, and joy to dwell in you.

"For the Kingdom of God is not a matter of what we eat or drink, but of living a life of goodness and peace and joy in the Holy Spirit" (Rom. 14:17).

12. He enables you to overflow with hope.

"I pray that God, the source of hope, will fill you completely with joy and peace because you trust in him. Then you will overflow with confident hope through the power of the Holy Spirit" (Rom. 15:13).

13. **He sanctifies you.**
" I am a special messenger from Christ Jesus to you Gentiles. I bring you the Good News so that I might present you as an acceptable offering to God, made holy by the Holy Spirit" (Rom. 15:16).

Based on these scriptures, write your Declaration of Faith about the Holy Spirit.
I believe that the Holy Spirit

_____

_____

_____

THE HOLY SPIRIT IS LIVING WATER:
"but whoever drinks of the water that I shall give him will never thirst. But the water that I shall give him will become in him a fountain of water springing up into everlasting life" (Jn. 4:14 NKJV).

The Holy Spirit is symbolized by Living Water.
"For I will pour out water to quench your thirst and to irrigate your parched fields. And I will pour out my Spirit on your descendants, and my blessing on your children. They will thrive like watered grass, like willows on a riverbank" (Isa. 44:3-4). "On the last day, the climax of the festival, Jesus stood and shouted to the crowds, "Anyone who is thirsty may come to me! Anyone who believes in me may come and drink! For the Scriptures declare, 'Rivers of living water will flow from his heart.'" (When he said "living water," he was speaking of the Spirit, who would be given to everyone believing in him. But the Spirit had not yet been given, because Jesus had not yet entered into his glory.)" (John 7:37-39). You cannot exist without water in your physical life. Without water, you would die. Think of things that water can do for you in your everyday life. The same water that hardens eggs can soften potatoes.

Make a list of things that water can do and then determine how that can apply to your spiritual life.

_____

_____

_____

THE HOLY SPIRIT PRODUCES FRUIT IN YOUR LIFE:
"For we through the Spirit wait for the hope of righteousness by faith" (Gal. 5:5 KJV).
"But the fruit of the Spirit is love, joy, peace, patience, kindness, goodness, faithfulness, gentleness, self-control; against such things there is no law" (Gal. 5:22-23 NASB).

How is the fruit produced in your life?
If a farmer owns an apple tree, he does not walk by and suddenly put apples on the tree. The farmer makes sure the tree is watered, pruned, has sunshine, and is cared for. It is the same as the fruit of the Spirit. He gives you living water, points out, and helps you remove things that hurt you, makes sure you have the light of Jesus in your life, He loves you and cares for you.

"So I say, let the Holy Spirit guide your lives. Then you won't be doing what your sinful nature craves. The sinful nature wants to do evil, which is just the opposite of what the Spirit wants. And the Spirit gives us desires that are the opposite of what the sinful nature desires. These two forces are constantly fighting each other, so you are not free to carry out your good intentions. But when you are directed by the Spirit, you are not under obligation to the law of Moses. When you follow the desires of your sinful nature, the results are very clear: sexual immorality, impurity, lustful pleasures, idolatry, sorcery, hostility, quarreling, jealousy, outbursts of anger, selfish ambition, dissension, division, envy, drunkenness, wild parties, and other sins like these. Let me tell you again, as I have before, that anyone living that sort of life will not inherit the Kingdom of God. But the Holy Spirit produces this kind of fruit in our lives: love, joy, peace, patience, kindness, goodness, faithfulness, gentleness, and self-control. There is no law against these things" (Gal. 5:16-23)!

How do you think the Holy Spirit produces fruit in your life?

_____

_____

_____

It is important to note that fruit is not given; fruit grows. The more you follow the leading and guiding of the Holy Spirit, the more fruit He can produce in your life.

Define each fruit listed and find one verse for each fruit. If you do not know how to do this, please ask one of your leaders.

1. Love _____
2. Joy _____
3. Peace _____
4. Patience _____
5. Kindness _____
6. Goodness _____
7. Gentleness _____
8. Faithfulness _____
9. Self-Control _____

"I am the true grapevine, and my Father is the gardener. He cuts off every branch of mine that doesn't produce fruit, and he prunes the branches that do bear fruit so they will produce even more. You have already been pruned and purified by the message I have given you. Remain in me, and I will remain in you. For a branch cannot produce fruit if it is severed from the vine, and you cannot be fruitful unless you remain in me. "Yes, I am the vine; you are the branches. Those who remain in me, and I in them, will produce much fruit. For apart from me you can do nothing. Anyone who does not remain in me is thrown away like a useless branch and withers. Such branches are gathered into a pile to be burned. But if you remain in me and my words remain in you, you may ask for anything you want, and it will be granted! When you produce much fruit, you are my true disciples. This brings great glory to my Father. "I have loved you even as the Father has loved me. Remain in my love. When you obey my commandments, you remain in my love, just as I obey my Father's commandments and remain in his love. I have told you these things so that you will be filled with my joy. Yes, your joy will overflow" (John 15:1-11)!

What is the key to bearing fruit in your life?

_____

_____

_____

"Even in old age they will still produce fruit; they will remain vital and green" (Ps. 92:14).

How long can you bear fruit? _____

"You didn't choose me. I chose you. I appointed you to go and produce lasting fruit, so that the Father will give you whatever you ask for, using my name" (John 15:16).

What kind of fruit did Jesus choose you to bear? _____

FRUIT OF THE HOLY SPIRIT:
"But the Holy Spirit produces this kind of fruit in our lives: love, joy, peace, patience, kindness, goodness, faithfulness, gentleness, and self-control. There is no law against these things" (Gal. 5:22-23)

LOVE
"Now hope does not disappoint, because the love of God has been poured out in our hearts by the Holy Spirit who was given to us" (Rom. 5:5 NKJV). "We love because He first loved us" (1 Jn. 4:19 NASB).
"For God so loved the world that He gave His only begotten Son, that whoever believes in Him should not perish but have everlasting life" (Jn. 3:16 NKJV). "He who does not love does not know God, for God is love" (1 Jn. 4:8 NKJV). "But above all these things put on love, which is the bond of perfection" (Col. 3:14 NKJV). "As the Father loved Me, I also have loved you; abide in My love. If you keep My commandments, you will abide in My love, just as I have kept My Father's commandments and abide in His love" (John 15:9-10 NKJV).

JOY
"These things I have spoken to you, that My joy may remain in you, and that your joy may be full" (John 15:11 NKJV). "Now may the God of hope fill you with all joy and peace in believing, that you may abound in hope by the power of the Holy Spirit" (Rom. 15:13 NKJV). "but whoever drinks of the water that I shall give him will never thirst. But the water that I shall give him will become in him a fountain of water springing up into everlasting life" (Jn. 4:14 NKJV). "Restore unto me the joy of thy salvation; and uphold me with thy free spirit". (Ps. 51:12 KJV).

PEACE
"Peace I leave with you, my peace I give unto you: not as the world giveth, give I unto you. Let not your heart be troubled, neither let it be afraid" (Jn. 14:27 KJV). "And I will pray the Father, and he shall give you another Comforter, that he may abide with you for ever" (Jn. 14:16 KJV); "And your feet shod with the preparation of the gospel of peace" (Eph. 6:15 KJV); "But now in Christ Jesus you who once were far off have been brought near by the blood of Christ. For He Himself is our peace, who has made both one, and has broken down the middle wall of separation" (Eph. 2:13-14 NKJV), "And let the peace of God rule in your hearts, to which also you were called in one body; and be thankful" (Col. 3:15 NKJV).

PATIENCE (Longsuffering)
"Always be humble and gentle. Be patient with each other, making allowance for each other's faults because of your love. Make every effort to keep yourselves united in the Spirit, binding yourselves together with peace" (Eph. 4:2-3). "The Lord isn't really being slow about his promise, as some people

think. No, he is being patient for your sake. He does not want anyone to be destroyed, but wants everyone to repent" (2 Peter 3:9).

KINDNESS (Gentleness)
"Therefore, as the elect of God, holy and beloved, put on tender mercies, kindness, humility, meekness, longsuffering; bearing with one another, and forgiving one another, if anyone has a complaint against another; even as Christ forgave you, so you also must do" (Col. 3:12-13 NKJV).

GOODNESS
"How God anointed Jesus of Nazareth with the Holy Ghost and with power: who went about doing good, and healing all that were oppressed of the devil; for God was with him" (Acts 10:38 KJV). "Surely goodness and mercy shall follow me all the days of my life: and I will dwell in the house of the Lord for ever" (Ps. 23:6 KJV).

FAITHFULNESS (Faith)
"Who then is a faithful and wise servant, whom his lord hath made ruler over his household, to give them meat in due season? Blessed is that servant, whom his lord when he cometh shall find so doing" (Mat 24:45-46 KJV).

GENTLENESS (Meekness)
"but sanctify Christ as Lord in your hearts, always being ready to make a defense to everyone who asks you to give an account for the hope that is in you, but with gentleness and respect" (1 Peter 3:15 KJV);

SELF-CONTROL (Temperance)
"For God has not given us a spirit of fear and timidity, but of power, love, and self-discipline" (2 Tim 1:7). "But also for this very reason, giving all diligence, add to your faith virtue, to virtue knowledge, to knowledge self-control, to self-control [patience]perseverance, to perseverance godliness, to godliness brotherly kindness, and to brotherly kindness love" (2 Peter 1:5-7 NKJV).

YOU ARE ANOINTED BY THE HOLY SPIRIT:
"The Spirit of the Lord is upon me, for he has anointed me to bring Good News to the poor. He has sent me to proclaim that captives will be released, that the blind will see, that the oppressed will be set free" (Luke 4:18), Jesus was quoting Isa. 61:1, when He spoke these Words over Himself. Jesus announced that He was and is the Messiah, which means Anointed One, the Son of God. Pay attention to what Jesus said in Luke 4:18, "The Spirit of the LORD is upon me…" When what is in you comes upon you, you will be baptized in the Holy Spirit. When you receive salvation, the Holy Spirit comes to live IN you. When you get baptized in the Holy Spirit, what is IN you (the Holy Spirit) comes UPON you. Then you begin to walk in your anointing with the dynamite power of the Holy Spirit.

THE HOLY SPIRIT GIVES YOU GIFTS:
"But the manifestation of the Spirit is given to each one for the profit of all: for to one is given the word of wisdom through the Spirit, to another the word of knowledge through the same Spirit, to another faith by the same Spirit, to another gifts of healings by the same Spirit, to another the working of miracles, to another prophecy, to another discerning of spirits, to another different kinds of tongues, to another the interpretation of tongues. But one and the same Spirit works all these things, distributing to each one individually as He wills" (1 Corinthians 12:7-11 NKJV).

1. **Word of Wisdom** – A message shared as an application or directive from the Holy Spirit for a specific situation, or a timely insight (specific application) illuminated by the Spirit from scripture concerning a person's future or going forward in a current situation.
"The Lord said, "Go over to Straight Street, to the house of Judas. When you get there, ask for a man from Tarsus named Saul. He is praying to me right now. I have shown him a vision of a man named Ananias coming in and laying hands on him so he can see again" (Acts 9:11-12). " Next Paul and Silas traveled through the area of Phrygia and Galatia because the Holy Spirit had prevented them from preaching the word in the province of Asia at that time. Then coming to the borders of Mysia, they headed north for the province of Bithynia, but again the Spirit of Jesus did not allow them to go there" (Acts 16:6-7). "He had to go through Samaria on the way" (John 4:4).

2. **Word of Knowledge** – A message from the Holy Spirit that includes knowledge, facts, or information that would not be known to the speaker beforehand, or a timely instruction (teaching) illuminated by the Spirit from scripture concerning something that pertains to a person's past or present.
"Then Peter said, "Ananias, why have you let Satan fill your heart? You lied to the Holy Spirit, and you kept some of the money for yourself. 4 The property was yours to sell or not sell, as you wished. And after selling it, the money was also yours to give away. How could you do a thing like this? You weren't lying to us but to God" (Acts 5:3-4)! "I have shown him a vision of a man named Ananias coming in and laying hands on him so he can see again." (Acts 9:12).

3. **Faith** – To be firmly persuaded of God's power and promises to accomplish His will and purpose and to display such a confidence in Him and His Word that circumstances and obstacles do not shake that conviction. Read: (Romans Chapter 4). "And he said to her, "Daughter, your faith has made you well. Go in peace. Your suffering is over." 36 But Jesus overheard them and said to Jairus, "Don't be afraid. Just have faith" (Mark 5:34, 36).

4. **Healing** – To be used as a means through which God makes people whole either physically, emotionally, mentally, or spiritually. "They will be able to handle snakes with safety, and if they drink anything poisonous, it won't hurt them. They will be able to place their hands on the sick, and they will be healed" (Mark 16:18). "As it happened, Publius's father was ill with fever and dysentery. Paul went in and prayed for him, and laying his hands on him, he healed him" (Acts 28:8).

5. **Miracles** – To be enabled by God to perform mighty deeds which witnesses acknowledge to be of supernatural origin and means. "And God confirmed the message by giving signs and wonders and various miracles and gifts of the Holy Spirit whenever he chose" (Heb. 2:4). "God gave Paul the power to perform unusual miracles" (Acts 19:11). "Holding her hand, he said to her, "Talitha koum," which means "Little girl, get up!" And the girl, who was twelve years old, immediately stood up and walked around! They were overwhelmed and totally amazed" (Mark 5:41-42).

6. **Prophecy** – To speak forth the message of God to His people.
"But one who prophesies strengthens others, encourages them, and comforts them. A person who speaks in tongues is strengthened personally, but one who speaks a word of prophecy strengthens the entire church" (1 Cor. 14:3-4). "In this way, all who prophesy will have a turn to speak, one after the other, so that everyone will learn and be encouraged. 39 So, my dear brothers and sisters, be eager to prophesy, and don't forbid speaking in tongues" (1 Cor. 14:31, 39). "In those days I will pour out my Spirit even on my servants—men and women alike and they will prophesy" (Acts 2:18). "When we returned to the ship at the end of the week, the entire congregation, including women and children, left

the city and came down to the shore with us. There we knelt, prayed" (Acts 21:5). "In his grace, God has given us different gifts for doing certain things well. So if God has given you the ability to prophesy, speak out with as much faith as God has given you" (Rom. 12:6). "But a woman dishonors her head if she prays or prophesies without a covering on her head, for this is the same as shaving her head" (1 Cor. 11:5).

7. **Discerning of Spirits** – To clearly distinguish truth from error by judging whether the behavior or teaching is from God, satan, human error, or human power. "Simon, Simon, Satan has asked to sift each of you like wheat. But I have pleaded in prayer for you, Simon, that your faith should not fail. So, when you have repented and turned to me again, strengthen your brothers." (Luke 22:31-32). This is how we know if they have the Spirit of God: If a person claiming to be a prophet acknowledges that Jesus Christ came in a real body, that person has the Spirit of God. But if someone claims to be a prophet and does not acknowledge the truth about Jesus, that person is not from God. Such a person has the spirit of the Antichrist, which you heard is coming into the world and indeed is already here. But you belong to God, my dear children. You have already won a victory over those people because the Spirit who lives in you is greater than the spirit who lives in the world. Those people belong to this world, so they speak from the world's viewpoint, and the world listens to them. But we belong to God, and those who know God listen to us. If they do not belong to God, they do not listen to us. That is how we know if someone has the Spirit of truth or the spirit of deception" (1 John 4:2-6).

"And the Father who knows all hearts knows what the Spirit is saying, for the Spirit pleads for us believers in harmony with God's own will" (Rom. 8:27). "But it was to us that God revealed these things by his Spirit. For his Spirit searches out everything and shows us God's deep secrets. No one can know a person's thoughts except that person's own spirit, and no one can know God's thoughts except God's own Spirit. And we have received God's Spirit (not the world's spirit), so we can know the wonderful things God has freely given us. When we tell you these things, we do not use words that come from human wisdom. Instead, we speak words given to us by the Spirit, using the Spirit's words to explain spiritual truths. But people who aren't spiritual can't receive these truths from God's Spirit. It all sounds foolish to them and they can't understand it, for only those who are spiritual can understand what the Spirit means. Those who are spiritual can evaluate all things, but they themselves cannot be evaluated by others. For, "Who can know the Lord's thoughts? Who knows enough to teach him" (1 Cor. 2:10-16)? "Give me an understanding heart so that I can govern your people well and know the difference between right and wrong. For who by himself is able to govern this great people of yours" (1 Kings 3:9)?

8. **Tongues** - To speak in a language not previously learned so unbelievers can hear God's message in their language or so the body can be edified. "On the day of Pentecost all the believers were meeting together in one place. Suddenly, there was a sound from heaven like the roaring of a mighty windstorm, and it filled the house where they were sitting. Then, what looked like flames or tongues of fire appeared and settled on each of them. And everyone present was filled with the Holy Spirit and began speaking in other languages, as the Holy Spirit gave them this ability. At that time there were devout Jews from every nation living in Jerusalem. 6 When they heard the loud noise, everyone came running, and they were bewildered to hear their own languages being spoken by the believers. They were completely amazed. "How can this be?" they exclaimed. "These people are all from Galilee, and yet we hear them speaking in our own native languages! Here we are—Parthians, Medes, Elamites, people from Mesopotamia, Judea, Cappadocia, Pontus, the province of Asia, Phrygia, Pamphylia, Egypt, and the areas of Libya around Cyrene, visitors from Rome (both Jews and converts to Judaism), Cretans, and Arabs. And we all hear these people speaking in our own languages about the wonderful

things God has done!" They stood there amazed and perplexed. "What can this mean?" they asked each other. But others in the crowd ridiculed them, saying, "They're just drunk, that's all" (Acts 2:1-13)!

"Then Peter replied, "I see very clearly that God shows no favoritism. In every nation he accepts those who fear him and do what is right. This is the message of Good News for the people of Israel—that there is peace with God through Jesus Christ, who is Lord of all. You know what happened throughout Judea, beginning in Galilee, after John began preaching his message of baptism. And you know that God anointed Jesus of Nazareth with the Holy Spirit and with power. Then Jesus went around doing good and healing all who were oppressed by the devil, for God was with him. "And we apostles are witnesses of all he did throughout Judea and in Jerusalem. They put him to death by hanging him on a cross, but God raised him to life on the third day. Then God allowed him to appear, not to the general public, but to us whom God had chosen in advance to be his witnesses. We were those who ate and drank with him after he rose from the dead. And he ordered us to preach everywhere and to testify that Jesus is the one appointed by God to be the judge of all—the living and the dead. He is the one all the prophets testified about, saying that everyone who believes in him will have their sins forgiven through his name." Even as Peter was saying these things, the Holy Spirit fell upon all who were listening to the message. The Jewish believers who came with Peter were amazed that the gift of the Holy Spirit had been poured out on the Gentiles, too. For they heard them speaking in other tongues and praising God. Then Peter asked, "Can anyone object to their being baptized, now that they have received the Holy Spirit just as we did?" So he gave orders for them to be baptized in the name of Jesus Christ. Afterward Cornelius asked him to stay with them for several days" (Acts 10:34-48).

"A person who speaks in tongues is strengthened personally, but one who speaks a word of prophecy strengthens the entire church. I wish you could all speak in tongues, but even more I wish you could all prophesy. For prophecy is greater than speaking in tongues, unless someone interprets what you are saying so that the whole church will be strengthened. Dear brothers and sisters, if I should come to you speaking in an unknown language, how would that help you? But if I bring you a revelation or some special knowledge or prophecy or teaching, that will be helpful. Even lifeless instruments like the flute or the harp must play the notes clearly, or no one will recognize the melody. And if the bugler doesn't sound a clear call, how will the soldiers know they are being called to battle? It's the same for you. If you speak to people in words they don't understand, how will they know what you are saying? You might as well be talking into empty space. There are many different languages in the world, and every language has meaning. But if I don't understand a language, I will be a foreigner to someone who speaks it, and the one who speaks it will be a foreigner to me. And the same is true for you. Since you are so eager to have the special abilities the Spirit gives, seek those that will strengthen the whole church. So, anyone who speaks in tongues should pray also for the ability to interpret what has been said. For if I pray in tongues, my spirit is praying, but I don't understand what I am saying. Well then, what shall I do? I will pray in the spirit, and I will also pray in words I understand. I will sing in the spirit, and I will also sing in words I understand. For if you praise God only in the spirit, how can those who don't understand you praise God along with you? How can they join you in giving thanks when they don't understand what you are saying? You will be giving thanks very well, but it won't strengthen the people who hear you. I thank God that I speak in tongues more than any of you. But in a church meeting I would rather speak five understandable words to help others than ten thousand words in an unknown language. Dear brothers and sisters, don't be childish in your understanding of these things. Be innocent as babies when it comes to evil but be mature in understanding matters of this kind. It is written in the Scriptures: "I will speak to my own people through strange languages and through the lips of foreigners. But even then, they will not listen to me," says the Lord. So, you see that speaking in tongues is a sign, not for believers, but for unbelievers. Prophecy, however, is for the benefit of believers, not unbelievers. Even so, if unbelievers or people who don't understand these things come into your church meeting and hear everyone speaking in an unknown language, they will think you are crazy. But if all of you are prophesying, and unbelievers or people who don't understand these things come into your meeting, they will be convicted of sin and judged by what you say. As they listen, their secret thoughts will be exposed, and they will fall to their knees and worship God, declaring, "God is truly here among you." Well, my brothers and sisters, let's summarize. When you meet together, one will sing, another will teach, another will tell some special revelation God has given, one will speak in tongues, and another will interpret what is said. But everything that is done must strengthen all of you. No more than two or three should speak in tongues. They must speak one at a time, and someone must interpret what they say. But if no one is present who can interpret, they must be silent in your church meeting and speak in tongues to God privately. Let two or three people prophesy, and let the others evaluate what is said. But if someone is prophesying and another person receives a revelation from the Lord, the one who is speaking must stop. In this way, all who prophesy will have a turn to speak, one after the other, so that everyone will learn and be encouraged. Remember that people who prophesy are in control of their spirit and can take turns. For God is not a God of disorder but of peace, as in all the meetings of God's holy people" (1 Cor. 14:4-33). "Then when Paul laid his hands on them, the Holy Spirit came on them, and they spoke in other tongues and prophesied" (Acts 19:6).

9. **Interpretation of Tongues** – To translate the message of someone who has spoken in tongues. "I wish you could all speak in tongues, but even more I wish you could all prophesy. For prophecy is greater than speaking in tongues, unless someone interprets what you are saying so that the whole church will be strengthened" (1 Cor. 14:5). "So anyone who speaks in tongues should pray also for the ability to interpret what has been said" (1 Cor. 14:13). "Well, my brothers and sisters, let's summarize. When you meet together, one will sing, another will teach, another will tell some special revelation God has given, one will speak in tongues, and another will interpret what is said. But everything that is done must strengthen all of you. No more than two or three should speak in tongues. They must speak one at a time, and someone must interpret what they say. But if no one is present who can interpret, they must be silent in your church meeting and speak in tongues to God privately" (1 Cor. 14:26-28).

Why are you given spiritual gifts?
"A spiritual gift is given to each of us so we can help each other" (1 Cor. 12:7).

_____
_____
_____
_____

Who decides which gift each person should have?
"It is the one and only Spirit who distributes all these gifts. He alone decides which gift each person should have" (1 Cor. 12:11).

_____
_____
_____

Is it alright for you to desire certain gifts?

"So you should earnestly desire the most helpful gifts. But now let me show you a way of life that is best of all" (1 Cor. 12:31).

_____
_____
_____

What should you seek more than any gift, and why?
"If I could speak all the languages of earth and of angels, but didn't love others, I would only be a noisy gong or a clanging cymbal. If I had the gift of prophecy, and if I understood all of God's secret plans and possessed all knowledge, and if I had such faith that I could move mountains, but didn't love others, I would be nothing. If I gave everything I have to the poor and even sacrificed my body, I could boast about it; but if I didn't love others, I would have gained nothing. Love is patient and kind. Love is not jealous or boastful or proud or rude. It does not demand its own way. It is not irritable, and it keeps no record of being wronged. It does not rejoice about injustice but rejoices whenever the truth wins out. Love never gives up, never loses faith, is always hopeful, and endures through every circumstance. Prophecy and speaking in unknown languages and special knowledge will become useless. But love will last forever! Now our knowledge is partial and incomplete, and even the gift of prophecy reveals only part of the whole picture! But when the time of perfection comes, these partial things will become useless. When I was a child, I spoke and thought and reasoned as a child. But when I grew up, I put away childish things. Now we see things imperfectly, like puzzling reflections in a mirror, but then we will see everything with perfect clarity. All that I know now is partial and incomplete, but then I will know everything completely, just as God now knows me completely. Three things will last forever—faith, hope, and love—and the greatest of these is love" (1 Cor. 13).

_____
_____
_____
_____

The gifts of the Spirit are a topic that can bring questions to some people. If that is you, write down your questions and try to answer your questions from the Word of God. Ask the Holy Spirit to teach you and then read the Bible. Search a concordance or Bible app for more scriptures on gifts, Holy Spirit, tongues, praying in the spirit, etc. After you have done this, ask a Godly person that you trust and respect for their thoughts, but always make sure what is said lines up with what the Bible says. Man's opinions may help, but God's Word is Truth. Base your beliefs on what God says about any topic.

LESSON SUMMARY:
- To stay filled with the Holy Spirit we must earnestly seek an intimate personal relationship. Our daily quiet time prayer devotion and one on one time in the Word with Holy Spirit are critical to our unity in the spirit, spiritual growth, and maturity in Christ.
- "Now He who has prepared us for this very thing is God, who also has given us the Spirit as a guarantee" (2 Cor. 5:5 NKJV).
- "To whom God would make known what is the riches of the glory of this mystery among the Gentiles, which is Christ in you, the hope of glory" (Col. 1:27 KJV):
- "Therefore, if anyone is in Christ, he is a new creation; old things have passed away; behold, all things have become new" (2 Cor. 5:17 NKJV).

- "We are made right with God by placing our faith in Jesus Christ. And this is true for everyone who believes, no matter who we are" (Rom. 3:22).
- "Let us therefore come boldly unto the throne of grace, that we may obtain mercy, and find grace to help in time of need" (Heb. 4:16 KJV).
- *Note: Lesson Slides end at this point.

OBEDIENCE PRECEDES BLESSING:

PRACTICE HIS PRESENCE:
This means carrying out an activity regularly, usually to improve whatever it is that you are doing. What do you think it means to practice His presence?

_____
_____
_____

"You will show me the way of life, granting me the joy of your presence and the pleasures of living with you forever" (Ps. 16:11). "There I will go to the altar of God, to God—the source of all my joy. I will praise you with my harp, O God, my God" (Ps. 43:4)!

What are some practical ways you can practice His Presence?

_____
_____
_____

What is one result of being in His Presence?

_____
_____
_____

The Holy Spirit is your Helper, your Friend, and He is not odd. He is your God. Begin to practice His presence by becoming aware of Him. You cannot see the wind, but it is there. You can feel the wind and see the effects of the wind. In the same way, you cannot see the Holy Spirit, but you can feel Him and see the effects of Him. When you feel the wind on your face, stop and smile at Him because He is smiling at you. "The wind blows wherever it wants. Just as you can hear the wind but can't tell where it comes from or where it is going, so you can't explain how people are born of the Spirit" (John 3:8). "Suddenly, there was a sound from heaven like the roaring of a mighty windstorm, and it filled the house where they were sitting" (Acts 2:2). "'May the Lord bless you and protect you. May the Lord smile on you and be gracious to you. May the Lord show you his favor and give you his peace" (Num. 6:24-26). When you see a dove, in person, or a picture, know that you are God's child, and He is well-pleased with you. "After his baptism, as Jesus came up out of the water, the heavens were opened, and he saw the Spirit of God descending like a dove and settling on him" (Matt. 3:16). Whenever you see oil, stop, and remind yourself that His anointing is upon you. "So as David stood there among his brothers, Samuel took the flask of olive oil he had brought and anointed David with the oil. And the Spirit of the Lord came powerfully upon David from that day on. Then Samuel returned to Ramah" (1 Sam. 16:13).

When you see fire, stop, and remember that He baptizes you with fire and that He wants you to fan into flames the spiritual gifts that He has chosen to give you. "John answered their questions by saying, "I baptize you with water; but someone is coming soon who is greater than I am-so much greater that I'm not even worthy to be his slave and untie the straps of his sandals. He will baptize you with the Holy Spirit and with fire" (Luke 3:16). "This is why I remind you to fan into flames the spiritual gift God gave you when I laid my hands on you" (2 Tim. 1:6). "Then, what looked like flames or tongues of fire appeared and settled on each of them" (Acts 2:3). When you see water, remember that living water will flow out of your heart. "On the last day, the climax of the festival, Jesus stood and shouted to the crowds, "Anyone who is thirsty may come to me! Anyone who believes in me may come and drink! For the Scriptures declare, 'Rivers of living water will flow from his heart.'" (When he said, "living water," he was speaking of the Spirit, who would be given to everyone believing in him. But the Spirit had not yet been given, because Jesus had not yet entered into his glory" (John 7:37-39). When you see a fruit tree, tell yourself that as you allow the Holy Spirit to lead, guide, and control you, He is producing the fruit of the Spirit in your life. "But the Holy Spirit produces this kind of fruit in our lives: love, joy, peace, patience, kindness, goodness, faithfulness, gentleness, and self-control. There is no law against these things" (Gal. 5:22-23)!

Begin to practice the Presence of the Holy Spirit every minute of every day, and you will never be the same! He loves you and wants to help you and let you know you are never alone because He is always with you. He is your Comforter, Teacher, Guide, Counselor, Advocate, Revealer, Spirit of Truth, and Intercessor when you don't know how to pray, and Giver of Words when you don't know what to say. He is the Giver of gifts and the Producer of fruits. What an exciting journey you are on!

MEMORY VERSE:
"Don't just listen to God's Word. You must do what it says" (James 1:22).

GROW DEEPER:
Baptism of The Holy Spirit: There is probably not a topic in the Bible that has brought more controversy than that of the Baptism of the Holy Spirit, but it is in the Bible numerous times. When a person is baptized in the Holy Spirit, he has power bestowed upon him. "But you will receive power when the Holy Spirit comes upon you. And you will be my witnesses, telling people about Me everywhere, in Jerusalem, throughout Judea, in Samaria, and to the ends of the earth" (Acts 1:8). Also, it is frequently accompanied by speaking in tongues. "And they were all filled with the Holy Spirit and began to speak with other tongues, as the Spirit was giving them utterance" (Acts 2:4). Read Acts chapters 1-2 to see the movement of the Holy Spirit upon the early church at Pentecost.

One question that comes up is whether the Baptism of the Holy Spirit happens at salvation or after. Jesus commanded that the disciples receive the Holy Spirit, and when He had said this, He breathed on them, and said to them, "Receive the Holy Spirit." This means that they were saved since the Holy Spirit is not received by the unsaved. "Then he breathed on them and said, "Receive the Holy Spirit" (John 20:22).

Then, later while they were gathered together, Jesus commanded them not to leave Jerusalem, but to wait for what the Father had promised, "Once when he was eating with them, he commanded them, "Do not leave Jerusalem until the Father sends you the gift he promised, as I told you before. John baptized with water, but in just a few days you will be baptized with the Holy Spirit" (Acts 1:4-5). Read the whole book of Acts to see what the Bible says about the Baptism of the Holy Spirit.

"I baptize with water those who repent of their sins and turn to God. But someone is coming soon who is greater than I am—so much greater that I'm not worthy even to be his slave and carry his sandals. He will baptize you with the Holy Spirit and with fire" (Matt. 3:11). "I baptize you with water, but he will baptize you with the Holy Spirit" (Mark 1:8)! "John answered their questions by saying, "I baptize you with water; but someone is coming soon who is greater than I am—so much greater that I'm not even worthy to be his slave and untie the straps of his sandals. He will baptize you with the Holy Spirit and with fire" (Luke 3:16). "I didn't know he was the one, but when God sent me to baptize with water, he told me, 'The one on whom you see the Spirit descend and rest is the one who will baptize with the Holy Spirit" (John 1:33). "John baptized with water, but in just a few days you will be baptized with the Holy Spirit" (Acts 1:5). "Then I thought of the Lord's words when he said, 'John baptized with water, but you will be baptized with the Holy Spirit" (Acts 11:16).

Names of The Holy Spirit:
He is the "Good Spirit"
"You sent your good Spirit to instruct them, and you did not stop giving them manna from heaven or water for their thirst" (Neh. 9:20).

He is "the Spirit of God"
"After his baptism, as Jesus came up out of the water, the heavens were opened and he saw the Spirit of God descending like a dove and settling on him" (Matt. 3:16).

He is called the "Counselor"
"And I will ask the Father, and he will give you another Advocate, who will never leave you. But when the Father sends the Advocate as my representative—that is, the Holy Spirit—he will teach you everything and will remind you of everything I have told you" (John 14:16, 26).

He is "the Spirit of Truth"
"When the Spirit of truth comes, he will guide you into all truth. He will not speak on his own but will tell you what he has heard. He will tell you about the future" (John 16:13).

He is referred to as "the Spirit of Christ"
"But you are not controlled by your sinful nature. You are controlled by the Spirit if you have the Spirit of God living in you. (And remember that those who do not have the Spirit of Christ living in them do not belong to him at all.)" (Rom. 8:9).

He is also called "the Spirit of Sonship"
"So, you have not received a spirit that makes you fearful slaves. Instead, you received God's Spirit when he adopted you as his own children. Now we call him, "Abba, Father" (Rom. 8:15).

He is "the Spirit of Grace"
"Just think how much worse the punishment will be for those who have trampled on the Son of God, and have treated the blood of the covenant, which made us holy, as if it were common and unholy, and have insulted and disdained the Holy Spirit who brings God's mercy to us" (Heb. 10:29).

GROW I
Journey to Freedom
Lesson 6

STAY CONNECTED AND STAY SUBMITTED

PURPOSE OF THIS LESSON:
The purpose of this lesson is to learn the importance and benefits of staying connected to God and other Christian believers and how staying submitted to God and people in spiritual authority provides a source of direction and protection. Fellowship with Him and One Another.

"This is the message which we have heard from Him and declare to you, that God is light and in Him is no darkness at all. If we say that we have fellowship with Him, and walk in darkness, we lie and do not practice the truth. But if we walk in the light as He is in "the light, we have fellowship with one another, and the blood of Jesus Christ His Son cleanses us from all sin" (1 John 1:5-7 NKJV). "Let us not neglect our meeting together as some people do, but encourage one another, especially now that the day of his return is drawing near" (Heb. 10:25).

INTRODUCTION:
The day you were saved or born again was very special. You never felt more accepted, connected, loved, and free in your life.

But for some people, they get saved and then do nothing else to grow in Christ to have an intimate personal relationship with the Lord. They never connect with the church or fellow believers and never submit their lives fully to God, Jesus is their Savior, but not their Lord. Many of these people do not stay free and, as a result, fall away from the Lord. "Then Jesus said to his disciples, "If any of you wants to be my follower, you must give up your own way, take up your cross, and follow me. If you try to hang on to your life, you will lose it. But if you give up your life for my sake, you will save it. And what do you benefit if you gain the whole world but lose your own soul? Is anything worth more than your soul" (Matt. 16:24-26)?

WHY IS THIS LESSON IMPORTANT TO YOUR LIFE?
Because you need to understand you are not alone in your journey to freedom. God is with you and has placed people in your life to help you continue to move forward.

"His purpose was for the nations to seek after God and perhaps feel their way toward him and find him—though he is not far from any one of us" (Acts 17:27). "Jesus answered and said to him, "If anyone loves Me, he will keep My word; and My Father will love him, and We will come to him and make Our home with him" John 14:23 NKJV "Now these are the gifts Christ gave to the church: the apostles, the prophets, the evangelists, and the pastors and teachers. Their responsibility is to equip God's people to do his work and build up the church, the body of Christ" (Eph. 4:11-12). "In his grace, God has given us different gifts for doing certain things well. So, if God has given you the ability to prophesy, speak out with as much faith as God has given you. If your gift is serving others, serve them well. If you are a teacher, teach well. If your gift is to encourage others, be encouraging. If it is giving, give generously. If God has given you leadership ability, take the responsibility seriously. And if you have a gift for showing kindness to others, do it gladly. Don't just pretend to love others. Really love them. Hate what is wrong. Hold tightly to what is good. Love each other with genuine affection and take delight in honoring each other" (Romans 12:6-10).

However, you must choose to connect with and submit to the people God places in your path. If you are not connected and submitted to God and other Christians, you will not survive spiritually and will fall. You will have no life because you will be disconnected from the power source of all life. Let's examine two areas to help you stay free, so you can fulfill the plans God has for you: staying connected and staying submitted.

STAY CONNECTED:
There are two areas where you must stay connected: first to God and then to other Christian believers. John 15:1-13 explains why you must stay connected to God.

"I am the true vine, and My Father is the vinedresser. Every branch in Me that does not bear fruit He takes away; and every branch that bears fruit He prunes, that it may bear more fruit. You are already clean because of the word which I have spoken to you. Abide in Me, and I in you. As the branch cannot bear fruit of itself, unless it abides in the vine, neither can you, unless you abide in Me. "I am the vine, you are the branches. He who abides in Me, and I in him, bears much fruit; for without Me you can do nothing. If anyone does not abide in Me, he is cast out as a branch and is withered; and they gather them and throw them into the fire, and they are burned. If you abide in Me, and My words abide in you, you will ask what you desire, and it shall be done for you. By this My Father is glorified, that you bear much fruit; so you will be My disciples. "As the Father loved Me, I also have loved you; abide in My love. If you keep My commandments, you will abide in My love, just as I have kept My Father's commandments and abide in His love. "These things I have spoken to you, that My joy may remain in you, and that your joy may be full. This is My commandment, that you love one another as I have loved you. Greater love has no one than this, than to lay down one's life for his friends" (John 15:1-13 NKJV).

This passage tells you that Jesus is the vine, and we are the branches. You, the branches, apart from the vine, can do nothing. If you do not stay connected, you wither and die and produce no fruit. However, if you abide in Jesus, the vine, you may ask anything you want, and it will be granted. The word "abide" means to live. It doesn't mean to just come for a visit but to live there in Christ. It means no turning back, no looking back, and staying the course no matter what the cost. If you abide or stay connected to God, you will fulfill the purpose you were created for. You will produce much fruit; you will be known as a true disciple; you will bring glory to the Father, and you will overflow with joy. As verses 10-13 explains, to truly connect and love others as Jesus loves us, we must keep His commandments to abide in His love remaining full of joy. Staying focused on the love of Jesus we can let His love flow through us to others, as we lay down our life (desires) serving others.

Let's take a closer look at staying connected is with other Christian believers.
Do you hang out with eagles or turkeys. This meeting together is not just about going to church. "For where two or three gather together as my followers, I am there among them" (Matt. 18:20). This tells us we can meet anywhere with other believers: church, homes, restaurant, coffee shop, park bench, etc. and Jesus will be there also. The point is to gather with other believers. God has put you in a loving family of believers that can help you stay free and strong. Believers Form a community. "All the believers devoted themselves to the apostles' teaching, and to fellowship, and to sharing in meals (including the Lord's Supper [the breaking of bread]), and to prayer. A deep sense of awe came over them all, and the apostles performed many miraculous signs and wonders. And all the believers met together in one place and shared everything they had. They sold their property and possessions and shared the money with those in need. They worshiped together at the Temple each day, met in homes for the Lord's Supper, and shared their meals with great joy and generosity [and sincere hearts.] all the

while praising God and enjoying the goodwill of all the people. And each day the Lord added to their fellowship those who were being saved" (Acts 2:42-47). This scripture shows us a beautiful picture of a church family. They worshiped together in the temple, met in homes, ate meals together, and shared all their possessions and money. When you stay connected to other believers, you are never alone. As part of a congregation, you receive pastoral care from the pastor, elders, and church leaders. However, it is in the setting of a small group where you receive individual care to grow into a disciple. This is also true through connections to a mentor, accountability partner, or prayer partner. Join a small group where you feel a connection. Find the one person who has been where you are and can give you guidance and correction.

Responsible parents care for, provide for, and protect their children. In this same way, your Heavenly Father has cared for you by placing godly people in your life that will encourage you when you are down and correct you when you need discipline. Even when Jesus sent the disciples out, He sent them out "two by two" He knew there was power in being connected to another believer. "And he called his twelve disciples together and began sending them out two by two, giving them authority to cast out evil spirits" (Mark 6:7). " The Lord now chose seventy-two other disciples and sent them ahead in pairs to all the towns and place he planned to visit" (Luke 10:1). God designed it, so we help each other, and many benefits come from these relationships. Being connected to others is the best way to be encouraged and built up. "So encourage each other and build each other up, just as you are already doing" (1 Thess. 5:11). A way to share your burdens. "Share each other's burdens, and in this way obey the law of Christ" (Gal. 6:2). To be comforted. "So, encourage each other with these words" (1 Thess. 4:18). To be taught and admonished. "Let the message about Christ, in all its richness, fill your lives. Teach and counsel each other with all the wisdom he gives. Sing psalms and hymns and spiritual songs to God with thankful hearts" (Col. 3:16). To get guidance and advice. "So don't go to war without wise guidance; victory depends on having many advisers" (Prov. 24:6). To have fellowship. "They worshiped together at the Temple each day, met in homes for the Lord's Supper, and shared their meals with great joy and generosity" (Acts 2:46). To get back on the right path when you sin. "Dear brothers and sisters, if another believer is overcome by some sin, you who are godly should gently and humbly help that person back onto the right path. And be careful not to fall into the same temptation yourself" (Gal. 6:1). To have companions. "I will search for faithful people to be my companions. Only those who are above reproach will be allowed to serve me" (Ps. 101:6). In short, you will become all you can be only as you stay connected to the body of Christ. Never be ashamed to admit, "I ain't got this" and to ask for help.

STAY SUBMITTED:
There are two types of submission that directly affect your journey with the Lord. One is staying submitted to God, and the other is staying submitted to godly spiritual leaders. Just as important as staying connected is staying submitted. Biblical submission is defined as a voluntary act of obedience and faith that comes from within a person. It means to trust and obey even when you do not want to, or you do not understand why. Have you ever heard a child tell an adult, "You're not my mama, so you can't tell me what to do?" That's what we are saying to God when we do not submit.

The first area of submission is staying submitted to God. Jesus demands that you be submissive if you are to follow Him. This requires you put him first. There is a Cost of Following Jesus, the following scriptures tells us the cost of being a submissive follower of Christ. "As they were walking along, someone said to Jesus, "I will follow you wherever you go." But Jesus replied, "Foxes have dens to live in, and birds have nests, but the Son of Man has no place even to lay his head." He said to another person, "Come, follow me." The man agreed, but he said, "Lord, first let me return home and bury my father." But Jesus told him, "Let the spiritually dead bury their own dead! Your duty is to go and preach about the Kingdom of God." Another said, "Yes, Lord, I will follow you, but first let me say good-bye to my family." But Jesus told him, "Anyone who puts a hand to the plow and then looks back is not fit for the Kingdom of God" (Luke 9:57-62). He calls you to submit now and not give excuses. "And if you do not carry your own cross and follow me, you cannot be my disciple" (Luke 14:27). Jesus tells you to be submissive as he was submissive. "I can do nothing on my own. I judge as God tells me. Therefore, my judgment is just, because I carry out the will of the one who sent me, not my own will" (John 5:30). He modeled the ultimate submission. "he humbled himself in obedience to God and died a criminal's death on a cross" (Phil. 2:8). "Father, if you are willing, please take this cup of suffering away from me. Yet I want your will to be done, not mine." (Luke 22:42). Jesus did not want to go to the cross. God had called him to do something hard, and he knew it would be painful and difficult, but His love for you was so great, he submitted to God's plan and died for you. His submission paid for your salvation and purchased your freedom. If Jesus submitted, you must do the same. "For God called you to do good, even if it means suffering, just as Christ suffered[died] for you. He is your example, and you must follow in his steps" (1 Peter 2:21). We are called by God to do good, even if it means suffering, just as Christ suffered for you. He is your example, and you MUST follow in his steps.

Submission is the core of man's relationship with God. Adam and Eve refused to submit, so sin and death came into the world. The Jews (God's chosen people) refused to submit to Jesus, the Messiah they had been waiting, seeking, and looking for their entire existence. Satan's fall and ongoing rebellion is his refusal to submit, and he tempts you to do the same. By submitting yourself to God, you have a source of direction, purpose, and protection. Nothing can happen to you that God did not design for his glory and your good. "So, humble yourselves before God. Resist the devil, and he will flee from you" (James 4:7). "Trust in the Lord with all your heart; do not depend on your own understanding. Seek his will in all you do, and he will show you which path to take" (Prov. 3:5-6). "Jesus replied, "'You must love the Lord your God with all your heart, all your soul, and all your mind'" (Matt. 22:37).

Not only do you submit to God, but you also submit to godly spiritual leaders. "Dear brothers and sisters, honor those who are your leaders in the Lord's work. They work hard among you and give you spiritual guidance. Show them great respect and wholehearted love because of their work. And live peacefully with each other." (1 Thessalonians 5:12-13). Within the local church, you receive pastoral care from the pastors, elders, and church leadership. These people have yielded themselves totally to God's divine authority and are stewards or overseers in the lives of God's people. "Obey your spiritual leaders and do what they say. Their work is to watch over your souls, and they are accountable to God. Give them a reason to do this with joy and not with sorrow. That would certainly not be for your benefit." (Heb. 13:17). Godly leaders are accountable to God for their work concerning your soul. From them, you receive the benefits of teaching, wisdom, protection, counsel, encouragement, prayer, care, and help. They do the work, and you receive the benefits by submitting to them and living your life so that the work concerning you is joyful. If you refuse to submit to the spiritual authorities that God has placed in your life, then you forfeit the blessings and benefits that God has in place to protect and guide you. Submission is not restrictive when you follow God and His leaders. Instead, it frees you and grants you authority, which is gained as you learn to submit to authority. This is the opposite of the world's philosophy because the world teaches you to be self-gratified and live life your way. Where has that philosophy gotten you? Do you want your way, or will you submit everything you are to God so you can stay free and be used by God to reach others?

The last area of submission is in the area of tithing. In the Bible, there are 500 verses on prayer and 500 on faith; but there are 2000 verses on money and possessions. Jesus talked about money in 16 of His 38 parables. Money is a test from God that reveals your priorities, affections, obedience, and submission. It is the primary way you acknowledge that God is first in your life. The priority of your financial budget is a good indication of where your heart is. If money and tithing are an issue and a struggle for you, seek guidance and help from someone in the church leadership. The tithe is the "first" tenth of your increase.

"As you harvest your crops, bring the very best of the first harvest to the house of the Lord your God...." (Exod. 23:19). "Honor the Lord with your wealth and with the best part of everything you produce. Then he will fill your barns with grain, and your vats will overflow with good wine" (Prov. 3:9-10). When you give your first 10% to God in faith, he will bless the rest (90%) and meet your needs. When you give God the tithe, you are merely returning what already belongs to Him, and He allows you to enjoy the remaining 90%. You are a steward, not the owner. Everything you have comes from God. Even the resources you must create wealth comes from Him.

Malachi talks about tithes and offerings. The offering is any amount you give above the tithe. "Give, and you will receive. Your gift will return to you in full – pressed down, shaken together to make room for more, running over, and poured in your lap. The amount you give will determine the amount you get back" (Luke 6:38). You are blessed to be a blessing. Remember this-a farmer who plants only a few seeds will get a small crop. But the one who plants generously will get a generous crop. You must each decide in your heart how much to give. And don't give reluctantly or in response to pressure. "For God loves a person who gives cheerfully." And God will generously provide all you need. Then you will always have everything you need, and plenty left over to share with others. As the Scriptures say" (2 Cor. 9:6-11), Tithing is the only place God invites you to test Him. "Bring all the tithes into the storehouse so there will be enough food in my Temple. If you do," says the Lord of Heaven's Armies, "I will open the windows of heaven for you. I will pour out a blessing so great you won't have enough room to take it in! Try it! Put me to the test" (Mal.3:10)! Putting God first in the tithe is the submission for releasing the blessings of God in your life. However, Malachi also tells you that keeping the tithe is robbing God and brings a curse on your finances. "Should people cheat God? Yet you have cheated me! "But you ask, 'What do you mean? When did we ever cheat you?' "You have cheated me of the tithes and offerings due to me. You are under a curse, for your whole nation has been cheating me" (Mal. 3:8-9). What will you choose: blessing or curse?

LESSON SUMMARY:

We must stay connected / submitted to God, our Spiritual Leaders and to other Christian believers.

- "For God called you to do good, even if it means suffering, just as Christ suffered[died] for you. He is your example, and you must follow in his steps" (1 Peter 2:21).
- "Obey your spiritual leaders and do what they say. Their work is to watch over your souls, and they are accountable to God. Give them reason to do this with joy and not with sorrow. That would certainly not be for your benefit" (Heb. 13:17).
- "Let us not neglect our meeting together as some people do, but encourage one another, especially now that the day of his return is drawing near" (Heb. 10:25).
- "Give, and you will receive. Your gift will return to you in full-pressed down, shaken together to make room for more, running over, and poured into your lap. The amount you give will determine the amount you get back." (Luke 6:38).
- *Note: Lesson Slides end at this point.

73

OBEDIENCE PRECEDES BLESSING:
"If ye abide in me, and my words abide in you, ye shall ask what ye will, and it shall be done unto you" (John 15:7 KJV). The word "abide" means to live. When you are in obedience, you will be submitted to God, He can bless you and your life.

MEMORY VERSE:
"Let us not neglect our meeting together as some people do, but encourage one another, especially now that the day of his return is drawing near" (Heb. 10:25).

GROW DEEPER:
God wants you to be connected to Godly believers. "As iron sharpens iron, so a friend sharpens a friend" (Prov. 27:17). This scripture tells us the advantage of choosing the right friends. He also warns us of the dangers of bad company. Read these scriptures to see what God says about choosing friends. "Run from anything that stimulates youthful lusts. Instead, pursue righteous living, faithfulness, love, and peace. Enjoy the companionship of those who call on the Lord with pure hearts" (2 Tim. 2:22). "Don't be fooled by those who say such things, for "bad company corrupts good character" (1 Cor. 15:33). "Don't team up with those who are unbelievers. How can righteousness be a partner with wickedness? How can light live with darkness? What harmony can there be between Christ and the devil[a]? How can a believer be a partner with an unbeliever? And what union can there be between God's temple and idols? For we are the temple of the living God. As God said: "I will live in them and walk among them. I will be their God, and they will be my people. Therefore, come out from among unbelievers, and separate yourselves from them, says the Lord. Don't touch their filthy things, and I will welcome you. And I will be your Father, and you will be my sons and daughters, says the Lord Almighty" (2 Cor. 6:14-18).

Why is it important for your spiritual growth to connect with other Christians? List ways someone else has helped you grow in your faith.

_____

_____

_____

"All the believers devoted themselves to the apostles' teaching, and to fellowship, and to sharing in meals (including the Lord's Supper), and to prayer. A deep sense of awe came over them all, and the apostles performed many miraculous signs and wonders. And all the believers met together in one place and shared everything they had" (Acts 2:42-44). "All the believers were united in heart and mind. And they felt that what they owned was not their own, so they shared everything they had. The apostles testified powerfully to the resurrection of the Lord Jesus, and God's great blessing was upon them all. There were no needy people among them, because those who owned land or houses would sell them and bring the money to the apostles to give to those in need" (Acts 4:32-35). "When he realized this, he went to the home of Mary, the mother of John Mark, where many were gathered for prayer" (Acts 12:12). "When Paul and Silas left the prison, they returned to the home of Lydia. There they met with the believers and encouraged them once more. Then they left town" (Acts 16:40). "Please give my greetings to our brothers and sisters at Laodicea, and to Nympha and the church that meets in her house" (Col 4:15).

Is there any encouragement from belonging to Christ? Any comfort from his love? Any fellowship together in the Spirit? Are your hearts tender and compassionate? Then make me truly happy by agreeing wholeheartedly with each other, loving one another, and working together with one mind and purpose. Don't be selfish; don't try to impress others. Be humble, thinking of others as better than yourselves. Don't look out only for your own interests, but take an interest in others, too. You must have the same attitude that Christ Jesus had. Though he was God, he did not think of equality with God as something to cling to. Instead, he gave up his divine privileges; he took the humble position of a slave and was born as a human being. When he appeared in human form, he humbled himself in obedience to God and died a criminal's death on a cross. Therefore, God elevated him to the place of highest honor and gave him the name above all other names, that at the name of Jesus every knee should bow, in heaven and on earth and under the earth, and every tongue declare that Jesus Christ is Lord, to the glory of God the Father. Dear friends, you always followed my instructions when I was with you. And now that I am away, it is even more important. Work hard to show the results of your salvation, obeying God with deep reverence and fear. For God is working in you, giving you the desire and the power to do what pleases him. Do everything without complaining and arguing, so that no one can criticize you. Live clean, innocent lives as children of God, shining like bright lights in a world full of crooked and perverse people. Hold firmly to the word of life; then, on the day of Christ's return, I will be proud that I did not run the race in vain and that my work was not useless. But I will rejoice even if I lose my life, pouring it out like a liquid offering to God, just like your faithful service is an offering to God. And I want all of you to share that joy. Yes, you should rejoice, and I will share your joy. If the Lord Jesus is willing, I hope to send Timothy to you soon for a visit. Then he can cheer me up by telling me how you are getting along. I have no one else like Timothy, who genuinely cares about your welfare. All the others care only for themselves and not for what matters to Jesus Christ. But you know how Timothy has proved himself. Like a son with his father, he has served with me in preaching the Good News. I hope to send him to you just as soon as I find out what is going to happen to me here. And I have confidence from the Lord that I myself will come to see you soon. Meanwhile, I thought I should send Epaphroditus back to you. He is a true brother, co-worker, and fellow soldier. And he was your messenger to help me in my need. I am sending him because he has been longing to see you, and he was very distressed that you heard he was ill. And he certainly was ill; in fact, he almost died. But God had mercy on him-and also on me, so that I would not have one sorrow after another. So, I am all the more anxious to send him back to you, for I know you will be glad to see him, and then I will not be so worried about you. Welcome him in the Lord's love and with great joy and give him the honor that people like him deserve. For he risked his life for the work of Christ, and he was at the point of death while doing for me what you couldn't do from far away" (Phil. 2)

Are small groups a biblical part of church life?

_____

_____

_____

Obtain a list of small groups and prayerfully choose the one that is right for you. Prayerfully seek out a mentor or accountability partner as soon as possible.

Submission is the key to unity and harmony in human relationships and society. "Is there any encouragement from belonging to Christ? Any comfort from his love? Any fellowship together in the Spirit? Are your hearts tender and compassionate? Then make me truly happy by agreeing wholeheartedly with each other, loving one another, and working together with one mind and purpose. Don't be selfish; don't try to impress others. Be humble, thinking of others as better than yourselves. Don't look out only for your own interests, but take an interest in others, too" (Phil. 2:1-4). Three types of human submissions were not discussed in this lesson. Study each area listed below.

Job Submission (employer/employee).

"Slaves, obey your earthly masters with deep respect and fear. Serve them sincerely as you would serve Christ. Try to please them all the time, not just when they are watching you. As slaves of Christ, do the will of God with all your heart. Work with enthusiasm, as though you were working for the Lord rather than for people. Remember that the Lord will reward each one of us for the good we do, whether we are slaves or free. Masters, treat your slaves in the same way. Don't threaten them; remember, you both have the same Master in heaven, and he has no favorites" (Eph. 6:5-9).

"You who are slaves must submit to your masters with all respect. Do what they tell you—not only if they are kind and reasonable, but even if they are cruel" (1 Pet. 2:18).

"Slaves, obey your earthly masters in everything you do. Try to please them all the time, not just when they are watching you. Serve them sincerely because of your reverent fear of the Lord. Work willingly at whatever you do, as though you were working for the Lord rather than for people. Remember that the Lord will give you an inheritance as your reward, and that the Master you are serving is Christ" (Col. 3:22-24).

Family Submission (wives/husbands and parents/children)

"In the same way, you wives must accept the authority of your husbands. Then, even if some refuse to obey the Good News, your godly lives will speak to them without any words. They will be won over by observing your pure and reverent lives. Don't be concerned about the outward beauty of fancy hairstyles, expensive jewelry, or beautiful clothes. You should clothe yourselves instead with the beauty that comes from within, the unfading beauty of a gentle and quiet spirit, which is so precious to God. This is how the holy women of old made themselves beautiful. They put their trust in God and accepted the authority of their husbands. For instance, Sarah obeyed her husband, Abraham, and called him her master. You are her daughters when you do what is right without fear of what your husbands might do. In the same way, you husbands must give honor to your wives. Treat your wife with understanding as you live together. She may be weaker than you are, but she is your equal partner in God's gift of new life. Treat her as you should so your prayers will not be hindered" (1 Pet. 3:1-7).

"And further, submit to one another out of reverence for Christ. For wives, this means submit to your husbands as to the Lord. For a husband is the head of his wife as Christ is the head of the church. He is the Savior of his body, the church. As the church submits to Christ, so you wives should submit to your husbands in everything. For husbands, this means love your wives, just as Christ loved the church. He gave up his life for her to make her holy and clean, washed by the cleansing of God's word. He did this to present her to himself as a glorious church without a spot or wrinkle or any other blemish. Instead, she will be holy and without fault. In the same way, husbands ought to love their wives as they love their own bodies. For a man who loves his wife actually shows love for himself. No one hates his own body but feeds and cares for it, just as Christ cares for the church. And we are members of his body. As the Scriptures say, "A man leaves his father and mother and is joined to his wife, and the two are united into one." This is a great mystery, but it is an illustration of the way Christ and the church are one. So again, I say, each man must love his wife as he loves himself, and the wife must respect her husband" (Eph. 5:21-33).

Children, obey your parents because you belong to the Lord, for this is the right thing to do. "Honor your father and mother." This is the first commandment with a promise: If you honor your father and mother, "things will go well for you, and you will have a long life on the earth." Fathers do not provoke your children to anger by the way you treat them. Rather, bring them up with the discipline and instruction that comes from the Lord" (Eph. 6:1-4).

"Wives, submit to your husbands, as is fitting for those who belong to the Lord. Husbands, love your wives and never treat them harshly. Children, always obey your parents, for this pleases the Lord. Fathers do not aggravate your children, or they will become discouraged" (Col. 3:18-21).

Government/Human Submission.

"Everyone must submit to governing authorities. For all authority comes from God, and those in positions of authority have been placed there by God. So anyone who rebels against authority is rebelling against what God has instituted, and they will be punished. For the authorities do not strike fear in people who are doing right, but in those who are doing wrong. Would you like to live without fear of the authorities? Do what is right, and they will honor you. The authorities are God's servants, sent for your good. But if you are doing wrong, of course you should be afraid, for they have the power to punish you. They are God's servants, sent for the very purpose of punishing those who do what is wrong. So you must submit to them, not only to avoid punishment, but also to keep a clear conscience. Pay your taxes, too, for these same reasons. For government workers need to be paid. They are serving God in what they do. Give to everyone what you owe them: Pay your taxes and government fees to those who collect them, and give respect and honor to those who are in authority" (Rom. 13:1-7).

"You know that Stephanas and his household were the first of the harvest of believers in Greece, and they are spending their lives in service to God's people. I urge you, dear brothers and sisters, to submit to them and others like them who serve with such devotion. I am very glad that Stephanas, Fortunatus, and Achaicus have come here. They have been providing the help you weren't here to give me. They have been a wonderful encouragement to me, as they have been to you. You must show your appreciation to all who serve so well" (1 Cor. 16:15-18).

"For the Lord's sake, submit to all human authority—whether the king as head of state, or the officials he has appointed. For the king has sent them to punish those who do wrong and to honor those who do right" (1 Pet. 2: 13-14).

List areas in your life where you need to learn to submit to God's authority and the authority of spiritual leaders.

_____

_____

_____

Pray about each area until submission comes.
Study 2 Cor. 8 and 9 to find what it means to be a generous giver.

"Now I want you to know, dear brothers and sisters, what God in his kindness has done through the churches in Macedonia. They are being tested by many troubles, and they are very poor. But they are also filled with abundant joy, which has overflowed in rich generosity. For I can testify that they gave not only what they could afford, but far more. And they did it of their own free will. They begged us again and again for the privilege of sharing in the gift for the believers in Jerusalem. They even did more than we had hoped, for their first action was to give themselves to the Lord and to us, just as God wanted them to do. So, we have urged Titus, who encouraged your giving in the first place, to return to you and encourage you to finish this ministry of giving. Since you excel in so many ways—in your faith, your gifted speakers, your knowledge, your enthusiasm, and your love from us—I want you to excel also in this gracious act of giving. I am not commanding you to do this. But I am testing how genuine your love is by comparing it with the eagerness of the other churches. You know the generous grace of our Lord Jesus Christ. Though he was rich, yet for your sakes he became poor, so that by his poverty he could make you rich. Here is my advice: It would be good for you to finish what you started a year ago. Last year you were the first who wanted to give, and you were the first to begin doing it. Now you should finish what you started. Let the eagerness you showed in the beginning be matched now by your giving. Give in proportion to what you have. Whatever you give is acceptable if you give it eagerly. And give according to what you have, not what you don't have. Of course, I don't mean your giving should make life easy for others and hard for yourselves. I only mean that there should be some equality. 14 Right now you have plenty and can help those who are in need. Later, they will have plenty and can share with you when you need it. In this way, things will be equal. As the Scriptures say, "Those who gathered a lot had nothing left over, and those who gathered only a little had enough." But thank God! He has given Titus the same enthusiasm for you that I have. Titus welcomed our request that he visit you again. In fact, he himself was very eager to go and see you. We are also sending another brother with Titus. All the churches praise him as a preacher of the Good News. He was appointed by the churches to accompany us as we take the offering to Jerusalem-a service that glorifies the Lord and shows our eagerness to help. We are traveling together to guard against any criticism for the way we are handling this generous gift. We are careful to be honorable before the Lord, but we also want everyone else to see that we are honorable. We are also sending with them another of our brothers who has proven himself many times and has shown on many occasions how eager he is. He is now even more enthusiastic because of his great confidence in you. If anyone asks about Titus, say that he is my partner who works with me to help you. And the brothers with him have been sent by the churches, and they bring honor to Christ. So, show them your love, and prove to all the churches that our boasting about you is justified" (2 Cor. 8).

"I really don't need to write to you about this ministry of giving for the believers in Jerusalem. For I know how eager you are to help, and I have been boasting to the churches in Macedonia that you in Greece were ready to send an offering a year ago. In fact, it was your enthusiasm that stirred up many of the Macedonian believers to begin giving. But I am sending these brothers to be sure you really are ready, as I have been telling them, and that your money is all collected. I don't want to be wrong in my boasting about you. We would be embarrassed—not to mention your own embarrassment-if some Macedonian believers came with me and found that you weren't ready after all I had told them! So, I thought I should send these brothers ahead of me to make sure the gift you promised is ready. But I want it to be a willing gift, not one given grudgingly. Remember this-a farmer who plants only a few seeds will get a small crop. But the one who plants generously will get a generous crop. You must each decide in your heart how much to give. And don't give reluctantly or in response to pressure. "For God loves a person who gives cheerfully." And God will generously provide all you need. Then you will always have everything you need, and plenty left over to share with others. As the Scriptures say, "They share freely and give generously to the poor. Their good deeds will be remembered forever." For God is the one who provides seed for the farmer and then bread to eat. In the same way, he will provide and increase your resources and then produce a great harvest of generosity in you. Yes, you will be enriched in every way so that you can always be generous. And when we take your gifts to those who need them, they will thank God. So, two good things will result from this ministry of giving—the needs of the believers in Jerusalem will be met, and they will joyfully express their thanks to God. As a result of your ministry, they will give glory to God. For your generosity to them and to all believers will prove that you are obedient to the Good News of Christ. And they will pray for you with deep affection because of the overflowing grace God has given to you. Thank God for this gift too wonderful for words" (2 Cor. 9)!

GROW I
Journey to Freedom
Lesson 7

STAY HUMBLE

PURPOSE OF THIS LESSON:
Is to compare the contrast pride and humility, showing the negative effects of the sin of pride and the blessings of staying humble.

"But the tax collector stood at a distance and dared not even lift his eyes to heaven as he prayed. Instead, he beat his chest in sorrow, saying, 'O God, be merciful to me, for I am a sinner.' I tell you, this sinner, not the Pharisee, returned home justified before God. For those who exalt themselves will be humbled, and those who humble themselves will be exalted" (Luke 18:13-14). "Though the Lord is great, he cares for the humble, but he keeps his distance from the proud" (Ps. 138:6).

INTRODUCTION:
In the Bible, there are about 800 verses that talk about humility and meekness and pride and arrogance. This tells us that these are important to God and should be important to us as well.

To compare the contrast of pride and humility, you need to know the definition of each. Webster defines pride as satisfaction or pleasure taken in one's own success or achievements; a high opinion of one's dignity, merit, or superiority; and excessive self-esteem which leads to conceit. The Bible describes pride as a person who is arrogant and consumed with self. Pride is putting yourself and what you want, think and feel above God and His will for your life.

The opposite of pride is humility or being humble. Webster defines humility as not proud or arrogant; modest; a feeling of being low in importance or dignity; and to be meek. Biblical humility is described as a person who shows dependence on God and love and respect for others. The Bible also describes it as meekness, lowliness, and absence of self. Being humble is a heart attitude, and staying humble is of the utmost importance in staying free. "God opposes the proud but gives grace to the humble. So, humble yourselves before God. Resist the devil, and he will flee from you. Come close to God, and God will come close to you" (James 4:6-8).

WHY IS THIS LESSON IMPORTANT TO YOUR LIFE?
This lesson is important because pride is a dangerous attitude affecting your walk with God, your relationships with others around you, and the decisions you make.

Pride is a sin, and it defiles a person. You must understand that this struggle between pride and humility is a battle of our flesh against our spirit, fleshly pride against spiritual humility. "For from within, out of a person's heart, come evil thoughts, sexual immorality, theft, murder, adultery, greed, wickedness, deceit, lustful desires, envy, slander, pride, and foolishness. All these vile things come from within; they are what defile you" (Mark 7:21-23). You must make a conscious effort to recognize your prideful attitudes. It has been said that the sin of pride in a person is obvious to everyone except the person with a prideful attitude. You need to know that God does not want to punish us for our pride but instead wants us to humble ourselves so that He can forgive and restore us. "For those who exalt themselves will be humbled, and those who humble themselves will be exalted" (Luke 14:11).

Know that God takes pleasure in you when you humble yourself so that He can exalt you. You must learn how to overcome it, so your life reflects Jesus and not yourself. Let's examine the areas of pride and humility.

PRIDE:

The best example of pride in the Bible is Lucifer. Lucifer was one of the three archangels created by God to live in His presence and to serve him with praise and worship. These angels were given the ability to think, feel, and make choices. Lucifer thought he was so handsome and glorious that he chose to rebel against God. "How you are fallen from heaven, O shining star, son of the morning! You have been thrown down to the earth, you who destroyed the nations of the world. For you said to yourself, 'I will ascend to heaven and set my throne above God's stars. I will preside on the mountain of the gods far away in the north. I will climb to the highest heavens and be like the Most High.' Instead, you will be brought down to the place of the dead, down to its lowest depths" (Isa. 14:12-15). Lucifer knew God had given him great beauty, power, and wisdom. These qualities caused him to become proud, and he was no longer content to worship and serve God. He wanted to be God and have the praise for himself that only God deserves.

This prideful attitude is called sin. "Haughty eyes, a proud heart, and evil actions are all sin" (Prov. 21:4). This was the first instance of sin against God. "You were blameless in all you did from the day you were created until the day evil was found in you. Your rich commerce led you to violence, and you sinned. So I banished you in disgrace from the mountain of God. I expelled you, O mighty guardian, from your place among the stones of fire. Your heart was filled with pride because of all your beauty. Your wisdom was corrupted by your love of splendor. So, I threw you to the ground and exposed you to the curious gaze of kings" (Ezek. 28:15-17).

Lucifer's sin was pride. When he rebelled against God in heaven, one-third of the angels joined him, and today he still entices all people to follow him in this sin. "Stay alert! Watch out for your great enemy, the devil. He prowls around like a roaring lion, looking for someone to devour" (1 Pet. 5:8). Interestingly, one definition of pride is "a group of lions." Your pride allows Satan to "devour" you like a lion devours its prey. You must stay alert and watch out for his schemes, or you face the same fate as Satan. "Pride goes before destruction and haughtiness before a fall" (Prov. 16:18). "But those who exalt themselves will be humbled, and those who humble themselves will be exalted" (Matt. 23:12).

The original sin in the Garden of Eden was one of pride. Lucifer, who is now known as Satan, enticed Eve with the lie that if she ate from the forbidden fruit of the Tree of Knowledge of Good and Evil, she would be like God. She made the choice to eat of the forbidden fruit, and Adam did likewise. "The serpent was the shrewdest of all the wild animals the Lord God had made. One day he asked the woman, "Did God really say you must not eat the fruit from any of the trees in the garden?" "Of course, we may eat fruit from the trees in the garden," the woman replied. "It's only the fruit from the tree in the middle of the garden that we are not allowed to eat. God said, 'You must not eat it or even touch it; if you do, you will die.'" "You won't die!" the serpent replied to the woman. "God knows that your eyes will be opened as soon as you eat it, and you will be like God, knowing both good and evil." The woman was convinced. She saw that the tree was beautiful, and its fruit looked delicious, and she wanted the wisdom it would give her. So, she took some of the fruit and ate it. Then she gave some to her husband, who was with her, and he ate it, too. At that moment their eyes were opened, and they suddenly felt shame at their nakedness. So, they sewed fig leaves together to cover themselves" (Gen. 3:1-7).

"When Adam sinned, sin entered the world. Adam's sin brought death, so death spread to everyone, for everyone sinned" (Romans 5:12). Through Adam's pride to be like God and know good and evil, sin entered the world.

As you can see, pride is demonic as it entered the world through Satan's actions. It is one of the fourteen root spirits named in the Bible and manifests itself in many ways. The personal spiritual profile contains an extensive list of the characteristics of pride. Any of these character traits can be detrimental to your relationships with others. They bring division, strife, and contention as self is determined to have his way and never considers the feelings of others. Pride makes you stubborn and unable to admit when you are wrong and thus keeps you in conflict with others. It also keeps you from saying you're sorry, which hurts others you love. "When you follow the desires of your sinful nature, the results are very clear: sexual immorality, impurity, lustful pleasures, idolatry, sorcery, hostility, quarreling, jealousy, outbursts of anger, selfish ambition, dissension, division, envy, drunkenness, wild parties, and other sins like these. Let me tell you again, as I have before, that anyone living that sort of life will not inherit the Kingdom of God" (Gal. 5:19-21). This passage gives a list of sins that result from following the desires of your sinful nature. Most of them deal with relational sins and are traits of pride: quarreling, jealousy, outbursts of anger, selfish ambition, dissension, division, and envy. Ultimately pride prevents the love of God from flowing out of you to others.

What prideful characteristics are destroying your relationships with others?

_____

_____

_____

There are three main ways pride destroys your relationship with God. First, pride separates you from God. "Though the Lord is great, he cares for the humble, but he keeps his distance from the proud" (Ps. 138:6). God will not come close to people who have prideful attitudes.

Next, pride keeps you from following Jesus. In Luke 9:23 Jesus says, "Then he said to the crowd, "If any of you wants to be my follower, you must give up your own way, take up your cross daily, and follow me." (Luke 9:23). You cannot be a follower of Jesus and be a Burger King Christian. You cannot have it your way. Pride always wants to have self on the throne, but Jesus is clear when he says that you must daily choose to be selfless.

Finally, pride keeps you from accepting Jesus as Savior and surrendering to Him as Lord. It makes you unwilling to admit you are a sinner. In your mind, you boast that you are righteous and good enough to be accepted by God and have no need for a savior. This is a lie of the devil because the Bible tells us that "We are all infected and impure with sin. When we display our righteous deeds, they are nothing but filthy rags. Like autumn leaves, we wither and fall, and our sins sweep us away like the wind. 7 Yet no one calls on your name or pleads with you for mercy. Therefore, you have turned away from us and turned us over to our sins." (Isa. 64:6-7). It is only in the righteousness of Christ that we are made right with God. "and become one with him. I no longer count on my own righteousness through obeying the law; rather, I become righteous through faith in Christ. For God's way of making us right with himself depends on faith" (Phil. 3:9). You also take credit for your abilities, accomplishments, and possessions instead of acknowledging that "For who sees anything different in you? What do you have that you did not receive? If then you received it, why do you boast as if you did not receive it" (1 Cor. 4:7 ESV)?

Pride causes us to have an intellectual knowledge of God instead of an intimate, heart-felt relationship with Him. When this happens, it keeps us from being close to Him; keeps us from being able to hear from Him; quenches the Holy Spirit and stops the flow of God's power and anointing in our lives. Pride keeps God's children from seeking Him. "The wicked are too proud to seek God. They seem to think that God is dead" (Ps. 10:4).

What pride traits are hindering your relationship with God?

_____

_____

_____

_____

The Bible tells us that God hates pride. "There are six things the Lord hates— no, seven things he detests: haughty eyes, a lying tongue, hands that kill the innocent, a heart that plots evil, feet that race to do wrong, a false witness who pours out lies, a person who sows discord in a family" (Prov. 6:16-19). God hates pride because it is one of the primary schemes Satan uses to destroy His children and their relationship with Him and others. The following scriptures emphasize God's hatred toward pride. Prov. "Therefore, I hate pride and arrogance, corruption and perverse speech" (Prov. 8:13b). "The Lord detests the proud; they will surely be punished" (Prov. 16:5). "I will not endure conceit and pride" (Ps. 101:5b). God is Holy and will not allow pride and arrogance to exist in His presence. "Therefore, the proud may not stand in your presence, for you hate all who do evil" (Ps. 5:5). People who continue to follow their desires and plans with no need for God will face the judgment of God.

HUMILITY:
If anyone ever had a reason to be prideful, it was Jesus. Yet, he displayed humility in every area of his life. He is our best example of humility. "You must have the same attitude that Christ Jesus had. Though he was God, he did not think of equality with God as something to cling to. Instead, he gave up his divine privileges; he took the humble position of a slave and was born as a human being. When he appeared in human form, he humbled himself in obedience to God and died a criminal's death on a cross. Therefore, God elevated him to the place of highest honor and gave him the name above all other names, that at the name of Jesus every knee should bow, in heaven and on earth and under the earth, and every tongue declare that Jesus Christ is Lord, to the glory of God the Father" (Phil. 2:5-11). Jesus' life on earth began in humility as He left heaven and gave up His equality with God to take on human flesh and be born in a humble stable to a humble family. "And because Joseph was a descendant of King David, he had to go to Bethlehem in Judea, David's ancient home. He traveled there from the village of Nazareth in Galilee. He took with him Mary, to whom he was engaged, who was now expecting a child. And while they were there, the time came for her baby to be born. She gave birth to her firstborn son. She wrapped him snugly in strips of cloth and laid him in a manger, because there was no lodging available for them" (Luke 2:4-7).

He continually demonstrated humility throughout His life. He described Himself as humble and gentle. "Take my yoke upon you. Let me teach you, because I am humble and gentle at heart, and you will find rest for your souls. For my yoke is easy to bear, and the burden I give you is light" (Matt. 11:29-30). Jesus had compassion for people. "Jesus saw the huge crowd as he stepped from the boat, and he had compassion on them because they were like sheep without a shepherd. So he began teaching them many things" (Mark 6:34). He took on the role of servant as He washed the feet of His disciples. "Jesus knew that the Father had given him authority over everything and that he had come from God and would return to God. So, he got up from the table, took off his robe, wrapped a towel around his waist, and poured water into a basin. Then he began to wash the disciples' feet, drying them with the

83

towel he had around him. When Jesus came to Simon Peter, Peter said to him, "Lord, are you going to wash my feet?" Jesus replied, "You don't understand now what I am doing, but someday you will" (John 13:3-7). He gave comfort to the brokenhearted, He built up and encouraged hurting people. "The Spirit of the Sovereign Lord is upon me, for the Lord has anointed me to bring good news to the poor. He has sent me to comfort the brokenhearted and to proclaim that captives will be released, and prisoners will be freed. He has sent me to tell those who mourn that the time of the Lord's favor has come, and with it, the day of God's anger against their enemies. To all who mourn in Israel, he will give a crown of beauty for ashes, a joyous blessing instead of mourning, festive praise instead of despair. In their righteousness, they will be like great oaks that the Lord has planted for his own glory." (Isa. 61:1-3).

He had a great love for all people, and He demonstrated His love when He laid His life down for all mankind. "I have loved you even as the Father has loved me. Remain in my love. When you obey my commandments, you remain in my love, just as I obey my Father's commandments and remain in his love. I have told you these things so that you will be filled with my joy. Yes, your joy will overflow! This is my commandment: Love each other in the same way I have loved you. There is no greater love than to lay down one's life for one's friends. You are my friends if you do what I command. I no longer call you slaves because a master doesn't confide in his slaves. Now you are my friends, since I have told you everything the Father told me. You didn't choose me. I chose you. I appointed you to go and produce lasting fruit, so that the Father will give you whatever you ask for, using my name. This is my command: Love each other" (John 15:9-17). Jesus cared for and thought more of others than He did of Himself. He was selfless as He went about healing, delivering, teaching, preaching, and saving the lost.

Jesus knew the Father and completely trusted Him and His plan. "just as my Father knows me and I know the Father. So, I sacrifice my life for the sheep" (John 10:15). Where Lucifer said in his heart, "I will, I will, I will," Jesus' heart was set on "Thy will" as He submitted in obedience to the Father in every area of His life even unto death. He voluntarily left the highest place to come to the lowest place to save us. He was ridiculed, falsely accused, disrespected, shamed, deserted, beaten, and ultimately killed, but he didn't say a word. "He was oppressed and treated harshly, yet he never said a word. He was led like a lamb to the slaughter. And as a sheep is silent before the shearers, he did not open his mouth" (Isa. 53:7). He endured all things with a spirit of humility. Humility is the key to building and maintaining relationships with others. "Always be humble and gentle. Be patient with each other, making allowance for each other's faults because of your love" (Eph. 4:2).

Jesus was humble (meek) but not weak. He was a strong man of conviction. He had no problem speaking the truth to others; He had no problem taking a stand against the spirit of religion; He had no problem proclaiming the word of God with boldness, and He had no problem enduring the pain of the cross to save you. People tend to believe that being humble means you must be weak. But, to be humble in the Greek means to have "strength under control." In Biblical times the word "meek" was used to describe a wild stallion that has been tamed. The horse still has as much power as he did when he was wild, but now that power is under control, and the horse can be used as his master wills. "For God has not given us a spirit of fear and timidity, but of power, love, and self-discipline" (2 Tim. 1:7). Jesus' life and ministry, shows you that you can be meek without being weak. Jesus lived a life of humility from the manger to the cross. As you follow His example some characteristics of humility that you need to develop in your life are trusting, sympathetic, compassionate, forgiving, teachable, servants, peacemakers, friendly, content, helpful, worshipful, obedient, selfless, joyful, secure, quiet, repentant, respectful. So, how do you develop these characteristics of a humble servant? You must be willing to have a teachable spirit; be willing to ask for help and counsel; be willing to be obedient to authority; be willing to be a servant; be willing to wait on God and be willing to pray and ask the Holy Spirit to change you.

Humility is impossible to achieve overnight; instead, it takes diligence and commitment to become more like Jesus. Jesus sent the Holy Spirit so we could be empowered to live a life of humility. Only when you are humble to God are you able to exhibit the nine fruits of the spirit. "But the Holy Spirit produces this kind of fruit in our lives: love, joy, peace, patience, kindness, goodness, faithfulness, gentleness, and self-control. There is no law against these things" (Gal. 5:22-23)! You should note that the characteristics of humility are the opposite of the traits of pride. Humility traits build up your relationships with others and draw you closer to God, whereas pride tears down and destroys your relationships and separate you from God.

If you walk in humility, you will: rejoice with others. "Be happy with those who are happy, and weep with those who weep. Live in harmony with each other. Don't be too proud to enjoy the company of ordinary people. And don't think you know it all" (Rom. 12:15-16)! Strive for unity and harmony with others. "Make every effort to keep yourselves united in the Spirit, binding yourselves together with peace" (Eph. 4:3). Forgive others quickly. "Since God chose you to be the holy people he loves, you must clothe yourselves with tenderhearted mercy, kindness, humility, gentleness, and patience. Make allowance for each other's faults, and forgive anyone who offends you. Remember, the Lord forgave you, so you must forgive others. Above all, clothe yourselves with love, which binds us all together in perfect harmony" (Col. 3:12-14). Build up others through encouragement. "Don't use foul or abusive language. Let everything you say be good and helpful, so that your words will be an encouragement to those who hear them" (Eph. 4:29). Genuinely love and care for others. "Finally, all of you should be of one mind. Sympathize with each other. Love each other as brothers and sisters. Be tenderhearted and keep a humble attitude. Don't repay evil for evil. Don't retaliate with insults when people insult you. Instead, pay them back with a blessing. That is what God has called you to do, and he will grant you, his blessing" (1 Peter 3:8-9). Paul tells us. "Don't be selfish; don't try to impress others. Be humble, thinking of others as better than yourselves. Don't look out only for your interests but take an interest in others too. You must have the same attitude that Christ Jesus had" (Phil. 2:3-5). Jesus' attitude was one of a servant. He taught you to put others before self.

Jesus said, "But among you it will be different. Whoever wants to be a leader among you must be your servant, and whoever wants to be first among you must be the slave of everyone else. For even the Son of Man came not to be served but to serve others and to give his life as a ransom for many" (Mark 10:43-45). When you operate out of a servant's heart you become the hands and feet of Jesus reaching out to broken and hurting people. It will require a sacrifice of self, but being selfless is part of being humble and is a command of Jesus to "deny yourself."

"Love is patient and kind. Love is not jealous or boastful or proud or rude. It does not demand its own way. It is not irritable, and it keeps no record of being wrong" (1 Cor. 13:4-5).

What are the traits of humility listed in this passage that help build up relationships?

_____

_____

_____

While humility builds relationships with others, it also draws you closer to God. "God opposes the proud but gives grace to the humble. So, humble yourselves before God. Resist the devil, and he will flee from you. Come close to God, and God will come close to you" (James 4:6-8). You cannot come to Christ for salvation unless you come in humility. You must admit and confess that you are a sinner, something that pride would never do. You must acknowledge that you can do nothing to save yourself, and you have nothing to give except your sin. You must admit your need for a savior and then accept the grace of God in humble gratitude. You must die to self and surrender your prideful will and life to God. When you do this, you will experience an intimate relationship with God that will help you walk out your newfound freedom in Christ.

The key to a closer walk with God is to choose daily to be dependent on the Holy Spirit so that humility grows in your life, and pride diminishes. Read the story of John the Baptist. "Then Jesus and his disciples left Jerusalem and went into the Judean countryside. Jesus spent some time with them there, baptizing people. At this time John the Baptist was baptizing at Aenon, near Salim, because there was plenty of water there; and people kept coming to him for baptism. (This was before John was thrown into prison.) A debate broke out between John's disciples and a certain Jew over ceremonial cleansing. So John's disciples came to him and said, "Rabbi, the man you met on the other side of the Jordan River, the one you identified as the Messiah, is also baptizing people. And everybody is going to him instead of coming to us." John replied, "No one can receive anything unless God gives it from heaven. You yourselves know how plainly I told you, 'I am not the Messiah. I am only here to prepare the way for him.' It is the bridegroom who marries the bride, and the bridegroom's friend is simply glad to stand with him and hear his vows. Therefore, I am filled with joy at his success. He must become greater and greater, and I must become less and less. "He has come from above and is greater than anyone else. We are of the earth, and we speak of earthly things, but he has come from heaven and is greater than anyone else. He testifies about what he has seen and heard, but how few believe what he tells them! Anyone who accepts his testimony can affirm that God is true. For he is sent by God. He speaks God's words, for God gives him the Spirit without limit. The Father loves his Son and has put everything into his hands. And anyone who believes in God's Son has eternal life. Anyone who doesn't obey the Son will never experience eternal life but remains under God's angry judgment" (John 3:22-26). It shows you a beautiful example of a humble person, but it also tells you the way to become humble and grow closer to the Lord. He said in verse 30, "He (Jesus) must become greater and greater, and I must become less and less." Less of self-equals more of humility.

Name a trait of humility that John the Baptist displayed. _____

LESSON SUMMARY:
- The key to a closer walk with God is to choose daily to be dependent on the Holy Spirit so that humility grows in your life, and pride diminishes.
- "He must become greater and greater, and I must become less and less" (John 3:30).
- "Though the Lord is great, he cares for the humble, but he keeps his distance from the proud" (Ps. 138:6).
- "For those who exalt themselves will be humbled, and those who humble themselves will be exalted" (Luke 14:11).
- "God opposes the proud but gives grace to the humble. So humble yourselves before God. Resist the devil, and he will flee from you. Come close to God, and God will come close to you" (James 4:6-8).

OBEDIENCE PRECEDES BLESSINGS:

So, why can't you live a life of humility? Sin! There is a war between your flesh (pride) and your spirit (humility). Paul tells about this war. "So, the trouble is not with the law, for it is spiritual and good. The trouble is with me, for I am all too human, a slave to sin. I don't really understand myself, for I want to do what is right, but I don't do it. Instead, I do what I hate. But if I know that what I am doing is wrong, this shows that I agree that the law is good. So, I am not the one doing wrong; it is sin living in me that does it. And I know that nothing good lives in me, that is, in my sinful nature. I want to do what is right, but I can't. I want to do what is good, but I don't. I don't want to do what is wrong, but I do it anyway. But if I do what I don't want to do, I am not really the one doing wrong; it is sin living in me that does it. I have discovered this principle of life—that when I want to do what is right, I inevitably do what is wrong. I love God's law with all my heart. But there is another power within me that is at war with my mind. This power makes me a slave to the sin that is still within me. Oh, what a miserable person I am! Who will free me from this life that is dominated by sin and death? Thank God! The answer is in Jesus Christ our Lord. So you see how it is: In my mind I really want to obey God's law, but because of my sinful nature I am a slave to sin" (Romans 7:14-25). Pride affects everyone's life and must be kept in check. It is willful disobedience, and all people fall to it at times. When you fall, you need to humble yourself and repent?

Why does pride keep you from admitting and confessing your sin?

_____

_____

_____

Humility comes when you choose to do the right and good things God has asked you to do. This is obedience. Proud people cannot be obedient because their sinful nature is in control. You must be humble in order to obey. In obedience and surrender to God you become humbler and the humbler you become, the less prideful you are. You must dethrone pride and enthrone humility. As pride diminishes, blessings of God come. "Pride leads to disgrace, but with humility comes wisdom" (Prov. 11:2). "Whoever loves a pure heart and gracious speech will have the king as a friend" (Prov. 22:4). " In the same way, you who are younger must accept the authority of the elders. And all of you, dress yourselves in humility as you relate to one another, for "God opposes the proud but gives grace to the humble." So, humble yourselves under the mighty power of God, and at the right time he will lift you up in honor. Give all your worries and cares to God, for he cares about you" (1 Peter 5:5-7). "Humble yourselves before the Lord, and he will lift you up in honor" (James 4:10). These eternal blessings are far greater than any temporal, physical blessing you could ever hope to get". Grace, honor, wisdom, and care can only come from God and are only available when you humble yourself. Which would you prefer, destruction or blessing? It's your choice!

MEMORY VERSE:
"For those who exalt themselves will be humbled, and those who humble themselves will be exalted" (Luke 14:11).

GROW DEEPER:

PRIDE DEFINITIONS
- **Contentious** = tending to argument or strife; quarrelsome
- **Cynicism** = cynical disposition, character, or belief. [Cynical = bitterly or sneeringly distrustful, contemptuous, or pessimistic.
- **Dictatorial** = inclined to dictate or command, overbearing, arrogant, bossy, domineering
- **Egotistical** = given to talking about oneself, vain, boastful, opinionated, selfish
- **Mockery** = ridicule, contempt; something absurdly or offensively inadequate or unfitting
- **Oppressive** = burdensome, unjustly harsh, distressing, or grievous.
- **Seditious** = rebellious, disobedient, disorderly, disloyal, defiance.

Answer the following questions.
1. Actively seek to obey God out of humility. How do you consciously choose daily to be dependent on God and obey Him?
2. List areas of pride that are keeping you in disobedience to what God has commanded you to do.
3. Ask people you trust where they see the pride in you. Be humble and accept what they say without resentment.
4. Pride is anything that relies on self rather than on God. List areas where you are self-sufficient. How can you replace this behavior with one of humility?
5. Ask the Lord to reveal to you what He sees. Ask Him to show you the pride in your heart. As He reveals areas to you, humble yourself and repent or agree with God.
6. Read about each person listed below. Decide if they have a spirit of pride or a spirit of humility. Identify the specific trait or characteristics. How did the pride or humility affect their lives?
7. King Nebuchadnezzar – Daniel Chapter 4
8. Haman – Esther chapters 5-8
9. Saul – 1 Samuel 18: 1-16
10. Abraham – Genesis chapter 13
11. Jacob – Genesis chapter 33
12. Isaac and the wells – Genesis 26:12-25
13. Joseph – Genesis chapter 45 (Joseph's entire life – chapters 37-50)
14. Joseph's brothers – Genesis chapter 48
15. Tower of Babel – Genesis chapter 11
16. Naaman – 2 Kings chapter 5
17. Prodigal son, his father, and his brother – Luke 15: 11-32
18. Tax Collector and the Pharisee – Luke 18:9-14
19. Rich Young Ruler – Luke 18:18-25
20. Rich Fool – Luke 12:16-21

How Much Pride Do You Have?
Answer **Yes** or **No** to each of the following questions to identify issues of pride in your life.
1. Do you look down on those who are less educated or less affluent than yourself? _____
2. Do you feel that you are too important to take time to serve others? _____
3. Do you have a judgmental spirit toward those who don't make the same lifestyle choices that you do? _____
4. Do you think of yourself as more spiritual than your mate or other believers that you know? _____
5. Are you quick to find fault with others? _____

6. Do you have a sharp, critical tongue toward others? _____
7. Do you blame others for your faults and sins? _____
8. Do you feel guilty for your sins? _____
9. Do you frequently correct or criticize your mate or other people in leadership? _____
10. Do you give undo time or attention to your physical appearance? _____
11. Are you proud of the schedule you keep and what you can accomplish? _____
12. Do you accept all the praise instead of sharing it with others? _____
13. Are you driven to receive approval, praise, or acceptance from others? _____
14. Are you argumentative? _____
15. Are you easily angered? _____
16. Are you easily annoyed by other people? _____
17. Do you generally think that your way is the right way, the only way, or the best way? _____
18. Do you have a touchy, sensitive spirit and are easily offended? _____
19. Are you guilty of trying to leave a better impression of yourself than is honestly
20. true? _____
21. Do you compare yourself to others rather than God? _____
22. When people disagree with you, do you feel the need to argue and prove your position? _____
23. Do you have a hard time admitting when you are wrong? _____
24. Do you have a hard time confessing your sin to God or others? _____
25. Do you find it difficult to submit your will to another person? _____
26. Do you have a hard time expressing your real spiritual needs and struggles with others? _____
27. Are you excessively shy? _____
28. Do you have a hard time reaching out and being friendly to people that you don't know? _____
29. Do you become defensive when you are criticized or corrected? _____
30. Are you a perfectionist? _____
31. Do you tend to be controlling of your mate? _____
32. Do you frequently interrupt people when they are speaking? _____
33. Are you hurt when those you dislike are honored? _____
34. Do you enjoy sharing and boasting about your accomplishments? _____
35. Do you publicly put others down to make yourself look superior or more important than they are? _____
36. Do you want others to be intimidated by your spirituality? _____
37. Are you more concerned about your reputation than God's? _____
38. Do you give the impression that you have no problems? _____
39. Do you feel that friends and family can never measure up to your expectations? _____
40. Do you often complain about your health, your church, your job, your circumstances, etc.? _____
41. Are you more concerned about your problems, your needs, and your burdens, than about other people's concerns? _____
42. Do you worry about what others think of you? _____
43. Do you neglect to express gratitude to God, your mate, or others for the little things? _____
44. Do you neglect prayer and the Word because you feel you can manage without them? _____
45. Do you do things for praise and compliments? _____
46. Do you get hurt if your accomplishments or your acts of service are not recognized or rewarded at home, at work, or church? _____

47. Do you get hurt if your opinions are not considered when decisions are made? _____
48. Do you have a hard time following rules and being told what to do? _____
49. Do you avoid participating in certain events for fear of being embarrassed or looking foolish? ___
50. Do you avoid being around certain people because you feel inferior compared to them? _____
51. Do you dislike inviting people to your home because you don't think it's nice enough? _____
52. Is it hard for you to let others know when you need help? _____
53. Do you quickly forgive others who have wronged you? _____
54. Are you reading this test and thinking about how many of these questions apply to someone you know? _____

Demonic Stronghold Prayer
I address you, the evil spirit of <u>PRIDE,</u> in the name of Jesus Christ. I bind you by the power of the blood of Jesus, the authority of the word of God, and the mighty anointing of the Holy Spirit! I have repented of the sin that let you in, and I have closed the door. I put the ax of the Holy Spirit to your roots. I pull you up by the roots. I command you to leave me now in the name of Jesus!

Are You Free?
Father, I thank you for this newfound freedom, and in the place vacated by the spirit of PRIDE, we now receive a humble and contrite Spirit to flood and fill our life.

GROW I
Journey to Freedom
Lesson 8

MOVING FORWARD

PURPOSE OF THIS LESSON:
To remind you of what you have learned since the Encounter and to make sure that you have the tools to stay free after you leave this class.

Every tool in your heavenly kit will serve you well if you are faithful to apply them throughout your spiritual journey in Christ. Jesus has already paid for and equipped you with everything you will ever need to be successful in your holy calling. Jesus said, "You didn't choose me. I chose you. I appointed you to go and produce lasting fruit, so that the Father will give you whatever you ask for, using my name" (John 15:16). Yes, I am the vine; you are the branches. Those who remain in me, and I in them, will produce much fruit. For apart from me you can do nothing" (John 15:5). "This means that anyone who belongs to Christ has become a new person. The old life is gone; a new life has begun" (2 Cor. 5:17)! "For by grace you have been saved through faith, and that not of yourselves; it is the gift of God" (Eph. 2:8 NKJV), "Jesus replied, You must love the Lord your God with all your heart, all your soul, and all your mind" (Matt. 22:37). "Guard your heart above all else, for it determines the course of your life" (Prov. 4:23). Blessed are those who hunger and thirst for righteousness, For they shall be filled (Mat. 5:6 NKJV).

INTRODUCTION:
God's Word has the answer for every problem and every need.

"Jesus said to the people who believed in him, "You are truly my disciples if you remain faithful to my teachings. And you will know the truth, and the truth will set you free" (John 8:31-32). Your challenge is to determine in your heart whether you believe God's truth over any lie of the enemy and then start applying His truth to your life. Jesus said, "As the Father loved Me, I also have loved you; abide in My love. If you keep My commandments, you will abide in My love, just as I have kept My Father's commandments and abide in His love" (John 15:9-10 NKJV). Discern what he says in the very next verse, "These things I have spoken to you, that My joy may remain in you, and that your joy may be full" (John 15:11 NKJV). Jesus said, we will abide in His love and remain full of Joy, if we receive the truth of His word and obey His commandments. The key is God's grace, if we mess up. We must instantly ask forgiveness and repent, in doing so we remain in the love of God and full of joy! "If we confess our sins, He is faithful and just to forgive us our sins and to cleanse us from all unrighteousness" (1 John 1:9 NKJV).

This is God's Word for you, "So Christ has truly set us free. Now make sure that you stay free and don't get tied up again in slavery to the law" (Gal. 5:1). "For if you are trying to make yourselves right with God by keeping the law, you have been cut off from Christ! You have fallen away from God's grace" (Gal. 5:4). If you believe this truth, then you need to establish what your part is in staying free and begin to do it. Seeking an intimate personal relationship with Jesus nurtures spiritual maturity. Your heart's desire to remain in His presence will cause old things to fade away and with every truth comes more freedom from the lies and oppression of the enemy. We grow in the spirit by spending time in the Word with our heavenly teacher the Holy Spirit drawing ever closer to God in an intimate personal relationship in Christ. "For the word of God is living and powerful, and sharper than any two-edged sword, piercing even to the division of soul and spirit, and of joints and marrow, and is a discerner of the thoughts and intents of the heart" (Heb. 4:12 NKJV). "All Scripture is inspired by God and is useful to teach us what is true and to make us realize what is wrong in our lives. It corrects us when we are wrong and teaches us to do what is right. God uses it to prepare and equip his people to do every good work" (2 Tim. 3:16-17). "But when the Father sends the Advocate as my representative—that is, the Holy Spirit—he will teach you everything and will remind you of everything I have told you" (John 14:26).

WHY IS THIS LESSON IMPORTANT IN YOUR LIFE?

Because the principle Stay Filled with the Holy Spirit, which we studied in a previous lesson, is so important it is necessary to repeat it. This principle is revealed in the following scripture. "When an evil spirit leaves a person, it goes into the desert, seeking rest but finding none. Then it says, 'I will return to the person I came from.' So it returns and finds its former home empty, swept, and in order. Then the spirit finds seven other spirits more evil than itself, and they all enter the person and live there. And so that person is worse off than before. That will be the experience of this evil generation" (Matt 12:43-45). If one has not filled the temple with the Holy Spirit and the Word of God, that evil spirit will return after finding seven other spirits, more evil than itself and they will all enter that person and live there. "Don't you realize that your body is the temple of the Holy Spirit, who lives in you and was given to you by God? You do not belong to yourself" (1 Cor. 6:19), The bottom line to this is: leave no room for the enemy and keep the doors locked! This is the only way to STAY FREE! "But you belong to God, my dear children. You have already won a victory over those people because the Spirit who lives in you is greater than the spirit who lives in the world" (1 John 4:4). "Since we are living by the Spirit, let us follow the Spirit's leading in every part of our lives" (Gal. 5:25). "For God called you to do good, even if it means suffering, just as Christ suffered for you. He is your example, and you must follow in his steps" (1 Peter 2:21). "Let us therefore come boldly unto the throne of grace, that we may obtain mercy, and find grace to help in time of need" (Heb. 4:16 KJV).

KEYS TO THE KINGDOM:

Keys can be used to lock doors as well as open them. The following are some keys that open doors to the Kingdom of God for access to the victory, wisdom, success, life, joy, love, knowledge, and so much more that God has prepared for you. You are also being given some keys that will lock doors. Which will keep the enemy from stealing your identity in Christ, killing your authority in Christ, and destroying your calling in Christ, your witness, gifts, and relationships. Some of the things in this lesson were previously studied in other lessons. Whenever God wants us to know something in His Word, He repeats it, so we will do well to take notice of these important principles to help you STAY FREE.

RENEW YOUR MIND:

"Don't copy the behavior and customs of this world, but let God transform you into a new person by changing the way you think. Then you will learn to know God's will for you, which is good and pleasing and perfect" (Rom. 12:2). Changing to a new way of living demands, you change the way you think and changing the way you think requires filling your mind with the Word of God. We studied this in more detail in Lesson 5, Stay in the Word. Refer to that lesson to refresh your mind and to remind you that you need time with the Lord daily to be at your strongest. If you have not done this yet, you need to get a daily plan that includes the following:

- **Secret Place:**
  - "Those who live in the shelter of the Most High will find rest in the shadow of the Almighty" (Ps. 91:1).
  - "Then no one will notice that you are fasting, except your Father, who knows what you do in private. And your Father, who sees everything, will reward you" (Matt. 6:18).

- **Set Time:**
  - "I rise early, before the sun is up; I cry out for help and put my hope in your words" (Ps. 119:147).
  - "Before daybreak the next morning, Jesus got up and went out to an isolated place to pray" (Mark 1:35).
- **Strategic Plan:**
  - "Commit your actions to the Lord, and your plans will succeed" (Prov. 16:3).
  - "Make the most of every opportunity in these evil days. Don't act thoughtlessly but understand what the Lord wants you to do. Don't be drunk with wine because that will ruin your life. Instead, be filled with the Holy Spirit, singing psalms and hymns and spiritual songs among yourselves, and making music to the Lord in your hearts. And give thanks for everything to God the Father in the name of our Lord Jesus Christ" (Eph. 5:16-20).
- **Be Still and Worship:**
  - "Be still and know that I am God! I will be honored by every nation. I will be honored throughout the world" (Ps. 46:10).
  - "But you will not even need to fight. Take your positions; then stand still and watch the Lord's victory. He is with you, O people of Judah and Jerusalem. Do not be afraid or discouraged. Go out against them tomorrow, for the Lord is with you!" After consulting the people, the king appointed singers to walk ahead of the army, singing to the Lord and praising him for his holy splendor. This is what they sang: "Give thanks to the Lord; his faithful love endures forever" (2 Chron. 20:17, 21)
  - "One day as these men were worshiping the Lord and fasting, the Holy Spirit said, "Appoint Barnabas and Saul for the special work to which I have called them" (Acts 13:2).
- **Pray and Read:**
  - "Before daybreak the next morning, Jesus got up and went out to an isolated place to pray" (Mark 1:35).
  - "I rise early, before the sun is up; I cry out for help and put my hope in your words" (Ps. 119:147).
- **Read the Word:**
  - "All Scripture is inspired by God and is useful to teach us what is true and to make us realize what is wrong in our lives. It corrects us when we are wrong and teaches us to do what is right. 17 God uses it to prepare and equip his people to do every good work" (2 Tim 3:16-17).
- **Listen and Write:**
  - "Beautiful words stir my heart. I will recite a lovely poem about the king, for my tongue is like the pen of a skillful poet" (Ps. 45:1).
  - "Every part of this plan," David told Solomon, "was given to me in writing from the hand of the Lord" (1 Chron. 28:19).
  - "Write my answer plainly on tablets, so that a runner can carry the correct message to others" (Hab. 2:2).

- Where is your Secret Place? _____

- When is your Set Time? _____

- What is your Strategic Plan? _____

GODLY BELIEFS:

A Godly Belief is anything that lines up with God's Word, His character, His nature, and His ways. There may be times when you go through new seasons, and doubts may come back. Get your Godly beliefs back out and proclaim them over your life every day until you sense you are strong in this area. It is also a good idea to regularly review these Godly Beliefs, so no Ungodly Beliefs creep back in. If an Ungodly Belief creeps in, write it down, then write a new Godly Belief and say it out loud daily until you have changed your mind and have replaced it with your new Godly Belief. This is part of renewing your mind.

DO THE NEXT RIGHT THING:

Sometimes in life, you can begin to feel overwhelmed, and that can prevent you from doing anything. There is a saying that would be good for you to adopt. Do the next right thing. So, begin to make a habit of "doing the next right thing." During those times, when you do not know what to do, stop, and ask yourself, "What is the next right thing?" When you get an answer, do it. If you do not know the next step, ask yourself, "What was the last right thing that I did not do?" When that comes to your mind, then do that right thing. Just realize that you only must do one right thing at a time. Then, do the next right thing. Then, keep on doing the next right thing. Sometimes, you may feel overwhelmed, but just stop and do the next right thing. There are so many things that scream at us to get our attention every day. Some things are good, and some are not. How do we choose? Ask God what the next right thing is. One thing at a time, one step at a time, one day at a time. "So don't worry about tomorrow, for tomorrow will bring its own worries. Today's trouble is enough for today" (Matt. 6:34). Doing the next right thing begins with a choice.

Just make up your mind that you will choose to do the next right thing. To help you get started, following is a list of things that you can choose to do when you do not know what to do:

Today, I choose to do the next right thing "By the time this child is old enough to choose what is right and reject what is wrong, he will be eating yogurt and honey" (Isa. 7:15).

Today, I choose to seek God first above everything "Seek the Kingdom of God above all else, and live righteously, and he will give you everything you need" (Matt. 6:33).

Today, I choose to serve God, to serve my family and those in my path "But if you refuse to serve the Lord, then choose today whom you will serve. Would you prefer the gods your ancestors served beyond the Euphrates? Or will it be the gods of the Amorites in whose land you now live? But as for me and my family, we will serve the Lord" (Josh. 24:15).

Today, I choose to be thankful in every circumstance "Be thankful in all circumstances, for this is God's will for you who belong to Christ Jesus" (1 Thes. 5:18).

Today, I choose to wear a garment of praise "To all who mourn in Israel, he will give a crown of beauty for ashes, a joyous blessing instead of mourning, festive praise instead of despair. In their righteousness, they will be like great oaks that the Lord has planted for his own glory" (Isa. 61:3).

Today, I choose to be in awe of and amazed by God for who He is and what He does "For they hated knowledge and chose not to fear the Lord" (Prov. 1:29).

Today, I choose to forgive and to love and to let the peace of Christ rule in my heart "Make allowance for each other's faults and forgive anyone who offends you. Remember, the Lord forgave you, so you must forgive others. Above all, clothe yourselves with love, which binds us all together in perfect harmony. And let the peace that comes from Christ rule in your hearts. For as members of one body, you are called to live in peace. And always be thankful" (Col. 3:13-15).

Today, I choose God's instruction, knowledge, wisdom, and understanding through His Word and prayer "Choose my instruction rather than silver, and knowledge rather than pure gold" (Prov. 8:10). "How much better to get wisdom than gold, and good judgment than silver" (Prov. 16:16)!

Today, I choose to do God's will "Anyone who wants to do the will of God will know whether my teaching is from God or is merely my own" (John 7:17).

Today, I choose to be friends with God "You adulterers! Don't you realize that friendship with the world makes you an enemy of God? I say it again: If you want to be a friend of the world, you make yourself an enemy of God" (James 4:4).

Today, I choose to find pleasure in this day and be full of joy "This is the day the Lord has made. We will rejoice and be glad in it" (Ps. 118:24).

Today, I choose life and blessings "Today I have given you the choice between life and death, between blessings and curses. Now I call on heaven and earth to witness the choice you make. Oh, that you would choose life, so that you and your descendants might live" (Deut. 30:19)!

Today, I choose to speak life over every circumstance "The tongue can bring death or life; those who love to talk will reap the consequences" (Prov. 18:21). "The Spirit alone gives eternal life. Human effort accomplishes nothing. And the very words I have spoken to you are spirit and life" (John 6:63).

Today, I choose what pleases God and hold fast to His covenant "For this is what the Lord says: I will bless those eunuchs who keep my Sabbath days holy and who choose to do what pleases me and commit their lives to me" (Isa. 56:4).

Today, I choose faith because it pleases God "And it is impossible to please God without faith. Anyone who wants to come to him must believe that God exists and that he rewards those who sincerely seek him" (Heb. 11:6).

What would happen if you made these right choices each day?

_____

_____

_____

Will you commit to read this list each day for the next 30 days and choose to do the next right thing! _____

FIGHT BACK:

When the enemy attacks you, don't just lay down and cry like a victim. FIGHT BACK! God did not expect you to fight back without weapons. He has already given you everything you need to win this war! "We are human, but we don't wage war as humans do. We use God's mighty weapons, not worldly weapons, to knock down the strongholds of human reasoning and to destroy false arguments. We destroy every proud obstacle that keeps people from knowing God. We capture their rebellious thoughts and teach them to obey Christ" (2 Cor. 10:3-5). There is a story in the Old Testament that shows us a picture of how we can win. "He picked up five smooth stones from a stream and put them into his shepherd's bag. Then, armed only with his shepherd's staff and sling, he started across the valley to fight the Philistine. 48 As Goliath moved closer to attack, David quickly ran out to meet him. 49 Reaching into his shepherd's bag and taking out a stone, he hurled it with his sling and hit the Philistine in the forehead. The stone sank in, and Goliath stumbled and fell face down on the ground. 50 So David triumphed over the Philistine with only a sling and a stone, for he had no sword. 51 Then David ran over and pulled Goliath's sword from its sheath. David used it to kill him and cut off his head" (1 Sam. 17:40, 48-51). Notice David selected five stones smooth from the stream yet, in one single stone he was victorious. Five is the number of Grace, in God's Grace through faith in Jesus Christ our cornerstone we are made smooth in His living water and are victorious over sin and the evil giants we face daily. "This High Priest of ours understands our weaknesses, for he faced all of the same testings we do, yet he did not sin. 16 So let us come boldly to the throne of our gracious God. There we will receive his mercy, and we will find grace to help us when we need it most" (Heb. 4:15-16), "And of His fullness we have all received, and grace for grace. For the law was given through Moses, but grace and truth came through Jesus Christ" (John 1:16-17 NKJV). "Sin is no longer your master, for you no longer live under the requirements of the law. Instead, you live under the freedom of God's grace. (Rom. 6:14). "But by the grace of God I am what I am, and His grace toward me did not prove vain; but I labored even more than all of them, yet not I, but the grace of God with me" (1 Cor. 15:10 NASB). By Grace through faith in Christ we are victorious! Be prepared to discuss why you think David defeated his enemy, Goliath (a giant), with only a stone instead of the world's weapons. What traits did David have that helped him to fight back when he was faced with a battle?

_____

_____

_____

WEAPONS THAT GOD HAS GIVEN US TO OVERCOME TEMPTATIONS:
Read the scriptures below and write out your thoughts on how you can personally use each weapon in your life.

Word – "I have hidden your word in my heart, that I might not sin against you" (Ps. 119:11).

_____

_____

_____

Prayer – "Put on salvation as your helmet, and take the sword of the Spirit, which is the word of God. Pray in the Spirit at all times and on every occasion. Stay alert and be persistent in your prayers for all believers everywhere" (Eph. 6:17-18).

_____

_____

Praise – "You have taught children and infants to tell of your strength, silencing your enemies and all who oppose you" (Ps. 8:2). "Be thankful in all circumstances, for this is God's will for you who belong to Christ Jesus" (1 Thes. 5:18).

_____

_____

_____

_____

_____

Righteousness (the act of doing the next right thing) – "We faithfully preach the truth. God's power is working in us. We use the weapons of righteousness in the right hand for attack and the left hand for defense" (2 Cor. 6:7).

_____

_____

_____

Personal check-ups – "Search me, O God, and know my heart; test me and know my anxious thoughts. Point out anything in me that offends you and lead me along the path of everlasting life" (Ps. 139:23-24).

_____

_____

_____

Accountability and Prayer Partner – "Confess your sins to each other and pray for each other so that you may be healed. The earnest prayer of a righteous person has great power and produces wonderful results" (James 5:16).

_____

_____

_____

Do you have an accountability/prayer partner? _____

If yes, how has this helped you?

_____

_____

_____

If no, stop right now and ask God to show you who you should ask? _____

As soon as you have an answer, make a phone call. Make this a priority!

STAY FREE!
Come prepared to discuss how you have implemented these 6 "Stays" into your life.

STAY Filled with the Holy Spirit "Don't be drunk with wine, because that will ruin your life. Instead, be filled with the Holy Spirit" (Eph. 5:18),

This means to be controlled by the Holy Spirit. If you do not truly believe this and obey it, you will start making your own choices that are contrary to the Holy Spirit. You will begin making bad choices which lead to hard consequences and a loss of freedom.

STAY in the Word "Study this Book of Instruction continually. Meditate on it day and night so you will be sure to obey everything written in it. Only then will you prosper and succeed in all you do" (Josh. 1:8). "I have hidden your word in my heart, that I might not sin against you" (Ps. 119:11).

If you do not stay in the Word, you cannot renew your mind, and if you do not renew your mind, you start listening to the enemy's lies, and then again, you will make bad choices.

STAY in Prayer and Worship "Don't worry about anything; instead, pray about everything. Tell God what you need and thank him for all he has done. Then you will experience God's peace, which exceeds anything we can understand. His peace will guard your hearts and minds as you live in Christ Jesus" (Phil. 4:6-7).

It is so necessary to stay in prayer to stay free. It is the vehicle that God uses to bring the answers you need. If you are weak, you ask for strength. If you need direction, you ask, and He guides. If you are tempted, ask where the door is to get out of this temptation. Ask, ask, ask, and He gives.

STAY Connected "And let us not neglect our meeting together, as some people do, but encourage one another, especially now that the day of his return is drawing near" (Heb. 10:25). "Dear brothers and sisters, if another believer is overcome by some sin, you who are godly should gently and humbly help that person back onto the right path. And be careful not to fall into the same temptation yourself. Share each other's burdens, and in this way obey the law of Christ. If you think you are too important to help someone, you are only fooling yourself. You are not that important" (Gal. 6:1-3).

This is one of the ways that can help you to stay free and strong. Do you hang out with eagles or turkeys? Surround yourself with Godly people that will encourage you when you are down and will correct you when you need it. God designed it so that we help each other in this journey called life.

STAY Submitted "So humble yourselves before God. Resist the devil, and he will flee from you" (James 4:7). "Everyone must submit to governing authorities. For all authority comes from God, and those in positions of authority have been placed there by God. So anyone who rebels against authority is rebelling against what God has instituted, and they will be punished. For the authorities do not strike fear in people who are doing right, but in those who are doing wrong. Would you like to live without fear of the authorities? Do what is right, and they will honor you" (Rom. 13:1-3). "You know that Stephanas and his household were the first of the harvest of believers in Greece, and they are spending their lives in service to God's people. I urge you, dear brothers and sisters, to submit to them and others like them who serve with such devotion" (1 Cor. 16:15-16). "Obey your spiritual leaders, and do what they say. Their work is to watch over your souls, and they are accountable to God. Give them reason to do this with joy and not with sorrow. That would certainly not be for your benefit" (Heb. 13:17).

Submit yourself to God, resist the devil, and he will flee from you. You must submit yourself to God first and then to Godly leaders who will watch over you and help you to grow stronger. When people think they don't need anyone, they are setting themselves up for a fall.

STAY Humble "Pride goes before destruction, and haughtiness before a fall" (Prov. 16:18). "Fear of the Lord teaches wisdom; humility precedes honor" (Prov. 15:33). "Humble yourselves before the Lord, and he will lift you up in honor" (James 4:10).

In the church, we see this happen over and over. When someone gets set free, the first few months, they are so grateful to God and everyone for everything, and then gradually, as time goes by, they start slipping on the first five "stays," and then pride creeps in. The Bible warns against this. "Pride goes before destruction." The only way to avoid this is to STAY humble before God and man. Pride precedes destruction. Humility precedes honor. Which would you prefer? Destruction or honor?

God's Word has the answer for every problem and every need. Your challenge, as stated earlier, is to determine in your heart whether you believe God's truth over any lie of the enemy and then start applying His truth to your lives.

If you choose to believe the lie, instead of believing and applying God's truth, you set yourself up for a fall. It is time to see freedom brought into the House of God for the Children of God. It is time to believe God and that His Word is the final authority on everything. He has a good plan for your life, and it is time to start living the abundant life that Jesus came to give you instead of the evil plan that the enemy wants for you. The enemy came to steal, kill, and destroy, but JESUS CAME to give you abundant life.

LESSON SUMMARY:
- Seeking an intimate personal relationship with Jesus nurtures spiritual maturity.
- "For if you are trying to make yourselves right with God by keeping the law, you have been cut off from Christ! You have fallen away from God's grace" (Gal. 5:4).
- Your heart's desire to remain in the Lord's presence will cause old things to fade away and with every truth comes more freedom from the lies of the enemy.
- "Don't copy the behavior and customs of this world, but let God transform you into a new person by changing the way you think. Then you will learn to know God's will for you, which is good and pleasing and perfect" (Rom. 12:2).

*Note: Lesson Slides end at this point.

OBEDIENCE PRECEDES BLESSING:
Be a doer of the Word. "Don't just listen to God's Word. You must do what it says" (James 1:22).

MEMORY VERSE:
"Christ has truly set us free. Now make sure that you STAY FREE" (Gal. 5:1).

GROW DEEPER:
"Then, Christ will make His home in your hearts as you trust in Him. Your roots will GROW down into God's love and keep you strong" (Eph. 3:17).

The best way to grow is by sharing what you know with someone else. Your challenge is to share this lesson with at least one other person as soon as possible!

Grow II
Lessons

"Foundations"

IDENTITY IN CHRIST

PURPOSE OF THIS LESSON:
To gain a thorough understanding of who you are in Christ.

What the cross of Calvary and the resurrection of Jesus means to us when we accept Jesus as our Lord and Savior. Understanding our benefits as believers empowers us to live victoriously every day in Christ, because we now belong to the Lord Jesus. Our freedom has been purchased with His blood and the ultimate price. Jesus sacrificed Himself for each of us, all charges have been dropped and our debt of sin has been paid in full!

"He personally carried our sins in his body on the cross so that we can be dead to sin and live for what is right. By his wounds, you are healed. Once you were like sheep who wandered away. But now you have turned to your Shepherd, the Guardian of your souls" (1 Pet. 2:24-25).

"However, it was our sicknesses that He Himself bore, And our pains that He carried; Yet we ourselves assumed that He had been afflicted, Struck down by God, and humiliated. But He was pierced for our offenses, He was crushed for our wrongdoings; The punishment for our well-being was laid upon Him, And by His wounds we are healed" (Isaiah 53:4-5 NASB).

Between His hand and the wood, there was a list. A long list. A list of our mistakes: our lusts and lies and greedy moments and prodigal years. A list of our sins. Dangling from the cross is an itemized catalog of your sins. The bad decisions from last year. The bad attitudes from last week. There, in broad daylight for all of heaven to see, is a list of your mistakes. The list God has made, however, cannot be read. The words can't be deciphered. The mistakes are covered. The sins are hidden. Those at the top are hidden by His hand; those down the list are covered by His blood. —HE CHOSE THE NAILS, Max Lucado

INTRODUCTION:
When Jesus was about to die on the cross and uttered, "It is finished," many spiritual transactions took place.

In those six hours that He was nailed to the tree, our entire sin debt was settled. We will explore everything Jesus purchased for us so that we might experience an abundant life and what we have received because of our salvation. We will examine the crucifixion of Jesus on the cross so that we, as believers, will be empowered with the knowledge and understanding of our new inheritance. "The thief comes only to steal and kill and destroy; I came so that they would have life and have it abundantly" (John 10:10).

WHY IS THIS LESSON IMPORTANT TO YOUR LIFE?
- The cross is a divine exchange.
- Jesus was punished and suffered death that we might be forgiven.

- Jesus was wounded that we might be healed.
- Jesus was made sin with our sinfulness that we might become righteous with His righteousness.
- Jesus died our death that we might share His life.
- Jesus became poor that we might become rich with His riches.
- Jesus bore our shame that we might share His glory.
- Jesus was rejected that we might be accepted.
- Jesus became a curse that we might receive a blessing.

We are Co-Heir's. What is an heir? The literal meaning of an heir is "someone who has been appointed to receive an inheritance." An heir is a person who receives something of value from a father. An heir receives the title to His father's property even though he is not the one who has labored to secure the property. He has a legal right to ownership based on His relationship with His father, the owner.

The Bible sometimes uses the word heir to describe us as recipients of a gift from God. "Now you are no longer a slave but God's own child. And since you are his child, God has made you, his heir" (Gal.4:7). "and if children, then heirs-heirs of God and joint heirs with Christ, if indeed we suffer with Him, that we may also be glorified together" (Rom. 8:17 NKJV).

We are Victor's. We have victory because of Christ's sacrifice. Jesus took on our sin and gave us His righteousness and salvation. "We know that our old sinful selves were crucified with Christ so that sin might lose its power in our lives. We are no longer slaves to sin" (Rom. 6:6). The Word of God tells us that "But in all these things we overwhelmingly conquer through Him who loved us" (Rom. 8:37 NASB). To conquer is to be victorious over an adversary. To be "more than a conqueror" means we not only achieve victory, but we are overwhelmingly victorious.

We are Children of God. What does it mean to be a Child of God? "Therefore, come out from among unbelievers, and separate yourselves from them, says the Lord. Don't touch their filthy things, and I will welcome you. And I will be your Father, and you will be my sons and daughters, says the Lord Almighty" (2 Cor. 6:17-18).

"For his Spirit joins with our spirit to affirm that we are God's children. And since we are his children, we are his heirs. In fact, together with Christ we are heirs of God's glory. But if we are to share his glory, we must also share his suffering" (Rom. 8:16-17).

"By his divine power, God has given us everything we need for living a godly life. We have received all of this by coming to know him, the one who called us to himself by means of his marvelous glory and excellence. And because of his glory and excellence, he has given us great and precious promises. These are the promises that enable you to share his divine nature and escape the world's corruption caused by human desires" (2 Pet. 1:3-4 NASB). "and he has identified us as his own by placing the Holy Spirit in our hearts as the first installment that guarantees everything he has promised us" (2 Cor. 1:22).
- All charges have been dropped. "He canceled the record of the charges against us and took it away by nailing it to the cross" (Col. 2: 14).
- Our freedom was legally purchased from our previous master, the devil, and all demonic influences. *Redemption (Bought back).

- "In this way, he disarmed the spiritual rulers and authorities. He shamed them publicly by His victory over them on the cross" (Col. 2:15).
- "I am crucified with Christ: nevertheless I live; yet not I, but Christ liveth in me: and the life which I now live in the flesh I live by the faith of the Son of God, who loved me, and gave himself for me" (Gal. 2:20 KJV).
- We were a slave to sin, separated from the Father.
- "We know that our old sinful selves were crucified with Christ so that sin might lose its power in our lives. We are no longer slaves to sin" (Rom. 6:6).
- We are a new creation in Jesus!
- "This means that anyone who belongs to Christ has become a new person. The old life is gone; a new life has begun" (2 Cor. 5:17)!
- "I give them eternal life, and they will never perish. No one can snatch them away from me, for my Father has given them to me, and he is more powerful than anyone else. No one can snatch them from the Father's hand" (John 10:28-29).

LESSON SUMMARY:
- To thorough understanding who you are in Christ is critical to your spiritual growth, maturity, survival, and salvation.
- "Don't you realize that your body is the temple of the Holy Spirit, who lives in you and was given to you by God? You do not belong to yourself, for God bought you with a high price. So, you must honor God with your body" (1 Cor. 6:19-20).
- "Therefore, if anyone is in Christ, he is a new creation; old things have passed away; behold, all things have become new" (2 Cor. 5:17 NKJV).
- "And they overcame him by the blood of the Lamb and by the word of their testimony, and they did not love their lives to the death" (Rev. 12:11 NKJV).
- *Note: Lesson Slides end at this point.

OBEDIENCE PRECEDES BLESSING:
- Do you know what brings God pleasure? _____
- What makes God happy? _____
- Making wise decisions. Speaking what is right.
  - "My child, if your heart is wise, my own heart will rejoice! Everything in me will celebrate when you speak what is right" (Prov. 23:15-16).
  - Always aiming to please the Lord.
  - "So, whether we are here in this body or away from this body, our goal is to please him" (2 Cor. 5:9).
  - He delights in you.
  - "He takes no pleasure in the strength of a horse or in human might. No, the Lord's delight is in those who fear him, those who put their hope in his unfailing love" (Ps. 147:10-11).
  - He takes pleasure in His people.
  - "For the Lord delights in his people; he crowns the humble with victory" (Ps. 149:4).

MEMORY VERSE: "Therefore, if anyone is in Christ, he is a new creation; old things have passed away; behold, all things have become new" (2 Cor. 5: 17 NKJV).

GROW DEEPER:

Here are the blessings Jesus died to give you. The forgiveness of sins: He was pierced for your transgressions.

"He personally carried our sins in his body on the cross so that we can be dead to sin and live for what is right. By his wounds, you are healed" (1 Pet. 2:24).

"But if we confess our sins to him, he is faithful and just to forgive us our sins and to cleanse us from all wickedness" (1 John 1:9).

Peace in your heart. The punishment that brings you peace was laid upon Him. Your thought life can be renewed. The crown of thorns that Jesus wore is symbolic of the curse: "Cursed is the ground. It will produce thorns and thistles for you. By the sweat of your brow, you will eat your food" (Gen. 3: 17-19).

Jesus took the curse upon His brow so that your thought life could be freed. You no longer must live with destructive, habitual thoughts.

Learning to live in the peace of God is essential for a believer. Peace is the foundation for the rest of your life as a child of God. Jesus said: "Peace I leave with you, my peace I give to you; not as the world gives do, I give to you. Let not your heart be troubled; neither let it be afraid" (John 14:27 NKJV).

Healing for your physical body: By His wounds, you are healed.
The complete work of the cross is that every aspect of sin and disease has been dealt with.

Jesus heals all sickness. There is not any disease that Jesus cannot heal. "Jesus traveled through all the towns and villages of that area, teaching in the synagogues and announcing the Good News about the Kingdom. And he healed every kind of disease and illness" (Matt. 9:35).

This same ability to heal has been entrusted to us as believers. "He called His twelve disciples to him and gave them authority to drive out evil spirits and to heal every disease and sickness" (Matt. 10:1 NIV).

Even the fear of God keeps our bodies free of disease. "Don't be impressed with your own wisdom. Instead, fear the Lord and turn away from evil. Then you will have healing for your body and strength for your bones" (Prov. 3:7-8).

YOU CAN OVERCOME TEMPTATION:
- "The temptations in your life are no different from what others experience. And God is faithful. He will not allow the temptation to be more than you can stand. When you are tempted, he will show you a way out so that you can endure" (1 Cor. 10:13).
- "So, you see, the Lord knows how to rescue godly people from their trials, even while keeping the wicked under punishment until the day of final judgment" (2 Pet. 2:9).

OVERCOME TEMPTATION WITH PRAYER:
- Jesus said to pray that you would not be led into temptation.
- "There he told them, "Pray that you will not give in to temptation" (Luke 22:40).

- Jesus taught that the prayer of forgiveness would deliver from temptation.
- "And don't let us yield to temptation but rescue us from the evil one. "If you forgive those who sin against you, your heavenly Father will forgive you. But if you refuse to forgive others, your Father will not forgive your sins" (Matt. 6:13-15).

OVERCOME TEMPTATION WITH THE WORD OF GOD:
- Every time Jesus was confronted with temptation, He answered with the Word of God.
- "Then Jesus was led by the Spirit into the wilderness to be tempted there by the devil. For forty days and forty nights he fasted and became very hungry. During that time the devil came and said to him, "If you are the Son of God, tell these stones to become loaves of bread." But Jesus told him, "No! The Scriptures say," 'People do not live by bread alone, but by every word that comes from the mouth of God.'" Then the devil took him to the holy city, Jerusalem, to the highest point of the Temple, and said, "If you are the Son of God, jump off! For the Scriptures say, 'He will order his angels to protect you. And they will hold you up with their hands so you won't even hurt your foot on a stone.'" Jesus responded, "The Scriptures also say, 'You must not test the Lord your God.'" Next the devil took him to the peak of a very high mountain and showed him all the kingdoms of the world and their glory. "I will give it all to you," he said, "if you will kneel down and worship me." "Get out of here, Satan," Jesus told him. "For the Scriptures say, 'You must worship the Lord your God and serve only him.'" Then the devil went away, and angels came and took care of Jesus" (Matt. 4:1-11).
- The Word of God is a weapon you can use to overcome the attacks of the enemy.
- "Put on salvation as your helmet, and take the sword of the Spirit, which is the word of God" (Eph. 6:17).

OVERCOME TEMPTATION WITH THE BLOOD OF THE LAMB:
- "And they overcame him by the blood of the Lamb and the word of their testimony" (Rev. 12:11 NKJV).
- Proclaiming the power of the blood of Christ in your life releases supernatural force on your behalf. Nothing is more powerful than the precious blood of the Lamb that paid for your redemption.

OVERCOME TEMPTATION BY FELLOWSHIPPING WITH STRONG BELIEVERS:
- You must "Run from anything that stimulates youthful lusts. Instead, pursue righteous living, faithfulness, love, and peace. Enjoy the companionship of those who call on the Lord with pure hearts" (2 Tim. 2:22).
- "But you, Timothy, are a man of God; so run from all these evil things. Pursue righteousness and a godly life, along with faith, love, perseverance, and gentleness" (1 Tim. 6: 11).
- Remember that bad company will corrupt good morals.
- "Don't be fooled by those who say such things, for "bad company corrupts good character" (1 Cor. 15:33).
- You cannot be in partnership with unbelievers who don't want to serve God.
- "Don't team up with those who are unbelievers. How can righteousness be a partner with wickedness? How can light live with darkness? What harmony can there be between Christ and the devil[a]? How can a believer be a partner with an unbeliever? And what union can there be between God's temple and idols? For we are the temple of the living God. As God said: "I will live in them and walk among them. I will be their God, and they will be my people. Therefore, come out from among unbelievers, and separate yourselves from them, says the Lord. Don't touch their filthy things, and I will welcome you. And I will be your Father, and you will be my sons and daughters,

says the Lord Almighty Don't team up with those who are unbelievers. How can righteousness be a partner with wickedness? How can light live with darkness? What harmony can there be between Christ and the devil? How can a believer be a partner with an unbeliever? And what union can here be between God's temple and idols? For we are the temple of the living God. As God said: "I will live in them and walk among them. I will be their God, and they will be my people. Therefore, come out from among unbelievers, and separate yourselves from them, says the Lord. Don't touch their filthy things, and I will welcome you. And I will be your Father, and you will be my sons and daughters, says the Lord Almighty" (2 Cor. 6:14-18).

QUESTIONS:

How does understanding your position in Christ give you boldness to approach God?

What does it mean to be a co-heir with Christ? What is your inheritance?

What are you most tempted by? What are you doing to overcome it?

Foundations
In Christ
Lesson 2

PUTTING GOD FIRST

PURPOSE OF THIS LESSON:
- To understand life's priorities based on Scripture.
- You shall have no other gods before Me.
- You shall not make for yourself an idol.
- You shall not worship them nor serve them.
- You shall not take the name of the Lord your God in vain.
- Remember the Sabbath day, to keep it holy.

The former are the first five of the Ten Commandments. The definition of a commandment is a rule that must be obeyed. It is clear from these commandments where God should fit in our lives. Where does He fit in yours?

The Ten Commandments:
"Then God spoke all these words, saying, "I am the Lord your God, who brought you out of the land of Egypt, out of the house of slavery. "You shall have no other gods before Me. "You shall not make for yourself an idol, or any likeness of what is in heaven above or on the earth beneath, or in the water under the earth. You shall not worship them nor serve them; for I, the Lord your God, am a jealous God, inflicting the punishment of the fathers on the children, on the third and the fourth generations of those who hate Me, but showing favor to thousands, to those who love Me and keep My commandments. "You shall not take the name of the Lord your God in vain, for the Lord will not leave him unpunished who takes His name in vain. "Remember the Sabbath day, to keep it holy. For six days you shall labor and do all your work, but the seventh day is a Sabbath of the Lord your God; on it you shall not do any work, you, or your son, or your daughter, your male slave or your female slave, or your cattle, or your resident who stays with you. For in six days the Lord made the heavens and the earth, the sea and everything that is in them, and He rested on the seventh day; for that reason the Lord blessed the Sabbath day and made it holy. "Honor your father and your mother, so that your days may be prolonged on the land which the Lord your God gives you. "You shall not murder. "You shall not commit adultery. "You shall not steal. "You shall not give false testimony against your neighbor. "You shall not covet your neighbor's house; you shall not covet your neighbor's wife, or his male slave, or his female slave, or his ox, or his donkey, or anything that belongs to your neighbor" (Exodus 20:1-17 NASB).

INTRODUCTION:
Before surrendering your life to Christ, you lived; however, you wanted, most likely, giving little or no thought to the consequences of your actions.

But now, as a child of God, you are called to be Christ-like and Holy, as He is Holy. This only happens through the building and continued growth of your relationship with the Father. Your intimacy with Him will grow by spending time with Him, by reading His Word and by praising and worshipping

Him. When you put Him first, all other things will fall into their proper order. "Dear friends, we are already God's children, but he has not yet shown us what we will be like when Christ appears. But we do know that we will be like him, for we will see him as he really is. And all who have this eager expectation will keep themselves pure, just as he is pure" (1 John 3:2-3).

"Don't you realize that those who do wrong will not inherit the Kingdom of God? Don't fool yourselves. Those who indulge in sexual sin, or who worship idols, or commit adultery, or are male prostitutes, or practice homosexuality, or are thieves, or greedy people, or drunkards, or are abusive, or cheat people – none of these will inherit the Kingdom of God. Some of you were once like that. But you were cleansed; you were made holy; you were made right with God by calling on the name of the Lord Jesus Christ and by the Spirit of our God" (1 Cor. 6:9-11). "This means that anyone who belongs to Christ has become a new person. The old life is gone; a new life has begun" (2 Cor. 5:17)!

"Imitate God, therefore, in everything you do, because you are His dear children. Live a life filled with love, following the example of Christ. He loved us and offered Himself as a sacrifice for us, a pleasing aroma to God. Let there be no sexual immorality, impurity, or greed among you. Such sins have no place among God's people. Obscene stories, foolish talk, and coarse jokes – these are not for you. Instead, let there be thankfulness to God. You can be sure that no immoral, impure, or greedy person will inherit the Kingdom of Christ and God. For a greedy person is an idolater, worshiping the things of this world. Don't be fooled by those who try to excuse these sins, for the anger of God will fall on all who disobey Him. Don't participate in the things these people do. For once, you were full of darkness, but now you have light from the Lord. So, live as people of light! For this light within you produces only what is good and right and true. Carefully determine what pleases the Lord. Take no part in the worthless deeds of evil and darkness; instead, expose them. It is shameful even to talk about the things that ungodly people do in secret. But their evil intentions will be exposed when the light shines on them, for the light makes everything visible. Therefore, it is said, 'Awake, O sleeper, rise up from the dead, and Christ will give you light.' So be careful how you live. Don't live like fools, but like those who are wise. Make the most of every opportunity in these evil days. Don't act thoughtlessly but understand what the Lord wants you to do. Don't be drunk with wine, because that will ruin your life. Instead, be filled with the Holy Spirit, singing psalms and hymns and spiritual songs among yourselves, and making music to the Lord in your hearts. And give thanks for everything to God the Father in the name of our Lord Jesus Christ" (Eph. 5:1-20).

WHY IS THIS LESSON IMPORTANT TO YOUR LIFE? In today's culture, so many of life's priorities are dictated by external sources.

Daily, the news media, social media, society, and tradition affect your perception of what is most important. Many times, without even realizing it, you have structured your lives accordingly.

"Don't copy the behavior and customs of this world, but let God transform you into a new person by changing the way you think. Then you will learn to know God's will for you, which is good and pleasing and perfect" (Rom. 12:2).

"So, prepare your minds for action and exercise self-control. Put all your hope in the gracious salvation that will come to you when Jesus Christ is revealed to the world. So, you must live as God's obedient children. Don't slip back into your old ways of living to satisfy your desires. You didn't know any better. But now you must be holy in everything you do, just as God who chose you is holy. For the Scriptures say, 'You must be holy because I am holy" (1 Pet. 1:13-16).

PRIORITIES:
Priority 1: God and Your Relationship with Him
Devotion to God and His Word is essential to your Christian walk. A heart that is devoted to God is the rudder that steers the Christian life, and the Word of God is the key ingredient to your success in Christ.

"And a small rudder makes a huge ship turn wherever the pilot chooses to go, even though the winds are strong" (James 3:4).

The Word is a daily mirror What are you reflecting on? Are you walking away and forgetting what you are seeing and doing?

"But don't just listen to God's word. You must do what it says. Otherwise, you are only fooling yourselves. For if you listen to the word and don't obey, it is like glancing at your face in a mirror. You see yourself, walk away, and forget what you look like. But if you look carefully into the perfect law that sets you free, and if you do what it says and don't forget what you heard, then God will bless you for doing it" (James 1:22-25).

The Word of God gives you your marching orders. What road are you marching on?

"Your word is a lamp to guide my feet and a light for my path" (Ps.119:105).

The Word is your daily bread. The bread represents the necessities of life. The Word of God is our spiritual food.

"During that time the devil came and said to him, "If you are the Son of God, tell these stones to become loaves of bread." 4 But Jesus told him, "No! The Scriptures say, 'People do not live by bread alone, but by every word that comes from the mouth of God'" (Matthew 4:3-4)

"Yes, he humbled you by letting you go hungry and then feeding you with mana, a food previously unknown to you and your ancestors. He did it to teach you that people do not live by bread alone; rather, we live by every word that comes from the mouth of the Lord" (Deut. 8:3).

The Word of God is your daily defense and your offensive weapon against the enemy.

"Put on salvation as your helmet, and take the sword of the Spirit, which is the word of God" (Eph 6:17).

Priority 2: Maintaining Your Body, Soul, and Spirit
There is a direct correlation between the prosperity of your soul and the prosperity of your physical body. As you maintain your spiritual life and keep it well-tuned, your physical life will also prosper.

"Dear friend, I hope all is well with you and that you are as healthy in body as you are strong in spirit" (3 John 2).

You must realize and know that the source of your strength is Almighty God.
"Have you never heard? Have you never understood? The Lord is the everlasting God, the Creator of all the earth. He never grows weak or weary. No one can measure the depths of His understanding. He gives power to the weak and strength to the powerless. Even youths will become weak and tired, and young men will fall in exhaustion" (Is. 40:28-30).

Cleanse your spirit with the Word of God. How do you cleanse your spirit? By obeying His word

" How can a young person stay pure? By obeying your word" (Ps. 119:9).

Ask God today to cleanse your heart and renew your spirit.

"Create in me a clean heart, O God. Renew a loyal spirit within me" (Ps. 51:10).

Maintain your physical body, knowing that it is the temple of the Holy Spirit, and it belongs to the Lord.

"Don't you realize that your body is the temple of the Holy Spirit, who lives in you and was given to you by God? You do not belong to yourself, for God bought you with a high price. So, you must honor God with your body" (1 Cor. 6:19-20).

Priority 3: Your Home – The Pillars of Success
"Wisdom has built her house; she has carved its seven columns" (Prov. 9:1).

What foundation is your home built upon? The Word says anything built on a poor foundation will not stand. The only foundation for life and marriage is the finished works of Jesus Christ.

Building on a Solid Foundation:
"Anyone who listens to my teaching and follows it is wise, like a person who builds a house on solid rock. Though the rain comes in torrents and the floodwaters rise and the winds beat against that house, it won't collapse because it is built on bedrock. But anyone who hears my teaching and doesn't obey it is foolish, like a person who builds a house on sand. When the rains and floods come and the winds beat against that house, it will collapse with a mighty crash" (Matthew 7:24-27).

When Jesus is the foundation of your life, all that you do will be built on Him. This includes the way you speak to your spouse, the care of your home, and the discipline of your children. Everything must be built on Him.

Priority 4: Your Ministry – A Life of Purpose
You were created by God for good works. "For we are His workmanship, created in Christ Jesus for good works, which God prepared beforehand that we should walk in them" (Eph. 2:10 NKJV). Your goal as a believer should be to walk in the ministry God has for you.

Priority 5: Your Vocation
In scripture we are warned against idleness. The apostle Paul referred to it as being disorderly.

"For even when we were with you, we commanded you this: If anyone will not work, neither shall he eat. For we hear that there are some who walk among you in a disorderly manner, not working at all, but are busybodies" (2 Thes. 3:10-11).

Whatever your vocation, you should do it diligently and to the best of your ability.

"Work willingly at whatever you do, as though you were working for the Lord rather than for people" (Col. 3:23).

Your vocation has its place in your life to support you and your family as well as to enable you to fulfill the other priorities in your life. Your vocation is not, nor should it ever become your identity. It is simply a tool to help you accomplish more important goals and priorities.

"My old self has been crucified with Christ! It is no longer I who live, but Christ lives in me. So, I live in this earthly body by trusting in the Son of God, who loved me and gave himself for me" (Gal. 2:20).

"He must become greater and greater, and I must become less and less" (John 3:30).

"Since you have been raised to new life with Christ, set your sights on the realities of heaven, where Christ sits in the place of honor at God's right hand. Think about the things of heaven, not the things of earth. For you died to this life, and your real life is hidden with Christ in God. And when Christ, who is your life, is revealed to the whole world, you will share in all his glory" (Col. 3:1-4).

"For those who live according to the flesh set their minds on the things of the flesh, but those who live according to the Spirit, the things of the Spiri." (Rom. 8:5).

"Jesus replied, "'You must love the Lord your God with all your   heart, all your soul, and all your mind. This is the first and greatest commandment" A second is equally important: 'Love your neighbor as yourself'" (Matt. 22:37-39).

LESSON SUMMARY:

- Your Devotion to God and His Word are essential to your spiritual maturity, Christian walk and personal intimate relationship in Christ.

- A heart devoted to God is the rudder that steers the Christian life, and the Word of God is the key ingredient to your success in Christ.

- "Therefore, having been justified by faith, we have peace with God through our Lord Jesus Christ, through whom also we have access by faith into this grace in which we stand, and rejoice in hope of the glory of God" (Romans 5:1-2 NKJV).

- "Seek the Kingdom of God above all else, and live righteously, and he will give you everything you need" (Matt. 6:33).

- "and be renewed in the spirit of your mind, and that you put on the new man which was created according to God, in true righteousness and holiness" (Eph. 4:23-24 NKJV).

*Note: Lesson Slides end at this point.

OBEDIENCE PRECEDES BLESSING:
"But if you look carefully into the perfect law that sets you free, and if you do what it says and don't forget what you heard, then God will bless you for doing it" (Jam. 1:25).

The following acronym "F.I.R.S.T." will help you to remember five important places where you need to put God first.

- **F**inances – If you want God to bless your finances, even during a recession, you must tithe. Sorry! There's no other alternative.

- **I**nterests – Put Him first in your hobbies, your career, and your recreation. Give God first consideration in every decision.

- **R**elationships – Put Him first in your family, your marriage, and your friendships.

- **S**chedule – That means you should give Him the first part of every day. You should get up and sit on the side of your bed every morning and say, "God, if I don't get anything else done today, I just want to love you a little bit more and know you a little bit better."

- **T**roubles – You need to turn to God first when you have a problem. Prayer should never be your last resort. It should be your first choice.

MEMORY VERSE: "Seek the Kingdom of God above all else, and live righteously, and he will give you everything you need" (Matt. 6:33).

GROW DEEPER:
"Then, Christ will make His home in your hearts as you trust in Him. Your roots will GROW down into God's love and keep you strong" (Eph. 3:17).

Living a balanced life should be a goal for all believers. One of Satan's primary goals is to get your lives out of balance so that you begin to focus on the secondary and lose sight of what is primary. At the end of your lives, you will want to look back and be able to say that you gave God your best, not just the little that was leftover. A rich and intimate walk with the Lord will pay great dividends in this life and throughout eternity.

Always remember and be careful to apply Josh. 1:8: "Study this Book of Instruction continually. Meditate on it day and night so you will be sure to obey everything written in it. Only then will you prosper and succeed in all you do."

QUESTIONS:

What is your daily routine?

Where does God fit into your daily routine? Is He first? Is He last?

What can you remove from or change about your daily routine to make room for God?

GROW II
**Foundations
In Christ
Lesson 3**

I AM A WATCHMAN: PRAYER AND INTERCESSION

PURPOSE OF THIS LESSON:
To understand the importance of prayer. To discover the different types of prayer. To learn the keys to praying effectively, the importance of spending time with the Lord, and how to implement this spiritual discipline into our lives. "Never stop praying" (1 Thes. 5:17).

One evening, I arrived home and didn't have the key to the door. My husband, who I love, was inside sleeping like a rock. He didn't hear me knocking on the door like the police. He didn't hear me ringing the doorbell repeatedly. He didn't hear me throw a bucket next to the window. That man was completely knocked out. So, I yelled next to the bedroom window, "Baby, open the door!" Seconds later, there he was standing at the front door. I asked him, "You didn't hear all of the noise I was making?" He said, "No!" "So, what woke you up, I asked?" He said, "I heard your voice."

It is not our emotional fits, demands, tantrums, and pouting that gets God's attention. His ears are attentive to our voice. One thing is for sure, God hears you, and if you know He hears you, you know you have the petition you have asked of Him. "And we are confident that he hears us whenever we ask for anything that pleases him. And since we know he hears us when we make our requests, we also know that he will give us what we ask for" (1 John 5:14-15). His ears are attentive to your prayers, and when you draw near to Him, He will draw near to you. Let God hear the cry of your heart, let God hear your voice! -Daughters of the King Devotion. "Come close to God, and God will come close to you. Wash your hands, you sinners; purify your hearts, for your loyalty is divided between God and the world" (James 4:8). "The eyes of the Lord watch over those who do right; his ears are open to their cries for help" (Ps. 34:15 KJV).

INTRODUCTION:
In any relationship that is of value, and that is going to grow and develop, communication is essential.

So, it is in your relationship with God. If you want to grow spiritually, you must devote time to talking to the Lord and learning how to listen as He speaks to you. In this way, you will build a relationship with the very source of life and truth; that is, God the Father, God the Son, and God the Holy Spirit. "My sheep listen to my voice; I know them, and they follow me" (John 10:27). "Jesus told him, "I am the way, the truth, and the life. No one can come to the Father except through me" (John14:6).

WHY IS THIS LESSON IMPORTANT TO YOUR LIFE?
Prayer is the way we communicate with God. Jesus often withdrew to lonely places and prayed.

"But Jesus often withdrew to the wilderness for prayer" (Luke 5:16). Often means regularly. How often are you praying? If Jesus (the Son of God) prayed, how much more should we? Prayer is how we build our relationship with God. Prayer is a relationship, wherein we humbly communicate, worship, and sincerely seek God's face, knowing that He hears us, loves us, and will respond, though not always in a manner we may expect or desire. Prayer can encompass adoration, praise, thanksgiving, confession, repentance, supplication, petition, proclamation, intercession, and more. Prayer is a vital part of your relationship with God. It helps you grow in your knowledge of Him and is also a way of showing your love and commitment to Him. "You can ask for anything in my name, and I will do it, so that the Son can bring glory to the Father. Yes, ask me for anything in my name, and I will do it" (John 14:13-14)! Prayer helps you receive direction and encouragement from the Father. In prayer, you can ask Him for wisdom in situations and be renewed in your spirit in times of trials. Jesus taught us how to pray. "Pray like this: Our Father in heaven, may your name be kept holy. May your Kingdom come soon. May your will be done on earth, as it is in heaven. Give us today the food we need, and forgive us our sins, as we have forgiven those who sin against us. And don't let us yield to temptation but rescue us from the evil one" (Matt. 6:9-13).

TYPES OF PRAYER:
Intercessory prayer allows you to "stand in the gap" in prayer for situations and people.
Crisis intercessors pray almost exclusively on assignments that come from the Father.
Warfare intercessors are called specially to engage the enemy in high-level spiritual warfare.

Apostle Paul instructs us to make supplications, prayers, and intercessions and to give thanks to God. "Therefore, I exhort first of all that supplications, prayers, intercessions, and giving of thanks be made for all men" (1 Tim 2:1 NKJV), Jesus was and is the great intercessor. He ever lives to make intercession for His people. "Therefore, he is able, once, and forever, to save those who come to God through him. He lives forever to intercede with God on their behalf" (Heb. 7:25). "Who then will condemn us? No one-for Christ Jesus died for us and was raised to life for us, and he is sitting in the place of honor at God's right hand, pleading for us" (Rom. 8:34).

In ripple prayer, you first lift-up areas concerning you and your relationship with the Lord. Then you move outward as if you had tossed a stone into a pool of water. Your prayer focus moves outward the same as a ripple moves through a pool of water. You can include the following areas: your family, your church, your neighborhood, your city, your state, your nation, and the world.

In his epistles, Paul made numerous requests for prayer for himself and for those who labored with him. "Dear brothers and sisters, pray for us" (1 Thes. 5:25). "Dear brothers and sisters, I urge you in the name of our Lord Jesus Christ to join in my struggle by praying to God for me. Do this because of your love for me, given to you by the Holy Spirit" (Rom.15:30). "And you are helping us by praying for us. Then many people will give thanks because God has graciously answered so many prayers for our safety" (2 Cor. 1:11). "For I know that as you pray for me and the Spirit of Jesus Christ helps me, this will lead to my deliverance" (Phil. 1:19). "One more thing—please prepare a guest room for me, for I am hoping that God will answer your prayers and let me return to you soon" (Philemon 22).

A WATCHMAN:
What does it mean to be a "Watchman?" A Watchman is a person who is to be on the lookout for any signs of disturbance or the activities and schemes of the enemy. "Be of sober spirit, be on the alert. Your adversary, the devil, prowls around like a roaring lion, seeking someone to devour" (1 Pet.5:8 NASB).
A Watchman is also to keep watch of "the exposed places."

"But when Sanballat, Tobiah, the Arabs, the Ammonites and the men of Ashdod heard that the repairs to Jerusalem's walls had gone ahead and that the gaps were being closed, they were very angry. They all plotted together to come and fight against Jerusalem and stir up trouble against it. But we prayed to our God and posted a guard day and night to meet this threat. Meanwhile, the people in Judah said, "The strength of the laborers is giving out, and there is so much rubble that we cannot rebuild the wall." Also, our enemies said, "Before they know it or see us, we will be right there among them and will kill them and put an end to the work." Then the Jews who lived near them came and told us ten times over, "Wherever you turn, they will attack us." Therefore, I stationed some of the people behind the lowest points of the wall at the exposed places, posting them by families, with their swords, spears, and bows. After I looked things over, I stood up and said to the nobles, the officials and the rest of the people, "Don't be afraid of them. Remember the Lord, who is great and awesome, and fight for your brothers, your sons and your daughters, your wives, and your homes" (Neh. 4:7-14).

Prayer is a war tactic. We fight for ourselves and our families through prayer. "For we are not fighting against flesh-and-blood enemies, but against evil rulers and authorities of the unseen world, against mighty powers in this dark world, and against evil spirits in the heavenly places" (Eph. 6:12).

You are worth fighting for. Your family is worth fighting for. Fight for yourself. Fight for them. Fight in prayer!

RENEWING YOUR MIND:
"Now this is the confidence that we have in Him, that if we ask anything according to His will, He hears us. And if we know that He hears us, whatever we ask, we know that we have the petitions that we have asked of Him" (1 John 5:14-15 NKJV). "Call to Me, and I will answer you, and show you great and mighty things, which you do not know" (Jer. 33:3). "I pray that the eyes of your heart may be enlightened so that you may know the hope to which he has called you, the riches of his glorious inheritance in his holy people" (Eph. 1:18). "Devote yourselves to prayer with an alert mind and a thankful heart" (Col. 4:2).

"No matter what! Let us then approach the throne of grace with confidence, so that we may receive mercy and find grace to help us in our time of need" (Heb. 4:16). "Then if my people who are called by my name will humble themselves and pray and seek my face and turn from their wicked ways, I will hear from heaven and will forgive their sins and restore their land" (2 Chron. 7:14).

"And Jabez called on the God of Israel saying, "Oh, that You would bless me indeed, and enlarge my territory, that Your hand would be with me, and that You would keep me from evil, that I may not cause pain!" So, God granted him what he requested" (1 Chron. 4:10).

LESSON SUMMARY:
- Prayer is the way we communicate with God.

- Prayer is a vital part of our relationship with God.

- Prayer showing our love and commitment to God's will.

- "No matter what! Let us then approach the throne of grace with confidence, so that we may receive mercy and find grace to help us in our time of need" (Heb. 4:16).

- "Devote yourselves to prayer with an alert mind and a thankful heart" (Col. 4:2).

- "For nothing is impossible with God" (Luke 1:37).

- *Note: Lesson slides end at this point.

OBEDIENCE PRECEDES BLESSING:

Quite often, we hear, "What would Jesus do?" Yet the better question is, "What did Jesus do?" Asking, what would Jesus do is subjective to what we think He did. Asking what Jesus did is objective because we have the Gospel record. What did Jesus do? Jesus prayed often and consistently. To maintain our relationship with the Father as born-again believers, consistent, fervent prayer is essential. It is the one piece of the armor that God provides us that energizes each of the other pieces. "Put on all of God's armor so that you will be able to stand firm against all strategies of the devil. For we are not fighting against flesh-and-blood enemies, but against evil rulers and authorities of the unseen world, against mighty powers in this dark world, and against evil spirits in the heavenly places. Therefore, put on every piece of God's armor so you will be able to resist the enemy in the time of evil. Then after the battle you will still be standing firm. Stand your ground, putting on the belt of truth and the body armor of God's righteousness. For shoes, put on the peace that comes from the Good News so that you will be fully prepared. In addition to all of these, hold up the shield of faith to stop the fiery arrows of the devil. Put on salvation as your helmet, and take the sword of the Spirit, which is the word of God. Pray in the Spirit at all times and on every occasion. Stay alert and be persistent in your prayers for all believers everywhere" (Eph. 6:11-18). Why did Jesus pray? He prayed to teach us that as children of God, our obedient submission to the will of the Father will bring us a spiritual blessing.

MEMORY VERSE:

"Devote yourselves to prayer with an alert mind and a thankful heart" (Col 4:2).

GROW DEEPER:

Prayer is our sustenance; it is the place of refreshing. Only in the secret place do we touch the very face of God. That's how precious prayer is!

The first part of the prayer time is to listen to God. Prayer is meant to be two-way communication with God. That is why it is important to not only speak to God but to also set aside time to listen and allow Him to speak to you.

Reading the Word of God is the second part. Allow God to speak to your heart as you read His Word. The Scriptures will challenge you to grow in your relationship with the Lord.
Prayer is one of the greatest privileges we have as believers. A daily time of prayer and communion with the Father is a discipline that we all must cultivate in our lives.

As you grow in this wonderful relationship with God, you will receive direction, encouragement, and strength from the source of life. As you intercede, you will experience the joy of seeing God at work in the lives of others as difficult life situations turn around

Praying is simply having a conversation with God. It is that simple.
A.C.T.S. is an easy example of a way to pray:

- **Adoration** is the first part of this type of prayer. Spend time praising the Lord and adoring Him for who He is. Love and cherish His presence and allow Him to work through your life. You may choose to praise Him by praying Scripture or singing hymns to Him.
    - o "Our Father in heaven, may your name be kept holy" (Matt. 6:9).

- o "'I am the God of Abraham, the God of Isaac, and the God of Jacob.' So, he is the God of the living, not the dead" (Matt. 22:32).
- o "How lovely is your dwelling place, O Lord of Heaven's Armies. I long, yes, I faint with longing to enter the courts of the Lord. With my whole being, body and soul, I will shout joyfully to the living God. Even the sparrow finds a home, and the swallow builds her nest and raises her young at a place near your altar, O Lord of Heaven's Armies, my King and my God! What joy for those who can live in your house, always singing your praises. What joy for those whose strength comes from the Lord, who have set their minds on a pilgrimage to Jerusalem. When they walk through the Valley of Weeping, it will become a place of refreshing springs. The autumn rains will clothe it with blessings. They will continue to grow stronger, and each of them will appear before God in Jerusalem. O Lord God of Heaven's Armies, hear my prayer. Listen, O God of Jacob. O God, look with favor upon the king, our shield! Show favor to the one you have anointed. A single day in your courts is better than a thousand anywhere else! I would rather be a gatekeeper in the house of my God than live the good life in the homes of the wicked. For the Lord God is our sun and our shield. He gives us grace and glory. "The Lord will withhold no good thing from those who do what is right. O Lord of Heaven's Armies, what joy for those who trust in you" (Ps.84).
- o "Each of these living beings had six wings, and their wings were covered all over with eyes, inside and out. Day after day and night after night they keep on saying, "Holy, holy, holy is the Lord God, the Almighty-the one who always was, who is, and who is still to come" (Rev. 4:8).
- o "And they sang a new song with these words: "You are worthy to take the scroll and break its seals and open it. For you were slaughtered, and your blood has ransomed people for God from every tribe and language and people and nation. And you have caused them to become a Kingdom of priests for our God. And they will reign on the earth" (Rev. 5:9-10).

- **Confession** comes next. Spend time asking Christ to search your heart for areas that displease Him and allow Christ to cleanse you of any unconfessed sin. Accept His forgiveness and cleansing.
  - o "Search me, O God, and know my heart; test me and know my anxious thoughts. Point out anything in me that offends you and lead me along the path of everlasting life" (Ps. 139:23-24).
  - o "Create in me a clean heart, O God. Renew a loyal spirit within me. Do not banish me from your presence, and don't take your Holy Spirit from me. Restore to me the joy of your salvation and make me willing to obey you. Then I will teach your ways to rebels, and they will return to you" (Ps. 51:10-13).
  - o "And they will not need to teach their neighbors, nor will they need to teach their relatives, saying, 'You should know the Lord.' For everyone, from the least to the greatest, will know me already," says the Lord. "And I will forgive their wickedness, and I will never again remember their sins" (Jer. 31:34).

- **Thanksgiving** comes next. Give God thanks for specific things He has done for you, such as certain blessings, people, open doors, guidance, etc. Also, give Him thanks for His goodness, loving-kindness, faithfulness, and for being a wonderful Savior.
  - o "Enter his gates with thanksgiving; go into his courts with praise. Give thanks to him and praise his name. For the Lord is good. His unfailing love continues forever, and his faithfulness continues to each generation" (Ps. 100:4-6).
  - o "Let all that I am praise the Lord; with my whole heart, I will praise his holy name. Let all

that I am praise the Lord; may I never forget the good things he does for me. He forgives all my sins and heals all my diseases. He redeems me from death and crowns me with love and tender mercies. He fills my life with good things. My youth is renewed like the eagle's! The Lord gives righteousness and justice to all who are treated unfairly. He revealed his character to Moses and his deeds to the people of Israel. The Lord is compassionate and merciful, slow to get angry and filled with unfailing love. He will not constantly accuse us, nor remain angry forever. He does not punish us for all our sins; he does not deal harshly with us, as we deserve. For his unfailing love toward those who fear him is as great as the height of the heavens above the earth. He has removed our sins as far from us as the east is from the west. The Lord is like a father to his children, tender and compassionate to those who fear him. For he knows how weak we are; he remembers we are only dust. Our days on earth are like grass; like wildflowers, we bloom and die. The wind blows, and we are gone-as though we had never been here. But the love of the Lord remains forever with those who fear him. His salvation extends to the children's children of those who are faithful to his covenant, of those who obey his commandments! The Lord has made the heavens his throne; from there he rules over everything. Praise the Lord, you angels, you mighty ones who carry out his plans, listening for each of his commands. Yes, praise the Lord, you armies of angels who serve him and do his will! Praise the Lord, everything he has created, everything in all his kingdom. Let all that I am praise the Lord" (Ps. 103).

- **Supplication**. Come to the Lord on behalf of others. Spend time praying for specific people, events, states, countries, missionaries, etc.
  - "And so, dear brothers and sisters, we can boldly enter heaven's Most Holy Place because of the blood of Jesus. By his death, Jesus opened a new and life-giving way through the curtain into the Most Holy Place. And since we have a great High Priest who rules over God's house, let us go right into the presence of God with sincere hearts fully trusting him. For our guilty consciences have been sprinkled with Christ's blood to make us clean, and our bodies have been washed with pure water. Let us hold tightly without wavering to the hope we affirm, for God can be trusted to keep his promise. Let us think of ways to motivate one another to acts of love and good works. And let us not neglect our meeting together, as some people do, but encourage one another, especially now that the day of his return is drawing near" (Heb. 10:19-25).
  - "But while Peter was in prison, the church prayed very earnestly for him" (Acts 12:5).
  - "Dear brothers and sisters, the longing of my heart and my prayer to God is for the people of Israel to be saved" (Rom. 10:1)'

QUESTIONS:
Do you have a quiet time?

When you pray, do you come boldly into God's presence as His child, or do you find yourself holding back?

Share some answered prayers in your life. Ask the Lord to lead you to situations that will allow you to minister the power of God in prayer to others.

GROW II
Foundations
In Christ
Lesson 4

I AM A PART OF SOMETHING BIGGER

PURPOSE OF THIS LESSON:
To learn the importance of being a part of the church family and utilizing the gifts within you.

Have you ever needed prayer? Have you ever needed someone to encourage you? Have you ever just needed someone to come alongside you and help you?

"While the people of Israel were still at Rephidim, the warriors of Amalek attacked them. Moses commanded Joshua, "Choose some men to go out and fight the army of Amalek for us. Tomorrow, I will stand at the top of the hill, holding the staff of God in my hand." So, Joshua did what Moses had commanded and fought the army of Amalek. Meanwhile, Moses, Aaron, and Hur climbed to the top of a nearby hill. As long as Moses held up the staff in his hand, the Israelites had the advantage. But, whenever he dropped his hand, the Amalekites gained the advantage. Moses' arms soon became so tired he could no longer hold them up. So, Aaron and Hur found a stone for him to sit on. Then they stood on each side of Moses, holding up his hands. So, his hands held steady until sunset. As a result, Joshua overwhelmed the army of Amalek in battle" (Exod. 17:8-13). As this scripture in Exodus tells us, it is important to surround yourself with people who will encourage you. Do you have the kind of friends that will hold your arms up to defeat the enemy when you are weary?

INTRODUCTION:
We the church are, the body of Christ, made up of many different members.

"All of you together are Christ's body, and each of you is a part of it" (1 Cor. 12:27). God has given each member gifts of grace in our natural skills and abilities, and a passion to serve others with these gifts. "Just as our bodies have many parts and each part has a special function, so it is with Christ's body. We are many parts of one body, and we all belong to each other" (Romans 12:4-5).

Gifts of Grace from God:
In his grace, God has given us different gifts for doing certain things well. So, if God has given you the ability to prophesy, speak out with as much faith as God has given you. If your gift is serving others, serve them well. If you are a teacher, teach well. If your gift is to encourage others, be encouraging. If it is giving, give generously. If God has given you leadership ability, take the responsibility seriously. And if you have a gift for showing kindness to others, do it gladly" (Romans 12:6-8).

"There are different kinds of spiritual gifts, but the same Spirit is the source of them all" (1 Cor. 12:4).

Gifts of the Holy Spirit:
"A spiritual gift is given to each of us so we can help each other. To one person the Spirit gives the ability to give wise advice [word of wisdom]; to another the same Spirit gives a message of special knowledge. [word of knowledge] The same Spirit gives great faith to another, and to someone else the one Spirit gives the gift of healing. He gives one person the power to perform miracles, and another the

ability to prophesy. He gives someone else the ability to discern whether a message is from the Spirit of God or from another spirit. Still another person is given the ability to speak in unknown languages, [various tongues] while another is given the ability to interpret what is being said. It is the one and only Spirit who distributes all these gifts. He alone decides which gift each person should have" (1 Cor. 12:7-11). "Yes, the body has many different parts, not just one part. If the foot says, "I am not a part of the body because I am not a hand," that does not make it any less a part of the body. And if the ear says, "I am not part of the body because I am not an eye," would that make it any less a part of the body" (1 Cor. 12:14-16)? Each member has gifts of the Spirit to serve the common good of the body of Christ. Each Spiritual gift serves a different purpose, yet all bring glory to God, revealing Christ to the world.

Together we form a more effective healthy functioning body serving as the hands and feet of Christ on the earth. No individual member of the body is as effective at home alone. Yet, assembled each member can serve, pray, build up, edify, and exhort other members of the body of Christ. Scripture shows we, members of the body of Christ, need each other to be completely functional and effective in our calling to share the Gospel of Christ.

WHY IS THIS LESSON IMPORTANT TO YOUR LIFE?
Satan will try to convince you that you do not need to be concerned about other people.

He will tell you that if you have God, you don't need other Christians. "But if we are living in the light, as God is in the light, then we have fellowship with each other, and the blood of Jesus, his Son, cleanses us from all sin" (1 John 1:7). "Together, we are his house, built on the foundation of the apostles and the prophets. And the cornerstone is Christ Jesus himself. We are carefully joined together in him, becoming a holy temple for the Lord. Through him you Gentiles are also being made part of this dwelling where God lives by his Spirit" (Eph. 2:20-22). The truth is, you are one of the living stones that God is using to build a spiritual house. "And you are living stones that God is building into his spiritual temple. What's more, you are his holy priests. Through the mediation of Jesus Christ, you offer spiritual sacrifices that please God" (1 Pet. 2:5). The house would be incomplete without you. You need other Christians, and they need you.

Fellowship translated in Greek is koinonia, it means "sharing in common" or communion. "All the believers devoted themselves to the apostles' teaching, and to fellowship, and to sharing in meals (including the Lord's Supper [the breaking of bread]), and to prayer" (Acts 2:42). This word describes how Christians should live; that is, as a community of people who share the selfless, sacrificial agape love of God, support, encourage and provide accountability to one another. "And this hope will not lead to disappointment. For we know how dearly God loves us, because he has given us the Holy Spirit to fill our hearts with his love" (Rom. 5:5). "So now I am giving you a new commandment: Love each other. Just as I have loved you, you should love each other" (John 13:34)."And this is his commandment: We must believe in the name of his Son, Jesus Christ, and love one another, just as he commanded us" (1 John 3:23).

John Wesley once said, "The Bible knows nothing of solitary religion." Christianity is a religion of fellow-ship. Following Christ means living in love, righteousness, and service, and these things can be achieved only through the social relationships found in the church. Nothing can take the place of being a part of the local church.

CHRISTIAN FELLOWSHIP BRINGS THREE SPECIFIC RESULTS:
We are not to forsake the assembling of ourselves together to stir up love and good works. "Let us think of ways to motivate one another to acts of love and good works. And let us not neglect our meeting together, as some people do, but encourage one another, especially now that the day of his return is drawing near" (Heb. 10:24-25). How do we encourage or stir up love if we are not together in fellowship?

1. Fellowship Brings Fruitfulness.
The psalmist in Ps. 133 says that unity is like the dew of Hermon falling on Mount Zion. The dew of Hermon is the source of water and life for the land, bringing refreshment and sustenance and enabling the people to produce their crops. Fellowship does the same for you in that it brings refreshment and nourishment to your soul, enabling you to be spiritually fruitful. "How wonderful and pleasant it is when brothers live together in harmony! 2 For harmony is as precious as the anointing oil that was poured over Aaron's head, that ran down his beard and onto the border of his robe. 3 Harmony is as refreshing as the dew from Mount Hermon that falls on the mountains of Zion. And there the Lord has pronounced his blessing, even life everlasting" (Ps. 133).

2. Fellowship Provides Spiritual Equipping.
There are many areas in your Christian life where you cannot function properly without fellowship with other believers. In the end, Christian fellowship is not an individual exercise, but a corporate one. Your gift is best utilized when you serve on a team.

The Holy Spirit moves to bring unity in the body of Christ, and He gives gifts as they are needed to build up and keep the body whole. There should be no poverty of spirit or lack of spiritual gift in the body, and everyone should be enriched and built up as spiritual gifts are shared in mutual love and service. "God has given each of you a gift from his great variety of spiritual gifts. Use them well to serve one another. Do you have the gift of speaking? Then speak as though God himself were speaking through you. Do you have the gift of helping others? Do it with all the strength and energy that God supplies. Then everything you do will bring glory to God through Jesus Christ. All glory and power to him forever and ever! Amen" (1 Pet. 4:10-11).

3. Fellowship Provides Safety.
Responsible parents do not abandon their children. They make sure to care and provide for them. God is your heavenly Father, and He cares for you and each person who comes to Him. God shows His love for you by putting you into the safety of a loving and caring family of believers that can help you grow to spiritual maturity. Within the local church congregation, you receive pastoral oversight from the senior pastor and staff pastors. "Their work is to watch over your souls, and they know they are accountable to God" (Heb. 13:17).

In addition to receiving pastoral oversight, you should be part of a small group that meets weekly in a home. In that group, you can receive the individual care and attention that you need to grow into an effective disciple of God. "We know what real love is because Jesus gave up his life for us. So, we also ought to give up our lives for our brothers and sisters. If someone has enough money to live well and sees a brother or sister in need but shows no compassion—how can God's love be in that person? Dear children, let's not merely say that we love each other; let us show the truth by our actions. Our actions will show that we belong to the truth, so we will be confident when we stand before God" (1 John 3:16-19).

RENEWING YOUR MIND:

"And do not be conformed to this [age] world, but be transformed by the renewing of your mind, so that you may [discover] prove what the will of God is, that which is good and [pleasing]acceptable and perfect" (Rom. 12:2 NASB).

As Christians, we need to maintain the right attitude towards others in the body of Christ.

Christians Should:

1. Love one another.

"So now I am giving you a new commandment: Love each other. Just as I have loved you, you should love each other. Your love for one another will prove to the world that you are my disciples" (John 13:34-35).

"This is my commandment: Love each other in the same way I have loved you. 17 This is my command: Love each other" (John 15:12, 17).

"And may the Lord make your love for one another and for all people grow and overflow, just as our love for you overflows" (1 Thess. 3:12).

"But we don't need to write to you about the importance of loving each other, for God himself has taught you to love one another" (1 Thess. 4:9).

"Dear children, let's not merely say that we love each other; let us show the truth by our actions" (1 John 3:18).

"Dear friends, let us continue to love one another, for love comes from God. Anyone who loves is a child of God and knows God" (1 John 4:7).

"Dear friends, since God loved us that much, we surely ought to love each other. 12 No one has ever seen God. But if we love each other, God lives in us, and his love is brought to full expression in us" (1 John 4:11-12).

2. Encourage one another.

"So, encourage each other with these words" (1 Thess. 4:18).

"You must warn each other every day, while it is still "today," so that none of you will be deceived by sin and hardened against God" (Heb. 3:13).

"And let us not neglect our meeting together, as some people do, but encourage one another, especially now that the day of his return is drawing near" (Heb. 10:25).

3. Edify one another.

"So then, let us aim for harmony in the church and try to build each other up" (Rom. 14:19).

4. Admonish one another.

"Let the message about Christ, in all its richness, fill your lives. Teach and counsel each other with all the wisdom he gives. Sing psalms and hymns and spiritual songs to God with thankful hearts" (Col. 3:16).

5. Serve one another.

"For you have been called to live in freedom, my brothers and sisters. But don't use your freedom to satisfy your sinful nature. Instead, use your freedom to serve one another in love" (Gal. 5:13).

"God has given each of you a gift from his great variety of spiritual gifts. Use them well to serve one another" (1 Pet. 4:10).

6. Bear with one another.

"Always be humble and gentle. Be patient with each other, making allowance for each other's faults because of your love" (Eph. 4:2).

"bearing with one another, and forgiving one another, if anyone has a complaint against another; even as Christ forgave you, so you also must do" (Col. 3:13 NKJV).

7. Forgive one another.

"If you forgive those who sin against you, your heavenly Father will forgive you. 15 But if you refuse to forgive others, your Father will not forgive your sins" (Matt. 6:14-15).

"Instead, be kind to each other, tenderhearted, forgiving one another, just as God through Christ has forgiven you" (Eph. 4:32).

"Make allowance for each other's faults and forgive anyone who offends you. Remember, the Lord forgave you, so you must forgive others" (Col. 3:13).

Be kind to one another.

"And be kind to one another, tenderhearted, forgiving one another, even as God in Christ forgave you" (Eph. 4:32 NKJV).

8. Be compassionate to one another.

"Be kind to one another, compassionate, forgiving each other, just as God in Christ also has forgiven you" (Eph. 4:32 NASB).

"Finally, all of you should be of one mind. Sympathize with each other. Love each other as brothers and sisters. Be tenderhearted and keep a humble attitude" (1 Pet. 3:8).

9. Accept one another.

"Therefore, accept each other just as Christ has accepted you so that God will be given glory" (Rom. 15:7).

10. Pray for one another.

"Confess your sins to each other and pray for each other so that you may be healed. The earnest prayer of a righteous person has great power and produces wonderful results" (Jam. 5:16).

11. Carry one another's burdens.

"Share each other's burdens, and in this way obey the law of Christ" (Gal. 6:2).

Christians should not:

1. Bite or devour one another.

"But if you are always biting and devouring one another, watch out! Beware of destroying one another" (Gal. 5: 15).

2. Provoke or envy one another.

"Let us not become conceited, or provoke one another, or be jealous of one another" (Gal. 5:26).

3. Hate one another.

"Once we, too, were foolish and disobedient. We were misled and became slaves to many lusts and pleasures. Our lives were full of evil and envy, and we hated each other" (Tit. 3:3).

4. Judge one another.

"So, let's stop condemning each other. Decide instead to live in such a way that you will not cause another believer to stumble and fall" (Rom. 14:13).

5. Lie to one another.

"Don't lie to each other, for you have stripped off your old sinful nature and all its wicked deeds" (Col. 3:9).

6. Slander or speak evil about one another.

"Don't speak evil against each other, dear brothers and sisters. If you criticize and judge each other, then you are criticizing and judging God's law. But your job is to obey the law, not to judge whether it applies to you" (Jam. 4: 11).

LESSON SUMMARY:

- Being part of a church family is critical to your spiritual development.
- "In his grace, God has given us different gifts for doing certain things well...." (Romans 12:6).
- Utilizing the gifts within us to serve the body of Christ manifest our maturity in Christ.
- "There are different kinds of spiritual gifts, but the same Spirit is the source of them all" (1Cor. 12:4).
- "But to each one is given the manifestation of the Spirit for the common good" (1 Cor. 12:7 NASB).

*Note: Lesson Slides end at this point.

OBEDIENCE PRECEDES BLESSING:

The English poet John Donne said, "No man is an island," and that is particularly true in the body of Christ. When you are born again, you become part of a spiritual family that is just as real as your natural family. You will grow in love, unity, and spiritual maturity as you flow with your church family. You will be equipped, protected, and encouraged so that you can become fruitful in God's kingdom. In short, you will become all that you can be only as you stay connected to the corporate body of Christ.

MEMORY VERSE:

"There is no greater love than to lay down one's life for one's friends" (John 15:13).

GROW DEEPER:

"When Jesus returned to Capernaum several days later, the news spread quickly that he was back home. Soon the house where he was staying was so packed with visitors that there was no more room, even outside the door. While he was preaching God's word to them, four men arrived carrying a paralyzed man on a mat. They couldn't bring him to Jesus because of the crowd, so they dug a hole through the roof above his head. Then they lowered the man on his mat, right down in front of Jesus. Seeing their faith, Jesus said to the paralyzed man, "My child, your sins are forgiven" (Mark 2:1-5).

Do you have these kinds of friends? Do you have friends that will pray with you? Carry you? War with you?

We urge you to get into a small group where you can build relationships and forge friendships that will help and encourage you through this journey. We learned earlier that no man is an island. Your church family will become an extended part of your natural family. A family that you can count on, lean on, and depend.

QUESTIONS:

Did Jesus have friends?

Did Jesus have close friends?

Why do you need other Christians for your spiritual growth?

Share how someone else has helped you grow in your faith.

Your position in Christ affords you many wonderful privileges, but it also brings with it responsibility. What are some ways you should be reflecting this in your relationships with those who don't know Christ?

GROW II
Foundations
A Christian Family
Lesson 5

BE A PEACEMAKER: LEARNING COMMUNICATION

PURPOSE OF THIS LESSON:

To learn the necessity of effective communication in all relationships, including the family unit and how to develop good communication skills.

As you apply specific ways of communicating, you will find your homes becoming healthier, happier places to live. Learning how to communicate is one of the main keys to making your family life successful. Poor communication skills lead to disharmony, hurt feelings, and misunderstandings with your spouse and children. Don't use foul or abusive language. In contrast, effective communication skills promote harmony, foster bonding, and increase love and understanding with them. "A gentle answer deflects anger, but harsh words make tempers flare" (Prov. 15:1).

Communication consists of two primary components: speaking and listening. Both are necessary, and there are a time and place for both. "Understand this, my dear brothers and sisters: you must all be quick to listen, slow to speak, and slow to get angry" (James. 1:19). If you truly want to nurture your relationship and grow closer together, learn to be a better communicator. "Let everything you say be good and helpful so that your words will be an encouragement to those who hear them" (Eph. 4:29).

INTRODUCTION:

A general definition for communication as supplied by Merriam Webster's Collegiate Dictionary is "a process by which information is exchanged between individuals through a common system of symbols, signs or behavior." Communication for Christians can be narrowed down to mean the use of the body, mind, and spirit to minister the grace of God to others.

Communication involves the physical body and the messages transmitted through words, gestures, utterances, and body language. It also involves the mind with its expressed emotions, feelings, and listening skills. Finally, communication involves the spirit, as demonstrated in attitudes and actions of forgiveness, love, and tenderness.

Poor communication is one of the primary problems faced by families. Too many husbands tune out their wives, and too many wives' resort to nagging and cajoling (persuading by making insincere compliments or promises) to try to communicate their needs. Children sulk and pout. Teenagers stop talking to everyone. Do you occupy the same residence with your family but have very little in common with them? Do you know or even care how to talk to your spouse and children? Do you open up and share your hopes, hurts, and dreams with them?

Husbands, wives, and children should be living in peace and harmony, supporting and caring for one another. Good conversation should flow, and laughter abounds. Home should be a place for resolving differences. For this scenario to occur, however, you must communicate. This lesson will help you to learn how to make the ideal become a reality in your home.

WHY IS THIS LESSON IMPORTANT TO YOUR LIFE?

"The tongue can bring death or life; those who love to talk will reap the consequences" (Prov. 18:21).

"And I tell you this, you must give an account on judgment day for every idle word you speak. The words you say will either acquit you or condemn you" (Mat. 12:36-37).

"The heart of the godly thinks carefully before speaking; the   mouth of the wicked overflows with evil words" (Prov. 15:28).

"Some people make cutting remarks, but the words of the wise bring healing" (Prov. 12:18).

TYPES OF COMMUNICATION:

Corrupt Communication (Negative)

In the physical realm, corrupt communication comes out in the form of profanity, foolish talking, coarse jesting, sarcasm, unholy gestures, or negative body language. It is often masked in humor.

In the soulish (mind) realm, corrupt communication manifests itself in arrogance and superiority, anger and rage, ignoring others or not showing interest in them, and rebellious actions.

In the spiritual realm, corrupt communication spews out bitterness, un-forgiveness, and hardness of heart. Of the three types of corrupt communication, the spiritual type is the worst.

Edifying Communication (Positive)

Positive communication in the physical realm is full of words of grace; it shows control of speech, gestures, and touch; and it overflows with praise and thanksgiving.

Positive communication in the realm of the mind exhibits itself in a humble, calm, controlled, attentive, and submitted manner.

Positive communication in the spiritual realm reflects a heart attitude of sweetness, tenderness, and forgiveness.

MAIN COMPONENTS OF POSITIVE COMMUNICATION:

Physical:

There is a difference between information and communication. Information is quick, neutral, and impersonal. This is the level at which many busy families live today in the so-called information age. They are primarily interested in their schedules and events.

Real communication, however, takes time. Since it involves body, mind, and spirit, real communication requires a perception of the physical signals, the soulish emotions and the spiritual attitudes being communicated. Words may come out quickly, but emotions and attitudes take time to surface and to be delivered. Words that take only five minutes to verbalize may take two hours to properly communicate.

Listening:

Listening takes discipline. "Spouting off before listening to the facts is both shameful and foolish" (Prov. 18:13).

Listening means to take seriously what is being said. If you disregard or belittle someone's conversation, you are not listening. You must listen to six specific areas:

1. Hurts – It hurt when_____.

2. Fears – You are afraid that_____.

3. Frustrations – It frustrates you when_____.

4. Disappointments – You wish this would/would not have happened_____.

5. Burdens – Your biggest problem is_____.

6. Dreams – You would love to _____.

Expression:

Affirmation and validation are vital, and the first type of expression is necessary. Active and verbal love must be communicated to your spouse and children.

Intimacy in communication is also needed. It means moving beyond concepts and current events to feelings; moving past feelings to attitudes; and moving past attitudes to vision, closeness, dreams and communion.

Forgiveness in the realm of communication is essential. You must release your partner or children from wrong words, emotions, and attitudes that they may have expressed.

BECOMING SKILLFUL IN THE ART OF LISTENING:

Hearing and listening:

In the Old Testament, the priest and leper both had blood applied to the ear, thumb, and big toe. "Then the priest will slaughter the lamb for the guilt offering. He will take some of its blood and apply it to the lobe of the right ear, the thumb of the right hand, and the big toe of the right foot of the person being purified" (Lev. 14:25). This symbolic act has an application to listening skills since listening begins with the ear.

There is a vast difference between hearing and listening. You can hear words being spoken without really listening to the person who is speaking. The husband, who absently utters "Uh-huh" while his wife is talking to him, maybe hearing her voice, but he is not listening. Your mind can tune out what you are not interested in. You should not try to do something else and listen to someone at the same time. Turn in the direction of the one speaking to you and look directly into his eyes as he speaks. Give your undivided attention to the person speaking and concentrate on what is being said. Your mind should be reconstructing what you are being told as you are listening. If not, you will be tuning the person out – nodding your head, murmuring your approval and pretending as though you are listening – all the while having no idea what was said.

Grasping and understanding:
Grasping or understanding the message is critical. The second-place God placed the blood and oil was on the thumb, the place for grasping. Listening means concentrating on the words heard. Grasping the message means understanding at a deeper level what is behind the spoken words. You must listen for the message your partner, parent, or child is trying to communicate. Observe body language, expressions, and emotions. Restate the message you are hearing to make sure you understand what the person is trying to say. Restate the message with interest – not with frustration.

Acting:
The third place the blood was applied was to the big toe, which represents the place of acting. Effective communication uses words that bring appropriate actions. A person knows he has been heard when he sees you responding appropriately. Acting upon what is heard demonstrates that true communication has occurred. When there is no corresponding action, there is no true communication.
The Lord told the prophet, Ezekiel, that he was being heard, but there was no corresponding action from the people. "So, my people come pretending to be sincere and sit before you. They listen to your words, but they have no intention of doing what you say" (Ezek. 33:31).

Listening but not acting on the words spoken will not produce the results you want in your family. Eventually, your loved ones will stop trying to communicate if they never see an appropriate response from you. You have not truly communicated until you have received the message in the same spirit in which the message was delivered and respond accordingly.

SPEAKING IS AS IMPORTANT AS LISTENING:

Gender wars:
Men generally do not listen very well because they tend to want to problem solve. They feel most comfortable giving a quick answer before they are even asked for advice. Women, however, often like to verbalize a problem and discuss it in detail. Many times, they are looking for understanding, not a solution. A man's greatest insecurity is a crying woman. His problem-solving nature makes him want to "fix it." On the other hand, a distressed woman would rather be held than lectured.

A woman's greatest frustration is her husband's lack of communication about direction and decisions. He may know what he wants to do, or he may not, but he does not want to say it until he is ready, not pushed. A man would prefer that he and his wife set a mutually agreed upon time for a decision to be reached. When a man delays in making decisions, this delay shakes his wife's security level. A wife sees her spouse as a procrastinator, and she becomes insecure in his ability to make good, sound decisions. The husband sees his wife's frustration as a lack of trust and respect in him.

"Apples of Gold"
Use pictures and parables to communicate. Jesus and the prophets used illustrations of God's feelings to communicate. Come up with creative stories and examples that will help others to understand the message you are trying to convey. Choose the time and place to communicate. "Timely advice is lovely, like golden apples in a silver basket" (Prov. 25:11). Lengthy, deep subjects need special, undisturbed time. The length of time the problem has been going on determines the length of time

needed to talk it out. If emotions flare, you will not want to be interrupted. You are not likely to fix every problem in one conversation – several may be necessary "like peeling an onion." Communication moves through levels. It moves from casual (the weather) to contemplative (weather patterns) to confrontational (global warming). You need all three levels (experience, ideas, and opinions) to enjoy true communication.

Words:

Do your words show humility, or are they filled with pride? "The tongue can bring death or life; those who love to talk will reap the consequences" (Prov. 18:21). Words have the power to build up or to tear down. "A good person produces good things from the treasury of a good heart, and an evil person produces evil things from the treasury of an evil heart. What you say flows from what is in your heart" (Luke 6:45). Once a word has been spoken, you will never be able to convince someone that you did not mean it. You can never take words back even when you wish it were possible. Like a video, words are imprinted on the memory bank. Ponder this thought: If the words you speak every day were visibly written on your body, would you still be beautiful?

Paul said, "Don't use foul or abusive language. Let everything you say be good and helpful so that your words will be an encouragement to those who hear them" (Eph. 4:29). Every word you speak either builds or destroys. We all need praise. A woman needs praise because she establishes her sense of worth by her family's daily reaction to her. "Her children stand and bless her. Her husband praises her" (Prov. 31:28). A child needs affirmation because he or she establishes their confidence in those words. A man needs praise to avoid feeling insecure, foolish, or inferior. "A time to tear and a time to mend. A time to be quiet and a time to speak" (Ecc. 3:7). May God forgive us for the negative words we have used to wound, and may He help us to use positive words to foster healthy family relationships.

LESSON SUMMARY:

- Effective Communication consists of both Speaking and Listening.

- Learn to be a better communicator to nurture relationships and grow closer.

- "Understand this, my dear brothers and sisters: You must all be quick to listen, slow to speak, and slow to get angry" (James 1:19).

- "Let everything you say be good and helpful so that your words will be an encouragement to those who hear them" (Eph. 4:29).

- "A gentle answer deflects anger, but harsh words make tempers flare" (Prov. 15:1).

- "The tongue can bring death or life; those who love to talk will reap the consequences" (Prov. 18:21).

- "And I tell you this, you must give an account on judgment day for every idle word you speak. The words you say will either acquit you or condemn you" (Mat. 12:36-37).

*Note: Lesson slides end at this point.

OBEDIENCE PRECEDES BLESSING:
"But if you look carefully into the perfect law that sets you free, and if you do what it says and don't forget what you heard, then God will bless you for doing it" (James 1:25).

- Cling to wisdom, not the words of evil people.

- "Wisdom will save you from evil people, from those whose words are twisted" (Prov. 2:12).

- "If you claim to be religious but don't control your tongue, you are fooling yourself, and your religion is worthless" (James 1:26).

- "The tongue can bring death or life; those who love to talk will reap the consequences" (Prov. 18:21).

- Speak the truth and build each other up."So, stop telling lies. Let us tell our neighbors the truth, for we are all parts of the same body. And "don't sin by letting anger control you." Don't let the sun go down while you are still angry, for anger gives a foothold to the devil. If you are a thief, quit stealing. Instead, use your hands for good hard work, and then give generously to others in need. Don't use foul or abusive language. Let everything you say be good and helpful, so that your words will be an encouragement to those who hear them" (Eph. 4:25-29).

- "So then, let us aim for harmony in the church and try to build each other up" (Rom. 14:19).

- "We should help others do what is right and build them up in the Lord" (Rom. 15:2).

- Be a good listener.

- "Understand this, my dear brothers and sisters: You must all be quick to listen, slow to speak, and slow to get angry" (James 1:19).

- Consider others more significant than yourselves.

- "Do nothing from selfish ambition or conceit, but in humility count others more significant than yourselves" (Phil 2:3 ESV).

MEMORY VERSE:
"Then keep your tongue from speaking evil and your lips from telling lies" (Ps. 34:13).

GROW DEEPER:
"Then, Christ will make His home in your hearts as you trust in Him. Your roots will GROW down into God's love and keep you strong" (Eph. 3:17).

QUESTIONS:
- What is the difference between hearing and listening?
- How can you increase your listening skills?
- What conveys to others that you are listening to them?
- How does body language provide clues of what a person is trying to communicate? Give examples.
- How can you deepen the level of communication in your family?

- Do you talk about things beyond asking, "How was your day?"
- Do you communicate thoughts, feelings, and fears?
- What are some life-affirming words you can say to your spouse and children?
- What kinds of words tear them down?

The New Testament says that your words reflect what is in your heart. Discuss the truth of this statement. Words can build up or destroy.

Read "Hung by the Tongue: What You Say is What You Get," by Francis P. Martin.

ACHIEVING TRUE INTIMACY:
BUILDING AND REBUILDING FOUNDATIONS

PURPOSE OF THIS LESSON:
In this lesson, you will learn what true intimacy in marriage is and how true intimacy can be attained in your families.

God designed marriage and the family to be the place where ultimate intimacy on earth would occur. That is the ideal. "For I know the plans I have for you," says the LORD. "They are plans for good and not for disaster, to give you a future and a hope" (Jer. 29:11). Although some families have attained that level of closeness, many others greatly struggle to find their identity as one family with shared values and aspirations.

When intimacy in marriage is mentioned, many people immediately jump to the conclusion that intimacy refers to the sexual aspect of marriage. Though sex in marriage is important, it is by no means the primary way of achieving true intimacy in marriage. True intimacy goes far beyond the physical union. The physical relationship in marriage is simply a reflection of the uniting and blending of the heart and soul of husband and wife. "As the Scriptures say, "A man leaves his father and mother and is joined to his wife, and the two are united into one" (Eph. 5:31).

After the creation of man, the entire second and third chapters of Genesis refer only to social, emotional, and spiritual intimacy and give no reference to physical intimacy between Adam and Eve. Not until the fourth chapter is physical intimacy finally mentioned: "Now Adam had sexual relations with his wife, Eve, and she became pregnant. When she gave birth to Cain, she said, "With the Lord's help, I have produced a man" (Gen. 4:1). Sex is not intimacy. Intimacy in a relationship happens when two people become one in spirit, mind, and then the body. It is through this unity in spirit, soul, and body that parents are able to nurture their children in true intimacy. "Fathers, [Parents] do not provoke your children to anger by the way you treat them. Rather, bring them up with the discipline and instruction that comes from the Lord" (Eph. 6:4).

INTRODUCTION:
True intimacy begins in the love of God.

"We love each other because he loved us first" (1 John 4:19). "For God so loved the world that He gave His only begotten Son, that whoever believes in Him should not perish but have everlasting life" (John 3:16). "God himself has prepared us for this, and as a guarantee he has given us his Holy Spirit" (2 Cor. 5:5). "And this hope will not lead to disappointment. For we know how dearly God loves us, because he has given us the Holy Spirit to fill our hearts with his love" (Rom. 5:5). However, if we do not know Jesus as our Lord and Savior there is no way we can know true love to have true intimate relationships. "But anyone who does not love does not know God, for God is love" (1 Jn 4:8). True intimacy in your home will come only when you learn to sacrificially die to yourselves. "This is My commandment, that you love one another as I have loved you. Greater love has no one than this, than to lay down one's life for his friends" (John 15:12-13). Become sensitive to the needs of your family members and are flexible to the seasons of change that occur in family relationships. "Always be humble and gentle. Be patient with each other, making allowance for each other's faults because of your love. Make every effort to keep yourselves united in the Spirit, binding yourselves together with peace" (Eph. 4:2-3). Intimacy grows when you learn the "love language" of your spouse and children and begin reaching out to them in that way. "Above all, clothe yourselves with love, which binds us all together in perfect harmony." (Col. 3:14). It's all about becoming "one" in place of "two." A united, committed couple, raising their children in a godly, secure environment, presents to the world the best picture of God and His desire for healthy families. " Who then is a faithful and wise servant, whom his lord hath made ruler over his household, to give them meat in due season? Blessed is that servant, whom his lord when he cometh shall find so doing" (Matt. 24:45-46 KJV).

WHY IS THIS LESSON IMPORTANT TO YOUR LIFE?

God's purpose for marriage is to teach intimacy. Marriage is the Ultimate in Intimacy.

The marriage relationship teaches you how to interact with and share your life with another. If you are married and your life is still all about "you" (independence) instead of "us" (interdependence), then you and your spouse are not an intimate unit, but simply two married singles. This is a marital arrangement, not a marriage. "Don't copy the behavior and customs of this world, but let God transform you into a new person by changing the way you think. Then you will learn to know God's will for you, which is good and pleasing and perfect" (Rom. 12:2).

People marry for many different reasons. Why did you get married in the first place? Was it for sexual gratification? Was it for financial security? Was it to have children? Was it to have someone care for you? Was it to escape loneliness? The reasons why people marry are many and varied, and not all of them are good ones. Sexual gratification, financial security, children and companionship are all by-products of marriage, but, in and of themselves, they do not guarantee intimacy. That is because intimacy always involves an inner bonding and not just outward acts.

True intimacy in marriage can be achieved. True intimacy comes only when you die to your selfish desires and ambitions and become "one" with your spouse. There are three main values recognized in marriages having true intimacy. They are:

- **Sacrifice – "I live for you"** – With this value, both partners have died to self and think of themselves as a unit, rather than as separate individuals. They have become one in flesh and spirit. They willingly sacrifice their happiness for the growth and development of their partner.

- **Sensitivity – "I listen to you"** – Partners in an intimate marriage relationship focus their attention on the needs of the other. They are sensitive to the needs of their spouse and aware of their loneliness, insecurity, fear, pain, and desires. They want to help in whatever means they can.

- **Surrender – "I learn about you"** – Spouses in a marriage must realize that both parties are constantly changing, and they must be willing to adapt to those changes. A rigid, compartmentalized view of marriage leaves no room for growth or change. Couples who are committed to each other, however, make necessary adjustments to times and seasons to maintain marital unity.

Intimacy is the result unity in the Spirit, manifesting the Power of "One." "One" is the number of God. "I pray that they will all be one, just as you and I are one-as you are in me, Father, and I am in you. And may they be in us so that the world will believe you sent me" (John 17:21). God is one! "Hear, Israel! The Lord is our God, the Lord is one" (Deu. 6:4 NASB)! He is three distinct persons (Father, Son, and Holy Spirit), but one essence. There is no strife, competition, jealousy or selfishness between the three persons of the Godhead. Their relationship is the most intimate in the universe. They are one. Jesus prayed that we would be one just as He and the Father are one. When Satan tried to start "two" in heaven, God could not tolerate it and removed him from His presence. Unity releases the blessing and power of God. "And I will give you the keys of the Kingdom of Heaven. Whatever you forbid on earth will be forbidden in heaven, and whatever you permit on earth will be permitted in heaven" (Matt. 16:19). Satan knows that his kingdom and power will come to an end under the power of "one." That is why Satan causes division and hates oneness and agreement, whether in a government, a church, a family, or a community. "As the Scriptures say, "A man leaves his father and mother and is joined to his wife, and the two are united into one." (Eph. 5:31). Marriage is not "two" who are each doing their own things and who are focused on their own agendas. In a marriage, the partners are mutually respected as unique individuals, but they have decided to enter "oneness." Divorce is Satan's effort to destroy "one," He knows that "one" brings the power and blessing of God into the earth. "You cry out, "Why doesn't the Lord accept my worship?" I'll tell you why! Because the Lord witnessed the vows you and your wife made when you were young. But you have been unfaithful to her, though she remained your faithful partner, the wife of your marriage vows. Didn't the Lord make you one with your wife? In body and spirit you are his. And what does he want? Godly children from your union. So guard your heart; remain loyal to the wife of your youth. "For I hate divorce!" says the Lord, the God of Israel. "To divorce your wife is to overwhelm her with cruelty," says the Lord of Heaven's Armies. "So guard your heart; do not be unfaithful to your wife." You have wearied the Lord with your words. "How have we wearied him?" you ask. You have wearied him by saying that all who do evil are good in the Lord's sight, and he is pleased with them. You have wearied him by asking, "Where is the God of justice" (Mal. 2:14-17)? God hates the practice of divorce – not the persons who are divorced. He knows that divorce destroys the potential of the most powerful relationship on earth: "one."

STEPS TO BECOMING "ONE" IN A FAMILY:

Brokenness, "Meanwhile, Jesus was in Bethany at the home of Simon, a man who had previously had leprosy. While he was eating, a woman came in with a beautiful alabaster jar of expensive perfume made from essence of nard. She broke open the jar and poured the perfume over his head" (Mark 14:3). The only way to make two solids become one is to crush them into the smallest of pieces and then mix them together. God does a crushing and a breaking of your will in marriage to bring you into deeper intimacy with your mate. "The sacrifice you desire is a broken spirit. You will not reject a broken and repentant heart, O God" (Psalm 51:17). Jesus taught that divorce is a matter of the "hardness of your hearts." "Jesus replied, "Moses permitted divorce only as a concession to your hard hearts, but it was not what God had originally intended" (Matt.19:8). The Lord must crush your will to make you and your mate one. Pride, independence, rights, and agendas are held in a "box," like the alabaster box the woman had. This box contains your secrets, feelings, mistakes, and private self. As long as your box remains unbroken, there will be no intimacy. You must learn to live "outside the box." Only when you open it and reveal the inner contents can you attain intimacy. To submit to one another requires brokenness. "The Lord is close to the brokenhearted; he rescues those whose spirits are crushed" (Psalm 34:18). Every member of the family needs to submit and lay down his life for other family members.

Covering, "And further, submit to one another out of reverence for Christ" (Eph. 5:21). God has ordained divine roles in the family to provide protection. This order is called headship or covering. "For wives, this means submit to your husbands as to the Lord. For a husband is the head of his wife as Christ is the head of the church. He is the Savior of his body, the church. As the church submits to Christ, so you wives should submit to your husbands in everything" (Eph. 5:22-24). It is not control or smothering. A wife is told to allow her husband to cover her (protect her) from the dangers, stresses, and attacks of the world similar to the way you would look to a policeman for protection. Ruth asked Boaz to cover her. "Who are you?" he asked. "I am your servant Ruth," she replied. "Spread the corner of your covering over me, for you are my family redeemer" (Ruth 3:9). She was asking for protection, provision, and intimacy. A woman has a deep desire to be taken care of and thought about by her husband. When a woman feels covered, she thrives and develops into the beautiful person God intended her to be.

If a husband neglects or manipulates his wife, her feelings of intimacy will quickly disappear. She needs her mate to protect her physically, emotionally, and financially. Jesus illustrated the perfect husband and father when He laid down His life for us. "For husbands, this means love your wives, just as Christ loved the church. He gave up his life for her" (Eph. 5:25).

Communication. Gary Chapman, the author of The Five Love Languages, outlines the importance of knowing how to meaningfully convey love to your spouses and children in such a way as to foster true intimacy. He has identified five primary ways that we all express and receive love. Though all five "languages" are important, you will probably find one way that is more meaningful to you than the others. That is your primary love language.

Knowing and understanding the love languages of your family members will help tremendously in knowing how to express love to them in an effective manner and increase intimacy in the home. They are:

- **Words of Affirmation.** This is the giving of verbal compliments and words of appreciation. When a person's love language is affirmation, and no words of affirmation are received, such a person will feel unappreciated, isolated, and distant. When affirming words are regularly given, however, he feels loved, appreciated, and connected.

- **Quality Time**. This means focusing your undivided attention on your spouse or child, hearing what he is saying, and understanding the meaning behind the words. It means sharing hopes, dreams, fears, and concerns. Quality time tells a person that he is important, and during that time, nothing matters as much as he does.

- **Receiving Gifts**. Simple, thoughtful gifts such as roadside flowers, humorous cards, and special treats sometimes mean more than expensive gifts to the person who craves this love language. The gift says that he is special, thought of, and appreciated.

- **Acts of Love.** To some people, acts such as mowing the grass, taking out the garbage, vacuuming, or bathing the children speak volumes to them. They are thrilled beyond measure when their spouse or children pitch in and help them, serving them through practical demonstrations of love.

- **Physical Touch.** Physical touch can include loving gestures such as a hug, a squeeze of the hand, a stroking of the hair, a caress of the face, and any other physical expression of love. Between husband and wife, physical touch can also include the sexual relationship, but not always.

- When you discover and express your spouse and children's love language, you will help to build their confidence and self-esteem. They will feel loved and appreciated. These acts of love lead to real intimacy and a spirit of oneness and unity.

LESSON SUMMARY:

- For I know the plans I have for you," says the LORD. "They are plans for good and not for disaster, to give you a future and a hope (Jer. 29:11).

- As the Scriptures say, "A man leaves his father and mother and is joined to his wife, and the two are united into one (Eph. 5:31).

- "And further, submit to one another out of reverence of Christ" (Eph. 5:21).

- "Fathers, [Parents] do not provoke your children to anger by the way you treat them. Rather, bring them up with the discipline and instruction that comes from the Lord" (Eph. 6:4).

- Always be humble and gentle. Be patient with each other, making allowance for each other's faults because of your love. Make every effort to keep yourselves united in the Spirit, binding yourselves together with peace (Eph 4:2-3).

- "This is My commandment, that you love one another as I have loved you. Greater love has no one than this, than to lay down one's life for his friends" (John 15:12-13).

- "Who then is a faithful and wise servant, whom his lord hath made ruler over his household, to give them meat in due season? Blessed is that servant, whom his lord when he cometh shall find so doing" (Matt. 24:45-46 KJV).

*Note: Lesson Slides end at this point.

OBEDIENCE PRECEDES BLESSING:

"But if you look carefully into the perfect law that sets you free, and if you do what it says and don't forget what you heard, then God will bless you for doing it," (James 1:25).

- Put your family's interests first.
  - "Don't be selfish; don't try to impress others. Be humble, thinking of others as better than yourselves. Don't look out only for your own interests, but take an interest in others, too" (Phil. 2:3-4).
  - "There is no greater love than to lay down one's life for one's friends" (John 15:13).
- Learn to listen.
  - "Understand this, my dear brothers and sisters: You must all be quick to listen, slow to speak, and slow to get angry" (James 1:19).
- Esteem others better than yourselves.
  - "Love each other with genuine affection, [with brotherly love.] and take delight in honoring each other" (Rom. 12:10).

- "Don't be selfish; don't try to impress others. Be humble, thinking of others as better than yourselves" (Phil. 2:3).
- Be willing to surrender your will.
  - "Love each other with genuine affection, [with brotherly love.] and take delight in honoring each other" (Rom. 12:10).
  - "Don't be selfish; don't try to impress others. Be humble, thinking of others as better than yourselves" (Phil. 2:3).

- Read Gary Chapman's book, The Five Love Languages, begin applying them with your spouse and children.

MEMORY VERSE:
"And further, submit to one another out of reverence of Christ" (Eph. 5:21).

GROW DEEPER:
"Then, Christ will make His home in your hearts as you trust in Him. Your roots will GROW down into God's love and keep you strong" (Eph. 3:17).

How does marriage teach interdependence rather than independence?

Is there a place for independence in marriage?

Under what circumstances and to what degree does independence have a place in marriage?

What are some of the reasons why people get married?

Which are good ones, and which are not?

"As the Scriptures say, "A man leaves his father and mother and is joined to his wife, and the two are united into one" (Eph. 5:31).

What are some of the ways that marriage "breaks" us? How can this lead to increased intimacy?

Discuss the five love languages. Which is your primary language? Which is your spouse's? Do you make an effort to speak your spouse's love language?

QUESTIONS
What main point do you want to remember from this lesson?

Do you recognize areas that need attention in your relationship with your husband, wife, or children? What are they?

What actions will you take to apply this lesson to daily living?

GROW II
Foundations
A Christian Family
Lesson 7

UNDERSTANDING GOD'S DESIGN FOR THE FAMILY: BUILDING AND REBUILDING FOUNDATIONS

PURPOSE OF THIS LESSON:

This lesson will help you to understand God's original plan and design for your family and the Godly influence it should have on advancing the Kingdom of God. Christian families should mirror Christ to the world. Nothing means more to you than your family. Nothing means more to God, who created families. God's design for the family is first shown in creation. After all the physical elements of earth, sky, vegetation, and animal life were created, God desired to create a being with the nature of God planted within him. God gave Adam dominion over everything on the earth. "So, God created human beings in His image. In the image of God, He created them; male and female, He created them. Then God blessed them and said, 'Be fruitful and multiply. Fill the earth and govern it. Reign over the fish in the sea, the birds in the sky, and all the animals that scurry along the ground" (Gen. 1:27-28).

Our lives are marked and shaped by experiences that happen to us in our families – both good and bad. Those experiences, whether wonderful, traumatic, or somewhere between survival and existence, all become part of our testimonies making us stronger in preparation of what's to come. "and He made from one man every nation of mankind to live on all the face of the earth, having determined their appointed times and the boundaries of their habitation, that they would seek God, if perhaps they might feel around for Him and find Him, though He is not far from each one of us" Acts 17:26-27 NASB).

Our families can be the source of great joy or sources of deep pain, havens of refuge, or prisons of terror, or they can be life-giving and nourishing or life-draining and unhealthy. When your families are fragmented and dysfunctional, family members become bogged down and find themselves continually struggling to survive. Your families should serve as firm foundations for every member as well as a springboard for their personal development and involvement in the things of God. When your families are functioning properly according to God's design, they present to the world a beautiful picture of life as God intended it. "This is my command: Love each other" (John 15:17).

INTRODUCTION:

God's original plan for mankind is filled with life, power, and fruitfulness and it is being fulfilled through the redemption in Christ. "For God saved us and called us to live a holy life. He did this, not because we deserved it, but because that was his plan from before the beginning of time-to show us his grace through Christ Jesus" (2 Tim. 1:9). "But it is due to Him that you are in Christ Jesus, who became to us wisdom from God, and righteousness and sanctification, and redemption" (1 Cor. 1:30 NASB). "For He made Him who knew no sin to be sin for us, that we might become the righteousness of God in Him" (2 Cor. 5:21 NKJV). "We are made right with God by placing our faith in Jesus Christ. And this is true for everyone who believes, no matter who we are" (Rom. 3:22).

WHY IS THIS LESSON IMPORTANT TO YOUR LIFE?

Because most families are dysfunctional at some level. But far too many that don't know Jesus are self-destructive. "Satan, who is the god of this world, has blinded the minds of those who don't believe. They are unable to see the glorious light of the Good News. They don't understand this message about the glory of Christ, who is the exact likeness of God" (2 Cor. 4:4). "What is causing the quarrels and fights among you? Don't they come from the evil desires at war within you? You want what you don't have, so you scheme and kill to get it. You are jealous of what others have, but you can't get it, so you fight and wage war to take it away from them. Yet you don't have what you want because you don't ask God for it. And even when you ask, you don't get it because your motives are all wrong-you want only what will give you pleasure" (James 4:1-3).

Dysfunction was not part of God's plan. "Don't copy the behavior and customs of this world, but let God transform you into a new person by changing the way you think. Then you will learn to know God's will for you, which is good and pleasing and perfect" (Rom. 12:2). Just as God knew beforehand, His original plan would be and was compromised when Adam and Eve sinned in the Garden. God intended for man and woman to live together in peace, harmony, and unity. "This is my commandment: Love each other in the same way I have loved you. There is no greater love than to lay down one's life for one's friends" (John15:12-13). His original plan included partnership, healthy family relationships, and intimacy on all levels. "Now may the God of hope fill you with all joy and peace in believing, that you may abound in hope by the power of the Holy Spirit" (Rom. 15:13 NKJV).

Many families need to exchange their guilt, fear, and blame for forgiveness, peace, and healing, which are all found in the atoning work of Jesus Christ on the cross. Your families can be restored to God's original design when the path to forgiveness is chosen. "But if you refuse to forgive others, your Father will not forgive your sins" (Matt. 6:15). "And we know that God causes everything to work together for the good of those who love God and are called according to his purpose for them" (Rom.8:28). "For the Lord your God is living among you. He is a mighty savior. He will take delight in you with gladness. With his love, he will calm all your fears. He will rejoice over you with joyful songs" (Zeph. 3:17). "For I know the plans I have for you," says the Lord. "They are plans for good and not for disaster, to give you a future and a hope" (Jer. 29:11). "Finally, brothers and sisters, whatever is true, whatever is honorable, whatever is right, whatever is pure, whatever is lovely, whatever is commendable, if there is any excellence and if anything, worthy of praise, think about these things. (Philippians 4:8 NASB). "Remember, it is sin to know what you ought to do and then not do it" (James 4:17).

GOD'S VISION FOR THE FAMILY:

- **Partnership.** "Then the Lord God said, "It is not good for the man to be alone. I will make a helper who is just right for him" (Gen. 2:18). Help meet means "someone standing opposite as a counterpart." Eve was not created to be a doormat, a tagalong, or a clone, but to help, assist, encourage, and compliment him. She was not created to be mistreated or abused by Adam, but to be the completion of him.

- "So, the Lord God caused the man to fall into a deep sleep. While the man slept, the Lord God took out one of the man's ribs and closed up the opening. Then the Lord God made a woman from the rib, and he brought her to the man" (Gen. 2:21-22). Rather than creating her only from the dust of the earth as He did Adam, God formed Eve by using a part of Adam's body, a rib from his side. In other words, Eve cost Adam something, and she was created to be a part of him. "So, husbands also ought to love their own wives as their own bodies. He who loves his own wife loves himself" (Eph. 5:28 NASB).

- Eve's creation is the first vision of the family: a man and woman, who perfectly complement each other, respect each other, are thankful for each other, are excited about and embrace their differences, and are thrilled to have each other as life partners.

- **Multiplication.** From the very beginning, God envisioned man and woman joined together to form their family unit. "This explains why a man leaves his father and mother and is joined to his wife, and the two are united into one" (Gen. 2:24). He saw a complete picture of a father, mother, and children. His original plan was one of a whole family reflecting His image – not one of lone, solitary lives intersecting with no one. His plan for the family is pure, wholesome, and fulfilling, and He looks forward to spending eternity with them.

- **Intimacy.** Adam and Eve were to be partners. They were also to be united in every way – physically, emotionally, and spiritually. Intimacy refers to a relationship characterized by total transparency and openness with no shame, no fear, and no barriers. "Live in harmony with each other. Don't be too proud to enjoy the company of ordinary people. And don't think you know it all" (Rom. 12:16)!

- Too many people equate intimacy with sex only, but the physical relationship is only a small part of what intimacy means in a marriage. True intimacy is so much greater. True intimacy occurs when both husband and wife are one in spirit, soul, and body. "Always be humble and gentle. Be patient with each other, making allowance for each other's faults because of your love. Make every effort to keep yourselves united in the Spirit, binding yourselves together with peace" (Eph. 4:2-3). That is the kind of intimacy God intended for marriage. His design desires a husband's life to be so intertwined with that of his wife that the two become one in every meaning of the word. Husband and wife are to be confidants, best friends, and lovers, not two people simply occupying the same residence.

SATAN POLLUTES GOD'S PLAN FOR THE FAMILY:
- **Guilt pollutes relationships.** Immediately after Adam and Eve sinned by eating the forbidden fruit of the Tree of the Knowledge of Good and Evil, their innocence was lost. Eve persuaded Adam to partake. Guilt and shame flooded their minds for the first time. They then attempted to cover themselves by sewing together fig leaves to cover their nakedness "At that moment their eyes were opened, and they suddenly felt shame at their nakedness. So, they sewed fig leaves together to cover themselves" (Gen. 3:7).

- Sin and disobedience are always followed by guilt and shame. Because guilt and shame are weapons of the devil. The Holy Spirit will bring conviction upon us, drawing us to confess our sins, ask forgiveness and seek repent. The devil will condemn us of sin to bring guilt and shame, to isolate us as we hide and pull away from the Lord. Sometimes it can be difficult to tell the difference between conviction and condemnation. Here is biblical principle that will help you determine with confidence whether the Holy Spirit bringing conviction or if the enemy is spewing condemnation. Holy Spirit was given to us to witness and glorify Christ in us. He will never bring guilt and shame upon our new identity in Christ, he will only lift us up in Christ. "When the Spirit of truth comes, he will guide you into all truth. He will not speak on his own but will tell you what he has heard. He will tell you about the future. He will bring me glory by telling you whatever he receives from me" (John 16:13-14). The enemy will put guilt and shame upon you to still your identity in Christ, kill your ability to operate in your authority in Christ and destroy your calling in Christ by hindering your spiritual maturity.

- If you fall to sin, you will have a choice to make. Will you face your failures and deal with them in a God-honoring fashion? "So, humble yourselves before God. Resist the devil, and he will flee from you. Come close to God, and God will come close to you. Wash your hands, you sinners; purify your hearts, for your loyalty is divided between God and the world" (James 4:7-8). Will you attempt to cover up your failures by hiding, running, lying, and denying? Will you try to hide and cover your failures with "fig leaves?" "Finally, I confessed all my sins to you and stopped trying to hide my guilt. I said to myself, "I will confess my rebellion to the Lord." And you forgave me! All my guilt is gone" (Ps. 32:5). Fig leaves are anything you use to defend yourselves from guilt and shame. Anger, blame-shifting, manipulation, lying, and denial are all fig leaves. Most family conflicts are the direct result of denying wrongs, defending wrongs with fig leaves, or refusing to accept responsibility for wrongs committed. "The thief's purpose is to steal and kill and destroy. My purpose is to give them a rich and satisfying life" (John10:10).

- **Fear breaks communion.** Although Adam and Eve tried to cover their guilt with fig leaves, they were still fearful of the repercussions of their sin. "When the cool evening breezes were blowing, the man and his wife heard the Lord God walking about in the garden. So, they hid from the Lord God among the trees. Then the Lord God called to the man, "Where are you?" He replied, "I heard you walking in the garden, so I hid. I was afraid because I was naked" (Gen. 3:8-10). When they lost their innocence, they also lost their unhindered communion with the Father. After they ate the fruit and covered their nakedness with fig leaves, they hid from God, being afraid to face Him. "At that moment their eyes were opened, and they suddenly felt shame at their nakedness. So, they sewed fig leaves together to cover themselves" (Gen. 3:7).

- Every choice you make in life will have consequences. Guilt and shame, fear, no communion with God, and hiding or covering up all describe the natural progression of sin. Yet, "If we confess our sins, He is faithful and just to forgive us our sins and to cleanse us from all unrighteousness" (1 John 1:9). Fear destroys trust and isolates and separates. It takes away peace, unity, and the simplicity of life. Fear, as a primary or first pollutant of the family, hinders members from moving into the unity God designed in the beginning. "Peace, I leave you, My peace I give you; not as the world gives, do I give to you. Do not let your hearts be troubled, nor fearful" (John 14:27).

- Fears within a family are many and varied. Some fear rejection from a spouse or parent. Others struggle with the fear of verbal, physical, or sexual abuse. Some fear their marriages will fail and end in divorce. Others fear financial bankruptcy and poverty. Many others battle fear of death, fear of consequences from their sinful past, fear of illness, fear of unemployment, fear of failure, or fear of "what-ifs" – the list is endless. Unresolved fear can lead to addictions, uncontrollable jealousy, sexual unhappiness or withdrawal, lack of communication, and a host of other problems. Fear was never a part of God's design for your family. "For God has not given us a spirit of fear, but of power and of love and of a sound mind" (2 Tim. 1:7).

- **Blame destroys intimacy.** The ultimate or last pollutant of families is to blame. When God asked Adam if he had eaten of the tree, he immediately responded, "It was the woman you gave me who

142

gave me the fruit, and I ate it" (Gen. 3:12). Adam first blamed God for giving him Eve, and then he blamed Eve for giving him the fruit.

- Blaming others for your failures is human, but 100% unacceptable. It destroys intimacy and leads to suspicion. When you justify your sinful actions rather than repenting, you are demonstrating a life filled with pride. God hates pride and arrogance. "The fear of the Lord is to hate evil; Pride and arrogance and the evil way And the perverse mouth I hate" (Prov. 8:13 NKJV). Being defensive will result in a "war" in your home. There is a major difference between saying you are sorry and truly repent. Did you ever say "I am sorry" for convenience's sake or to quickly end an argument without repenting? True repentance is two-fold: turning from sin and turning to God. When you truly repent from sin, you will completely turn your back on sin, never wanting to return to that sinful life again. "Now repent of your sins and turn to God, so that your sins may be wiped away. Then times of refreshment will come from the presence of the Lord, and he will again send you Jesus, your appointed Messiah" (Acts 3:19-20). Your heart's desire and focus turn to please God.

- When you continue in the "hardening of the heart." "Jesus replied, "Moses permitted divorce only as a concession to your hard hearts, but it was not what God had originally intended" (Matt. 19:8). God hates divorce, "For I hate divorce!" says the Lord, the God of Israel. "To divorce your wife is to overwhelm her with cruelty," says the Lord of Heaven's Armies. "So, guard your heart; do not be unfaithful to your wife" (Mal. 2:16). Therefore, how much more do you think He will help you to restore your marriage?

GOD'S SOLUTION FOR FAMILY RESTORATION:

- **Satan's defeat is sure.** Even though Adam and Eve sinned grievously against God, in His great love and mercy, made a way of redemption. "And I will cause hostility between you and the woman, and between your offspring and her offspring. He will strike[bruise] your head, and you will strike his heel" (Gen. 3:15). God promised Eve would produce a seed that would crush Satan's head. "Look, I have given you authority over all the power of the enemy, and you can walk among scorpions and snakes and crush them. Nothing will injure you" (Luke 10:19). That seed was Christ. "For I can do everything through Christ, who gives me strength" (Phil. 4:13). He was already making provision for the guilt, fear, and blame that resulted from our sin. Christ can come into any polluted family where Satan has worked his evil plan and bring righteousness, peace, healing and restoration. God plans to heal through the power of the cross of Christ will bring wholeness, no matter what problem your family faces.

- In your families, your partners and your children are not your enemies – Satan is! When you and your spouse join forces against Satan's influence in your home, you become a powerful force, able to withstand any attack from the devil. "Again, I say to you, that if two of you agree on earth about anything that they may ask, it shall be done for them by My Father who is in heaven. For where two or three have gathered together in My name, I am there in their midst" (Matt. 18:19-20 NASB). In unity, you begin taking back territory the enemy stole from you. You also begin moving forward into God's purpose for your family.

- **Divine order protects family unity.** Adam's failure in his role as a husband had disastrous consequences for not only Eve and him, but also for all humanity. "But those who won't care for their relatives, especially those in their own household, have denied the true faith. Such people are worse than unbelievers" (1 Tim. 5:8). When can certainly debate whether the fall of humanity could have possibly been prevented if Adam had adequately protected Eve from the serpent's influence. Based on the husband's position as head of household alone we can clearly see he failed in his duties and responsibilities. Although, it is somewhat sad to say often in life we can learn as much from all the bad examples of what not to do. "Don't copy the behavior and customs of this world, but let God   transform you into a new person by changing the way you think. Then you will learn to know God's will for you, which is good and pleasing and perfect" (Rom. 12:2).

- Satan knows the power of a family that lives in divine order. "I tell you the truth, whatever you forbid on earth will be forbidden in heaven, and whatever you permit on earth will be permitted in heaven" (Matt. 18:18). He hates it and works actively to undermine order in the home because he knows it is God's tool to protect and unify the family. "The thief's purpose is to steal, kill, and destroy. My purpose is to give them a rich and satisfying life" (John 10:10). Satan has no room to maneuver or hinder God's design for a family when a husband is leading his family as a servant-leader, the wife is respecting her husband's leadership, and the children are honoring their parents.

- **Total forgiveness restores any relationship.** After Adam and Eve's sin, God provided them with clothing made from animal skins. "And the Lord God made clothing from animal skins for Adam and his wife" (Gen. 3:21). This is the first time we see the shedding of blood to atone for sin. "In fact, according to the law of Moses, nearly everything was purified with blood. For without the shedding of blood, there is no forgiveness" (Heb. 9:22). Only the blood of Jesus can atone for our sins, wash away our past failures, and restore God's original intent for our marriages and families. "He is so rich in kindness and grace that he purchased our freedom with the blood of his Son and forgave our sins" (Eph. 1:7). "For He made Him who knew no sin to be sin for us, that we might become the righteousness of God in Him" (2 Cor. 5:21). "For we through the Spirit wait for the hope of righteousness by faith" (Gal. 5:5). "Now hope does not disappoint, because the love of God has been poured out in our hearts by the Holy Spirit who was given to us" (Rom. 5:5).

LESSON SUMMARY:

o God's original plan for mankind is filled with life, power, and fruitfulness and it is being fulfilled through the redemption in Christ.

o "Then God blessed them and said, "Be fruitful and multiply. Fill the earth and govern it" (Gen. 1:28a.b.).

o "For God saved us and called us to live a holy life. He did this, not because we deserved it, but because that was his plan from before the beginning of time-to show us his grace through Christ Jesus" (2 Tim. 1:9).

o "But it is due to Him that you are in Christ Jesus, who became to us wisdom from God, and righteousness and sanctification, and redemption" (1 Cor. 1:30 NASB).

o "We are made right with God by placing our faith in Jesus Christ. And this is true for everyone who believes, no matter who we are" (Rom. 3:22).

o "This is my commandment: Love each other in the same way I have loved you." (John 15:12).

*Note: Lesson slides end at this point.

OBEDIENCE PRECEDES BLESSING:

- "But if you look carefully into the perfect law that sets you free, and if you do what it says and don't forget what you heard, then God will bless you for doing it" (James 1:25).
- Restrain from every evil way.
  - "I have refused to walk on any evil path, so that I may remain obedient to your word" (Ps. 119:101).
- Follow God's safe path that will lead you away from evil.
  - "The path of the virtuous leads away from evil; whoever follows that path is safe" (Prov. 16:17).
- Trust God's Word as being right and hate every false way.
  - "Each of your commandments is right. That is why I hate every false way" (Ps. 119:128).
- Forgive.
  - "Even if that person wrongs you seven times a day and each time turns again and asks forgiveness, you must forgive" (Luke 17:4).
- Recognize your real enemy is Satan, not flesh and blood.
  - "For we are not fighting against flesh-and-blood enemies, but against evil rulers and authorities of the unseen world, against mighty powers in this dark world, and against evil spirits in the heavenly places: (Eph. 6:12).

MEMORY VERSE:
"If you forgive those who sin against you, your heavenly Father will forgive you. But if you refuse to forgive others, your Father will not forgive your sins" (Mt. 6:14-15).

GROW DEEPER:
"Then Christ will make His home in your hearts as you trust in Him. Your roots will grow down into God's love and keep you strong" (Eph. 3:17).

How does God's plan for the family differ from the world's view of family?

How has your view of the family been influenced by television, movies, and other aspects of the media?

Is your family falling short of God's divine order? Why?

How do guilt, fear, and blame pollute a family? If not dealt with, what is their result in the family?

Who is the real enemy of your family? How can you fight your real enemy rather than one another?

Why is forgiveness so vital to family relationships? Are there family members you need to forgive?

Will you decide today to walk in forgiveness in all your family relationships?

QUESTIONS:
Before studying this lesson, did you believe your family had a purpose?

After studying this lesson, do you believe your family has a purpose? What is it?

Was there any point in this lesson where you said "ouch" or "oh me?"

Has this lesson helped you to see that God's plan can make your family better and stronger? How?

GROW II
Foundations
A Christian Family
Lesson 8

ROLES IN THE FAMILY:
BUILDING AND REBUILDING FOUNDATIONS

PURPOSE OF THIS LESSON:
To take a closer look at the roles God has set in place for husbands and wives.

In a marriage, when a husband and wife accept and follow their God-ordained roles, they will complement each other and enjoy a more fulfilling marriage. God's plan is always best.

God created men and women uniquely different yet complementary. Each has a special role to play in the family. When each assumes their God-ordained role, the family becomes what it is meant to be. The husband's primary role is to be the head of the family. He is to guide, protect, and serve his wife and children. A wife's role is primarily one of submission, by willingly accepting her husband's covering, by honoring his rightful position as head, and by adapting herself to her husband. A husband who loves as Christ loves the church and a woman who understands her role as helpmate form a dynamic team – one that is a picture of Christian love and unity.

"And further, submit to one another out of reverence for Christ. For wives, this means submit to your husbands as to the Lord. For husbands, this means love your wives, just as Christ loved the church. He gave up His life for her" (Eph. 5:21-22, 25).

INTRODUCTION:
When God created the first family, He desired for them to function as one unit.

"Always be humble and gentle. Be patient with each other, making allowance for each other's faults because of your love. Make every effort to keep yourselves united in the Spirit, binding yourselves together with peace" (Eph. 4:2-3). Although the roles and responsibilities of husband and wife are uniquely different, their equality in the Lord is unquestionable. Peace and harmony rule in the home when both husband and wife are committed to fulfilling their specific roles within the family. Confusion and strife run rampant when selfishness rules at the expense of the other.

WHY IS THIS LESSON IMPORTANT TO YOUR LIFE?
The understanding of the roles of husband and wife is critical to a successful marriage.

More and more couples look to divorce as their only solution to marital conflict. Today, husbands and wives are reversing their God-ordained roles, many do not understand their roles, many refuse to yield and own up to their roles, and others force their spouses into attempting to meet their ideal expectations or fantasies. None of these will bring fulfillment in marriage. God has a perfect plan, and His plan has not changed. When both husband and wife fulfill God's roles in marriage, the entire family is strengthened. Only then can love and peace reign in the home.

"Don't copy the behavior and customs of this world, but let God transform you into a new person by changing the way you think. Then you will learn to know God's will for you, which is good and pleasing and perfect" (Rom. 12:2).

WHAT IS A MAN?

A real man rejects passivity, accept responsibility, leads courageously, and expects the greater reward, God's reward! "I have glorified You on the earth. I have finished the work which You have given Me to do" (John 17:4). "looking unto Jesus, the author and finisher of our faith, who for the joy that was set before Him endured the cross, despising the shame, and has sat down at the right hand of the throne of God" (Hebrew 12:2 NKJV). Man was God's first human creation, and he was the originator of the family. He was designated the head of the family by God. God created men with certain qualities that help them to fulfill their role of headship within the family. The first man was named Adam, which means "red dirt." God fashioned man in His image and likeness from the dust of the ground. He gave him specific physical, emotional, and spiritual characteristics. In Abraham, the basic character traits of a man are identified. A look at Abraham in the Old Testament gives us insight into the qualities that distinguish men from women. Men and women were purposely created uniquely different by God.

WHAT ARE THE BASIC CHARACTER TRAITS OF A MAN?

A man is adventurous. "The Lord had said to Abram, "Leave your native country, your relatives, and your father's family, and go to the land that I will show you" (Gen. 12:1). Abraham (Abram) was instructed to leave his country and go to a place that God would show him. The Bible simply states, "So Abram departed as the Lord had instructed, and Lot went with him. Abram was seventy-five years old when he left Haran" (Gen. 12:4). This shows that Abram was obedient to God's direction, possessed a basic sense of security that enabled him to leave home and launch out into the unknown. Although, he was disobedient to the Lord's full instruction as he was to leave his relatives and father's family behind. Yet he took Lot with him, possibly not wanting to leave him at Haran by himself, as His grandfather Terah had already passed away. However, this basic sense of security makes a man a risk-taker. He is challenged by risk, preferring to attempt and fail rather than to never try at all. This trait may make his family very uncomfortable as he tries to find and obey his life's calling, but it is a deeply ingrained part of him.

A man is territorial. Most men have a sense of territory or turf. If uncontrolled, this sense of territory can cause men to adopt a dog-eat-dog attitude or become defensive about what they perceive as their turf. "So, disputes broke out between the herdsmen of Abram and Lot. (At that time Canaanites and Perizzites were also living in the land.) Finally, Abram said to Lot, "Let's not allow this conflict to come between us or our herdsmen. After all, we are close relatives! The whole countryside is open to you. Take your choice of any section of the land you want, and we will separate. If you want the land to the left, then I'll take the land on the right. If you prefer the land on the right, then I'll go to the left." Lot took a long look at the fertile plains of the Jordan Valley in the direction of Zoar. The whole area was well watered everywhere, like the garden of the Lord or the beautiful land of Egypt. (This was before the Lord destroyed Sodom and Gomorrah.) Lot chose for himself the whole Jordan Valley to the east of them. He went there with his flocks and servants and parted company with his uncle Abram. So, Abram settled in the land of Canaan, and Lot moved his tents to a place near Sodom and settled among the cities of the plain" (Gen. 13:7-12). If surrendered to the Holy Spirit, this natural aggressiveness will spur the man to do those things that his family needs him to do. Lot took a "long look at the fertile plains." He lusted after the things of the world and was willing to move his family in the direction of what he perceived as better territory. This aggressiveness and striving for more are found in many men.

Again, it is not bad in and of itself. Only when a continual striving for material possessions and temporal earthly goals develops does this striving become corrupted. "Think about the things of heaven, not the things of earth" (Col. 3:2).

A man is militant. Men are naturally militant. Abram took 318 men from his household and chased down four kings and their armies to rescue Lot after being taken captive by the invading armies. "But one of Lot's men escaped and reported everything to Abram the Hebrew, who was living near the oak grove belonging to Mamre the Amorite. Mamre and his relatives, Eshcol and Aner, were Abram's allies. When Abram heard that his nephew Lot had been captured, he mobilized the 318 trained men who had been born into his household. Then he pursued Kedorlaomer's army until he caught up with them at Dan. There he divided his men and attacked during the night. Kedorlaomer's army fled, but Abram chased them as far as Hobah, north of Damascus. Abram recovered all the goods that had been taken, and he brought back his nephew Lot with his possessions and all the women and other captives" (Gen. 14:13-16). Men love all types of competition, such as football, baseball, arm wrestling, video games, fishing contests, and other such things that feed their continual desire to conquer.

A man is skeptical. Men are generally visual learners rather than abstract thinkers. God told Abram that he would have a son born to him in his old age. He brought Abram outside and made him look at the stars so that he could visualize what He was promising to him. "Then the Lord said to him, "No, your servant will not be your heir, for you will have a son of your own who will be your heir." Then the Lord took Abram outside and said to him, "Look up into the sky and count the stars if you can. That's how many descendants you will have!" And Abram believed the Lord, and the Lord counted him as righteous because of his faith. Then the Lord told him, "I am the Lord who brought you out of Ur of the Chaldeans to give you this land as your possession." But Abram replied, "O Sovereign Lord, how can I be sure that I will actually possess it" (Gen. 15:4-8)? Men, by nature, are very left-brained (rational) and require conclusive proof of everything. "O Sovereign Lord, how can I be sure that I will possess it?" This was Abram's first question regarding the promise. Men question everything because of their naturally skeptical nature.

A man is exalted. God changed Abram's name "exalted father" to Abraham, "father of a multitude." "What's more, I am changing your name. It will no longer be Abram. Instead, you will be called Abraham, for you will be the father of many nations. I will make you extremely fruitful. Your descendants will become many nations, and kings will be among them" (Gen. 17:5-6)! This new name revealed his royal position before God. Every man has a divine calling and destiny to rule, govern, and multiply into a spiritual nation. Because Sarai treated Abram like a king, God changed her name to Sarah "princess." Sarah even made a practice of referring to Abram as "master" "For instance, Sarah obeyed her husband, Abraham, and called him her master. You are her daughters when you do what is right without fear of what your husbands might do" (1 Pet. 3:6). She acknowledged his headship and walked in submission to him, honoring him in his role as a husband. "So, she laughed silently to herself and said, "How could a worn-out woman like me enjoy such pleasure, especially when my master-my husband-is also so old" (Gen. 18:12)?

A man is redeemed. Abraham obeyed God and took Isaac up the mountain to be sacrificed. "So, Abraham placed the wood for the burnt offering on Isaac's shoulders, while he himself carried the fire and the knife. As the two of them walked on together, Isaac turned to Abraham and said, "Father?" "Yes, my son?" Abraham replied. "We have the fire and the wood," the boy said, "but where is the sheep for the burnt offering?" "God will provide a sheep for the burnt offering, my son," Abraham answered. And they both walked on together. When they arrived at the place where God had told him to go, Abraham built an altar and arranged the wood on it. Then he tied his son, Isaac, and laid him on the altar on top of the wood. And Abraham picked up the knife to kill his son as a sacrifice. At that moment the angel of the Lord called to him from heaven, "Abraham! Abraham!" "Yes," Abraham replied. "Here I am!" "Don't lay a hand on the boy!" the angel said. "Do not hurt him in any way, for now I know that you truly fear God. You have not withheld from me even your son, your only son" (Gen. 22:6-12). God was showing a picture of what He would have to do to His Son Jesus on the cross thousands of years later.

Christ knew what was in each person's heart. "No one needed to tell him about human nature, for he knew what was in each person's heart" (John 2:25). He knew, left to his own devices, man would fall, connive, disobey, and manipulate. However, He made adequate provision for man to be redeemed. Every man must be born again, as Christ told Nicodemus. "Jesus replied, "I tell you the truth, unless you are born again, you cannot see the Kingdom of God" (John 3:3). Only then can he hope to take his rightful place in the family and provide the type of leadership his family needs.

THE HUSBAND'S ROLE IN THE FAMILY IS CRITICAL:
Husbands are to honor their wives. God made a woman to be honored. "In the same way, you husbands must give honor to your wives. Treat your wife with understanding as you live together. She may be weaker than you are, but she is your equal partner in God's gift of new life. Treat her as you should so your prayers will not be hindered" (1 Pet. 3:7). She was created uniquely beautifully, and her husband should see her uniqueness as valuable and worthy of honor. God will bless a man who understands his wife and honors her. God created a woman with less physical power than a man—not less emotional, spiritual, or intellectual ability. A good wife makes her husband twice the man he would be without her. She completes his insufficiencies. God did not create a woman to be exploited or abused. Anyone who neglects or disregards his wife is, in effect, disconnecting his prayers from God's answers. She is just as loved, valuable, and worthy of God's attention as is the husband. A man brings a curse upon himself when he does not honor his wife.

Husbands are the established heads of their homes.
The authority in the home was given to the husband by God. "For a husband is the head of his wife as Christ is the head of the church. He is the Savior of His body, the church" (Eph. 5:23). This privilege was also given the challenging responsibility of loving their wives like Christ loved the church. "For husbands, this means love your wives, just as Christ loved the church. He gave up His life for her" (Eph. 5:25).

Husbands are Christ's representatives to their families.
The husband is to be a picture of Christ-like love to his wife and children. He is a servant-leader, constantly looking for ways to make his family more secure and grounded in Christ. He sets the direction of the family and serves as protector, provider, confidant, and friend.

What is a Woman? The beauty of a woman is "a gentle and quiet spirit," as described by Peter. "In the same way, you wives must accept the authority of your husbands. Then, even if some refuse to obey the Good News, your godly lives will speak to them without any words. They will be won over by observing your pure and reverent lives. Don't be concerned about the outward beauty of fancy hairstyles, expensive jewelry, or beautiful clothes. You should clothe yourselves instead with the beauty that comes from within, the unfading beauty of a gentle and quiet spirit, which is so precious to

God. This is how the holy women of old made themselves beautiful. They put their trust in God and accepted the authority of their husbands. For instance, Sarah obeyed her husband, Abraham, and called him her master. You are her daughters when you do what is right without fear of what your husbands might do" (1 Pet. 3:1-6). Peter reminds women that this is the highest quality they can demonstrate. A gentle and quiet spirit is contrary to a woman's natural tendency toward passion. Just as a man must work at releasing his passionate side (right-brain function), a woman must work at controlling her passionate side. A woman with a gentle and quiet spirit is one who has her emotions, desires, and words under the total control of the Holy Spirit. The worldly woman is passionate about clothes, jewelry, external objects, and is actively pursuing external values. The godly woman is passionately developing her inward woman and actively pursuing eternal values.

FIVE MAIN PASSIONS OF A WOMAN ARE:

To Protect. Pharaoh ordered the two Hebrew midwives to kill every baby boy. Instead, they disobeyed Pharaoh and helped protect the children. "Then Pharaoh, the king of Egypt, gave this order to the Hebrew midwives, Shiphrah and Puah: "When you help the Hebrew women as they give birth, watch as they deliver. If the baby is a boy, kill him; if it is a girl, let her live." But because the midwives feared God, they refused to obey the king's orders. They allowed the boys to live, too" (Exod. 1:15-17). God has given women a natural desire to protect and nurture. "So, God was good to the midwives, and the Israelites continued to multiply, growing more and more powerful. And because the midwives feared God, he gave them families of their own" (Exod. 1:20-21). This same passion to protect was seen in Moses' mother, his sister, and Pharaoh's daughter, all of whom had a part in saving his life. "But when she could no longer hide him, she got a basket made of papyrus reeds and waterproofed it with tar and pitch. She put the baby in the basket and laid it among the reeds along the bank of the Nile River. The baby's sister then stood at a distance, watching to see what would happen to him. Soon Pharaoh's daughter came down to bathe in the river, and her attendants walked along the riverbank. When the princess saw the basket among the reeds, she sent her maid to get it for her. When the princess opened it, she saw the baby. The little boy was crying, and she felt sorry for him. "This must be one of the Hebrew children," she said. Then the baby's sister approached the princess. "Should I go and find one of the Hebrew women to nurse the baby for you?" she asked. "Yes, do!" the princess replied. So, the girl went and called the baby's mother. "Take this baby and nurse him for me," the princess told the baby's mother. "I will pay you for your help." So, the woman took her baby home and nursed him. Later, when the boy was older, his mother brought him back to Pharaoh's daughter, who adopted him as her own son. The princess named him Moses, for she explained, "I lifted him out of the water" (Exod. 2:3-10).

This passion to protect, however, can get out of control, and women can become overprotective and manipulative. Rebekah was like this with Jacob when she helped Jacob fool his father Isaac into giving him the blessing of the firstborn. "She covered his arms and the smooth part of his neck with the skin of the young goats. Then she gave Jacob the delicious meal, including freshly baked bread. So, Jacob took the food to his father. "My father?" he said. "Yes, my son," Isaac answered. "Who are you—Esau or Jacob?" Jacob replied, "It's Esau, your firstborn son. I've done as you told me. Here is the wild game. Now sit up and eat it so you can give me your blessing." Isaac asked, "How did you find it so quickly, my son?" "The Lord your God put it in my path!" Jacob replied. Then Isaac said to Jacob, "Come closer so I can touch you and make sure that you really are Esau." So, Jacob went closer to his father, and Isaac touched him. "The voice is Jacob's, but the hands are Esau's," Isaac said. But he did not recognize Jacob, because Jacob's hands felt hairy just like Esau's. So, Isaac prepared to bless Jacob. "But are you really my son Esau?" he asked. "Yes, I am," Jacob replied. Then Isaac said, "Now, my son, bring me the wild game. Let me eat it, and then I will give you, my blessing." So, Jacob took the food to his father, and Isaac ate it. He also drank the wine that Jacob served him. Then Isaac said to Jacob, "Please come a little closer and kiss me, my son." So, Jacob went over and kissed him. And when Isaac caught the smell of his clothes, he was finally convinced, and he blessed his son. He said, "Ah! The smell of my son is like the smell of the outdoors, which the Lord has blessed! "From the dew of heaven and the richness of the earth, may God always give you abundant harvests of grain and bountiful new wine. May many nations become your servants, and may they bow down to you. May you be the master over your brothers and may your mother's sons bow down to you. All who curse you will be cursed, and all who bless you will be blessed" (Gen. 27:16-29). James and John's mother was like this when she asked for high positions for them in the kingdom of Christ. "Then the mother of James and John, the sons of Zebedee, came to Jesus with her sons. She knelt respectfully to ask a favor. "What is your request?" he asked. he replied, "In your Kingdom, please let my two sons sit in places of honor next to you, one on your right and the other on your left" (Matt. 20:20-21).

To Praise. The second quality of a godly woman is her passion for expressing praises to God. Miriam and the women were the first to take a tambourine and begin to dance on the shore of the Red Sea after Pharaoh's defeat. "Then Miriam the prophet, Aaron's sister, took a tambourine and led all the women as they played their tambourines and danced" (Exod. 15:20). Miriam was a prophetess, and the prophetic mantle is usually more easily released through a woman. She must guard this passion, however, and not let it get out of order, as did Miriam later in her life. That is why Paul tells women to release their prophetic gifts under the covering of proper authority. A man must appreciate this passionate release of praise and prophecy within the woman.   She can sense spiritual forces at work, both heavenly and demonic. A wise husband will avail himself of this natural ability within his wife.

To Pray. Because of her greater spiritual sensitivity, a godly woman feels prayer with a passion. "Once after a sacrificial meal at Shiloh, Hannah got up and went to pray. Eli the priest was sitting at his customary place beside the entrance of the Tabernacle. Hannah was in deep anguish, crying bitterly as she prayed to the Lord. And she made this vow: "O Lord of Heaven's Armies, if you will look upon my sorrow and answer my prayer and give me a son, then I will give him back to you. He will be yours for his entire lifetime, and as a sign that he has been dedicated to the Lord, his hair will never be cut." As she was praying to the Lord, Eli watched her. Seeing her lips moving but hearing no sound, he thought she had been drinking. "Must you come here drunk?" he demanded. "Throw away your wine!" "Oh no, sir!" she replied. "I haven't been drinking wine or anything stronger. But I am very discouraged, and I was pouring out my heart to the Lord" (1 Sam. 1:9-15). Hannah was in "deep anguish, crying bitterly as she prayed to the Lord," vs. 10. She said, "I was pouring out my heart to the Lord" vs. 15.

In the same way, a woman incubates a child before birth; she can travail in prayer for a situation, an idea, or a request to be birthed. A woman's faith is tenacious, like the Syro-Phoenician woman who asked for her daughter's deliverance. "and she begged him to cast out the demon from her daughter. Since she was a Gentile, born in Syrian Phoenicia" (Mark 7:26). or the Shunammite woman who asked for her son's resurrection. "But when she came to the man of God at the mountain, she fell to the ground before him and caught hold of his feet. Gehazi began to push her away, but the man of God said, "Leave her alone. She is deeply troubled, but the Lord has not told me what it is." Then she said, "Did I ask you for a son, my lord? And didn't I say, 'Don't deceive me and get my hopes up'?" Then Elisha said to Gehazi, "Get ready to travel; take my staff and go! Don't talk to anyone along the way. Go quickly and lay the staff on the child's face." But the boy's mother said, "As surely as the Lord lives and you yourself live, I won't go home unless you go with me." So, Elisha returned with her. (2 Kings 4:27-30).

To Give. A godly woman is passionate about working hard to provide for her household and those in need. "She finds wool and flax and busily spins it. She is like a merchant's ship, bringing her food from afar. She gets up before dawn to prepare breakfast for her household and plan the day's work for her servant girls. She goes to inspect a field and buys it; with her earnings she plants a vineyard. She is energetic and strong, a hard worker. She makes sure her dealings are profitable; her lamp burns late into the night. Her hands are busy spinning thread, her fingers twisting fiber. She extends a helping hand to the poor and opens her arms to the needy" (Prov. 31:13-20). Jesus had women who followed Him for the express purpose of contributing from their resources to support Jesus and His disciples. "Joanna, the wife of Chuza, Herod's business manager; Susanna; and many others who were contributing from their own resources support Jesus and his disciples" (Luke 8:3). Mary, the sister of Martha, poured an entire bottle of spikenard (worth a year's salary) on the head of Jesus in preparation for His burial. "Then Mary took a twelve-ounce jar of expensive perfume made from essence of nard, and she anointed Jesus' feet with it, wiping his feet with her hair. The house was filled with the fragrance" (John 12:3). The Prov. 31 woman epitomizes a loving, caring woman who is concerned not only for her family but also for the poor and needy. She is a generous woman with a kind and giving heart.

To Love. The Samaritan woman reveals the passionate desire of a woman to express her love to a man. "I don't have a husband," the woman replied. Jesus said, "You're right! You don't have a husband" (John 4:17). God created a woman with the ability to express her passion for her husband. She must always do her best to make sure that this expression does not turn seductive and is reserved only for her husband. The Samaritan woman had been taken advantage of by many men who misinterpreted her passion for love. (Love gives at the expense of self; lust takes at the expense of others). Affection, courtship, and romance are inward gifts God has given the woman to enhance the marriage relationship. Solomon spoke of his bride's ability to "capture his heart." "You have captured my heart, my treasure, my bride. You hold it hostage with one glance of your eyes, with a single jewel of your necklace" (Song of Solomon 4:9).

The Pharisees caught a woman in adultery who had misused her passion for love. They brought her out both to stone her and trap Jesus. After briefly discussing the law of the mater with stones in hand they were ready to kill her. Jesus said, he without sin cast the first stone. One by one they drop their rock and departed. Jesus asks her does any accuse you, she replied none. "No, Lord," she said. And Jesus said, "Neither do I. Go and sin no more" (John 8:11). Jesus ministered to the prostitute at His feet. "Then Jesus said to the woman, "Your sins are forgiven" (Luke 7:48). God's desire to minister to every broken, destroyed woman and to elevate her to her true position as His "princess."

A WIFE'S ROLE IN THE FAMILY IS EQUALLY IMPORTANT:
The wife's role of submission. "Wives submit to your husbands, as to the Lord" (Eph. 5:22 NKJV). Just as the husband's primary role is one of headship, the wife's primary role is one of submission. This does not make her inferior to him, but rather this is God's design to promote order and harmony in the home. Where there is a tug-a-war for control, there is no one leading the family.

Authority and order are a part of life, and the home is no exception. There must always be someone with the ultimate authority in any situation, whether a teacher in a class, a pastor in a church, an employer on the job, or a husband in the home. The wife's role of yielding to her husband's authority is equal in importance to her husband's role of headship. Submission "as to the Lord" is powerful. Christ Himself taught us the power of submission and the victory of a submitted life when He submitted to His Father's will and gave His life on the cross.

The wife receives covering. God's roles in the family provide protection. We call this order "headship," or "covering." It is not control or smothering. A wife is told to allow her husband to cover her (protect her) from the dangers, stresses, and attacks of the world. In the story of Ruth in the Old Testament, Ruth asked Boaz to cover her, "Who are you?" he asked. "I am your servant Ruth," she replied. "Spread the corner of your covering over me, for you are my family redeemer" (Ruth 3:9). She was asking her kinsman for protection, provision, and intimacy. Like Ruth, women have a deep desire to be taken care of, thought about, and "worried over" by their husbands. When a woman feels covered, she will thrive and develop into the beautiful person God intended her to be. On the other hand, if a husband neglects or manipulates his wife, her feelings of intimacy and desire to submit to his leadership will quickly disappear. She needs a man who will protect her physically, emotionally, and spiritually. Jesus illustrated as a perfect man what it meant to lay down His life for us. "Husbands, love your wives, just as Christ also loved the church and gave Himself for her" (Eph. 5:25 NKJV). A woman needs to see that she is so valued and important in her husband's eyes that he will sacrificially and willingly give of his time, love, resources, and even his life for her, if necessary.

Wives are to respect their husbands. "Nevertheless, let each one of you in particular so love his own wife as himself, and let the wife see that she respects her husband," (Eph. 5:33 NKJV). We often overlook this verse because it goes against today's society which has created a mindset of having to "earn" respect before it is given, and after all, we've already heard twice before this verse that our husbands should love us. "For husbands, this means love your wives, just as Christ loved the church. He gave up his life for her. In the same way, husbands ought to love their wives as they love their own bodies. For a man who loves his wife actually shows love for himself" (Eph. 5:25, 28). This worldly way of thinking leads wives to absent-mindedly neglect to give and show respect to their husbands – the one thing husbands crave most. Imagine how awful it would be to have to "earn" his love – the one thing you crave most. It's simply NOT God's design for our lives. He never says respect your husband if he behaves, if he checks off everything on your honey-do list, if he meets all your wants and dreams or if he never makes a mistake as the leader of your home. Rather, He commands wives to respect their husbands just as husbands are to love their wives. The two complement one another perfectly in a way that could only be designed by God. "Then the Lord God said, "It is not good for the man to be alone. I will make a helper who is just right for him" (Gen. 2:18). Tells us God created a "helper" comparable to Adam speaking of Eve. How likely are you to accept help, advice, or consider the opinion of someone you feel does not respect you? God designed the wife intending to create a helper. Without being on purpose to freely give respect, we cannot fulfill this God-designed responsibility as a wife. God not only gave us this responsibility, but we were created to respect our husbands from the very beginning.

You may be wondering what that looks like in real life and simply put, it is trusting God. For example, what if you notice your husband's priorities are falling out of order, and you feel his wrong priorities are going to cause your family problems. Respecting him does not mean you cannot lovingly talk to him and communicate your feelings to your husband. He may not even notice what is happening, and any loving husband is going to hear you out if you talk to him in a respectful, loving way. Now, what if he does not take action to realign his priorities immediately? Your job as a respectful wife, is to support him in whatever he is pouring his focus into while trusting God to sort his misdirected priorities out.

Pray for your husband instead of nagging him about the problem and stand firm on the knowledge that God will work it out.

Roles for Single Adults. Trust your future to God. "Don't worry about anything; instead, pray about everything. Tell God what you need and thank Him for all He has done. Then you will experience God's peace, which exceeds anything we can understand. His peace will guard your hearts and minds as you live in Christ Jesus" (Phil. 4:6-7).

Be equally yoked with believers. "Don't team up with those who are unbelievers. How can righteousness be a partner with wickedness? How can light live with darkness" (2 Cor. 6:14).

Give your undivided devotion to the Lord. "I want you to be free from the concerns of this life. An unmarried man can spend his time doing the Lord's work and thinking about how to please Him. But a married man must think about his earthly responsibilities and how to please his wife. His interests are divided. In the same way, a woman who is no longer married or has never been married can be devoted to the Lord and holy in body and spirit. But a married woman must think about her earthly responsibilities and how to please her husband. I am saying this for your benefit, not to place restrictions on you. I want you to do whatever will help you serve the Lord best, with as few distractions as possible" (1 Cor. 7:32-35).

"For your Creator will be your husband; the Lord of Heaven's Armies is His name! He is your Redeemer, the Holy One of Israel, the God of all the earth" (Isa. 54:5).

Refrain from immorality. "…Yes, it is good to abstain from sexual relations. But because there is so much sexual immorality, each man should have his own wife, and each woman should have her own husband" (1 Cor. 7:1-2).

"So, I say to those who aren't married and to widows – it's better to stay unmarried, just as I am. But if they can't control themselves, they should go ahead and marry. It's better to marry than to burn with lust" (1 Cor. 7:8-9).

LESSON SUMMARY:
- "And further, submit to one another out of reverence for Christ. For wives, this means submit to your husbands as to the Lord. For husbands, this means love your wives, just as Christ loved the church. He gave up His life for her" (Eph. 5:21-22, 25).
- "Always be humble and gentle. Be patient with each other, making allowance for each other's faults because of your love. Make every effort to keep yourselves united in the Spirit, binding yourselves together with peace" (Eph. 4:2-3).
- "Imitate God, therefore, in everything you do because you are His dear children. Live a life filled with love, following the example of Christ" (Eph. 5:1-2).

*Note: Lesson Slides end at this point.

OBEDIENCE PRECEDES BLESSING:
- "But if you look carefully into the perfect law that sets you free, and if you do what it says and don't forget what you heard, then God will bless you for doing it," (James 1:25).

- Husbands – "For husbands, this means love your wives, just as Christ loved the church. He gave up his life for her" (Eph. 5:25).

- Husbands – "In the same way, husbands ought to love their wives as they love their own bodies. For a man who loves his wife actually shows love for himself" (Eph. 5:28).

- Husbands - "Christ is also the head of the church, which is his body. He is the beginning, supreme over all who rise from the dead. So, he is first in everything" (Col. 1:18). "God has put all things under the authority of Christ and has made him head over all things for the benefit of the church" (Eph 1:22).

- "For a husband is the head of his wife as Christ is the head of the church. He is the Savior of his body, the church" (Eph. 5:23).

- Wives - "As the church submits to Christ, so you wives should submit to your husbands in everything" (Eph 5:24).

- "In the same way, you wives must accept the authority of your husbands. Then, even if some refuse to obey the Good News, your godly lives will speak to them without any words. They will be won over 2 by observing your pure and reverent lives" (1 Pet. 3:1-2).

- "Keep your lives pure before God "And all who have this eager expectation will keep themselves pure, just as he is pure" (1 John 3:3).

- "For I am jealous for you with the jealousy of God himself. I promised you as a pure bride to one husband—Christ" (2 Cor. 11:2).

MEMORY VERSE:
"Imitate God, therefore, in everything you do because you are His dear children. Live a life filled with love, following the example of Christ" (Eph. 5:1-2).

GROW DEEPER:
"Then, Christ will make His home in your hearts as you trust in Him. Your roots will GROW down into God's love and keep you strong" (Eph. 3:17).

How do the roles of husband and wife complement each other?

What happens when marriage partners do not understand their God-given roles?

What are some of the ways that men and women differ from each other? How does understanding these differences enhance the marriage relationship?

Why do wives often fight for leadership in their homes? What is God's role for wives?

Why do husbands often turn over the leadership of their homes to their wives? What is God's role for husbands?

What are the limits to a woman's submission to her husband?

Husbands are instructed to love their wives as "Christ loved the church." How will this type of love affect a godly man's treatment of his wife and children?

How will this type of love affect his wife's ability to submit to him?

I am a single woman. Who is my husband?

If a single couple cannot control their sexual desires, God says it is better they should marry than burn with what? What is lust? How does lust differ from love?

QUESTIONS:

Before this lesson, how would you describe your role as a husband? A wife?

Had the world greatly influenced what your roles had become in your home? How?

How has this lesson helped you realign your roles to God's design?

For single individuals, has this lesson changed your desire to put the Lord first, trusting Him with your future?

GROW II
Foundations
A Christian Family
Lesson 9

CHILDREN ARE A BLESSING:
PARENTING, BUILDING AND REBUILDING FOUNDATIONS

PURPOSE OF THIS LESSON: To understand that children are a blessing from God and to learn effective ways of raising children in a godly manner.

Children can be funny. After the christening of his baby brother in church, little Johnny sobbed all the way home in the back seat of the car. His father asked him three times what was wrong. Finally, the boy replied, "That priest said he wanted us brought up in a Christian home, and I want to stay with you guys!"

A Sunday school teacher asked her children, as they were on the way to church service, "And why is it necessary to be quiet in church?" One bright little girl replied, "Because a lot of people are sleeping."

A father was at the beach with his children when his four-year-old son ran up to him, grabbed his hand, and led him to the shore where a seagull lay dead in the sand. "Daddy, what happened to him?" the son asked. "He died and went to Heaven," the Dad replied. The boy thought a moment and then said, "Did God throw him back down?"

INTRODUCTION: God created the family. His design was for a man and a woman to marry for life and raise children to know and honor Him.

"Let no one split apart what God has joined together" (Mark. 10:9). Adoption is also God's idea, and He models this in His adoption of us as His children. "So, you have not received a spirit that makes you fearful slaves. Instead, you received God's Spirit when he adopted you as his own children. Now we call him, "Abba, Father" (Rom. 8:15). "And we believers also groan, even though we have the Holy Spirit within us as a foretaste of future glory, for we long for our bodies to be released from sin and suffering. We, too, wait with eager hope for the day when God will give us our full rights as his adopted children, including the new bodies he has promised us" (Rom. 8:23). "God decided in advance to adopt us into his own family by bringing us to himself through Jesus Christ. This is what he wanted to do, and it gave him great pleasure" (Eph. 1:5).

Regardless of how they enter a family, children are a gift from God, and He cares about how they are raised. "Children are a gift from the Lord; they are a reward from him" (Ps. 127:3). "Come, my children, and listen to me, and I will teach you to fear the Lord" (Ps. 34:11). "Don't fail to discipline your children. The rod of punishment won't kill them. Physical discipline may well save them from death" (Prov. 23:13-14). When God gives us gifts, He also gives clear instructions about their use.

WHY IS THIS LESSON IMPORTANT TO YOUR LIFE? "Children are a gift from the Lord; they are a reward from him" (Ps. 127:3). He places them in families and guides parents in how they are to be raised. The goal of good parenting is to produce wise children who know and honor

157

God with their lives. "The father of godly children has cause for joy. What a pleasure to have children who are wise" (Prov. 23:24). The former verse shows the result of raising children according to God's plan and what a pleasure it is to have children who are fun-loving and kind.

All our relationships are important, and all of them require certain responsibilities as well as affording certain privileges. As marriage partners, we play the role of husband or wife. One unique role many of us assume at some point in our lives is that of a parent. The parent-child bond is a unique one, evoking strong emotion unparalleled in other relationships. We have all witnessed the tenacity of a mothers' love, the fierce protectiveness of a father for his child's physical safety, and the stalwart refusal of parents to give up on their most wayward child. The parent-child relationship, when it is healthy and God-centered, probably gives us the clearest picture on earth of what unconditional love is like.

Children are a blessing from the Lord, as the Scriptures declare. They are not a nuisance, inconvenience, or setback to our plans. They are precious, vital, and cherished treasures. As Christians, we must learn to view our children as God sees them and develop healthy ways of relating to them and training them to be that godly seed that brings honor to God.

Children are indeed a gift from God - precious and valuable in all respects. Our responsibility as parents, however, is not just to love them unconditionally, but also to train them to become a "godly seed" "Didn't the Lord make you one with your wife? In body and spirit, you are his. And what does he want? Godly children from your union. So, guard your heart; remain loyal to the wife of your youth" (Mal. 2:15). We have the task of teaching them the right standards of conduct, common courtesy, good manners, character training, and, most importantly, the ways of the Lord. "We will not hide these truths from our children; we will tell the next generation about the glorious deeds of the Lord, about his power and his mighty wonders" (Ps. 78:4). This is our primary goal as Christian parents.

Keep in mind that we are not raising sons and daughters. We are raising Kings and Queens.

DISCIPLINE:
"Fathers do not provoke your children to anger by the way you treat them. Rather, bring them up with the discipline and instruction that comes from the Lord" (Eph. 6:4).

Discipline is intended primarily for character building. Parents must understand that their goal is to shape their child's will while building their spirit. Parents must train the moral conscience of a child to move from thinking, "I must do what is right or be punished" to "I want to do right." A parent must build an atmosphere of trust with a child through spending quality time with him, speaking encouraging words, being a part of his private world, and guarding the words and tone of voice used in speaking to him. Discipline will correct. The goal of correction is restoration.

THERE ARE THREE LEVELS OF CORRECTION USED BY GOD AND PARENTS:
- **Rebuke**. This is a verbal correction. Expect an immediate response, require eye contact, and refuse to threaten, repeat, bribe, or negotiate.
- **Chastening**. This punishment allows our children to suffer the consequences of their actions. This may include isolating them, taking away privileges, or making them take personal responsibility.
- **Scourging**. This is corporal punishment reserved for correcting rebellion, as evidenced in disrespect, defiance, or disobedience. Spanking should always be done in a very controlled, precise

158

manner. Proverbs teach us the merits of carefully applying the rod. "Those who spare the rod of discipline hate their children. Those who love their children care enough to discipline them" (Prov. 13:24). "My child, if your heart is wise, my own heart will rejoice" (Prov. 22:15)! "Don't fail to discipline your children. The rod of punishment won't kill them" (Prov. 23:13). "Discipline your children, and they will give you peace of mind and will make your heart glad" (Prov. 29:17).

TEN COMMANDMENTS OF TRAINING CHILDREN:

1. Establish your authority from birth. Parents must be the ones with the most and ultimate authority.
2. Understand your child's temperament. There is no "one size fits all" method in child-rearing.
3. Place the most emphasis on character and values. When you take the time to form your child's character, it is as though you are indelibly engraving upon him those things that are important.
4. Limit the number of rules. Choose a few important rules and stick to them.
5. Listen to your child before passing judgment. Do not jump to conclusions. Discipline according to what the child has done, not according to why.
6. Discipline corporally for rebellion, stubbornness, and outright disobedience. Corporal discipline should be reserved for the greatest offenses, not every minor infraction.
7. Discipline to establish self-control. Laws are made to control people who cannot control themselves.
8. Teach your child to deny himself. A child must learn how to control his appetites and desires. Delayed gratification will teach him self-discipline.
9. Follow the progression of "master," "guide," and "friend" in relating to your child. Young children need someone in authority, a master. Teenagers should be allowed to make choices and mistakes, but they need a guide. As a child becomes an adult, your relationship should progress to that of friendship.
10. Walk-in forgiveness. No matter what your child has done, he is still your child. Never withhold forgiveness. There is no better example of tender forgiveness than the story of the father and the Prodigal Son.

We are responsible for shaping our children's will without breaking their spirits. One of the most important ways this is done is through teaching them obedience. When we are successful in raising our children with the discipline and instruction that comes from Lord, "Fathers, do not provoke your children to anger by the way you treat them. Rather, bring them up with the discipline and instruction that comes from the Lord" (Eph. 6:4). we have the wonderful privilege of seeing a godly seed for the Lord raised through our efforts.

LESSON SUMMARY:

* Children are a gift from the Lord; they are a reward from him (Ps. 127:3).

* Train up a child in the way he should go, and when he is old, he will not depart from it (Prov. 22:6 NKJV).

* Don't fail to discipline your children. The rod of punishment won't kill them. Physical discipline may well save them from death (Prov. 23:13-14).

* We will not hide these truths from our children; we will tell the next   generation about the glorious deeds of the Lord, about his power and his mighty wonders (Ps. 78:4).

* Fathers do not provoke your children to anger by the way you treat them. Rather, bring them up with the discipline and instruction that comes from the Lord (Eph. 6:4).

*Note: Lesson Slides end at this point.

OBEDIENCE PRECEDES BLESSING:
"But if you look carefully into the perfect law that sets you free, and if you do what it says and don't forget what you heard, then God will bless you for doing it" (James 1:25).

Jesus learned obedience, and he became the source of eternal salvation for all those who obey him. "Even though Jesus was God's Son, he learned obedience from the things he suffered. In this way, God qualified him as a perfect High Priest, and he became the source of eternal salvation for all those who obey him" (Heb. 5:8-9). Obedience is important.

God ordained the family as the place where the will could be shaped so that Satan could not rule. "Didn't the Lord make you one with your wife? In body and spirit, you are his. And what does he want? Godly children from your union. So, guard your heart; remain loyal to the wife of your youth" (Mal. 2:15). God said, The whole earth would be cursed unless parents and children came together. "His preaching will turn the hearts of fathers to their children, and the hearts of children to their fathers. Otherwise, I will come and strike the land with a curse" (Mal. 4:6).

Parents are a family before they ever have children. "This is how Jesus the Messiah was born. His mother, Mary, was engaged to be married to Joseph. But before the marriage took place, while she was still a virgin, she became pregnant through the power of the Holy Spirit" (Mt. 1:18). The first lesson a child must learn is that the parents are in charge, rule over them for their own go and are the center of the home. The child is welcome to join the family, but not to rule it. God never intended for a family to become child centered.

Obedience has three stages:
- **Obey.** "Children obey your parents because you belong to the Lord, for this is the right thing to do" (Eph. 6:1).
- **Submit**. Jesus submitted to John to "fulfill all righteousness" by being baptized. "But Jesus said, "It should be done, for we must carry out all that God requires." So, John agreed to baptize him" (Mat. 3:15).
- **Honor**. "Honor your father and mother." This is the first commandment with a promise" (Eph. 6:2):

MEMORY VERSE:
"Train up a child in the way he should go, and when he is old, he will not depart from it" (Prov. 22:6 NKJV).

GROW DEEPER:
"Then Christ will make His home in your hearts as you trust in Him. Your roots will grow down into God's love and keep you strong" (Eph. 3:17).

Why is obedience such an important part of training children?

What happens to children who never learn to obey?

How does failure to teach your children obedience carry over into their relationships with others and with God?

What are the rights of children in a family? What are other things that are nice to provide, but not essential?

How much do you owe your children materially?

What is the purpose of discipline in the parent-child relationship?

What role does corporal punishment play?

What are other effective ways of discipline?

Which methods are effective?

Discuss how your relationship with your child should change as he ages. What does he need from you as a very small child? When school-aged? As a teenager? As an adult?

How does having a strong marriage benefit your children? How does a weak marriage affect them? What is the priority relationship in your home? Husband/wife or parent/child? Why?

QUESTIONS:

Do you presently teach your children the importance of obedience? If so, how?

Many parents have made the mistake of improperly disciplining their children. How would you describe your form of discipline with your children? Do you see ways you can improve the way you discipline them?

What would you say is your greatest revelation from this lesson? What actions will you take to walk out what you have learned?

FAMILY BONDING AND MINISTERING AS A FAMILY: BUILDING AND REBUILDING FOUNDATIONS

PURPOSE OF THIS LESSON:

You will gain a picture of what healthy family interaction looks like and how it fosters the development of strong family bonds.

You will also learn the blessing and privilege of ministering together as a family. God wants your families to be wonderful sources of strength and fulfillment, not places of stress, trauma, and difficulty. When you begin bonding with others in your families, the atmosphere in your homes begins changing as you grow closer to one another. "Always keep yourselves united in the Holy Spirit and bind yourselves together with peace" (Eph. 4:3).

Bonding in your family takes place in several ways. First, serve each other and put others' needs before your own. Second, play together. Third, plan projects and set times for working together and achieving common goals. Fourth, stand together through trials. As you grow in these four areas, your family will bond and connect in ways that unite you and make you stronger as a family. "Two people are better off than one, for they can help each other succeed. If one person falls, the other can reach out and help. But someone who falls alone is in real trouble" (Eccles. 4:9-10). Being married with all its demands does not exempt you from discovering a way to contribute to the body of Christ. The way you serve God may vary at different times in your life, but a firm commitment to be actively involved in His work should never waver.

Ministering together as husband and wife is one of the greatest thrills a couple can experience. When you accept the challenge to let God use you and partner with your mate to see that challenge come to pass, you move into a deeper level of ministry than if you minister alone. Your unique gifts and talents will enhance those of your mate and vice versa. The two of you together are better than one, and with the presence of the Holy Spirit, you will form a triple-braided cord. "A person standing alone can be attacked and defeated, but two can stand back-to-back and conquer. Three are even better, for a triple-braided cord is not easily broken" (Eccl. 4:12).

INTRODUCTION:

Mom no longer dusts the house clad in a freshly pressed dress with a string of pearls around her neck, and Dad does not always know best, like in the "perfect" television families of the '60s. Today, those images are just illusions. The good news is, however, that you can create an atmosphere in your home where individual family members have a sense of belonging to a loving, caring unit. This is achieved when your family members begin to learn how to bond with one another through shared activities, goals, work, and ministry to the Lord.

You were not created by God to travel through your earthly lives alone, independent of everyone else, and doing your own thing. In the family, you were meant to find your deepest, most fulfilling connections of all. Serving God through ministering together fulfills a Christian family's purpose, and it brings new meaning to your relationships. There is no deeper joy for your family than seeing souls saved, needs met, and lives transformed because of ministering together.

WHY IS THIS LESSON IMPORTANT TO YOUR LIFE?
Bonding is Important to Families. Christ taught the principles of bonding.

He had healthy relationships with His disciples that were demonstrated in His unconditional, unchanging love for them. Isn't this the kind of relationship you want with your family? Don't you want to love and be loved unconditionally? Isn't it nice to know that home is the one place where you can truly be yourselves and where you are always welcome? "Before the Passover celebration, Jesus knew that his hour had come to leave this world and return to his Father. He had loved his disciples during his ministry on earth, and now he loved them to the very end" (John 13:1).

There is a huge difference between bondage and bonding. "Bondage" is the unwanted attachment that confines people in relationships and situations over which they have no control. "Bonding," on the other hand, is the life-giving, empowering aspect of relationships that supports, secures, and sustains. It is the process by which you develop trust and community. Your family experiences bonding when you are considerate of others, exercise trust, and intentionally share your lives with your spouse and children.

When you become isolated, lose trust and respect, never communicate, bondage occurs. Divorce is the result of the process by which the bonds (glue, adhesive) of the marriage relationship start coming apart, and the marriage deteriorates into bondage. However, there are things you can do to restore your marriage before it results in divorce.

FAMILIES BOND BY SERVING ONE ANOTHER:
The first aspect of family bonding is the process of serving and ministering to one another. "No," Peter protested, "you will never ever wash my feet!" Jesus replied, "Unless I wash you, you won't belong to me." And since I, your Lord and Teacher, have washed your feet, you ought to wash each other's feet" (John 13:8, 14). Bonding occurs when a family member recognizes that you have sacrificed a special time and paid attention to his needs. Are you aware of the needs and hurts of all the members in your household? Washing symbolizes taking the lowest position and serving others. How about washing your spouse's car? Doing the laundry? Cooking dinner one evening. This list could go on and on. All bonding begins with an obvious effort to serve. Serving others speaks of love, care, and commitment and is the first step to bonding in your family.

FAMILIES BOND BY PLAYING TOGETHER:
"Don't let your hearts be troubled. Trust in God, and trust also in me" (John 14:1). Today's life is filled with pressure and stress. "Then Jesus said, "Let's go off by ourselves to a quiet place and rest awhile." He said this because there were so many people coming and going that Jesus and his apostles didn't even have time to eat" (Mark 6:31). He knew the necessity and value of taking the time to get away from everything to be refreshed and rejuvenated. He often retreated with His disciples to mountains, isolated places, and private retreats. There the disciples spent time away from others, bonding with Christ and one another as His primary group of disciples. Family bonding grows when there are times of play. The family that plays together stays together. Never think that God only intends for you to work to keep your household running. He also wants you to take time to rest and have fun with your family. Your family should sit down and decide which activities each member enjoys the

163

most. Then you should schedule activities you can do together so that everyone's "fun" side is released (camping, hunting, swimming, fishing, visiting museums, having cookouts, etc.) These activities will vary, depending upon the ages of your children, the income level of your family, and personal schedules. With a little effort, you can find activities that are relevant, affordable, and meaningful to your family.

FAMILIES BOND BY WORKING TOGETHER:

Bonding occurs when family members share common goals and passions. When you work together with your spouse and children, you can be much more fruitful than if you work alone. Bonding takes place in your family when its members not only minister to one another but also work together successfully on a joint project. "Every branch in Me that does not bear fruit He [lifts up] takes away; and every branch that bears fruit He prunes, that it may bear more fruit" (John 15:2). Parents and siblings may need to lift up other family members by encouraging them. Every member of your family should feel needed. All should have a part in the upkeep of the home: doing dishes, cleaning, and working together on behalf of others. Children should be given age-appropriate chores and know that their contributions are essential to the proper functioning of the home.

You must be careful not to let times of work become times of stress. Ownership of a project means that your entire family has all bought into it, and all are willingly doing their share. You and your spouse may need to help your children see the value and fun that comes from shared responsibility.

In addition to working in the home together, you will want to find ways that you can reach outside of the confines of the home to the community and body of Christ. Ministering for the Lord together is a vital part of family bonding. As a family, you might travel to outreach together, go Christmas caroling to shut-ins, bring groceries to the needy, do yardwork for an elderly relative, etc. These are tremendously rewarding and cultivate feelings of shared accomplishment. Paul often referred to individual people as "my fellow laborer." You should be laboring with your family in the kingdom of God.

FAMILIES BOND BY FACING DIFFICULTIES TOGETHER:

"But the time is coming-indeed it's here now-when you will be scattered, each one going his own way, leaving me alone. Yet I am not alone because the Father is with me" (John 16:32). All families face difficulties of one type or another: financial, physical, emotional, vocational, educational, etc. Up until now, Christ's disciples had stayed with Him through all His trials. "You have stayed with me in my time of trial" (Luke. 22:28). During the trying times of life, you will bond with those who encourage, assist, and strengthen you.

Paul often referred to certain people as his "fellow soldier" or "fellow prisoner." Because they had been imprisoned with him, they shared a common bond. Bonds that are formed during hardships are not easily severed. "Many waters cannot quench love, nor can rivers drown it. If a man tried to buy love with all his wealth, his offer would be utterly scorned" (Song of Sol. 8:7).

When your family faces a trial, it will either bring you closer or drive you apart. The result depends upon how you respond to the trial, support one another, shoulder the burden, and seek solutions. When you face a problem in your family, don't waste time blaming other family members for it (even if their actions were a factor in it). Instead, draw close to one another and determine to walk through the trial together; those families can stand against anything.

TEN LAWS THAT GOVERN FAMILY MINISTRY:

1. Law of Agreement: Acts 5. When you and your spouse love the Lord and are committed to serving Him together, you become a powerful force that accomplishes great things in God's kingdom. "Two people are better off than one, for they can help each other succeed" (Eccl. 4:9). Husband and wife are the most powerful form of agreement on earth. Examples: Ananias and Sapphira acted in the principle of agreement (even though in the wrong way), and that is why they were both judged; Adam and Eve agreed together to sin, and it cost the world suffering. "I also tell you this: If two of you agree here on earth concerning anything you ask, my Father in heaven will do it for you. For where two or three gather together as my followers, I am there among them" (Matt. 18:19-20).

2. Law of Purpose:

God calls both husband and wife to a common purpose – to win souls and make disciples. "There he became acquainted with a Jew named Aquila, born in Pontus, who had recently arrived from Italy with his wife, Priscilla. They had left Italy when Claudius Caesar deported all Jews from Rome. 26 When Priscilla and Aquila heard him preaching boldly in the synagogue, they took him aside and explained the way of God even more accurately" (Acts 18:2, 26). You will answer for how you serve in the kingdom of God. You and your spouse are partners in everything, including ministry. Many times, wives are first to recognize ways to minister together in the body of Christ. If husbands are open to the discernment of their wives and do not shut them out, avenues of joint ministry can open. "Give my greetings to Priscilla and Aquila, my co-workers in the ministry of Christ Jesus. In fact, they once risked their lives for me. I am thankful to them, and so are all the Gentile churches. Also give my greetings to the church that meets in their home. Greet my dear friend Epenetus. He was the first person from the province of Asia to become a follower of Christ" (Rom. 16:3-5). A wife is an heir of Christ, along with her husband. She has a unique contribution to make to the body of Christ. "In the same way, you husbands must give honor to your wives. Treat your wife with understanding as you live together. She may be weaker than you are, but she is your equal partner in God's gift of new life. Treat her as you should so your prayers will not be hindered" (1 Pet. 3:7). Example: Aquila and Priscilla opened a house church, and together they ministered in it.

3. Law of Failure:

The strength of your partner is there to help you when you fail and encourage you when you are tempted to quit. You will be able to go the distance in ministry when you have a supportive spouse by your side. If one person falls, the other can reach out and help. But someone who falls alone is in real trouble. (Eccl. 4:10). When your ministry is not bearing fruit or achieving what you thought it would, it can be easy to think you missed God. A godly partner in ministry will help keep you on the right track and will balance your perspective during struggling times.

4. Law of Hospitality:

The Word of God instructs you to, "When God's people are in need, be ready to help them. Always be eager to practice hospitality" (Rom. 12:13). This is a very easy way for you and your family to begin ministering to others. Fruitfulness and favor come upon couples who offer hospitality to further God's kingdom. Example: The couple in 2 Kings decided to add an addition to their home for the prophet Elisha. The woman "felt" the need, and her husband "built" the need. This couple was blessed with a miracle child, despite the husband's advanced age. "She said to her husband, "I am sure this man who stops in from time to time is a holy man of God. Let's build a small room for him on the roof and furnish it with a bed, a table, a chair, and a lamp. Then he will have a place to stay whenever he comes by" (2 Kings 4:9-10).

5. Law of Order:
The passive husband (Ahab) and the domineering and controlling wife (Jezebel) are a prescription for disaster. Jezebel was able to incite Ahab to do evil because he was passive and would not take the lead. Their marriage was out of order. "(No one else so completely sold himself to what was evil in the Lord's sight as Ahab did under the influence of his wife Jezebel" (1 Kings 21:25). When a husband relinquishes his responsibility of leadership to his wife, this will destroy any of their attempts at the ministry. The home must be in order if couples want to minister effectively for the Lord. Couples who accept their roles in the home are powerful tools in the hand of God. Unity, overflowing from their home into ministry, will become an unstoppable force against the enemy.

Example: Joseph and Mary were in order. Mary submitted to Joseph's direction from the angel of the Lord. "After the wise men were gone, an angel of the Lord appeared to Joseph in a dream. "Get up! Flee to Egypt with the child and his mother," the angel said. "Stay there until I tell you to return, because Herod is going to search for the child to kill him." That night Joseph left for Egypt with the child and Mary, his mother" (Mt. 2:13-14).

6. Law of Balance: A wife balances her husband's anger, and a husband balances his wife's fear. She provides him with tenderness since she is "grace" while he is "law." He provides her with confidence and faith since he is "conquest" while she is "compassion." A couple who ministers continue to look for "our way," which is in submission to "His way," – never "my way" or "your way." "David replied to Abigail, "Praise the Lord, the God of Israel, who has sent you to meet me today! Thank God for your good sense! Bless you for keeping me from murder and from carrying out vengeance with my own hands" (1 Sam. 25:32-33).

7. Law of Priesthood: Your ministry begins in your home. Ministry to each other and then the nurturing and training of your children are the basis from which all other ministry is derived.
Examples: Noah and his wife lived according to God's standard of holiness, and their three sons and wives were all part of a priestly family. "When everything was ready, the Lord said to Noah, "Go into the boat with all your family, for among all the people of the earth, I can see that you alone are righteous" (Gen. 7:1). Zacharias and Elizabeth were righteous and produced John the Baptist, a spiritual Nazarite. "Zechariah and Elizabeth were righteous in God's eyes, careful to obey all of the Lord's commandments and regulations" (Luke 1:6).

8. Law of Inheritance: Part of a godly couple's ministry is to reproduce godly seed. "Didn't the Lord make you one with your wife? In body and spirit, you are his. And what does he want? Godly children from your union. So, guard your heart; remain loyal to the wife of your youth" (Mal 2:15). Throughout the Bible, godly couples raised the next generation of leaders. "His preaching will turn the hearts of fathers to their children, and the hearts of children to their fathers. Otherwise, I will come and strike the land with a curse" (Mal. 4:6). Your desire for your children should not be just passing on a financial inheritance, but more importantly, a spiritual one. Find the best way for your family to serve God together and then make it a top priority. "Your wife will be like a fruitful grapevine, flourishing within your home. Your children will be like vigorous young olive trees as they sit around your table" (Psa. 128:3).

10. **Law of Peace:** Being married to an unsaved person does not mean you can divorce him just because he is not saved. Joseph was married to a heathen priestess and remained in the marriage. "Then Pharaoh gave Joseph a new Egyptian name, Zaphenath-Paneah. He also gave him a wife, whose name

166

was Asenath. She was the daughter of Potiphera, the priest of On. So Joseph took charge of the entire land of Egypt" (Gen. 41:45). God can greatly use your presence as an influence on your children and your unsaved partner. "and all of them drank the same spiritual water. For they drank from the spiritual rock that traveled with them, and that rock was Christ" (1 Cor. 10:4). If the unbelieving spouse is abusive, you can separate but not divorce. Divorce is scriptural only in cases of adultery. "And I tell you this, whoever divorces his wife and marries someone else commits adultery—unless his wife has been unfaithful" (Mt. 19:9). Then and only then is remarriage an option. The general rule is maintaining "peace" at all costs.

10. Law of Self-Control: To those who are single or who find themselves single again, the rule is self-control. The key to living a spiritually pure single life is to be devoted to the Lord, as married people are to their partners. "So, I say to those who aren't married and to widows—it's better to stay unmarried, just as I am. 9 But if they can't control themselves, they should go ahead and marry. It's better to marry than to burn with lust" (1 Cor. 7:8-9).

If sexual passions are burning, Paul taught that you should marry rather than burn with lust. "I want you to be free from the concerns of this life. An unmarried man can spend his time doing the Lord's work and thinking how to please him. But a married man has to think about his earthly responsibilities and how to please his wife. His interests are divided. In the same way, a woman who is no longer married or has never been married can be devoted to the Lord and holy in body and in spirit. But a married woman has to think about her earthly responsibilities and how to please her husband. I am saying this for your benefit, not to place restrictions on you. I want you to do whatever will help you serve the Lord best, with as few distractions as possible. But if a man thinks that he's treating his fiancée improperly and will inevitably give in to his passion, let him marry her as he wishes. It is not a sin. But if he has decided firmly not to marry and there is no urgency and he can control his passion, he does well not to marry. So, the person who marries his fiancée does well, and the person who doesn't marry does even better. A wife is bound to her husband as long as he lives. If her husband dies, she is free to marry anyone she wishes, but only if he loves the Lord. But in my opinion, it would be better for her to stay single, and I think I am giving you counsel from God's Spirit when I say this" (1 Cor. 7:32-40). However, a single can choose to put ministry over marriage—even permanently—if he or she so desires.

LESSON SUMMARY:
- "Always keep yourselves united in the Holy Spirit and bind yourselves together with peace" (Eph. 4:3).

- "A person standing alone can be attacked and defeated, but two can stand back-to-back and conquer. Three are even better, for a triple-braided cord is not easily broken" (Eccl. 4:12).

- "No," Peter protested, "you will never ever wash my feet!" Jesus replied, "Unless I wash you, you won't belong to me." 14 And since I, your Lord and Teacher, have washed your feet, you ought to wash each other's feet" (John 13:8, 14).

- "Every branch in Me that does not bear fruit He [lifts up] takes away; and every branch that bears fruit He prunes, that it may bear more fruit" (John 15:2).

*Note: Lesson Slides end at this point.

OBEDIENCE PRECEDES BLESSING:
"But if you look carefully into the perfect law that sets you free, and if you do what it says and don't forget what you heard, then God will bless you for doing it" (James 1:25).

MEMORY VERSE:
"Always keep yourselves united in the Holy Spirit and bind yourselves together with peace" (Eph. 4:3).

GROW DEEPER:
"Then, Christ will make His home in your hearts as you trust in Him. Your roots will GROW down into God's love and keep you strong" (Eph. 3:17).

QUESTIONS

Describe your mental image of the ideal family. Is it a realistic one?

What are some concrete things people can do to foster family closeness? Which ones have you tried?

Why is playing together important to family bonding?

Why do some Christians have a problem with this?

Does God want you to have fun?

What are some ways to have fun that don't compromise your faith?

What kinds of activities should you avoid?

Can a family be too close? What are some unhealthy ways of bonding?

How can trials and difficulties bring a family closer?

What has been your experience in your family?

There is nothing more fulfilling than a family that serves God together.

What are some things you could start doing in your family that would achieve that goal?

What do you think it means to minister together as husband and wife?

Does it always mean leading a small group or teaching a Bible study?

What are some other ways couples can minister together?

How can you include your children in ministry? How does age factor into this?

A passive husband and a domineering wife make a poor combination for ministry. Why?

How can couples change this pattern?

What steps can you take to ensure that your children are receiving a spiritual inheritance?

How does your ministry affect the future of your children's ministry?

Do you regard ministry as an integral part of your Christian life or as something optional?

If you have never ventured forth to serve God in a definite, specific way, where could you begin?

Have you had a desire to minister?

Has your spouse?

Have you made any attempts to minister to others in the past? How did that go?

Moving forward, assuming both husband and wife are now fulfilling their God-designed roles, how will you take steps to serve others?

How will you train your children to minister to others?

Grow III
Lessons

"God's Heartbeat"

GROW III
God's Heartbeat
Lesson 1

DISCOVERING GOD'S HEARTBEAT:
FOR HOLINESS AND WALKING AS JESUS WALKED

PURPOSE OF THIS LESSON:
To know and believe God is completely and indisputably Holy, and He calls and equips us to be Holy as He is.

"But now you must be holy in everything you do, just as God who chose you is holy. For the Scriptures say, "You must be holy because I am holy" (1 Pet. 1:15-16). "All praise to God, the Father of our Lord Jesus Christ, who has blessed us with every spiritual blessing in the heavenly realms because we are united with Christ. Even before he made the world, God loved us and chose us in Christ to be holy and without fault in his eyes" (Eph. 1:3-4).
*(See Appendix, Teaching Note 1)

INTRODUCTION:
What does Holiness look like in our day-to-day lives, and how do we take this truth from the abstract to the concrete?

"Many who became believers confessed their sinful practices. A number of them who had been practicing sorcery brought their incantation books and burned them at a public bonfire. The value of the books was several million dollars. So, the message about the Lord spread widely and had a powerful effect" (Acts 19:18-20).
*(See Appendix, Teaching Note 2)

WHY IS THIS LESSON IMPORTANT TO YOUR LIFE?
This lesson sets the foundation for living the abundant life Jesus came to give, a life filled with purpose, direction, and freedom from sin. "The thief's purpose is to steal and kill and destroy. My purpose is to give them a rich and satisfying life" (John 10:10). "Those who say they live in God should live their lives as Jesus did" (1 John 2:6). "But you are not like that, for you are a chosen people. You are royal priests, a holy nation, God's very own possession. As a result, you can show others the goodness of God, for he called you out of the darkness into his wonderful light" (1 Pet 1:9).

THE POWER TO BE HOLY:
Would you say we are living in a world that is marked by impurity with very few parameters of being pure in our thoughts and actions? Is it a world where "you're ok, and I'm ok" just "live and let live" or "to each his own" is a mindset of tolerance to all beliefs and lifestyles? A place with no plumb line or cornerstone of truth with which we can align our lives to? "If it feels good, then do it! If it is convenient and no one will get hurt or make judgments on your choices, then what's the harm? After all, no one is perfect!" Or how about this, "This is just the way I am! This is the way they have always been. What is Holiness? Frankly, I don't even care. That is just judgmental and legalistic." The sad truth is that these thoughts have crept into the church, into those who have been called to be set apart, sanctified, and Holy.

170

These questions must be asked, "What truth am I ordering my life after? Is there a different or better way? Is there any hope for a life not marked by sickness, sadness, hurt, dysfunction, divorce, poverty, or destruction? Is there anyone that has discovered what that is, what it looks like, and how to obtain it?

Of course, there is a different and better way! There is a plumb line of truth on which to build our lives! There is SOMEONE who has discovered what it is, what it looks like, and how to obtain it! Now the question is, will you go after that SOMEONE with all your heart? Will you say "yes" to that someone and help others to find Him as well? Discover who that SOMEONE is. "Jesus told him, "I am the way, the truth, and the life. No one can come to the Father except through me" (John 14:6).

Let's examine where you are with this very foundational truth of Holiness:
- First, take a few minutes to answer the following questions BEFORE you look up the Bible verses.
- Next, look up the verses and ask the Holy Spirit to teach you the Heartbeat of God the Father for these topics!

1. What comes to mind when you hear "Holy"? Define and give examples.

2. Is it important that God is Holy? Why or why not?

    "Reverence for the Lord is pure, lasting forever. The laws of the Lord are true; each one is fair" (Psalm. 19:9)

3. Is being Holy possible? Why or why not?

    *(See Appendix, Teaching Note 3)

    "Jesus looked at them intently and said, "Humanly speaking, it is impossible. But with God everything is possible" (Matt. 19:26).

    "For I can do everything through Christ, who gives me strength" (Phil. 4:13).

4. Do you believe God is just and Holy in ALL His ways?

    "He is the Rock; his deeds are perfect. Everything he does is just and fair. He is a faithful God who does no wrong; how just and upright he is" (Deut. 32:4)!

5. Do you believe God's creation was pure?

    "God called the dry ground "land" and the waters "seas." And God saw that it was good" (Gen. 1:10).

    "The land produced vegetation—all sorts of seed-bearing plants, and trees with seed-bearing fruit. Their seeds produced plants and trees of the same kind. And God saw that it was good" (Gen. 1:12).

    "to govern the day and night, and to separate the light from the darkness. And God saw that it was good" (Gen. 1:18).

    "So, God created great sea creatures and every living thing that scurries and swarms in the water, and every sort of bird—each producing offspring of the same kind. And God saw that it was good" (Gen. 1:21).

"God made all sorts of wild animals, livestock, and small animals, each able to produce offspring of the same kind. And God saw that it was good" (Gen. 1:25).

"So, God created human beings in his own image. In the image of God, he created them; male and female he created them.' Then God blessed them and said, "Be fruitful and multiply. Fill the earth and govern it. Reign over the fish in the sea, the birds in the sky, and all the animals that scurry along the ground" (Gen. 1:27-28).
"Then God looked over all he had made, and he saw that it was very good! And evening passed and morning came, marking the sixth day" (Gen. 1:31).

6. Do you believe man is corrupt?
"The Lord observed the extent of human wickedness on the earth, and he saw that everything they thought or imagined was consistently and totally evil" (Gen. 6:5).

"The human heart is the most deceitful of all things, and desperately wicked. Who really knows how bad it is" (Jer. 17:9)?

7. Do you believe God provided a way for man to escape corruption?

"But God showed his great love for us by sending Christ to die for us while we were still sinners" (Rom. 5:8).

8. What do you believe God feels about the wicked non-believer?

"As surely as I live, says the Sovereign Lord, I take no pleasure in the death of wicked people. I only want them to turn from their wicked ways so they can live. Turn! Turn from your wickedness, O people of Israel! Why should you die" (Ezek. 33:11)?

"The Lord isn't really being slow about his promise, as some people think. No, he is being patient for your sake. He does not want anyone to be destroyed but wants everyone to repent" (2 Pet. 3:9).

Now take a few minutes to meditate on what you heard the Holy Spirit say. Did you get any new insights? Is there a shift happening in your thinking, opinions, and beliefs about Holiness?

Now we are going to take this abstract view of Holiness to concrete where we look at what Holiness looks like in important areas of our lives. I believe you will be both encouraged and challenged as you examine your journey to Holiness.

THE PLUMB LINE:
"But the wisdom from above is first of all pure. It is also peace loving, gentle at all times, and willing to yield to others. It is full of mercy and the fruit of good deeds. It shows no favoritism and is always sincere" (James 3:17). God being Holy is the plumb line in OUR journey to Holiness. Here is what it says in Amos, "Then he showed me another vision. I saw the Lord standing beside a wall that had been built using a plumb line. He was using a plumb line to see if it was still straight. 8 And the Lord said to me, "Amos, what do you see?" I answered, "A plumb line." And the Lord replied, "I will test my people with this plumb line. I will no longer ignore all their sins" (Amos 7:7-8). So, you may ask, "What is a plumb line?" A plumb line is a weight, usually with a pointed tip at the bottom for marking a point. The weight is suspended from a string; gravity pulls the weight down and pulls the string tight. It is used by builders as a vertical reference point – to make sure that what they are building is straight. It is also used by builders for testing walls that are already built to see if they are still straight, to see if

they are bowing, or bulging, or sagging, or crooked, and if so, they need to be torn down. Now the Lord is using that image as one of righteousness and justice in Israel. He says that He will not pass by them anymore. A plumb line does not deviate, it does not provide excuses, it does not just tell you what you want to hear, and it does not change. It is unerringly straight and right. The Lord is going to measure Israel like that – the Lord measures us like that, and thus this is why God must be Holy.

Action Step: Begin to read the Bible through in one year and begin to implement what you learn. "But don't just listen to God's word. You must do what it says. Otherwise, you are only fooling yourselves. For if you listen to the word and don't obey, it is like glancing at your face in a mirror. You see yourself, walk away, and forget what you look like" (James 1:22-24). Recommend using One Year Bible www.oneyearbibleonline.com

The Holy Spirit:

"God has called us to live holy lives, not impure lives." (1 Thess. 4:7). How does it make you feel when you read this verse? I know for myself, there was hesitancy at first, because the thought of being perfect is hard to imagine! Once I realized that I had a helper in the Holy Spirit, I knew that it was possible. Do you realize that you have a helper that is there to always be your comforter, your guide, your teacher? Jesus said, "And I will pray the Father, and he shall give you another Comforter, that he may abide with you forever" (John 14:16 KJV); Jesus also said, "But when the Father sends the Advocate as my representative-that is, the Holy Spirit-he will teach you everything and will remind you of everything I have told you" (John 14:26). Do you see that being Holy is possible, but not in our strength! We must and need to rely on the teacher and comforter that Jesus calls the Holy Spirit. For further information on how real friendship with the Holy Spirit can change your life.

I highly recommend you read "The God I Never Knew: How Real Friendship with the Holy Spirit Can Change Your Life," by Robert Morris

Action Step: Go to a Christian bookstore or amazon.com to purchase the book and read it.

THE JUST GOD:

This question is one of the most important questions of the lesson because what you believe about God will determine your walk with Him. Most Christians today will say, "Of course God is just and Holy in all His ways!" But then when their lives start getting hard, they will start blaming Him and questioning His decision-making process. So, I ask you again, do you truly believe God is just and Holy in ALL His ways? Do you believe that God is just and Holy when you lose your job when your child dies in a car wreck when your spouse gets diagnosed with cancer when your sweet child turns her back on everything that you have taught her? There are many trials in this life, and when we know God can do something about it and He does not, we begin to question Him and what appears to be His lack of caring in our lives. We must have a firm foundation and belief that God is just and Holy in all His ways, just like Simon Peter: "Then Jesus turned to the Twelve and asked, "Are you also going to leave?" Simon Peter replied, "Lord, to whom would we go? You have the words that give eternal life" (John 6:67-69).

How about Shadrach, Meshach, and Abednego? "Shadrach, Meshach, and Abednego replied, "O Nebuchadnezzar, we do not need to defend ourselves before you. If we are thrown into the blazing furnace, the God whom we serve is able to save us. He will rescue us from your power, Your Majesty. But even if he doesn't, we want to make it clear to you, Your Majesty, that we will never serve your gods or worship the gold statue you have set up" (Dan. 3:16-18). How about when God gave permission to Satan to take everything from Job (his children, business, and wealth, community respect, and his health), but he could not kill him. We read Job's response, "Job stood up and tore his robe in grief. Then he shaved his head and fell to the ground to worship. He said, "I came naked from my mother's womb, and I will be naked when I leave. The Lord gave me what I had, and the Lord has taken it away. Praise the name of the Lord!" In all of this, Job did not sin by blaming God" (Job 1:20-22).

Action Step: Next time, God doesn't make sense, purpose in your heart to say out loud: "You, God are Just and Holy in all Your ways, and I will trust You!"

THE VITAL INPUTS:

"We destroy every proud obstacle that keeps people from knowing God. We capture their rebellious thoughts and teach them to obey Christ" (2 Cor. 10:5). Why is it so important that we take every thought captive? What forms a thought? How do we purify our thoughts? All these questions and more may be going through your mind when the phrase "take your thoughts captive" is read, and I understand! Taking your thoughts captive is no easy task, but it is doable. First and foremost, "For I can do everything through Christ, who gives me strength" (Phil. 4:13). Let's not lean on our own strength, but on our Savior's. Jesus has given us practical steps we can take in taking our thoughts captive. Jesus said, "Your eye is like a lamp that provides light for your body. When your eye is healthy, your whole body is filled with light. But when your eye is unhealthy, your whole body is filled with darkness. And if the light you think you have is actually darkness, how deep that darkness is! "No one can serve two masters. For you will hate one and love the other; you will be devoted to one and despise the other. You cannot serve God and be enslaved to money" (Matt. 6: 22-24). Who are we following or associating with? Jesus tells us that even this takes away or moves us toward holiness. "Oh, the joys of those who do not follow the advice of the wicked, or stand around with sinners, or join in with mockers" (Ps. 1:1). Then also in "Don't be fooled by those who say such things, for "bad company corrupts good character" (1 Cor. 15:33). Three critical questions we must ask ourselves are, "What are we watching? What are we listening to? Who are we associating with?"

Action Step: Start TODAY!!! Take inventory of what you watch, listen to, and associate with! Ask and answer this question BEFORE you watch, listen, and associate, "Will this move me into or take me away from becoming more like Jesus and a life marked by Holiness?"

THE IMPORTANT DECISION:

I believe one of the most important decisions you will ever make as a single person is to stay sexually pure until marriage and then, as a married person, is to continue to stay sexually pure in your marriage. This is a tough topic for believers and one that most churches can sweep under the rug if they are not careful because it can cause discomfort and hurt feelings. My prayer for you is that as we discussed sexual purity in this lesson that you saw how important it is in your life as a follower of Jesus. Once you made that commitment to accept Jesus Christ as your personal savior, He bought your body for a price, His sacrifice on the cross, and gave us the honor of housing the Holy Spirit. That's why Paul is stressing the importance of sexual purity in the following verse, "Run from sexual sin! No other sin so clearly affects the body as this one does. For sexual immorality is a sin against your own body. Don't you realize that your body is the temple of the Holy Spirit, who lives in you and was given to you by God? You do not belong to yourself" (1 Cor. 6:18-19), Maybe sexual purity was not on the top of your list, or you are just coming to know Christ, guess what! Jesus is our eraser, and all we must do is ask

His forgiveness and "flee immorality." If this is an area of great struggle for you, we have listed some important action steps that will help you overcome this stronghold.

LESSON SUMMARY:

• "Run from sexual sin! No other sin so clearly affects the body as this one does. For sexual immorality is a sin against your own body. Don't you realize that your body is the temple of the Holy Spirit, who lives in you and was given to you by God? You do not belong to yourself" (1 Cor. 6:18-19).

• "But you are not like that, for you are a chosen people. You are royal priests, a holy nation, God's very own possession. As a result, you can show others the goodness of God, for he called you out of the darkness into his wonderful light" (1 Pet 1:9).

• "But now you must be holy in everything you do, just as God who chose you is holy. For the Scriptures say, "You must be holy because I am holy" (1 Pet. 1:15-16).

• "For I can do everything through Christ, who gives me strength" (Phil. 4:13).

*Note: Lesson Slides end at this point.

OBEDIENCE PRECEDES BLESSING:
Rate from 1-5, with 5 being the best, of how you are personally doing in each step towards Holiness!

_____ Become a believer and begin the journey to becoming more like Jesus.

"to open their eyes, so they may turn from darkness to light and from the power of Satan to God. Then they will receive forgiveness for their sins and be given a place among God's people, who are set apart by faith in me" (Acts 26:18).

"For God knew his people in advance, and he chose them to become like his Son, so that his Son would be the firstborn among many brothers and sisters" (Rom. 8:29).

_____ Take your thoughts captive.

"Don't copy the behavior and customs of this world, but let God transform you into a new person by changing the way you think. Then you will learn to know God's will for you, which is good and pleasing and perfect" (Rom.12:2).

"We destroy every proud obstacle that keeps people from knowing God. We capture their rebellious thoughts and teach them to obey Christ" (2 Cor. 10:5).

"And now, dear brothers and sisters, one final thing. Fix your thoughts on what is true, and honorable, and right, and pure, and lovely, and admirable. Think about things that are excellent and worthy of praise" (Phil. 4:8).

"So, prepare your minds for action and exercise self-control. Put all your hope in the gracious salvation that will come to you when Jesus Christ is revealed to the world" (1 Pet. 1:13).

_____ Live out Integrity and Character.

"What sorrow awaits you teachers of religious law and you Pharisees. Hypocrites! For you are careful to tithe even the tiniest income from your herb gardens, but you ignore the more important aspects of the law—justice, mercy, and faith. You should tithe, yes, but do not neglect the more important things. Blind guides! You strain your water, so you won't accidentally swallow a gnat, but you swallow a camel! "What sorrow awaits you teachers of religious law and you Pharisees. Hypocrites! For you are so careful to clean the outside of the cup and the dish, but inside you are filthy—full of greed and self-indulgence! You blind Pharisee! First wash the inside of the cup and the dish, and then the outside will become clean, too. "What sorrow awaits you teachers of religious law and you Pharisees. Hypocrites! For you are like whitewashed tombs—beautiful on the outside but filled on the inside with dead people's bones and all sorts of impurity. Outwardly you look like righteous people, but inwardly your hearts are filled with hypocrisy and lawlessness. "What sorrow awaits you teachers of religious law and you Pharisees. Hypocrites! For you build tombs for the prophets your ancestors killed, and you decorate the monuments of the godly people your ancestors destroyed. Then you say, 'If we had lived in the days of our ancestors, we would never have joined them in killing the prophets.' "But in saying that, you testify against yourselves that you are indeed the descendants of those who murdered the prophets. Go ahead and finish what your ancestors started. Snakes! Sons of vipers! How will you escape the judgment of hell" (Matt. 23:23-33)?

Jesus replied, "You hypocrites! Isaiah was right when he prophesied about you, for he wrote, 'These people honor me with their lips, but their hearts are far from me. Their worship is a farce, for they teach man-made ideas as commands from God.' For you ignore God's law and substitute your own tradition" (Mark. 7:6-8).

_____ Keep sexually pure.

"Don't you realize that all of you together are the temple of God and that the Spirit of God lives in you? God will destroy anyone who destroys this temple. For God's temple is holy, and you are that temple" (1 Cor. 3:16-17).

"Run from sexual sin! No other sin so clearly affects the body as this one does. For sexual immorality is a sin against your own body. Don't you realize that your body is the temple of the Holy Spirit, who lives in you and was given to you by God? You do not belong to yourself, for God bought you with a high price. So, you must honor God with your body" (1 Cor. 6:18-20).

God's will is for you to be holy, so stay away from all sexual sin. Then each of you will control his own body and live in holiness and honor-not in lustful passion like the pagans who do not know God and his ways. Never harm or cheat a fellow believer in this matter by violating his wife, for the Lord avenges all such sins, as we have solemnly warned you before. God has called us to live holy lives, not impure lives. Therefore, anyone who refuses to live by these rules is not disobeying human teaching but is rejecting God, who gives his Holy Spirit to you. (1 Thess. 4:3-8).

"Give honor to marriage and remain faithful to one another in marriage. God will surely judge people who are immoral and those who commit adultery" (Heb. 13:4).

_____ Starve flesh and feed spirit.

So, I say, let the Holy Spirit guide your lives. Then you won't be doing what your sinful nature craves. The sinful nature wants to do evil, which is just the opposite of what the Spirit wants. And the Spirit gives us desires that are the opposite of what the sinful nature desires. These two forces are constantly fighting each other, so you are not free to carry out your good intentions. But when you are directed by the Spirit, you are not under obligation to the law of Moses. When you follow the desires of your sinful nature, the results are very clear: sexual immorality, impurity, lustful pleasures, idolatry, sorcery, hostility, quarreling, jealousy, outbursts of anger, selfish ambition, dissension, division, envy, drunkenness, wild parties, and other sins like these. Let me tell you again, as I have before, that anyone living that sort of life will not inherit the Kingdom of God. But the Holy Spirit produces this kind of fruit in our lives: love, joy, peace, patience, kindness, goodness, faithfulness, gentleness, and self-control. There is no law against these things! Those who belong to Christ Jesus have nailed the passions and desires of their sinful nature to his cross and crucified them there. Since we are living by the Spirit, let us follow the Spirit's leading in every part of our lives" (Gal. 5:16-25).

_____ Choose to stay on Journey to Holiness and let God be Lord of your life.

"But if you refuse to serve the Lord, then choose today whom you will serve. Would you prefer the gods your ancestors served beyond the Euphrates? Or will it be the gods of the Amorites in whose land you now live? But as for me and my family, we will serve the Lord" (Josh. 24:15).

"Above all, you must live as citizens of heaven, conducting yourselves in a manner worthy of the Good News about Christ. Then, whether I come and see you again or only hear about you, I will know that you are standing together with one spirit and one purpose, fighting together for the faith, which is the Good News" (Phil. 1:27).

"My old self has been crucified with Christ. It is no longer I who live, but Christ lives in me. So, I live in this earthly body by trusting in the Son of God, who loved me and gave himself for me" (Gal. 2:20).

"Finally, dear brothers and sisters, we urge you in the name of the Lord Jesus to live in a way that pleases God, as we have taught you. You live this way already, and we encourage you to do so even more" (1 Thess. 4:1).

*(See Appendix, Teaching Note 4)

MEMORY VERSE:
"But now you must be Holy in everything you do, just as God who chose you is Holy." 1 Pet. 1:15

GROW DEEPER:
"Then, Christ will make His home in your hearts as you trust in Him. Your roots will GROW down into God's love and keep you strong" (Eph. 3:17).

Have you ever thought that there is more to this life? Have you ever felt that your life falls into a routine and then into a rut? Even as a follower of Jesus, you can fall into despair, and you can easily drift to sources outside of Him to try to ease your burden. In this section of the lesson, we are going to give you some more in-depth information, thought-provoking questions, and action steps to move into Holiness as God so designed! Strap on your seat belt and let's go!

THE FIRST STEP:
Jesus came to give a life filled with purpose, direction, and freedom from sin. Do you believe that it is true for your life? Lao Tzu said, "The journey of a thousand miles begins with one step." When it comes to believing that Jesus came to give you a life filled with purpose, direction, and freedom from sin, it starts with you taking the first step forward towards Him.

Action Step: Using (When, Where, Who) write your testimony of becoming a born-again believer in Jesus.

Action Steps:

- Seek out an accountability partner that will not be afraid to ask you tough questions and keep you accountable in the sexual purity realm.
- Ask a member of your church's leadership about accountability software that you can sign up for that will send emails to your accountability partners if you choose to view pornography on the internet.
- Lastly and most important, GROW your relationship with God. I know this sounds like a typical churchy answer, but I promise you that as your grow your roots deeper down into who Jesus is and your relationship with Him becomes stronger, the desire to sin will become less. I know this has been true in my life.

Additional Resources:

"The Purity Principle" by Randy Alcorn
"Humility – The Beauty of Holiness" by Andrew Murray
"I Kissed Dating Goodbye" by Joshua Harris
"The Unsupervised Man" by Frank Mazzapica
"The God I Never Knew: How Real Friendship with the Holy Spirit Can Change Your Life," by Robert Morris

Action Step: Pick one of the additional resources and complete it!

GROW III
God's Heartbeat
Lesson 2

DISCOVERING GOD'S HEARTBEAT:
FOR WORSHIP AND WORSHIPPING AS GOD LIKES

PURPOSE OF THIS LESSON:

To give a clear, Biblical understanding of how God wants to be worshipped through our praise and worship. Jesus said, "But the time is coming-indeed it's here now-when true worshipers will worship the Father in spirit and in truth. The Father is looking for those who will worship him that way. For God is Spirit, so those who worship him must worship in spirit and in truth" (John 4:23-24). In the former scripture Jesus tells us we must worship God in Spirit and Truth. He goes on to say the Father is looking for those who will worship Him in this manner. Paul gives us the keys of true worship as he reveals, "For the Lord is the Spirit, and wherever the Spirit of the Lord is, there is freedom" (2 Cor. 3:17). It is our worship in Christ that the Father desires and Paul goes on to say, "God himself has prepared us for this, and as a guarantee he has given us his Holy Spirit" (2 Cor. 5:5). "Don't you realize that your body is the temple of the Holy Spirit, who lives in you and was given to you by God? You do not belong to yourself, for God bought you with a high price. So, you must honor God with your body" (1 Cor. 6:19-20).

The Spirit of the Lord resides within us. He is our guarantee of salvation and joins with our spirit providing unity in the spirit as evidence we are in Christ and children of God. "For his Spirit joins with our spirit to affirm that we are God's children" (Rom.8:16). In Christ we worship the Father through unity in the Spirit. Jesus promised, "When the Spirit of truth comes, he will guide you into all truth. He will not speak on his own but will tell you what he has heard. He will tell you about the future" (John 16:13). Through the Holy Spirit, Who is the Spirit of Truth, guiding us into all truth and teaching us the deeper truths of the Word of God we grow spiritually and become more mature in Christ. As Holy Spirit exposes the lies and deception of the devil with every new truth from God's Word our mind is renew and our soul restored.

We begin to have the humble mind and heart of Christ as compassion for others breaks our hearts, pouring out mercy and grace from the Holy Spirit. It is in the Word of God we find the truth which not only sets us free but, allows us the properly worship the Father in spirit and truth. "So, Jesus was saying to those Jews who had believed Him, "If you continue in My word, then you are truly My disciples; 32 and you will know the truth, and the truth will set you free." (John 8:31-32). We often refer to verse thirty-two without thirty-one. Notice however verse thirty-two start with the word and. Which means there is a prerequisite to knowing the truth and being set free by the truth. Jesus said, we must remain in His Word to find the truth which will set us free. It is in that truth we can worship the Father in Christ (in the spirit), and truth. "And the Lord—who is the Spirit—makes us more and more like him as we are changed into his glorious image" (2 Cor. 3:18b.).

*(See Appendix, Teaching Note 1)

INTRODUCTION:

True praise and worship will be your natural and automatic response when you have an up-close and personal experience of God's Holiness demonstrated in your life. After you have a personal encounter with the Lord worship becomes your life. "When the people of Israel saw the mighty power that the Lord had unleashed against the Egyptians, they were filled with awe before him. They put their faith in the Lord and in his servant Moses" (Exod. 14:31). "Then Moses and the people of Israel sang this song to the Lord: "I will sing to the Lord, for he has triumphed gloriously; he has hurled both horse and rider into the sea. The Lord is my strength and my song; he has given me victory. This is my God, and I will praise him-my father's God, and I will exalt him! The Lord is a warrior; Yahweh is his name" (Exod. 15:1-3)!

"You are blessed because you believed that the Lord would do what he said." Mary responded, "Oh, how my soul praises the Lord. How my spirit rejoices in God my Savior! For he took notice of his lowly servant girl, and from now on all generations will call me blessed. For the Mighty One is holy, and he has done great things for me. He shows mercy from generation to generation to all who fear him. (Luke 1:45-50).

WHY THIS LESSON IS IMPORTANT TO YOUR LIFE?

You cannot "fully" know the will of God unless worship is an integral part of your life! "And so, dear brothers and sisters, I plead with you to give your bodies to God because of all he has done for you. Let them be a living and holy sacrifice-the kind he will find acceptable. This is truly the way to worship him. Don't copy the behavior and customs of this world, but let God transform you into a new person by changing the way you think. Then you will learn to know God's will for you, which is good and pleasing and perfect" (Rom. 12:1-2).

"Always be joyful. Never stop praying. Be thankful in all circumstances, for this is God's will for you who belong to Christ Jesus" (1 Thes. 5:16-18).

POWER TO WORSHIP GOD'S WAY:

Take a few moments to ponder the following questions.

- Did God have an original plan for worship that was in existence before Gen. 1?
- Who were His worship leaders, and what were their roles?
- Do those leaders and their roles exist today?
- Did God have a plan for worship in heaven, past, present, and future?
- Did God have a worship plan for earth, past, present, or future?
- Where does His church fit into this plan?

FOUR BASIC TRUTHS ABOUT WORSHIP:

1. Everything was created through Jesus and for Jesus.

    - "for through him God created everything in the heavenly realms and on earth. He made the things we can see and the things we can't see-such as thrones, kingdoms, rulers, and authorities in the unseen world. Everything was created through him and for him" (Col. 1:16).

2. Since God is enthroned in praise, Worship is the key to entering fully into God's presence. Praise releases God's glory bringing worshipers response through the Holy Spirit.

    - "Yet you are holy, enthroned on the praises of Israel "(Ps. 22:3).

3. We worship and glorify Father God in Christ, giving Thanks through Jesus and in His mighty name.

    - "Let the message about Christ, in all its richness, fill your lives. Teach and counsel each other with all the wisdom he gives. Sing psalms and hymns and spiritual songs to God with thankful hearts. And whatever you do or say, do it as a representative of the Lord Jesus, giving thanks through him to God the Father" (Col. 3:16-17).

4. Ministering faithfully is the key to worship in the Kingdom of God.

- "However, the Levitical priests of the family of Zadok continued to minister faithfully in the Temple when Israel abandoned me for idols. These men will serve as my ministers. They will stand in my presence and offer the fat and blood of the sacrifices, says the Sovereign Lord. They alone will enter my sanctuary and approach my table to serve me. They will fulfill all my requirements" (Ezek. 44:15-16).

What would you say are some hindrances to the true worship of the one and only God of all creation?

Take a few minutes to look up the following six verses.

- "You must not worship any of the gods of neighboring nations, for the Lord your God, who lives among you, is a jealous God. His anger will flare up against you, and he will wipe you from the face of the earth" (Deut. 6:14-15).

- "Many people did believe in him, however, including some of the Jewish leaders. But they wouldn't admit it for fear that the Pharisees would expel them from the synagogue. For they loved human praise more than the praise of God" (John 12:42-43).

- "Therefore, let us offer through Jesus a continual sacrifice of praise to God, proclaiming our allegiance to his name" (Heb. 13:15).

- "Come close to God, and God will come close to you. Wash your hands, you sinners; purify your hearts, for your loyalty is divided between God and the world" (James 4:8).

- "Jesus replied, "And why do you, by your traditions, violate the direct commandments of God? For instance, God says, 'Honor your father and mother,' and 'Anyone who speaks disrespectfully of father or mother must be put to death.' But you say it is all right for people to say to their parents, 'Sorry, I can't help you. For I have vowed to give to God what I would have given to you.' In this way, you say they don't need to honor their parents. And so you cancel the word of God for the sake of your own tradition. You hypocrites! Isaiah was right when he prophesied about you, for he wrote, 'These people honor me with their lips, but their hearts are far from me. Their worship is a farce, for they teach man-made ideas as commands from God" (Matthew 15:3-9).

- "Shout with the voice of a trumpet blast. Shout aloud! Don't be timid. Tell my people Israel of their sins! Yet they act so pious! They come to the Temple every day and seem delighted to learn all about me. They act like a righteous nation that would never abandon the laws of its God. They ask me to take action on their behalf, pretending they want to be near me. 'We have fasted before you!' they say. 'Why aren't you impressed? We have been very hard on ourselves, and you don't even notice it!' "I will tell you why!" I respond. "It's because you are fasting to please yourselves. Even while you fast, you keep oppressing your workers. What good is fasting when you keep on fighting and quarreling? This kind of fasting will never get you anywhere with me. You humble yourselves by going through the motions of penance, bowing your heads like reeds bending in the wind. You dress in burlap and cover yourselves with ashes. Is this what you call fasting? Do you really think this will please the Lord? "No, this is the kind of fasting I want: Free those who are wrongly imprisoned; lighten the burden of those who work

- for you. Let the oppressed go free and remove the chains that bind people. Share your food with the hungry and give shelter to the homeless. Give clothes to those who need them, and do not hide from relatives who need your help. "Then your salvation will come like the dawn, and your wounds will quickly heal. Your godliness will lead you forward, and the glory of the Lord will protect you from behind. Then when you call, the Lord will answer. 'Yes, I am here,' he will quickly reply. "Remove the heavy yoke of oppression. Stop pointing your finger and spreading vicious rumors! Feed the hungry and help those in trouble. Then your light will shine out from the darkness, and the darkness around you will be as bright as noon. The Lord will guide you continually, giving you water when you are dry and restoring your strength. You will be like a well-watered garden, like an ever-flowing spring. Some of you will rebuild the deserted ruins of your cities. Then you will be known as a rebuilder of walls and a restorer of homes. "Keep the Sabbath day holy. Don't pursue your own interests on that day but enjoy the Sabbath and speak of it with delight as the Lord's holy day. Honor the Sabbath in everything you do on that day, and don't follow your own desires or talk idly. Then the Lord will be your delight. I will give you great honor and satisfy you with the inheritance I promised to your ancestor Jacob. I, the Lord, have spoken" (Isa 58:1-14)!

Match the scriptures with the top six hindrances listed below:

TOP SIX HINDRANCES TO A LIFE OF WORSHIP:
Tradition, Substitution, Hedonism, Spectator, Pride, or Sin?

Now ask yourself which ones are keeping you from worshipping God with your whole heart?

Read the following scripture and answer this question,
"Does Jesus encourage radical worship?" _____

- "When he reached the place where the road started down the Mount of Olives, all of his followers began to shout and sing as they walked along, praising God for all the wonderful miracles they had seen. "Blessings on the King who comes in the name of the Lord! Peace in heaven, and glory in highest heaven!" But some of the Pharisees among the crowd said, "Teacher, rebuke your followers for saying things like that!" He replied, "If they kept quiet, the stones along the road would burst into cheers" (Luke 19:37-40)!

To enter into worship is to enter into spiritual warfare against an enemy attack. Read the following verse and answer the next two questions:

- "And whenever the tormenting spirit from God troubled Saul, David would play the harp. Then Saul would feel better, and the tormenting spirit would go away" (1 Sam. 16:23).

(1) What action was taken? _____

(2) What was the result? _____

SEVEN HEBREW MEANINGS FOR THE WORD PRAISE:

During class, we will look at seven different Hebrew words (weapons) with different meanings, yet all translated to "praise"! For now, look up each of these verses, circling the word "praise" in each verse.

1. Halel: (Strong's 1984), to rave, boast, celebrate, to become clamorously foolish.

- "Then I will thank you in front of the great assembly. I will praise you before all the people" (Ps. 35:18).

2. <u>Yadah</u>: (Strong's 3034), to acknowledge in public with an extended hand.

- "I give you thanks, O Lord, with all my heart; I will sing your praises before the gods" (Ps. 138:1).

3. <u>Barak</u>: (Strong's 1288), to bless by kneeling or bowing.

- "Let all that I am praise the Lord; with my whole heart, I will praise his holy name" (Ps. 103:1).

4. <u>Shabach</u>: (Strong's 7623), to address in a loud tone, to shout.

- "Your unfailing love is better than life itself; how I praise you! I will praise you as long as I live, lifting up my hands to you in prayer" (Ps. 63:3-4).

5. <u>Zamar</u>: (Strong's 2167), making music to God with strings.

- "It is good to give thanks to the Lord, to sing praises to the Most High" (Ps. 92:1).

- "Praise him with a blast of the ram's horn; praise him with the lyre and harp! Praise him with the tambourine and dancing; praise him with strings and flutes! 5 Praise him with a clash of cymbals; praise him with loud clanging cymbals" (Ps. 150:3-5).

6. <u>Towdah</u>: (Strong's 8426), to lift hands in adoration.

- "But giving thanks is a sacrifice that truly honors me. If you keep to my path, I will reveal to you the salvation of God" (Ps. 50:23 NKJV).

7. <u>Tehilah</u>: (Strong's 8416), exuberant singing.

- "I will praise the Lord at all times. I will constantly speak his praises" (Ps. 34:1).

***All seven Hebrew words are expressed or specifically used in the following scripture.

- "My heart is confident in you, O God; no wonder I can sing your praises with all my heart! Wake up, lyre and harp! I will wake the dawn with my song. I will thank you, LORD, among all the people. I will sing your praises among the nations" (Ps. 108:1-3).

WHAT IS WORSHIP? WHAT IS PRAISE?
- Worship is commitment, recognizing who God is and faithful obedience.
  - "O Lord my God, how great you are! You are robed with honor and majesty." (Ps. 104:1).
  - "Then David praised the Lord in the presence of the whole assembly: "O Lord, the God of our ancestor Israel, may you be praised forever and ever! Yours, O Lord, is the greatness, the power, the glory, the victory, and the majesty. Everything in the heavens and on earth is yours, O Lord, and this is your kingdom. We adore you as the one who is over all things. Wealth and honor come from you alone, for you rule over everything. Power and might are in your hand, and at your discretion people are made great and given strength. "O our God, we thank you and praise your glorious name! (1 Chron. 29:10-13).
- Worship is exalting God.
  - "Come, let us tell of the Lord's greatness; let us exalt his name together" (Ps. 34:3).
  - "Exalt the LORD our God! Bow low before his feet, for he is holy" (Ps. 99:5)!
- Worship honoring God.

- "After this time had passed, I, Nebuchadnezzar, looked up to heaven. My sanity returned, and I praised and worshiped the Most High and honored the one who lives forever. His rule is everlasting, and his kingdom is eternal. 35 All the people of the earth are nothing compared to him. He does as he pleases among the angels of heaven and among the people of the earth. No one can stop him or say to him, 'What do you mean by doing these things?' 36 "When my sanity returned to me, so did my honor and glory and kingdom. My advisers and nobles sought me out, and I was restored as head of my kingdom, with even greater honor than before. 37 "Now I, Nebuchadnezzar, praise and glorify and honor the King of heaven. All his acts are just and true, and he is able to humble the proud" (Dan.4:34-37).

- Worship is magnifying God.

- "Mary responded, "Oh, how my soul praises the Lord" (Luke 1:46).

- "For they heard them speaking in other tongues and praising God. Then Peter asked" (Acts 10:46).

- Worship is marveling at God.
- "When he comes on that day, he will receive glory from his holy people—praise from all who believe. And this includes you, for you believed what we told you about him" (2 Thess. 1:10).

- Worship is glorifying God.

- "Who will not fear you, Lord, and glorify your name? For you alone are holy. All nations will come and worship before you, for your righteous deeds have been revealed" (Rev. 15:4).

- "Honor the Lord, you heavenly beings; honor the Lord for his glory and strength" (Ps. 29:1).

- Praise is thankfulness, acknowledging God for all He has done for us.

- "The Lord is good and does what is right; he shows the proper path to those who go astray. 9 He leads the humble in doing right, teaching them his way. 10 The Lord leads with unfailing love and faithfulness all who keep his covenant and obey his demands" (Ps. 25:8-10).

- "O Lord, I will honor and praise your name, for you are my God. You do such wonderful things! You planned them long ago, and now you have accomplished them" Isa. 25:1).

LESSON SUMMARY:

- "For God is Spirit, so those who worship him must worship in spirit and in truth" (John 4:24).

- "And the Lord—who is the Spirit—makes us more and more like him as we are changed into his glorious image" (2 Cor. 3:18).

- "God himself has prepared us for this, and as a guarantee he has given us his Holy Spirit" (2 Cor. 5:5).

- "For his Spirit joins with our spirit to affirm that we are God's children" (Romans 8:16).

- "When the Spirit of truth comes, he will guide you into all truth. He will not speak on his own but will tell you what he has heard. He will tell you about the future" (John 16:13).

- "So, Jesus was saying to those Jews who had believed Him, "If you continue in My word, then you are truly My disciples; and you will know the truth, and the truth will set you free." (John 8:31-32).

*Note: Lesson Slides end at this point.

OBEDIENCE PRECEDES BLESSING:
We have looked at God's original plan for worship, some hindrances to worship, and the ways God likes to be worshipped. Now, what do I do? What are my next steps?

Read the following verses and use the following words to fill in the blanks: Thank, Include, Love, Worship, Offer, Worship.

_____ is the ONLY thing God does not already have.

- "I have no complaint about your sacrifices or the burnt offerings you constantly offer. But I do not need the bulls from your barns or the goats from your pens. For all the animals of the forest are mine, and I own the cattle on a thousand hills. I know every bird on the mountains, and all the animals of the field are mine. If I were hungry, I would not tell you, for all the world is mine and everything in it. Do I eat the meat of bulls? Do I drink the blood of goats? Make thankfulness your sacrifice to God and keep the vows you made to the Most High. Then call on me when you are in trouble, and I will rescue you, and you will give me glory" (Ps 50:8-15).

_____ Him with sincere appreciation and heart fully committed.

- "The eyes of the Lord search the whole earth in order to strengthen those whose hearts are fully committed to him. What a fool you have been! From now on you will be at war" (2 Chron. 16:9).

_____ Him the control of your life.

- "And so, dear brothers and sisters, I plead with you to give your bodies to God because of all he has done for you. Let them be a living and holy sacrifice—the kind he will find acceptable. This is truly the way to worship him "(Rom. 12:1).

_____ Him in your everyday life.

- "You must not worship any of the gods of neighboring nations, for the Lord your God, who lives among you, is a jealous God. His anger will flare up against you, and he will wipe you from the face of the earth "(Deut. 6:14-15).

_____ Him using HIS love language.

- "My heart is confident in you, O God; no wonder I can sing your praises with all my heart! 3 I will thank you, LORD, among all the people. I will sing your praises among the nations" (Ps 108:1,3).

_____ Him with your all.

- Jesus replied, "The most important commandment is this: 'Listen, O Israel! The Lord our God is the one and only Lord. And you must love the Lord your God with all your heart, all your soul, all your mind, and all your strength "(Mark 12:29-30).

Read the flowing verse and then give yourself a heart check by honestly asking and answering the following 3 questions, and would your answers be backed by the evidence of your life?

185

- "If you look for me wholeheartedly, you will find me" (Jer. 29:13).
  - What do I love the most? _____
  - What do I think about the most? _____
  - What do I do the most? _____

*(See Appendix, Teaching Notes 2 & 3)

MEMORY VERSE:
- "And so, dear brothers and sisters,[a] I plead with you to give your bodies to God because of all he has done for you. Let them be a living and holy sacrifice-the kind he will find acceptable. This is truly the way to worship him" (Rom. 12:1).

GROW DEEPER:
- "Then, Christ will make His home in your hearts as you trust in Him. Your roots will grow down into God's love and keep you strong" (Eph. 3:17).

Have you ever thought that there is more to this life? Have you ever felt that your life falls into a routine and then into a rut? Even as a follower of Jesus, you can fall into despair, and you can easily drift to sources outside of Him to try to ease your burden.

In this section of the lesson, we are going to give you some more in-depth information, thought-provoking questions, and ACTION STEPS to move into Worshiping God in His love language! Jump onboard the ship; we are setting sail!

How important is Worship to you? I understand that most of you reading this lesson are coming from various religious backgrounds or no religious background, but I hope by this time you see how important and vital worship is to a Christian's life. Maybe you're still thinking, "I don't get what the big deal is with worship, and I surely am not going to worship a way that makes me uncomfortable." I encourage you to read the following 71 verses from the Bible on praise and worship and then ask yourself, how significant are praise and worship?

WHY SHOULD YOU WORSHIP AND PRAISE GOD?
- God is enthroned on the praises of His people.
  - "Yet you are holy, enthroned on the praises of Israel" (Ps. 22:3).
- Nothing else can praise God quite like man.
  - "What will you gain if I die if I sink into the grave? Can my dust praise you? Can it tell of your faithfulness" (Ps. 30:9)?
  - "The dead cannot sing praises to the Lord, for they have gone into the silence of the grave. 18 But we can praise the Lord both now and forever! Praise the Lord" (Ps. 115:17-18)!
- Praise lifts up and rejoices in God's great deeds, both now and in the past.
  - "O Lord my God, you have performed many wonders for us. Your plans for us are too numerous to list. You have no equal. If I tried to recite all your wonderful deeds, I would never come to the end of them" (Ps. 40:5).

- "Sing a new song to the Lord, for he has done wonderful deeds. His right hand has won a mighty victory; his holy arm has shown his saving power" (Ps. 98:1)!

- "Your right hand, O Lord, is glorious in power. Your right hand, O Lord, smashes the enemy" (Exod. 15:6).

- Praise proclaims God's greatness and majesty to the world.

  - "Come and see what our God has done, what awesome miracles he performs for people! 6 He made a dry path through the Red Sea, and his people went across on foot. There we rejoiced in him. 7 For by his great power he rules forever. He watches every movement of the nation; let no rebel rise in defiance. Interlude 8 Let the whole world bless our God and loudly sing his praises" (Ps. 66:5-8).

- Praise releases God's blessing to you.

  - "May the nations praise you, O God. Yes, may all the nations praise you. 6 Then the earth will yield its harvests, and God, our God, will richly bless us. 7 Yes, God will bless us, and people all over the world will fear him" (Ps. 67:5-7).

- Praise releases God's power.

  - "Let the praises of God be in their mouths, and a sharp sword in their hands-7 to execute vengeance on the nations and punishment on the peoples, 8 to bind their kings with shackles and their leaders with iron chains, 9 to execute the judgment written against them. This is the glorious privilege of his faithful ones. Praise the Lord" (Ps. 149:6-9)!

  - "O our God, won't you stop them? We are powerless against this mighty army that is about to attack us. We do not know what to do, but we are looking to you for help." 22 At the very moment they began to sing and give praise, the Lord caused the armies of Ammon, Moab, and Mount Seir to start fighting among themselves" (2 Chron. 20:12, 22).

- God created man to praise Him.

  - "I have made Israel for myself, and they will someday honor me before the whole world" (Isa. 43:21).

  - "All praise to God, the Father of our Lord Jesus Christ, who has blessed us with every spiritual blessing in the heavenly realms because we are united with Christ. Even before he made the world, God loved us and chose us in Christ to be holy and without fault in his eyes. God decided in advance to adopt us into his own family by bringing us to himself through Jesus Christ. This is what he wanted to do, and it gave him great pleasure. So, we praise God for the glorious grace he has poured out on us who belong to his dear Son. He is so rich in kindness and grace that he purchased our freedom with the blood of his Son and forgave our sins. He has showered his kindness on us, along with all wisdom and understanding. God has now revealed to us his mysterious will regarding Christ-which is to fulfill his own good plan. And this is the plan: At the right time he will bring everything together under the authority of Christ-everything in heaven and on earth. Furthermore, because we are united with Christ, we have received an inheritance from God, for he chose us in advance, and he makes everything work out according to his plan. God's purpose was that we Jews who were the first to trust in Christ would bring praise and glory to God. And now you Gentiles have also heard the truth, the Good News that God saves you. And when you believed in Christ, he identified you as his own by giving you the Holy Spirit, whom he promised long ago. The Spirit is God's guarantee that he will give us the inheritance he promised and that he has purchased us to be his own people. He did this so we would praise and glorify him" (Eph. 1:3-14).

- You have been instructed to praise God.
  - "Don't be drunk with wine because that will ruin your life. Instead, be filled with the Holy Spirit, 19 singing psalms and hymns and spiritual songs among yourselves and making music to the Lord in your hearts. 20 And give thanks for everything to God the Father in the name of our Lord Jesus Christ" (Eph. 5:18-20).
  - "Praise the Lord! Let all that I am praise the Lord" (Ps. 146:1). "Enter his gates with thanksgiving; go into his courts with praise. Give thanks to him and praise his name" (Ps. 100:4).

- Praise is a sacrifice that pleases God.
  - "Therefore, let us offer through Jesus a continual sacrifice of praise to God, proclaiming our allegiance to his name. 16 And don't forget to do good and to share with those in need. These are the sacrifices that please God" (Heb. 13:15-16).
  - "Let them praise the Lord for his great love and for the wonderful things he has done for them. Let them offer sacrifices of thanksgiving and sing joyfully about his glorious acts" (Ps. 107:21-22).
  - "But the king replied to Araunah, "No, I insist on buying it, for I will not present burnt offerings to the Lord my God that have cost me nothing." So, David paid him fifty pieces of silver for the threshing floor and the oxen" (2 Sam. 24:24).

- It comes from your whole being, not just from your lips.
  - "And so, dear brothers and sisters, I plead with you to give your bodies to God because of all he has done for you. Let them be a living and holy sacrifice—the kind he will find acceptable. This is truly the way to worship him" (Rom. 12:1).

- God is worthy to receive your praise.
  - "And they sang a new song with these words: "You are worthy to take the scroll and break its seals and open it. For you were slaughtered, and your blood has ransomed people for God from every tribe and language and people and nation. And you have caused them to become a Kingdom of priests for our God. And they will reign on the earth." Then I looked again, and I heard the voices of thousands and millions of angels around the throne and of the living beings and the elders. And they sang in a mighty chorus: "Worthy is the Lamb who was slaughtered-to receive power and riches and wisdom and strength and honor and glory and blessing." And then I heard every creature in heaven and on earth and under the earth and in the sea. They sang: "Blessing and honor and glory and power belong to the one sitting on the throne and to the Lamb forever and ever." And the four living beings said, "Amen!" And the twenty-four elders fell down and worshiped the Lamb" (Rev. 5:9-14).

GOD'S WAY TO WORSHIP – TAKE A STEP OF FAITH:
When you were going through the seven different meanings of "praise", did you start feeling uncomfortable thinking of acting out each meaning? Does raising your hand, dancing, bowing, seem

silly, impossible, absolutely not going to happen? If any of these thoughts are going through your head, we encourage you to take an action step this, Lesson!

Action Step: In your worship time, start acting out each meaning of praise, and then when you're worshiping corporately at your church, step out in faith and block out everyone around you and act out each meaning of praise to God. I know from personal experience that when you step out in faith and worship God with his love language, you will experience a new depth of meaning in your relationship with Him.

Additional Resources:

Additional scriptures on praise & worship:
- "When the Spirit of truth comes, he will guide you into all truth. He will not speak on his own but will tell you what he has heard. He will tell you about the future. He will bring me glory by telling you whatever he receives from me. All that belongs to the Father is mine; this is why I said, 'The Spirit will tell you whatever he receives from me'" (John 16:13-15).

- "These people honor me with their lips, but their hearts are far from me. Their worship is a farce, for they teach man-made ideas as commands from God" (Matt. 15:8-9).

- "singing psalms and hymns and spiritual songs among yourselves and making music to the Lord in your hearts" (Eph. 5:19).

- "You Samaritans know very little about the one you worship, while we Jews know all about him, for salvation comes through the Jews" (John 4:22).

- "So, Paul, standing before the council, addressed them as follows: "Men of Athens, I notice that you are very religious in every way, for as I was walking along, I saw your many shrines. And one of your altars had this inscription on it: 'To an Unknown God.' This God, whom you worship without knowing, is the one I'm telling you about" (Acts 17:22-23).

- "Well then, what shall I do? I will pray in the spirit, and I will also pray in words I understand. I will sing in the spirit, and I will also sing in words I understand" (1 Cor. 14:15).

- "It was in the year King Uzziah died that I saw the Lord. He was sitting on a lofty throne, and the train of his robe filled the Temple. Attending him were mighty seraphim, each having six wings. With two wings they covered their faces, with two they covered their feet, and with two they flew. They were calling out to each other, "Holy, holy, holy is the Lord of Heaven's Armies! The whole earth is filled with his glory!" Their voices shook the Temple to its foundations, and the entire building was filled with smoke. Then I said, "It's all over! I am doomed, for I am a sinful man. I have filthy lips, and I live among a people with filthy lips. Yet I have seen the King, the Lord of Heaven's Armies" (Isa. 6:1-5).

- "In front of the throne was a shiny sea of glass, sparkling like crystal. In the center and around the throne were four living beings, each covered with eyes, front and back. The first of these living beings was like a lion; the second was like an ox; the third had a human face; and the fourth was like an eagle in flight. Each of these living beings had six wings, and their wings were covered all over with eyes, inside and out. Day after day and night after night they keep on saying, "Holy, holy, holy is the Lord God, the Almighty-the one who always was, who is, and who is still to come." Whenever the living beings give glory and honor and thanks to the one sitting on the throne (the one who lives forever and ever), the twenty-four elders fall down and worship the one sitting on the throne (the one who lives forever and ever). And they lay their crowns before the throne and say, "You are worthy, O Lord our God, to receive glory and honor and power. For you created all things, and they exist because you created what you pleased" (Rev. 4:6-11).

- "In my vision, the man brought me back to the entrance of the Temple. There I saw a stream flowing east from beneath the door of the Temple and passing to the right of the altar on its south side. The man brought me outside the wall through the north gateway and led me around to the eastern entrance. There I could see the water flowing out through the south side of the east gateway. Measuring as he went, he took me along the stream for 1,750 feet and then led me across. The water was up to my ankles. He measured off another 1,750 feet and led me across again. This time the water was up to my knees. After another 1,750 feet, it was up to my waist. Then he measured another 1,750 feet, and the river was too deep to walk across. It was deep enough to swim in, but too deep to walk through. He asked me, "Have you been watching, son of man?" Then he led me back along the riverbank. When I returned, I was surprised by the sight of many trees growing on both sides of the river. Then he said to me, "This river flows east through the desert into the valley of the Dead Sea. The waters of this stream will make the salty waters of the Dead Sea fresh and pure. There will be swarms of living things wherever the water of this river flows. Fish will abound in the Dead Sea, for its waters will become fresh. Life will flourish wherever this water flows. Fishermen will stand along the shores of the Dead Sea. All the way from En-gedi to En-eglaim, the shores will be covered with nets drying in the sun. Fish of every kind will fill the Dead Sea, just as they fill the Mediterranean. But the marshes and swamps will not be purified; they will still be salty. Fruit trees of all kinds will grow along both sides of the river. The leaves of these trees will never turn brown and fall, and there will always be fruit on their branches. There will be a new crop every month, for they are watered by the river flowing from the Temple. The fruit will be for food and the leaves for healing" (Ezek. 47:1-12).

- "I will praise you, Lord, with all my heart; I will tell of all the marvelous things you have done" (Ps. 9:1).

- "Come, let us sing to the Lord! Let us shout joyfully to the Rock of our salvation" (Ps. 95:1).

- "Come, let us worship and bow down. Let us kneel before the Lord our maker" (Ps. 95:6).

- "I will sing to the Lord as long as I live. I will praise my God to my last breath" (Ps. 104:33)!

- "Let the godly sing for joy to the Lord; it is fitting for the pure to praise him" (Ps. 33:1).

- "Praise him with the tambourine and dancing; praise him with strings and flutes" (Ps. 150:4)!

- "Praise his name with dancing, accompanied by tambourine and harp" (Ps. 149:3).

- "Lift your hands toward the sanctuary and praise the Lord" (Ps. 134:2).

- "Praise him with a blast of the ram's horn; praise him with the lyre and harp! Praise him with the tambourine and dancing; praise him with strings and flutes! Praise him with a clash of cymbals; praise him with loud clanging cymbals" (Ps. 150:3-5).

- "Shout to the Lord, all the earth; break out in praise and sing for joy! Sing your praise to the Lord with the harp, with the harp and melodious song, with trumpets and the sound of the ram's horn. Make a joyful symphony before the Lord, the King" (Ps 98:4-6)!

- "For I fully expect and hope that I will never be ashamed, but that I will continue to be bold for Christ, as I have been in the past. And I trust that my life will bring honor to Christ, whether I live or die" (Phil. 1:20).

- "for God bought you with a high price. So, you must honor God with your body" (1 Cor. 6:20).

- "singing psalms and hymns and spiritual songs among yourselves and making music to the Lord in your hearts. And give thanks for everything to God the Father in the name of our Lord Jesus Christ" (Eph. 5:19-20

- "Always be joyful. Never stop praying. Be thankful in all circumstances, for this is God's will for you who belong to Christ Jesus" (1 Thess. 5:16-18).

- "Let the message about Christ, in all its richness, fill your lives. Teach and counsel each other with all the wisdom he gives. Sing psalms and hymns and spiritual songs to God with thankful hearts. And whatever you do or say, do it as a representative of the Lord Jesus, giving thanks through him to God the Father" (Col. 3:16-17).

- "So, we praise God for the glorious grace he has poured out on us who belong to his dear Son" (Eph. 1:6).

- "God's purpose was that we Jews who were the first to trust in Christ would bring praise and glory to God" (Eph. 1:12).

- "The Spirit is God's guarantee that he will give us the inheritance he promised and that he has purchased us to be his own people. He did this so we would praise and glorify him" (Eph. 1:14).

- "Always be full of joy in the Lord. I say it again-rejoice" (Phil. 4:4)!

- "I praise God for what he has promised. I trust in God, so why should I be afraid? What can mere mortals do to me? I praise God for what he has promised; yes, I praise the Lord for what he has promised. I trust in God, so why should I be afraid? What can mere mortals do to me? I will fulfill my vows to you, O God, and will offer a sacrifice of thanks for your help" (Ps. 56:4, 10-12).

- "After consulting the people, the king appointed singers to walk ahead of the army, singing to the Lord and praising him for his holy splendor. This is what they sang: "Give thanks to the Lord; his faithful love endures forever!" At the very moment they began to sing and give praise, the Lord caused the armies of Ammon, Moab, and Mount Seir to start fighting among themselves" (2 Chron. 20:21-22).

191

- "Around midnight Paul and Silas were praying and singing hymns to God, and the other prisoners were listening. Suddenly, there was a massive earthquake, and the prison was shaken to its foundations. All the doors immediately flew open, and the chains of every prisoner fell off" (Acts 16:25-26)!

- "You are worthy, O Lord our God, to receive glory and honor and power. For you created all things, and they exist because you created what you pleased" (Rev. 4:11).

- "And they sang in a mighty chorus: "Worthy is the Lamb who was slaughtered-to receive power and riches and wisdom and strength and honor and glory and blessing" (Rev. 5:12).

- "And so, dear brothers and sisters, we can boldly enter heaven's Most Holy Place because of the blood of Jesus. By his death, Jesus opened a new and life-giving way through the curtain into the Most Holy Place. And since we have a great High Priest who rules over God's house, let us go right into the presence of God with sincere hearts fully trusting him. For our guilty consciences have been sprinkled with Christ's blood to make us clean, and our bodies have been washed with pure water" (Heb. 10:19-22).

- "He has made us a Kingdom of priests for God his Father. All glory and power to him forever and ever! Amen" (Rev. 1:6).

- "But you are not like that, for you are a chosen people. You are royal priests, a holy nation, God's very own possession. As a result, you can show others the goodness of God, for he called you out of the darkness into his wonderful light" (1 Pet. 2:9).

- "But the time is coming—indeed it's here now—when true worshipers will worship the Father in spirit and in truth. The Father is looking for those who will worship him that way. For God is Spirit, so those who worship him must worship in spirit and in truth" (John 4:23-24).

- "We love each other because he loved us first" (1 John 4:19).

- "But it was to us that God revealed these things by his Spirit. For his Spirit searches out everything and shows us God's deep secrets. No one can know a person's thoughts except that person's own spirit, and no one can know God's thoughts except God's own Spirit. And we have received God's Spirit (not the world's spirit), so we can know the wonderful things God has freely given us. When we tell you these things, we do not use words that come from human wisdom. Instead, we speak words given to us by the Spirit, using the Spirit's words to explain spiritual truths. But people who aren't spiritual can't receive these truths from God's Spirit. It all sounds foolish to them, and they can't understand it, for only those who are spiritual can understand what the Spirit means. Those who are spiritual can evaluate all things, but they themselves cannot be evaluated by others. For, who can know the Lord's thoughts? Who knows enough to teach him?" But we understand these things, for we have the mind of Christ" 1 Cor. 2:10-16).

GROW III
God's Heartbeat
Lesson 3

DISCOVERING GOD'S HEARTBEAT:
FOR SPIRITUAL AUTHORITY AND WARRING AS GOD DESIGNED

PURPOSE OF THIS LESSON:
To know the meaning of authority, its origin, what it is and what it isn't; God's heartbeat for His church to walk, war, and win the battles of life against you, your family, friends, and beyond! "Look, I have given you authority over all the power of the enemy, and you can walk among snakes and scorpions and crush them. Nothing will injure you" (Luke 10:19).

"And Jesus came up and spoke to them, saying, "All authority in heaven and on earth has been given to Me. Go, therefore, and make disciples of all the nations, baptizing them in the name of the Father and the Son and the Holy Spirit, teaching them to follow all that I commanded you; and behold, I am with you always, to the end of the age" (Matt. 28:18-20 NASB). "These signs will accompany those who have believed: in My name they will cast out demons, they will speak with new tongues; they will pick up serpents, and if they drink any deadly poison, it will not harm them; they will lay hands on the sick, and they will recover" (Mark 16:17-18 NASB).

*(See Appendix, Teaching Note 1)

INTRODUCTION:
What does Authority look like in the lives of His children and those that are not; what does it take for both to be lined up to receive God's blessing and for victory in spiritual warfare? "Look, today I am giving you the choice between a blessing and a curse! You will be blessed if you obey the commands of the Lord your God that I am giving you today. But you will be cursed if you reject the commands of the Lord your God and turn away from him and worship gods you have not known before" (Deut. 11:26-28).

"God gave Paul the power to perform unusual miracles. When handkerchiefs or aprons that had merely touched his skin were placed on sick people, they were healed of their diseases, and evil spirits were expelled. A group of Jews was traveling from town to town casting out evil spirits. They tried to use the name of the Lord Jesus in their incantation, saying, "I command you in the name of Jesus, whom Paul preaches, to come out!" Seven sons of Sceva, a leading priest, were doing this. But one time when they tried it, the evil spirit replied, "I know Jesus, and I know Paul, but who are you?" Then the man with the evil spirit leaped on them, overpowered them, and attacked them with such violence that they fled from the house, naked and battered" (Acts 19:11-16).

WHY THIS LESSON IS IMPORTANT TO YOUR LIFE?
Jesus delegated His authority to us in Christ. So, we can fulfill a purpose driven life. Led by the Holy Spirit to share the Gospel of salvation in Jesus Christ. You will live a defeated, sad, lonely, and purposeless life ruled by everyone and everything without God's designed and powerful authority leading you! "You should know this, Timothy, that in the last days there will be very difficult times. For people will love only themselves and their money. They will be boastful and proud, scoffing at God, disobedient to their parents, and ungrateful. They will consider nothing sacred. They will be

unloving and unforgiving; they will slander others and have no self-control. They will be cruel and hate what is good. They will betray their friends, be reckless, be puffed up with pride, and love pleasure rather than God. They will act religious, but they will reject the power that could make them godly. Stay away from people like that" (2 Tim. 3:1-5)!

"Remind the believers to submit to the government and its officers. They should be obedient, always ready to do what is good. They must not slander anyone and must avoid quarreling. Instead, they should be gentle and show true humility to everyone. Once we, too, were foolish and disobedient. We were misled and became slaves to many lusts and pleasures. Our lives were full of evil and envy, and we hated each other. But-When God our Savior revealed his kindness and love, he saved us, not because of the righteous things we had done, but because of his mercy. He washed away our sins, giving us a new birth and new life through the Holy Spirit" (Titus 3:1-5).

THE POWER OF SPIRITUAL AND DELEGATED AUTHORITY:

What first comes to mind when you hear the word "authority"? How would you define it to another person that had no idea what it meant?

Now take a few minutes to read these verses and answer the correlating question using the truth in the verse you read:

- When do we first see authority in the Bible?
  - "Then God said, "Let there be light," and there was light" (Gen. 1:3).

- When was authority first given to man?
  - "Then God blessed them and said, "Be fruitful and multiply. Fill the earth and govern it. Reign over the fish in the sea, the birds in the sky, and all the animals that scurry along the ground" (Gen. 1:28).

- Who has it now?
  - "Satan, who is the god of this world, has blinded the minds of those who don't believe. They are unable to see the glorious light of the Good News. They don't understand this message about the glory of Christ, who is the exact likeness of God" (2 Cor. 4:4).
  - "You used to live in sin, just like the rest of the world, obeying the devil—the commander of the powers in the unseen world. He is the spirit at work in the hearts of those who refuse to obey God" (Eph. 2:2).

Let's take a few minutes and think on different kinds of authority:

- Have you ever heard the term "delegated authority"? What do you think it is, and who would hold this authority?

- Have you ever heard of spiritual authority? What do you think it is, and who would hold this authority?

Some people say that delegated authority comes from man, and spiritual authority comes from God.

How would you answer the following question?

Does all authority (both delegated and spiritual) come from God?

Now read the following scriptures to see if your view lines up with scripture.

194

- "Jesus came and told his disciples, "I have been given all authority in heaven and on earth" (Matt. 28:18).
- "Everyone must submit to governing authorities. For all authority comes from God, and those in positions of authority have been placed there by God. So, anyone who rebels against authority is rebelling against what God has instituted, and they will be punished. For the authorities do not strike fear in people who are doing right, but in those who are doing wrong. Would you like to live without fear of the authorities? Do what is right, and they will honor you. The authorities are God's servants, sent for your good. But if you are doing wrong, of course you should be afraid, for they have the power to punish you. They are God's servants, sent for the very purpose of punishing those who do what is wrong. So, you must submit to them, not only to avoid punishment, but also to keep a clear conscience. Pay your taxes, too, for these same reasons. For government workers need to be paid. They are serving God in what they do" (Rom. 13:1-6).

Spend some time looking up the following verses and answer the correlating questions:

- Do you always have to obey delegated authority, in all situations?
- "Remind the believers to submit to the government and its officers. They should be obedient, always ready to do what is good" (Titus 3:1).
- "For the Lord's sake, submit to all human authority—whether the king as head of state, 14 or the officials he has appointed. For the king has sent them to punish those who do wrong and to honor those who do right. 15 It is God's will that your honorable lives should silence those ignorant people who make foolish accusations against you. 16 For you are free, yet you are God's slaves, so don't use your freedom as an excuse to do evil" (1 Pet. 2:13-16).

Do you always have to obey spiritual authority, in all situations?

- "But you will receive power when the Holy Spirit comes upon you. And you will be my witnesses, telling people about me everywhere-in Jerusalem, throughout Judea, in Samaria, and to the ends of the earth" (Acts 1:8).

Is there ever a time you don't have to obey authority?

- "Shadrach, Meshach, and Abednego replied, "O Nebuchadnezzar, we do not need to defend ourselves before you. If we are thrown into the blazing furnace, the God whom we serve is able to save us. He will rescue us from your power, Your Majesty. But even if he doesn't, we want to make it clear to you, Your Majesty, that we will never serve your gods or worship the gold statue you have set up" (Dan. 3:16-18).

- "But Peter and the apostles replied, "We must obey God rather than any human authority. 40 The others accepted his advice. They called in the apostles and had them flogged. Then they ordered them never again to speak in the name of Jesus, and they let them go" (Acts 5:29,40).

Is it possible to live as an overcomer free from Satan's authority?

- "Who then will condemn us? No one-for Christ Jesus died for us and was raised to life for us, and he is sitting in the place of honor at God's right hand, pleading for us. Can anything ever separate us from Christ's love? Does it mean he no longer loves us if we have trouble or calamity, or are persecuted, or hungry, or destitute, or in danger, or threatened with death? (As the Scriptures say, "For your sake we are killed every day; we are being slaughtered like sheep.") No, despite all these things, overwhelming victory is ours through Christ, who loved us. And I am convinced that nothing can ever separate us from God's love. Neither death nor life, neither angels nor demons, neither our fears for today nor our worries about tomorrow—not even the powers of hell can separate us from God's love. No power in the sky above or in the earth below—indeed, nothing in all creation will ever be able to separate us from the love of God that is revealed in Christ Jesus our Lord" (Rom. 8:34-39).

How important would you say the topic of authority is?

Would you say that authority is crucial to understanding, or is it not a big deal?

Once again, take a few minutes to go into God's Word to discover what God says first by answering the question and then reading the correlating verses to see if your view lines up with God's:

When should we begin to teach about the why and how of authority?

- "Listen, O Israel! The Lord is our God, the Lord alone. And you must love the Lord your God with all your heart, all your soul, and all your strength. And you must commit yourselves wholeheartedly to these commands that I am giving you today. Repeat them again and again to your children. Talk about them when you are at home and when you are on the road, when you are going to bed and when you are getting up. Tie them to your hands and wear them on your forehead as reminders. Write them on the doorposts of your house and on your gates" (Deut. 6:4-9).

- "Direct your children onto the right path, and when they are older, they will not leave it" (Prov. 22:6).

- "Children, obey your parents because you belong to the Lord, for this is the right thing to do. "Honor your father and mother." This is the first commandment with a promise: If you honor your father and mother, "things will go well for you, and you will have a long life on the earth." Fathers do not provoke your children to anger by the way you treat them. Rather, bring them up with the discipline and instruction that comes from the Lord" (Eph. 6:1-4).

Without being taught and living out authority, what would the world look like?

- "In those days Israel had no king; all the people did whatever seemed right in their own eyes" (Judges 21:25).

- "But realize this, that in the last days difficult times will come. For people will be lovers of self, lovers of money, boastful, arrogant, slanderers, disobedient to parents, ungrateful, unholy, unloving, irreconcilable, malicious gossips, without self-control, brutal, haters of good, treacherous, reckless, conceited, lovers of pleasure rather than lovers of God, holding to a form of godliness although they have denied its power; avoid such people as these" (2 Tim. 3:1-5 NASB).

- "Remind them to be subject to rulers, to authorities, to be obedient, to be ready for every good deed, to slander no one, not to be contentious, to be gentle, showing every consideration for all people. For we too were once foolish, disobedient, deceived, enslaved to various lusts and pleasures, spending our life in malice and envy, hateful, hating one another. But when the kindness of God our Savior and His love for mankind appeared, He saved us, not on the basis of deeds which we did in righteousness, but in accordance with His mercy, by the washing of regeneration and renewing by the Holy Spirit" (Titus 3:1-5 NASB)

*SERVANT LEADER/UPENDED PYRAMID:

(Luke 22:25-26, John 13:12-13)

*(See Appendix, Teaching Note 2)

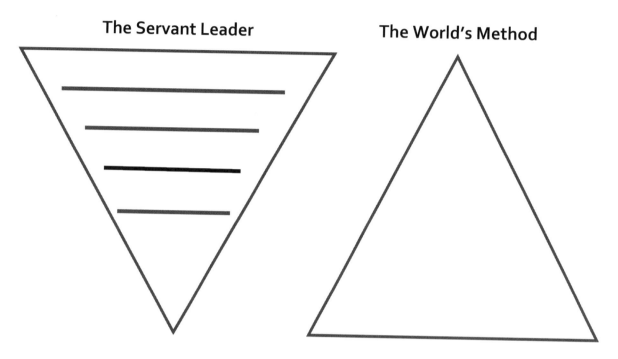

You must first learn to submit yourself to both delegated and spiritual authority before you can operate in the fullness of your God-given authority.

Jesus gave us an example of being a servant leader in Luke 22:25-26 and John 13:12-13.

- "Jesus told them, "In this world the kings and great men lord it over their people, yet they are called 'friends of the people.' But among you it will be different. Those who are the greatest among you should take the lowest rank, and the leader should be like a servant" (Luke 22:25-26).
- "After washing their feet, he put on his robe again and sat down and asked, "Do you understand what I was doing? You call me 'Teacher' and 'Lord,' and you are right, because that's what I am" (John 13:12-13).

When we learn to walk, war, and win as Jesus did, the truth of Acts 17:6 will be said of us, and our world will be a different place!!!!

- "Not finding them there, they dragged out Jason and some of the other believers instead and took them before the city council. "Paul and Silas have caused trouble all over the world," they shouted, "and now they are here disturbing our city, too" (Acts 17:6).

BE DIFFERENT, SO YOU CAN LIVE DIFFERENT SO THAT YOU CAN MAKE A DIFFERENCE!

*(See Appendix, Teaching Note 3)

LESSON SUMMARY:

- "Look, I have given you authority over all the power of the enemy, and you can walk among snakes and scorpions and crush them. Nothing will injure you" (Luke 10:19).
- "And Jesus came up and spoke to them, saying, "All authority in heaven and on earth has been given to Me. Go, therefore, and make disciples of all the nations, baptizing them in the name of the Father and the Son and the Holy Spirit, teaching them to follow all that I commanded you; and behold, I am with you always, to the end of the age" (Matt. 28:18-20 NASB).
- "These signs will accompany those who have believed: in My name they will cast out demons, they will speak with new tongues; they will pick up serpents, and if they drink any deadly poison, it will not harm them; they will lay hands on the sick, and they will recover" (Mark 16:17-18 NASB).

*Note: Lesson Slides end at this point.

OBEDIENCE PRECEDES BLESSING:

Sometimes we want to jump right to the end of a book to find out what happens, eat dessert before dinner, get an "A" on a test without studying, and win the game without practicing. The list of short cuts we all are tempted to take can go on and on. It doesn't take long, though, to realize that shortcuts don't get us where we want to go, and they cause us more harm than we thought, and the price was higher than we wanted to pay. It is true in having authority as well. We usually want to lead our own lives and not be told what and how to do something. Yet, scripture teaches us what life teaches us.

What do you think are the two steps to possessing, giving and walking in authority?

Read the following scriptures, then list the two steps.

- "Children, obey your parents because you belong to the Lord, for this is the right thing to do. "Honor your father and mother." This is the first commandment with a promise: If you honor your father and mother, "things will go well for you, and you will have a long life on the earth" (Eph. 6:1-3).

- "You must teach these things and encourage the believers to do them. You have the authority to correct them when necessary, so don't let anyone disregard what you say" (Titus 2:15).

- "When you obey my commandments, you remain in my love, just as I obey my Father's commandments and remain in his love. I have told you these things so that you will be filled with my joy. Yes, your joy will overflow" (John 15:10-11)!

1. _____
2. _____

God has a plan for us to begin to walk, war, and win the spiritual battles of life.

Read the following four verses: Can you identify the four steps in His plan? Please list them.

- "And this is the way to have eternal life—to know you, the only true God, and Jesus Christ, the one you sent to earth" (John 17:3).

- "So, I say, let the Holy Spirit guide your lives. Then you won't be doing what your sinful nature craves. The sinful nature wants to do evil, which is just the opposite of what the Spirit wants. And the Spirit gives us desires that are the opposite of what the sinful nature desires. These two forces are constantly fighting each other, so you are not free to carry out your good intentions" (Gal. 5:16-17).

- "For we are God's masterpiece. He has created us anew in Christ Jesus, so we can do the good things he planned for us long ago" (Eph. 2:10).

- "For even the Son of Man came not to be served but to serve others and to give his life as a ransom for many" (Mark 10:45).

1. _____
2. _____
3. _____
4. _____

We have looked at what authority is, its importance, and its rewards! You might be asking yourself what exactly I have spiritual authority over. It is time to match ourselves up with seven areas of authority so you can overcome the enemy of both God and man. Are you ready?
Read the following scriptures and draw a line to the word that matches with the Word of God.

- "Therefore, go and make disciples of all the nations, baptizing them in the name of the Father and the Son and the Holy Spirit. Teach these new disciples to obey all the commands I have given you. And be sure of this: I am with you always, even to the end of the age" (Matt. 28:19-20).
- "But you will receive power when the Holy Spirit comes upon you. And you will be my witnesses, telling people about me everywhere—in Jerusalem, throughout Judea, in Samaria, and to the ends of the earth" (Acts 1:8).
- "to open their eyes, so they may turn from darkness to light and from the power of Satan to God. Then they will receive forgiveness for their sins and be given a place among God's people, who are set apart by faith in me" (Acts 26:18).
- "One day Jesus called together his twelve disciples and gave them power and authority to cast out all demons and to heal all diseases" (Luke 9:1).
- "Look, I have given you authority over all the power of the enemy, and you can walk among snakes and scorpions and crush them. Nothing will injure you" (Luke 10:19).
- "Amazement gripped the audience, and they began to discuss what had happened. "What sort of new teaching is this?" they asked excitedly. "It has such authority! Even evil spirits obey his orders" (Mark 1:27)!
- "So, humble yourselves before God. Resist the devil, and he will flee from you" (James, 4:7).
- "But you belong to God, my dear children. You have already won a victory over those people because the Spirit who lives in you is greater than the spirit who lives in the world" (1 John 4:4).

- "We destroy every proud obstacle that keeps people from knowing God. We capture their rebellious thoughts and teach them to obey Christ" (2 Cor. 10:5).
- "By his divine power, God has given us everything we need for living a godly life. We have received all of this by coming to know him, the one who called us to himself by means of his marvelous glory and excellence. And because of his glory and excellence, he has given us great and precious promises. These are the promises that enable you to share his divine nature and escape the world's corruption caused by human desires. In view of all this, make every effort to respond to God's promises. Supplement your faith with a generous provision of moral excellence, and moral excellence with knowledge, and knowledge with self-control, and self-control with patient endurance, and patient endurance with godliness, and godliness with brotherly affection, and brotherly affection with love for everyone. The more you grow like this, the more productive and useful you will be in your knowledge of our Lord Jesus Christ" (2 Pet. 1:3-8).

1. Matt. 28:19-20, Acts 1:8, Acts 26:18	Sickness
2. Luke 9:1	Evil spirits
3. Luke 10:19	Souls of men
4. Mark 1:27	Your actions
5. Jas, 4:7, 1 John 4:4	Your thoughts
6. 2 Cor. 10:5	demonic oppression
7. 2 Pet. 1:3-8	devil

MEMORY VERSE:
- "We destroy every proud obstacle that keeps people from knowing God. We capture their rebellious thoughts and teach them to obey Christ" (2 Cor. 10:5).

GROW DEEPER:
- "Then, Christ will make His home in your hearts as you trust in Him. Your roots will GROW down into God's love and keep you strong" (Eph. 3:17).

How have your thoughts on authority changed since going through this lesson? Do you see the importance and vital role that authority plays in the life of a believer? Do you realize now that God has given us authority, so no one must live in sin and condemnation? In this Grow Deeper section, we will explore how King David, through submitting to his authority, King Saul, was able to prosper. This will allow us to see that when we trust in God's plans that we cannot go wrong! So, let's put on a humble spirit, like King David, and explore authority in more depth.

KING SAUL VS. KING DAVID:
King Saul was God's anointed ruler for the kingdom of Israel, but due to his disobedience, God chose to replace him with a man after His own heart, King David. David had to go on the run to keep from being killed by Saul, but throughout this time, he put his trust in the Lord. We are going to look at two instances where David put his trust in the Lord and respected the authority God placed on Saul's life.

1. "After Saul returned from fighting the Philistines, he was told that David had gone into the wilderness of En-gedi. 2 So Saul chose 3,000 elite troops from all Israel and went to search for David and his men near the rocks of the wild goats. 3 At the place where the road passes some sheepfolds, Saul went into a cave to relieve himself. But as it happened, David and his men were hiding farther back in that very cave! 4 "Now's your opportunity!" David's men whispered to him.

"Today the Lord is telling you, 'I will certainly put your enemy into your power, to do with as you wish.'" So David crept forward and cut off a piece of the hem of Saul's robe. 5 But then David's conscience began bothering him because he had cut Saul's robe. 6 He said to his men, "The Lord forbid that I should do this to my lord the king. I shouldn't attack the Lord's anointed one, for the Lord himself has chosen him." 7 So David restrained his men and did not let them kill Saul. After Saul had left the cave and gone on his way" (1 Sam. 24:1-7),

2. "Who will volunteer to go in there with me?" David asked Ahimelech the Hittite and Abishai son of Zeruiah, Joab's brother. "I'll go with you," Abishai replied. 7 So David and Abishai went right into Saul's camp and found him asleep, with his spear stuck in the ground beside his head. Abner and the soldiers were lying asleep around him. 8 "God has surely handed your enemy over to you this time!" Abishai whispered to David. "Let me pin him to the ground with one thrust of the spear; I won't need to strike twice!" 9 "No!" David said. "Don't kill him. For who can remain innocent after attacking the Lord's anointed one? 10 Surely the Lord will strike Saul down someday, or he will die of old age or in battle. 11 The Lord forbid that I should kill the one he has anointed! But take his spear and that jug of water beside his head, and then let's get out of here!" 12 So David took the spear and jug of water that were near Saul's head. Then he and Abishai got away without anyone seeing them or even waking up, because the Lord had put Saul's men into a deep sleep" (1 Sam. 26:6-12).

As you are reading these two instances, do you sit there thinking, "come on, kill Saul and take your place on the throne!" How easy it would have been for David to take the life of Saul, God delivered Saul into his hands, but he realized that to kill Saul would be disobeying the principle of authority that God established since the beginning of time. Is there an authority in your life right now that you want to be rebellious toward? I encourage you to take a lesson from King David and put your trust in God. Let Him deal with the authority over your life if they are defying Him.

Action Step: Starting today, submit yourself to your authority and perform the best you can for them, whether they are the spiritual or delegated authority.

Additional Resources:
1. "Under Cover" by John Bevere
2. "The Serving Leader" by John Stahl-Wert & Ken Jennings

Action Step: Purchase at least one of these books and make a commitment to read it this year.

GROW III
God's Heartbeat
Lesson 4

DISCOVERING GOD'S HEARTBEAT:
FOR THE SPOKEN WORD AND WIELDING THE SWORD AS JESUS MODELED

PURPOSE OF THIS LESSON:

To know, understand, and walk out the Biblical truth that EVERY word you speak, and your words do affect you now, tomorrow, and all eternity. "Some people make cutting remarks, but the words of the wise bring healing" (Prov. 12:18). "Let no corrupt communication proceed out of your mouth, but that which is good to the use of edifying, that it may minister grace unto the hearers. And grieve not the holy Spirit of God, whereby ye are sealed unto the day of redemption" Eph. 4:29-30 NKJV "But I tell you that for every [useless]careless word that people speak, they will give an account of it on the day of judgment"(Matt. 12:36 NASB).
*(See Appendix, Teaching Note 1)

INTRODUCTION:

The Bible teaches us how your words mirror your belief system and how they affect your life's direction as well as others you are connected to.

"This was their report to Moses: "We entered the land you sent us to explore, and it is indeed a bountiful country—a land flowing with milk and honey. Here is the kind of fruit it produces. 28 But the people living there are powerful, and their towns are large and fortified. We even saw giants there, the descendants of Anak! 29 The Amalekites live in the Negev, and the Hittites, Jebusites, and Amorites live in the hill country. The Canaanites live along the coast of the Mediterranean Sea and along the Jordan Valley." 30 But Caleb tried to quiet the people as they stood before Moses. "Let's go at once to take the land," he said. "We can certainly conquer it!" 31 But the other men who had explored the land with him disagreed. "We can't go up against them! They are stronger than we are!" 32 So they spread this bad report about the land among the Israelites: "The land we traveled through and explored will devour anyone who goes to live there. All the people we saw were huge. 33 We even saw giants [Nephilim] there, the descendants of Anak. Next to them we felt like grasshoppers, and that's what they thought, too" (Numbers 13:27-33)!

"Then the whole community began weeping aloud, and they cried all night. 2 Their voices rose in a great chorus of protest against Moses and Aaron. "If only we had died in Egypt, or even here in the wilderness!" they complained. 3 "Why is the Lord taking us to this country only to have us die in battle? Our wives and our little ones will be carried off as plunder! Wouldn't it be better for us to return to Egypt?" 4 Then they plotted among themselves, "Let's choose a new leader and go back to Egypt!" 5 Then Moses and Aaron fell face down on the ground before the whole community of Israel. 6 Two of the men who had explored the land, Joshua son of Nun and Caleb son of Jephunneh, tore their clothing. 7 They said to all the people of Israel, "The land we traveled through and explored is a wonderful land! 8 And if the Lord is pleased with us, he will bring us safely into that land and give it to us. It is a rich land flowing with milk and honey. 9 Do not rebel against the Lord, and don't be afraid of the people of the land. They are only helpless prey to us! They have no protection, but the Lord is with us! Don't be afraid of them!" (Numbers 14:1-9).

WHY THIS LESSON IS IMPORTANT TO YOUR LIFE?

Your life can be marked by success, prosperity, health, and power if you get control over your spoken words. "Study this Book of Instruction continually. Meditate on it day and night so you will be sure to obey everything written in it. Only then will you prosper and succeed in all you do" (Josh. 1:8). "Indeed, we all make many mistakes. For if we could control our tongues, we would be perfect and could also control ourselves in every other way" (James 3:2).

THE POWER TO SPEAK LIFE AND THUS CHANGE THE COURSE OF YOUR LIFE:

Is the old saying, "sticks and stone may break your bones, but names never hurt you!" true or false? I am sure that you have heard this saying during your childhood and parents or peers use it to show that we should not worry what is said to us, but what most people do not realize is that the words we use can either bring life or death not only to ourselves but to others. "The tongue can bring death or life; those who love to talk will reap the consequences" (Prov. 18:21) Reflect on the times in your own life when the words spoken to you have either built you up or torn you down.

If words can have such an impact on our lives and the lives of those around us, then what words should mostly come from our mouths? "And now, dear brothers and sisters, one final thing. Fix your thoughts on what is true, and honorable, and right, and pure, and lovely, and admirable. Think about things that are excellent and worthy of praise" (Phil. 4:8). Meditate on how we should be speaking. As you are meditating on these eight areas, read the following verse. "Timely advice is lovely, like golden apples in a silver basket" (Prov 25:11).

What do you think God is saying about the timing of our words?

Now that we know what types of words we should be speaking and that we need to use the right words at the right time, let's look at how we do this. What does the word "encourage" mean to you? I encourage you to look up the definition and decide what it means to you in your own life. We will be talking more in-depth about this word and its significance.

The Bible mentions five main areas in which we all need encouragement. Read the following verses and match up the verse with the areas in which people need encouragement.

- "So, encourage each other with these words" (1 Thes. 4:18).
- "So, encourage each other and build each other up, just as you are already doing" (1 Thes. 5:11).
- "When he arrived and saw this evidence of God's blessing, he was filled with joy, and he encouraged the believers to stay true to the Lord" (Acts 11:23).
- "Such things were written in the Scriptures long ago to teach us. And the Scriptures give us hope and encouragement as we wait patiently for God's promises to be fulfilled" (Romans 15:4).
- "Then Judas and Silas, both being prophets, spoke at length to the believers, encouraging and strengthening their faith" (Acts 15:32).

  1. True to God   1 Thess. 4:18
  2. God's Word   1 Thess. 5:11
  3. Judgment   Acts 11:23
  4. Death   Romans 15:4
  5. Have Hope   Acts 15:32

BASEBALL DIAGRAM FOR SPEAKING LIFE:

*(See Appendix, Teaching Note 2)

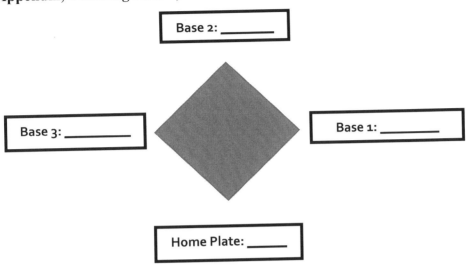

Some people brighten a room when they enter it; others when they leave. Which one are you?

SIX TIPS TO SPEAKING LIFE INTO OTHERS:
1. Don't be shy with encouraging words.
2. Send a gift, handwritten note.
3. Celebrate their victories.
4. Remind fellow Christians of God's promises.
5. Be specific with your praise.
6. Be with others (TIME) and add light.

Action Step: Pick one of these six tips and apply them this upcoming week.

LESSON SUMMARY:
- "Don't copy the behavior and customs of this world, but let God transform you into a new person by changing the way you think. Then you will learn to know God's will for you, which is good and pleasing and perfect" (Rom. 12:2).
- "and be renewed in the spirit of your mind, and that you put on the new man which was created according to God, in true righteousness and holiness" Eph. 4:23-24 NKJV
- "Put on salvation as your helmet, and take the sword of the Spirit, which is the word of God" (Eph. 6:17).
- "For the word of God is alive and powerful. It is sharper than the sharpest two-edged sword, cutting between soul and spirit, between joint and marrow. It exposes our innermost thoughts and desires" (Heb. 4:12).

*Note: Lesson Slides end at this point.

OBEDIENCE PRECEDES BLESSING:

Up to this point, we have seen how scripture tells us that our words are important and what kind of words we should be speaking. We have also looked at the importance of encouraging each other and what areas to focus on. Now let's look at some steps to living an encouraging life and being an encouragement to others. Read EACH verse and then fill in the blank using one of the following words: **Eternity, Throne, Good, Negativity, Faith, Hope, Prepare, Build, Bad, Guard**

- Avoid _____ in yourself and others.

  o "Oh, the joys of those who do not follow the advice of the wicked, or stand around with sinners, or join in with mockers. 2 But they delight in the law of the Lord, meditating on it day and night. 3 They are like trees planted along the riverbank, bearing fruit each season. Their leaves never wither, and they prosper in all they do" (Ps. 1:1-3).

  o "Walk with the wise and become wise; associate with fools and get in trouble" (Prov. 13:20).

  o "This kind of talk spreads like cancer, as in the case of Hymenaeus and Philetus" (2 Tim. 2:17).

  o "If people are causing divisions among you, give a first and second warning. After that, have nothing more to do with them" (Titus 3:10).

- _____ ahead of time.

  o "A good person produces good things from the treasury of a good heart, and an evil person produces evil things from the treasury of an evil heart. What you say flows from what is in your heart" (Luke 6:45).

  o Keep _____ always in your sights.

  o "Think about the things of heaven, not the things of earth" (Col 3:2).

- _____ your heart.

  o "Watch out! Don't let your hearts be dulled by carousing and drunkenness, and by the worries of this life. Don't let that day catch you unaware" (Luke 21:34).

- _____ your faith.

  o "But you, dear friends, must build each other up in your most holy faith, pray in the power of the Holy Spirit" (Jude 1:20).

- Maintain _____.

  o "Why am I discouraged? Why is my heart so sad? I will put my hope in God! I will praise him again-my Savior and my God" (Ps. 42:11)!

- Go to God's _____.

  o "So then, since we have a great High Priest who has entered heaven, Jesus the Son of God, let us hold firmly to what we believe. 15 This High Priest of ours understands our weaknesses, for he faced all of the same testings we do, yet he did not sin. 16 So let us come boldly to the throne of our gracious God. There we will receive his mercy, and we will find grace to help us when we need it most" (Heb. 4:14-16).

- Speak _____ over your circumstance.

○ "Then he said to me, "Speak a prophetic message to these bones and say, 'Dry bones, listen to the word of the Lord! Then he said to me, "Speak a prophetic message to the winds, son of man. Speak a prophetic message and say, 'This is what the Sovereign Lord says: Come, O breath, from the four winds! Breathe into these dead bodies so they may live again" (Ezek. 37:4,9).

▪ Encourage the _____ before you reprove the _____.

○ "I know all the things you do. I have seen your hard work and your patient endurance. I know you don't tolerate evil people. You have examined the claims of those who say they are apostles but are not. You have discovered they are liars. 3 You have patiently suffered for me without quitting. 4 "But I have this complaint against you. You don't love me or each other as you did at first" (Rev. 2:2-4)!

○ "I know that you live in the city where Satan has his throne, yet you have remained loyal to me. You refused to deny me even when Antipas, my faithful witness, was martyred among you there in Satan's city. 14 "But I have a few complaints against you. You tolerate some among you whose teaching is like that of Balaam, who showed Balak how to trip up the people of Israel. He taught them to sin by eating food offered to idols and by committing sexual sin" (Rev. 2:13-14).

○ "I know all the things you do. I have seen your love, your faith, your service, and your patient endurance. And I can see your constant improvement in all these things. 20 "But I have this complaint against you. You are permitting that woman—that Jezebel who calls herself a prophet— to lead my servants astray. She teaches them to commit sexual sin and to eat food offered to idols" (Rev. 2:19-20).

*(See Appendix, Teaching Note 3)

MEMORY VERSE:
"And I tell you this, you must give an account on judgment day for every idle word you speak" (Matt. 12:36).

GROW DEEPER:
"Then Christ will make his home in your hearts as you trust in him. Your roots will grow down into God's love and keep you strong" (Eph.3:17).

Wow, oh wow, what an amazing lesson we have had thus far on the power of the spoken Word of God! What an honor it is that we can speak life into other people and see them blossom into the man or woman God has called them to be! At this point, we want to give you some additional information and action steps that will help you speak life into yourself, your family, and everyone else you meet! So just like in our baseball diagram, let's start contacting the balls of life (our spoken words) and speed along the different bases so we can have a fulfilled life and bless others.

COMMUNICATION SKILLS:
Everyone we meet, whether they are spouses, family, friends, or strangers, will go through these four levels and four barriers of communication.
FOUR LEVELS OF COMMUNICATION:
1. Surface Communication - A nod of the head, a smile, asking how someone is doing but not expecting a response.
2. General Information - How's the weather doing, how's your day going, etc.

3. Deep Feelings - Feelings might not always be right, but they are real. We cannot ignore how someone feels, but we can understand and try to help them. Try saying, "this is how I feel" because no one can argue with how you feel, but they can argue with a "statement."
4. Deep Needs - This is where true progress and encouragement takes place. This is the place where we can help each other move beyond our hurts and start working together to walk out our Christian faith.

FOUR BARRIERS TO COMMUNICATION:
1. Withdrawal - We refuse to address how we feel out of fear, anger, personality, passive-aggressiveness, hate of conflict. Complete shutdown.
2. Escalation - We let our temper get the better of us, and after a certain point, we do not even want to resolve the conversation.
3. Belittling - At this point, we do not want to raise ourselves out of the pit we dug, so we bring the other person down lower than us. Hurting people hurt people.
4. False Belief - This is where we are starting to let Satan put lies in our heads about other people, which will hold us back from having meaningful communication.

Action Step: Reflect over these four levels and four barriers to communication and start looking at how you can apply this to your relationships.

Additional Resources:
"Tongue: A Creative Force" by Charles Capps
"How to Win Friends & Influence People" by Dale Carnegie
"How to have Confidence and Power in Dealing with People" by Les Giblin
"How I raised myself from Failure to Success in Selling" by Frank Bettger
"The 5 Love Languages" by Gary Chapman
"Personality Plus" by Florence Littauer

Action Step: Commit to purchase and read all these books in a year.

DISCOVERING GOD'S HEARTBEAT:
BEING HIS WITNESSES - WAKING UP TO THE BIGGER PICTURE

PURPOSE OF THIS LESSON:
To realize that all the people in the world are on death row without Jesus and you have the power to give them a permanent stay of execution by choosing to make sharing the Gospel a priority in your life.

"For "Everyone who calls on the name of the Lord will be saved." But how can they call on him to save them unless they believe in him? And how can they believe in him if they have never heard about him? And how can they hear about him unless someone tells them? And how will anyone go and tell them without being sent? That is why the Scriptures say, "How beautiful are the feet of messengers who bring good news" (Rom. 10:13-15)!

"Again, he said, "Peace be with you. As the Father has sent me, so I am sending you" (John 20:21). "And then he told them, "Go into all the world and preach the Good News to everyone" (Mark 16:15).

*(See Appendix, Teaching Note 1)

INTRODUCTION:
What does sharing the Gospel of Jesus Christ look like, and how much of the Bible am I responsible to know? "Study this Book of Instruction continually. Meditate on it day and night so you will be sure to obey everything written in it. Only then will you prosper and succeed in all you do" (Josh. 1:8).

"Now someone may argue, "Some people have faith; others have good deeds." But I say, "How can you show me your faith if you don't have good deeds? I will show you my faith by my good deeds" (James 2:18).

"And they overcame him by the blood of the Lamb and by the word of their testimony, and they did not love their lives to the death" (Rev. 12:11 NKJV).

"So, for the second time they called in the man who had been blind and told him, "God should get the glory for this, because we know this man Jesus is a sinner." "I don't know whether he is a sinner," the man replied. "But I know this: I was blind, and now I can see!" "But what did he do?" they asked. "How did he heal you?" "Look!" the man exclaimed. "I told you once. Didn't you listen? Why do you want to hear it again? Do you want to become his disciples, too" (John 9:24-27)?

WHY THIS LESSON IS IMPORTANT TO YOUR LIFE?
Being a part of the witnessing to ALL nations is the only thing you will ever do that leaves an eternal legacy both in heaven and on earth at the same time. "And all of this is a gift from God,

who brought us back to himself through Christ. And God has given us this task of reconciling people to him. For God was in Christ, reconciling the world to himself, no longer counting people's sins against them. And he gave us this wonderful message of reconciliation. So, we are Christ's ambassadors; God is making his appeal through us. We speak for Christ when we plead, "Come back to God" (2 Cor. 5:18-20)!

POWER AND PURPOSE TO CHANGE THE WORLD FOR ALL ETERNITY:
To discover what your purpose is, we must go back and discover Jesus' purpose.

"The Spirit of the Lord is upon me, for he has anointed me to bring Good News to the poor. He has sent me to proclaim that captives will be released, that the blind will see, that the oppressed will be set free, and that the time of the Lord's favor has come" (Luke 4:18-19). What was Jesus anointed to do while here on earth?

What is a Christian's purpose? According to "For God knew his people in advance, and he chose them to become like his Son, so that his Son would be the firstborn among many brothers and sisters" (Rom. 8:29). and "But you will receive power when the Holy Spirit comes upon you. And you will be my witnesses, telling people about me everywhere—in Jerusalem, throughout Judea, in Samaria, and to the ends of the earth" (Acts 1:8).

What are two basic ways can we witness the Kingdom of God?
Read the following scriptures and answer the former question.

"Listen! A farmer went out to plant some seeds. As he scattered them across his field, some seeds fell on a footpath, and the birds came and ate them. Other seeds fell on shallow soil with underlying rock. The seeds sprouted quickly because the soil was shallow. But the plants soon wilted under the hot sun, and since they didn't have deep roots, they died. Other seeds fell among thorns that grew up and choked out the tender plants. Still other seeds fell on fertile soil, and they produced a crop that was thirty, sixty, and even a hundred times as much as had been planted! Anyone with ears to hear should listen and understand" (Matt. 13:3-9).

"Now listen to the explanation of the parable about the farmer planting seeds: The seed that fell on the footpath represents those who hear the message about the Kingdom and don't understand it. Then the evil one comes and snatches away the seed that was planted in their hearts. The seed on the rocky soil represents those who hear the message and immediately receive it with joy. But since they don't have deep roots, they don't last long. They fall away as soon as they have problems or are persecuted for believing God's word. The seed that fell among the thorns represents those who hear God's word, but all too quickly the message is crowded out by the worries of this life and the lure of wealth, so no fruit is produced. The seed that fell on good soil represents those who truly hear and understand God's word and produce a harvest of thirty, sixty, or even a hundred times as much as had been planted" (Matt. 13:18-23)!

"Jesus called out to them, "Come, follow me, and I will show you how to fish for people" (Matt. 4:19)!

"And whatever you do, do it heartily, as to the Lord and not to men" (Col. 2:23 NKJV), "You did not choose Me, but I chose you and appointed you that you should go and bear fruit, and that your fruit should remain, that whatever you ask the Father in My name He may give you. These things I command you, that you love one another" (John 15:16-17 NKJV).

"Greater love has no one than this, than to lay down one's life for his friends" (John 15:13 NKJV). "In his grace, God has given us different gifts for doing certain things well. So, if God has given you the ability to prophesy, speak out with as much faith as God has given you. If your gift is serving others, serve them well. If you are a teacher, teach well" (Rom. 12:6-7).

"If your gift is to encourage others, be encouraging. If it is giving, give generously. If God has given you leadership ability, take the responsibility seriously. And if you have a gift for showing kindness to others, do it gladly. Don't just pretend to love others. Really love them. Hate what is wrong. Hold tightly to what is good. Love each other with genuine affection and take delight in honoring each other. Never be lazy but work hard and serve the Lord enthusiastically. Rejoice in our confident hope. Be patient in trouble and keep on praying. When God's people are in need, be ready to help them. Always be eager to practice hospitality. Bless those who persecute you. Don't curse them; pray that God will bless them. Be happy with those who are happy, and weep with those who weep. Live in harmony with each other. Don't be too proud to enjoy the company of ordinary people. And don't think you know it all" (Rom. 12:8-16 NLT)!

1. _____
2. _____

*(See Appendix, Teaching Note 2)

When in relationships with others, communication is so very crucial.
Are we saying what we mean, and are they hearing what we are saying? Now think about your relationships and ask yourself what type of listener you are now, and do you want to grow in this area to the next level. Not all relationships are at the same level of intimacy.

Place the following 4 words next to the correct definition:
Communion, Commitment, Conversational, and Confidence.
_____, (general exchange of info: weather, family, job)
_____, (fears, joys, feelings)
_____, (weaknesses, personal struggles)
_____, (confessions, all in no matter what)

Since the beginning of time, there has been a misconception as to how to differentiate between religion and Christianity. What do you think the difference is?

Is everyone called to witness by sharing the Gospel of Jesus Christ?
"Jesus called out to them, "Come, follow me, and I will show you how to fish for people" (Matt. 4:19)! "Jesus came and told his disciples, "I have been given all authority in heaven and on earth. Therefore, go and make disciples of all the nations, baptizing them in the name of the Father and the Son and the Holy Spirit. Teach these new disciples to obey all the commands I have given you. And be sure of this: I am with you always, even to the end of the age" (Matt. 28:18-20). If we are called to witness, then the question must be asked, is there only one way in which to accomplish this? How do we witness?

How would you rate the church in their on-purpose activity to be His witnesses?
Poor_____Fair _____Good _____Excellent_____

If you had to list the top two reasons Christians don't evangelize, what would you say?

*(See Appendix, Teaching Note 3)
*(See Appendix, Teaching Note 4)

Do you think there is a difference between the gift of evangelism and evangelizing?

"Are we all apostles? Are we all prophets? Are we all teachers? Do we all have the power to do miracles? Do we all have the gift of healing? Do we all have the ability to speak in unknown languages? Do we all have the ability to interpret unknown languages? Of course, not" (1 Cor. 12:29-30)! "Now these are the gifts Christ gave to the church: the apostles, the prophets, the evangelists, and the pastors and teachers" (Eph. 4:11).

Three essential ingredients one must possess to effectively witness of the Gospel of Jesus Christ?
Read the following verses and answer the question: What are three essential ingredients?

"Either way, Christ's love controls us. Since we believe that Christ died for all, we also believe that we have all died to our old life" (2 Cor. 5:14).

"But you shall receive power when the Holy Spirit has come upon you; and you shall be witnesses to Me in Jerusalem, and in all Judea and Samaria, and to the end of the earth" (Acts 1:8 NKJV).

"Don't be afraid of those who want to kill your body; they cannot touch your soul. Fear only God, who can destroy both soul and body in hell" (Matt. 10:28).

"Because we understand our fearful responsibility to the Lord, we work hard to persuade others. God knows we are sincere, and I hope you know this, too" (2 Cor. 5:11).

What are the four tools one must use when sharing the Gospel?
Read each verse and then use one of the following four words to fill in each blank.

Pray, Authenticity, Testimony, Word

1. Personal _____.

- "We proclaim to you what we ourselves have actually seen and heard so that you may have fellowship with us. And our fellowship is with the Father and with his Son, Jesus Christ. We are writing these things so that you may fully share our joy" (1 John 1:3-4).

- "And they have defeated him by the blood of the Lamb and by their testimony. And they did not love their lives so much that they were afraid to die" (Rev. 12:11).

2. The _____ of God.

- "All Scripture is inspired by God and is useful to teach us what is true and to make us realize what is wrong in our lives. It corrects us when we are wrong and teaches us to do what is right" (2 Tim. 3:16).

- "It is the same with my word. I send it out, and it always produces fruit. It will accomplish all I want it to, and it will prosper everywhere I send it" (Isa. 55:11).

3. _____ in words and actions.

- "Your love for one another will prove to the world that you are my disciples" (John 13:35).

- "When you produce much fruit, you are my true disciples. This brings great glory to my Father" (John 15:8).

- "Instead, you must worship Christ as Lord of your life. And if someone asks about your hope as a believer, always be ready to explain it. But do this in a gentle and respectful way. Keep your conscience clear. Then if people speak against you, they will be ashamed when they see what a good life you live because you belong to Christ" (1 Pet. 3:15-16).

4. _____ for the lost.

- "And pray for me, too. Ask God to give me the right words so I can boldly explain God's mysterious plan that the Good News is for Jews and Gentiles alike. I am in chains now, still preaching this message as God's ambassador. So, pray that I will keep on speaking boldly for him, as I should" (Eph. 6:19-20).

LESSON SUMMARY:

- "Instead, you must worship Christ as Lord of your life. And if someone asks about your hope as a believer, always be ready to explain it. But do this in a gentle and respectful way. Keep your conscience clear. Then if people speak against you, they will be ashamed when they see what a good life you live because you belong to Christ" (1 Pet. 3:15-16).

- "Your love for one another will prove to the world that you are my disciples" (John 13:35).

- When you produce much fruit, you are my true disciples. This brings great glory to my Father" (John 15:8).

- "Jesus came and told his disciples, "I have been given all authority in heaven and on earth. Therefore, go and make disciples of all the nations, baptizing them in the name of the Father and the Son and the Holy Spirit. Teach these new disciples to obey all the commands I have given you. And be sure of this: I am with you always, even to the end of the age" (Matt. 28:19-20).

*Note: Lesson Slides end at this point.

OBEDIENCE PROCEEDS BLESSING:
What do you believe, and what actions are you taking to prove it?
Read each verse and fill in the blank with the following words:

Involved, Have, Loves, Go, Wants, Send

1. God_____ ALL people.

- "For this is how God loved the world: He gave his one and only Son, so that everyone who believes in him will not perish but have eternal life" (John 3:16).

2. God _____ ALL people to become born again.

- "The Lord isn't really being slow about his promise, as some people think. No, he is being patient for your sake. He does not want anyone to be destroyed but wants everyone to repent" (2 Pet. 3:9).

3. God wants us to be _____ in missions both locally and worldwide.

- "but you will receive power when the Holy Spirit has come upon you; and you shall be My witnesses both in Jerusalem and in all Judea, and Samaria, and as far as the remotest part of the earth" (Acts 1:8 NASB).

4. God calls some to _____ and some to _____

- "One day as these men were worshiping the Lord and fasting, the Holy Spirit said, "Appoint Barnabas and Saul for the special work to which I have called them." So, after more fasting and prayer, the men laid their hands on them and sent them on their way" (Acts 13:2-3).

- "As you know, you Philippians were the only ones who gave me financial help when I first brought you the Good News and then traveled on from Macedonia. No other church did this. Even when I was in Thessalonica you sent help more than once. I don't say this because I want a gift from you. Rather, I want you to receive a reward for your kindness. At the moment I have all I need—and more! I am generously supplied with the gifts you sent me with Epaphroditus. They are a sweet-smelling sacrifice that is acceptable and pleasing to God. And this same God who takes care of me will supply all your needs from his glorious riches, which have been given to us in Christ Jesus" (Phil. 4:15-19).

5. God only asks us to do according to what we _____

- "If someone has enough money to live well and sees a brother or sister in need but shows no compassion—how can God's love be in that person? Dear children, let's not merely say that we love each other; let us show the truth by our actions" (1 John 3:17-18).

- "But someone who does not know, and then does something wrong, will be punished only lightly. When someone has been given much, much will be required in return; and when someone has been entrusted with much, even more will be required" (Luke 12:48).

MEMORY VERSE:
"Jesus called out to them, "Come, follow me, and I will show you how to fish for people" (Matt. 4:19)

*(See Appendix, Teaching Note 4)

GROW DEEPER:
"Jesus called out to them, "Come, follow me, and I will show you how to fish for people" (Eph. 3:17)!

What an amazing lesson on the power of sharing the gospel and the difference it can make in people's lives. Have you caught the bigger picture for sharing the gospel locally and worldwide?

Do you feel a tug on your heart to go on a mission trip outside your country? In this section, we are going to see how much our world is hurting and in need of the good news that saves!

GOD'S VIEW:
Have you ever stopped and asked God to show you how He views the lost? The Bible depicts exactly how He views the lost, and as we are becoming more like the image of His son Jesus, we need to ask God to change how we view the lost. Let look at three viewpoints of how God views the lost.

1. God does not want anyone to perish.

- "The Lord isn't really being slow about his promise, as some people think. No, he is being patient for your sake. He does not want anyone to be destroyed but wants everyone to repent" (2 Pet. 3:9).

- How well does seeing people die without knowing Jesus sit with you?

- If God was patient with us, should we not be patient and show love to the people around us until they come to repentance?

2. God loves each person on His Earth and has a purpose for them.

- "Look! I stand at the door and knock. If you hear my voice and open the door, I will come in, and we will share a meal together as friends" (Rev. 3:20).

- Some churches teach that only special people can be saved, but as we can see from scripture, God's perfect will is that every person hears the gospel and responds to His saving grace through Jesus.

3. God is Just, and Hell is the final destination for the lost.

- "Not at all! And you will perish, too, unless you repent of your sins and turn to God. And what about the eighteen people who died when the tower in Siloam fell on them? Were they the worst sinners in Jerusalem? No, and I tell you again that unless you repent, you will perish, too" (Luke 13:3-5).

- "The time came when the beggar died, and the angels carried him to Abraham's side. The rich man also died and was buried. In Hades, where he was in torment, he looked up and saw Abraham far away, with Lazarus by his side. So, he called to him, 'Father Abraham, have pity on me and send Lazarus to dip the tip of his finger in water and cool my tongue because I am in agony in this fire'" (Luke 16:22-24).

- We serve a Creator who is just in all His ways and cannot accept sin into Heaven. Do you realize that Hell is a real place, and through your obedience of sharing the gospel, lost souls can be saved from this horrible place?

THE REAL TRUTH:
We are about to look at some shocking statistics that are going to blow your mind. As you are reading over these, stop and ask yourself how can I help change this? Then go back to the meat of this lesson and do something! Our world will not change unless we start taking action today!
- There are 4.8 billion people without Christ on earth.
- Estimates are that 2.2 billion people know the Lord. In the United States, it may be more common for people to attend church and hear the gospel, but in many other nations, it is unheard of to have access to Bibles and gospel preaching.

- If you stood the 4.8 billion lost people in line, that line would stretch thirty-six times around the circumference of the earth. This would equate to driving around the world, at 60 mph, for 2 years seeing a dead person lined up shoulder to shoulder.
- There are still many unreached people groups. In these groups, 66,000 people who have never heard the gospel die every day.
- In 2006, 250,000 people died in a tsunami. In four days', time, the 66,000 that die daily in the unreached people groups is the equivalent of the loss experienced from the tsunami.
- Brazil has 67 tribes that have never been contacted by the modern world; they have only been seen from helicopters.
- Seventy percent of Asians have never heard the name of Jesus.
- Saudi Arabia, North Korea, Iran, and other nations prohibit the conversion of Muslims.
- The 10/40 Window is a region that presents special challenges. It has the most illiteracy and most languages. It includes 95 percent of the un-evangelized peoples of the world, and it is home to two out of every three people on earth. Of the 400 megacities on earth, 300 of them are in the 10/40 Window.
- There are three main religions in the world after Christianity.
- Islam: 1.5 billion followers
- Hinduism: 1 billion followers
- Buddhism: 350 million followers

GROW III
God's Heartbeat
Lesson 6

DISCOVERING GOD'S HEARTBEAT:
FOR THE HOLY SPIRIT AND WADING IN FOR A POWER

PURPOSE OF THIS LESSON:
To know and understand the importance of depending on the Holy Spirit when sharing the Gospel of Jesus Christ.

"And now I will send the Holy Spirit, just as my Father promised. But stay here in the city until the Holy Spirit comes and fills you with power from heaven" (Luke 24:49).

"But you will receive power when the Holy Spirit comes upon you. And you will be my witnesses, telling people about me everywhere—in Jerusalem, throughout Judea, in Samaria, and to the ends of the earth" (Acts 1:8).

"And they overcame him by the blood of the Lamb and by the word of their testimony, and they did not love their lives to the death" (Rev. 12:11 NKJV).

*(See Appendix, Teaching Note 1)

INTRODUCTION:
There is a difference between witnessing something you have heard about verses someone you have experienced.

"Then Peter, filled with the Holy Spirit, said to them, "Rulers and elders of our people, are we being questioned today because we've done a good deed for a crippled man? Do you want to know how he was healed? Let me clearly state to all of you and to all the people of Israel that he was healed by the powerful name of Jesus Christ the Nazarene, the man you crucified but whom God raised from the dead. For Jesus is the one referred to in the Scriptures, where it says, 'The stone that you builders rejected has now become the cornerstone.' There is salvation in no one else! God has given no other name under heaven by which we must be saved." The members of the council were amazed when they saw the boldness of Peter and John, for they could see that they were ordinary men with no special training in the Scriptures. They also recognized them as men who had been with Jesus" (Acts 4:8-13).

"A group of Jews was traveling from town to town casting out evil spirits. They tried to use the name of the Lord Jesus in their incantation, saying, "I command you in the name of Jesus, whom Paul preaches, to come out!" Seven sons of Sceva, a leading priest, were doing this. But one time when they tried it, the evil spirit replied, "I know Jesus, and I know Paul, but who are you?" Then the man with the evil spirit leaped on them, overpowered them, and attacked them with such violence that they fled from the house, naked and battered" (Acts 19:13-16).

WHY THIS LESSON IS IMPORTANT TO YOUR LIFE?

Walking in the knowledge and power of the Holy Spirit will exchange your fear for boldness and you will become fruitful, advancing the Kingdom of God, one person at a time.

"God raised Jesus from the dead, and we are all witnesses of this. Now he is exalted to the place of highest honor in heaven, at God's right hand. And the Father, as he had promised, gave him the Holy Spirit to pour out upon us, just as you see and hear today" (Acts 2:32-33). "Those who believed what Peter said were baptized and added to the church that day—about 3,000 in all" (Acts 2:41).

"After this prayer, the meeting place shook, and they were all filled with the Holy Spirit. Then they preached the word of God with boldness" (Acts 4:31).

POWER AND PRINCIPALS FOR COMMUNICATING THE GOSPEL EFFECTIVELY:
Make a list of the Behaviors of a Christian:
What would be some of the things you would put on the list?

Let me get you started: Pray, read Bible, tithe, how many you can list?
Now take a few minutes to prioritize your list with the most important at the top and so forth.
*(See Appendix, Teaching Note 2)

Why do Christians (by their actions) put "evangelism" at the bottom (if at all) on the list?"
Where do you think it would be on God's list?

"Now these are the gifts Christ gave to the church: the apostles, the prophets, the evangelists, and the pastors and teachers. Their responsibility is to equip God's people to do his work and build up the church, the body of Christ. This will continue until we all come to such unity in our faith and knowledge of God's Son that we will be mature in the Lord, measuring up to the full and complete standard of Christ" (Eph. 4:11-13).

"Yet preaching the Good News is not something I can boast about. I am compelled by God to do it. How terrible for me if I didn't preach the Good News! If I were doing this on my own initiative, I would deserve payment. But I have no choice, for God has given me this sacred trust" (1 Cor. 9:16-17).

"So, I am eager to come to you in Rome, too, to preach the Good News. For I am not ashamed of this Good News about Christ. It is the power of God at work, saving everyone who believes—the Jew first and also the Gentile. This Good News tells us how God makes us right in his sight. This is accomplished from start to finish by faith. As the Scriptures say, "It is through faith that a righteous person has life" (Rom. 1:15-17).

How would you define evangelist?
Do you think anyone can be an evangelist at any given moment?

"The Spirit of the Lord is upon me, for he has anointed me to bring Good News to the poor. He has sent me to proclaim that captives will be released, that the blind will see, that the oppressed will be set free, and that the time of the Lord's favor has come" (Luke 4:18-19).

If writing a job description for an evangelist, what would you put as the top two essential components?

1. _____

2. _____

Four truths about the Holy Spirit's role in evangelism.
Read each verse, then using the five words listed below, fill in the blanks that state Activated, Draw, Hopeless, Lift, Act

1. Apart from the power of the Holy Spirit, your evangelism is. ——————

2. The Holy Spirit must be _____ in your life.

- "And when they had prayed, the place where they were assembled together was shaken; and they were all filled with the Holy Spirit, and they spoke the word of God with boldness" (Acts 4:31).

3. The Holy Spirit must also _____ in those you are sharing the Gospel of Jesus.

- "For no one can come to me unless the Father who sent me draws them to me, and at the last day I will raise them up" (John 6:44).

4. The Holy Spirit will _____men when you _____ up the Name of Jesus.

- "And when I am lifted up from the earth, I will draw everyone to myself" (John 12:32).

Have you ever asked yourself, why do some people accept Jesus into their life and others do not? What is keeping them from receiving His love and abundant life? Have you ever wondered why you hesitated to receive the love and forgiveness of Jesus Christ?

Three hindrances that keep the Holy Spirit from working in a person's life.
Read each verse and fill in the blank with the word from below. Can you relate to one or all of these?   Approval, Darkness, Unbelief, God

1. Love the _____rather than light.

- "And the judgment is based on this fact: God's light came into the world, but people loved the darkness more than the light, for their actions were evil" (John 3:19).

2. _____ in the Word of God.

- "The Spirit alone gives eternal life. Human effort accomplishes nothing. And the very words I have spoken to you are spirit and life. But some of you do not believe me." (For Jesus knew from the beginning which ones didn't believe, and he knew who would betray him.)" (John 6:63-64a.).

3. Love the _____ of man more than the approval of _____

- "Many people did believe in him, however, including some of the Jewish leaders. But they wouldn't admit it for fear that the Pharisees would expel them from the synagogue. For they loved human praise more than the praise of God" (John 12:42-43).

LESSON SUMMARY:

- "The Spirit of the Lord is upon me, for he has anointed me to bring Good News to the poor. He has sent me to proclaim that captives will be released, that the blind will see, that the oppressed will be set free, and that the time of the Lord's favor has come" (Luke 4:18-19).

- "But you will receive power when the Holy Spirit comes upon you. And you will be my witnesses, telling people about me everywhere – in Jerusalem, throughout Judea, in Samaria, and to the ends of the earth" (Acts 1:8).

- "The Spirit alone gives eternal life. Human effort accomplishes nothing. And the very words I have spoken to you are spirit and life" (John 6:63).

- "And they overcame him by the blood of the Lamb and by the word of their testimony, and they did not love their lives to the death" (Rev. 12:11 NKJV).

*Note: Lesson Slides end at this point.

OBEDIENCE PRECEDES BLESSING:

Once again, we get to the challenging part of each lesson. How do we take the abstract of truths and move them into the concrete of our daily lives? You must activate the Holy Spirit in your life. What does that even look like?

Read each scripture, then choose one of the following from to fill in the blank:
Empowered, Discern, Expecting, Open, Sent, Receive, Filled

1. _____ the Holy Spirit.

    - "But you shall receive power when the Holy Spirit has come upon you; and you shall be witnesses to Me in Jerusalem, and in all Judea and Samaria, and to the end of the earth" (Acts 1:8 NKJV).

2. Be _____ with the Holy Spirit.

    - "Then Jesus, full of the Holy Spirit, returned from the Jordan River. He was led by the Spirit in the wilderness" (Luke 4:1).

3. Be _____ by the Holy Spirit.

    - "Then Jesus returned to Galilee, filled with the Holy Spirit's power. Reports about him spread quickly through the whole region" (Luke 4:14).

4. Be _____ out in the Holy Spirit.

    - "Not at all! And you will perish, too, unless you repent of your sins and turn to God. And what about the eighteen people who died when the tower in Siloam fell on them? Were they the worst sinners in Jerusalem" (Acts 13:3-4)?

5. _____ by the Holy Spirit.

- "I planted the seed in your hearts, and Apollos watered it, but it was God who made it grow. 7 It's not important who does the planting, or who does the watering. What's important is that God makes the seed grow. 8 The one who plants and the one who waters work together with the same purpose. And both will be rewarded for their own hard work. 9 For we are both God's workers. And you are God's field. You are God's building" (1 Cor.3:6-9).

- Planting

- Watering

- Harvesting

- Keep doors _____ by the Holy Spirit.

  "And the believers were filled with joy and with the Holy Spirit" (Acts 13:52).

  "The same thing happened in Iconium. Paul and Barnabas went to the Jewish synagogue and preached with such power that a great number of both Jews and Greeks became believers" (Acts 14:1).

6. Be _____ in the Holy Spirit.

- "Those who believed what Peter said were baptized and added to the church that day—about 3,000 in all. 47 all the while praising God and enjoying the goodwill of all the people. And each day the Lord added to their fellowship those who were being saved" (Acts 2:41,47).

- "But many of the people who heard their message believed it, so the number of men who believed now totaled about 5,000" (Acts 4:4).

- "Yet more and more people believed and were brought to the Lord—crowds of both men and women" (Acts 5:14).

- "The church then had peace throughout Judea, Galilee, and Samaria, and it became stronger as the believers lived in the fear of the Lord. And with the encouragement of the Holy Spirit, it also grew in numbers" (Acts 9:31).

  We have discussed many aspects of the Holy Spirit's role in witnessing.
  How can you secure the Holy Spirit in your life? Remember salvation is free, but blessing is conditional.

Read the following verses and choose the best word to fill in the blanks. Action, Prayer, Devotion

- _____ "And pray for me, too. Ask God to give me the right words so I can boldly explain God's mysterious plan that the Good News is for Jews and Gentiles alike" (Eph. 6:19).

- _____ "All the believers devoted themselves to the apostles' teaching, and to fellowship, and to sharing in meals (including the Lord's Supper), and to prayer. 46 They worshiped together at the Temple each day, met in homes for the Lord's Supper, and shared their meals with great joy and generosity— 47 all the while praising God and enjoying the goodwill of all the people. And each day the Lord added to their fellowship those who were being saved" (Acts 2:42, 46, 47).

- "Jesus traveled through all the towns and villages of that area, teaching in the synagogues and announcing the Good News about the Kingdom. And he healed every kind of disease and illness. 36 When he saw the crowds, he had compassion on them because they were confused and helpless, like sheep without a shepherd. 37 He said to his disciples, "The harvest is great, but the workers are few. 38 So pray to the Lord who is in charge of the harvest; ask him to send more workers into his fields" (Matt. 9:35-38).

- "Therefore, go and make disciples of all the nations, baptizing them in the name of the Father and the Son and the Holy Spirit. 20 Teach these new disciples to obey all the commands I have given you. And be sure of this: I am with you always, even to the end of the age" (Matt. 28:19-20).

Become familiar with the following "tools" that assist you in becoming the best witness for Jesus you can be.

*(See Appendix, Teaching Note 3 & 4)

1. Introduction and questions
2. Your 3-point testimony (short on point BC, when Jesus saved you, new Life in Christ).
3. Doorhanger
4. Ministries brochure

MEMORY VERSE:
"but you will receive power when the Holy Spirit has come upon you; and you shall be My witnesses both in Jerusalem and in all Judea, and Samaria, and as far as the remotest part of the earth" (Acts 1:8 NASB).

GROW DEEPER:
"By God's grace and mighty power, I have been given the privilege of serving him by spreading this Good News" (Eph. 3:17).

Do you realize now the power we as a believer can and have received from the Holy Spirit? We are not alone on this journey to become more Christ-like and to share the gospel to a hurting and dying world!

Read the following book for more information on just how amazing and powerful the Holy Spirit is in your life. **The God I Never Knew**: How Real Friendship with the Holy Spirit Can Change Your Life, by Robert Morris.

Practice sharing your testimony with a family member or friend.

Practice asking the introduction and diagnostic questions: Hello, my name is _____ with _____ Church in _____.

Suggestions:
We just came by to share the love of Jesus with you and see how you are doing. Then go from there based on answers given. The most important thing is to truly listen, and you will hear the key to the heart. There are endless possibilities. However, I truly believe an attempt to build relationships should be an open approach. Leading into, do you have a relationship with Jesus. Or I

am sorry to hear about (whatever bad thing they share) But, let me tell you what Jesus did for me, and He can do the same for you! Jesus loves you and wants the best for you!

Is there any reason why you would not want to receive Jesus and begin to experience His love and abundant life right now?

READ AND BEGIN TO MEMORIZE THE SEVEN SALVATION SCRIPTURES:

Salvation verses:

1. "For everyone has sinned; we all fall short of God's glorious standard" (Rom. 3:23).

2. "For the wages of sin is death, but the free gift of God is eternal life through Christ Jesus our Lord" (Rom. 6:23).

3. "And this is the way to have eternal life—to know you, the only true God, and Jesus Christ, the one you sent to earth" (John 17:3).

4. "But God showed his great love for us by sending Christ to die for us while we were still sinners" (Rom. 5:8).

5. "God saved you by his grace when you believed. And you can't take credit for this; it is a gift from God. 9 Salvation is not a reward for the good things we have done, so none of us can boast about it" (Eph. 2:8-9).

6. "If you openly declare that Jesus is Lord and believe in your heart that God raised him from the dead, you will be saved. 10 For it is by believing in your heart that you are made right with God, and it is by openly declaring your faith that you are saved" (Rom. 10:9-10).

7. "And now you Gentiles have also heard the truth, the Good News that God saves you. And when you believed in Christ, he identified you as his own by giving you the Holy Spirit, whom he promised long ago" (Eph. 1:13).

Two assurance verses:

1. "I have written this to you who believe in the name of the Son of God, so that you may know you have eternal life" (1 John 5:13).

2. "Prove by the way you live that you have repented of your sins and turned to God. Don't just say to each other, 'We're safe, for we are descendants of Abraham.' That means nothing, for I tell you, God can create children of Abraham from these very stones" (Luke 3:8).

DISCOVERING GOD'S HEARTBEAT:
FOR COMMUNICATING THE GOSPEL

PURPOSE OF THIS LESSON:
To be equipped to fulfill God's will and desire for all people to be saved.

"For this is how God loved the world: He gave his one and only Son, so that everyone who believes in him will not perish but have eternal life. God sent his Son into the world not to judge the world, but to save the world through him" (John 3:16-17).

"Now may the God of peace-who brought up from the dead our Lord Jesus, the great Shepherd of the sheep, and ratified an eternal covenant with his blood-may he equip you with all you need for doing his will. May he produce in you, through the power of Jesus Christ, every good thing that is pleasing to him. All glory to him forever and ever! Amen" (Heb. 13:20-21).

INTRODUCTION:
We can see through the life of both Peter and Paul the stark difference from before they were equipped and after they were equipped to fulfill the ministry of reconciliation.

- Peter Not Equipped.

- "But Peter denied it. "Woman," he said, "I don't even know him!" After a while someone else looked at him and said, "You must be one of them!" "No, man, I'm not!" Peter retorted. But Peter said, "Man, I don't know what you are talking about." And immediately, while he was still speaking, the rooster crowed" (Luke 22:57, 58, 60).

- Peter Equipped.

- "So, they called the apostles back in and commanded them never again to speak or teach in the name of Jesus. But Peter and John replied, "Do you think God wants us to obey you rather than him? We cannot stop telling about everything we have seen and heard" (Acts 4:18-20).

- Paul Not Equipped.
- "Meanwhile, Saul was uttering threats with every breath and was eager to kill the Lord's followers. So, he went to the high priest" (Acts 9:1)

- Paul Equipped.

- "Saul's preaching became more and more powerful, and the Jews in Damascus couldn't refute his proofs that Jesus was indeed the Messiah" (Acts 9:22).

*(See Appendix, Teaching Note 1) Read – Tag Changer.

WHY THIS LESSON IS IMPORTANT TO YOUR LIFE?

Proper training prepares us to minister, releasing the anointing of the Holy Spirit to flow through us. Producing the posture needed to share the gospel of the Kingdom of God and be a "tag changer."

"Yes, I am the vine; you are the branches. Those who remain in me, and I in them, will produce much fruit. For apart from me you can do nothing" (John 15:5).

"All the believers devoted themselves to the apostles' teaching, and to fellowship, and to sharing in meals (including the Lord's Supper), and to prayer. A deep sense of awe came over them all, and the apostles performed many miraculous signs and wonders. And all the believers met together in one place and shared everything they had. They sold their property and possessions and shared the money with those in need. They worshiped together at the Temple each day, met in homes for the Lord's Supper, and shared their meals with great joy and generosity-all the while praising God and enjoying the goodwill of all the people. And each day the Lord added to their fellowship those who were being saved" (Acts 2:42-47).

The power that equipping will accomplish in sharing the gospel.
When we go out next week to share the gospel, we will us the following guidelines.

You knock on the door, smile, and hold out your right hand to shake with doorhanger in the left hand as you speak the introduction statement. The handshake should be firm but not crushing or wimpy, which is saying, "I am glad to meet you."

The handshake should last no longer than stating your name, which at this time you should let go and place the doorhanger in their still extended hand. Then finish your introduction, ice breaker, diagnostic question and wait for their reply. You first validate their response and then proceed based on what they have said. Listen compassionately and you will hear the key to their heart. You will hold the key in your testimony and the love of Jesus, share boldly! If they are a Christian, in relationship with Jesus, celebrate in fellowship of exhortation and encouragement.

IF INDIVIDUAL IS SAVED:
You're sincerely thankful and excited for them being saved and share your 3-point testimony and then asked them when and where they accept Jesus as their savior and become born again. The leader can also ask the trainee to share their 3-point testimony. From there you determine if they have a church family, and they are connected to the body of Christ. If not, then give them a ministry flyer and invite them to church. Let them know you will meet them, show them around and sit together. Then you ask if you can pray for them about anything. Pray and thank them for their hospitality!

IF THE PERSON IS NOT SAVED:
First validate all answers and then proceed based on what they have said. Validating their answers is not coming into agreement with ungodly beliefs. When we are lost in the world we are deceived by the lies of the devil and that deception influences our belief system and becomes our reality. This is what we are validating. We want to validate their current reality. This allows the opportunity of hope to shine bright. Then through our testimony of how Jesus rescued us from this very thing and how Jesus will do the same thing for them will flood their heart. Show you're sincerely concerned about their pain, struggles, and broken heart. Listen compassionately and you will hear the key to their heart. You will hold the key in your testimony of the love of Jesus! Share

your 3-point testimony: Past, present, and future. Where, when, and how Jesus saved you. Remember we overcome by the blood of the lamb and the word of our testimony. Let them know, Jesus wants to do this for them too, to set them free, to love them! If they say something like I wish I had that. Ask them, is there any reason why you would not want to receive Jesus as your Lord and Savior and begin to experience His love and abundant life right now? Speak life, truth, ask Holy Spirit to be your words! Team members can be praying in the Spirit without anyone knowing. Follow-up, invite them to the church using a ministry flyer. Then ask how you can pray for them. Pray and thank them for their hospitality.

Sharing the gospel can take many ministry approaches. Often, a demonstration of the love of Jesus will soften the hardest of hearts. If the person is open to hear then proceed with the Gospel using the seven salvations answers and conclude with, "Is there any reason why you would not want to receive the Holy Spirit of promise and give your life to Jesus and begin to experience His love and abundant life right now? Pray with them for salvation restating the truths from the seven verses. End Gospel with two assurance verses. Give them a flyer and invite them to church, stating you will meet them, show them around and set with them. Ask how you can pray for them. Pray and thank them for their hospitality!

ALL visits have three components:
Knocking on the door maximum three times, leaving door knocker, and prayer.

- Introduction Statement: Hello, my name is _____ and We are from _____ Church. We just came by to share the love of Jesus with you and see how you are doing?

- Diagnostic Question: Is there any reason why you would not want to receive Jesus and begin to experience His love and abundant life right now?

- Take time this week in preparation for "going" to know the following from memory.

- Seven Salvation Verses:

1. "For everyone has sinned; we all fall short of God's glorious standard" (Rom. 3:23).

2. "For the wages of sin is death, but the free gift of God is eternal life through Christ Jesus our Lord" (Rom. 6:23).

3. "And this is the way to have eternal life—to know you, the only true God, and Jesus Christ, the one you sent to earth" (John 17:3).

4. "But God showed his great love for us by sending Christ to die for us while we were still sinners" (Rom. 5:8).

5. "God saved you by his grace when you believed. And you can't take credit for this; it is a gift from God. 9 Salvation is not a reward for the good things we have done, so none of us can boast about it" (Eph. 2:8-9).

6. "If you openly declare that Jesus is Lord and believe in your heart that God raised him from the dead, you will be saved. 10 For it is by believing in your heart that you are made right with God, and it is by openly declaring your faith that you are saved" (Rom. 10:9-10).

7. "And now you Gentiles have also heard the truth, the Good News that God saves you. And when you believed in Christ, he identified you as his own by giving you the Holy Spirit, whom he promised long ago" (Eph.1:13).

- Two Assurance & Grow Verses:

1. "I have written this to you who believe in the name of the Son of God, so that you may know you have eternal life" (1 John 5:13).

2. "Prove by the way you live that you have repented of your sins and turned to God. Don't just say to each other, 'We're safe, for we are descendants of Abraham.' That means nothing, for I tell you, God can create children of Abraham from these very stones" (Luke 3:8).

LESSON SUMMARY:

- "For this is how God loved the world: He gave his one and only Son, so that everyone who believes in him will not perish but have eternal life" (John 3:16).

- "Yes, I am the vine; you are the branches. Those who remain in me, and I in them, will produce much fruit. For apart from me you can do nothing" (John 15:5).

- "If you openly declare that Jesus is Lord and believe in your heart that God raised him from the dead, you will be saved. For it is by believing in your heart that you are made right with God, and it is by openly declaring your faith that you are saved" (Rom. 10:9-10).

- "but sanctify Christ as Lord in your hearts, always being ready to make a defense to everyone who asks you to give an account for the hope that is in you, but with gentleness and respect" (1 Pet. 3:15 NASB).

*Note: Lesson Slides end at this point.

*(See Appendix, Teaching Note 2).

OBEDIENCE PRECEDES BLESSING:
How are you feeling now since you have completed this lesson on Discovering God's Heartbeat for communicating His Gospel, Watering the seed? I know for me it was a game-changer when Holy Spirit gave me a revelation to His church's purpose and that He had left me the Holy Spirit to not only save me but to equip me to be His witness. Then when I learned these practical tools to share my faith and the Gospel, I realized that I could step into this at any time and quite simply.

MEMORY VERSE:
"For by grace you have been saved through faith; and this is not of yourselves, it is the gift of God; 9 not a result of works, so that no one may boast" (Eph. 2:8-9 NASB).

GROW DEEPER:
Now to practice, for like they say, "Practice makes perfect!" It also brings confidence. So, practice on your born-again family and friends and in front of the mirror. You can even practice on your unsaved family and friends, for who knows the timing might be perfect, and they are ready to receive Jesus' saving grace and forgiveness! So exciting for sure! "For God says, "At just the right time, I heard you. On the day of salvation, I helped you." Indeed, the "right time" is now. Today is the day of salvation" (2 Cor. 6:2).

So, for you to grow deeper, practice, Practice, Practice, and don't let the seeds of life and purpose die within you! "For "Everyone who calls on the name of the Lord will be saved." But how can they call on him to save them unless they believe in him? And how can they believe in him if they have never heard about him? And how can they hear about him unless someone tells them? And how will anyone go and tell them without being sent? That is why the Scriptures say, "How beautiful are the feet of messengers who bring good news!" But not everyone welcomes the Good News, for Isaiah the prophet said, "Lord, who has believed our message?" So, faith comes from hearing, that is, hearing the Good News about Christ" (Rom. 10:13-17).

GROW III
God's Heartbeat
Lesson 8

DISCOVERING GOD'S HEARTBEAT:
FOR THE HARVEST AND WALKING IT OUT AS GOD PLANNED

PURPOSE OF THIS LESSON:
To fulfill the great commission to go, make, baptize!

"Therefore, go and make disciples of all the nations, baptizing them in the name of the Father and the Son and the Holy Spirit. Teach these new disciples to obey all the commands I have given you. And be sure of this: I am with you always, even to the end of the age" (Matthew 28:19-20).

INTRODUCTION:
Jesus modeled the "going," and you are the answer to His prayer by "going" also!

"Jesus traveled through all the towns and villages of that area, teaching in the synagogues and announcing the Good News about the Kingdom. And he healed every kind of disease and illness. When he saw the crowds, he had compassion on them because they were confused and helpless, like sheep without a shepherd. He said to his disciples, "The harvest is great, but the workers are few. So, pray to the Lord who is in charge of the harvest; ask him to send more workers into his fields" (Matt. 9:35-38).

The class will be going out into the community, house-to-house, witnessing and inviting people to be born again and to attend church.

WHY THIS LESSON IS IMPORTANT TO YOUR LIFE?
Jesus was commissioned to model the Father. "I don't speak on my own authority. The Father who sent me has commanded me what to say and how to say it. And I know his commands lead to eternal life; so, I say whatever the Father tells me to say" (John 12:49-50). You were predestined to model Jesus. "For God knew his people in advance, and he chose them to become like his Son, so that his Son would be the firstborn among many brothers and sisters" (Rom. 8:29).

THE POWER THAT "GOING" WILL ACCOMPLISH FOR ALL ETERNITY:
The power that "going" will accomplish for all eternity. Jesus will have accomplished His purpose to make you a witness of his kingdom. "But you are not like that, for you are a chosen people. You are royal priests, a holy nation, God's very own possession. As a result, you can show others the goodness of God, for he called you out of the darkness into his wonderful light" (1 Pet. 2:9). "He has made us a Kingdom of priests for God his Father. All glory and power to him forever and ever! Amen' (Rev. 1:6).

"And they sang a new song with these words: "You are worthy to take the scroll and break its seals and open it. For you were slaughtered, and your blood has ransomed people for God from every tribe and language and people and nation. And you have caused them to become a Kingdom of priests for our God. And they will reign on the earth" (Rev. 5:9-10).

"So, Jesus said to them again, "Peace to you! As the Father has sent Me, I also send you" (John 20:21 NKJV).

- Introduction Statement: Hello, my name is_____ and We are from _____ Church. We just came by to share the love of Jesus with you and see how you are doing?

- Note: Suggestions, we just came by to share the love of Jesus with you and see how you are doing. Then go from there based on answers given. There are endless possibilities. However, I truly believe an attempt to build relationships should be the open approach. Leading into, do you have a relationship with Jesus. Or I am sorry to hear about (whatever bad thing they share) But, let me tell you what Jesus did for me, and He can do the same for you!

- Diagnostic Question: Is there any reason why you would not want to receive Jesus and begin to experience His love and abundant life right now?

Seven Salvation Verses:
1. "For everyone has sinned; we all fall short of God's glorious standard" (Rom. 3:23).

2. "For the wages of sin is death, but the free gift of God is eternal life through Christ Jesus our Lord" (Rom. 6:23).

3. "And this is the way to have eternal life—to know you, the only true God, and Jesus Christ, the one you sent to earth" (John 17:3).

4. "But God showed his great love for us by sending Christ to die for us while we were still sinners" (Rom. 5:8).

5. "God saved you by his grace when you believed. And you can't take credit for this; it is a gift from God. 9 Salvation is not a reward for the good things we have done, so none of us can boast about it" (Eph. 2:8-9).

6. "If you openly declare that Jesus is Lord and believe in your heart that God raised him from the dead, you will be saved. 10 For it is by believing in your heart that you are made right with God, and it is by openly declaring your faith that you are saved" (Rom. 10:9-10).

7. "And now you Gentiles have also heard the truth, the Good News that God saves you. And when you believed in Christ, he identified you as his own by giving you the Holy Spirit, whom he promised long ago" (Eph.1:13).

Two Assurance & Grow Verses:
1. "I have written this to you who believe in the name of the Son of God, so that you may know you have eternal life" (1 John 5:13).

2. "Prove by the way you live that you have repented of your sins and turned to God. Don't just say to each other, 'We're safe, for we are descendants of Abraham.' That means nothing, for I tell you, God can create children of Abraham from these very stones' (Luke 3:8).

LESSON SUMMARY:
The Great Commission:

- "And Jesus came and spoke to them, saying, "All authority has been given to Me in heaven and on earth. Go therefore and make disciples of all the nations, baptizing them in the name of the Father and of the Son and of the Holy Spirit, teaching them to observe all things that I have commanded you; and lo, I am with you always, even to the end of the age." Amen" (Matthew 28:18-20 NKJV).

- "And He said to them, "Go into all the world and preach the gospel to every creature" (Mark 16:15 NKJV).

- "Then He said to them, "Thus it is written, and thus it was necessary for the Christ to suffer and to rise from the dead the third day, and that repentance and remission of sins should be preached in His name to all nations, beginning at Jerusalem. And you are witnesses of these things" (Luke 24:46-48 NKJV).

- "So, Jesus said to them again, "Peace to you! As the Father has sent Me, I also send you" (John 20:21 NKJV).

- "But you shall receive power when the Holy Spirit has come upon you; and you shall be witnesses to Me in Jerusalem, and in all Judea and Samaria, and to the end of the earth" (Acts 1:8 NKJV).

*Note: Lesson Slides end at this point.

OBEDIENCE PRECEDES BLESSING:
The class will go out into the local community, door-to-door as an application to Week 7 training.

MEMORY VERSE:
"Therefore, go and make disciples of all the nations, baptizing them in the name of the Father and the Son and the Holy Spirit. Teach these new disciples to obey all the commands I have given you. And be sure of this: I am with you always, even to the end of the age" (Matthew 28:19-20).

GROW DEEPER:
Read the book of Acts in your favorite translation. Write down four things you learned about the history of the early church and how you can apply these revelations to your own life.

Now that your life is different, go and make a difference every day! Have fun! It is a great life!

DISCOVERING GOD'S HEARTBEAT:
FOR ETERNITY AND WINNING FOR TODAY AND BEYOND - Part 1

PURPOSE OF THIS LESSON:

To answer the question of how you would, could, and should live to give Jesus, the Lamb, the full reward for His suffering for you. Read the following verse. "I am crucified with Christ: nevertheless, I live; yet not I, but Christ liveth in me: and the life which I now live in the flesh I live by the faith of the Son of God, who loved me, and gave himself for me" (Gal. 2:20 KJV).

INTRODUCTION:

One day EVERY Christian will stand before the judgment seat of Jesus Christ and give an account for all we were entrusted to in this age.

"Again, the Kingdom of Heaven can be illustrated by the story of a man going on a long trip. He called together his servants and entrusted his money to them while he was gone. He gave five bags of silver to one, two bags of silver to another, and one bag of silver to the last-dividing it in proportion to their abilities. He then left on his trip. "The servant who received the five bags of silver began to invest the money and earned five more. The servant with two bags of silver also went to work and earned two more. But the servant who received the one bag of silver dug a hole in the ground and hid the master's money. "After a long time their master returned from his trip and called them to give an account of how they had used his money. The servant to whom he had entrusted the five bags of silver came forward with five more and said, 'Master, you gave me five bags of silver to invest, and I have earned five more.' "The master was full of praise. 'Well done, my good and faithful servant. You have been faithful in handling this small amount, so now I will give you many more responsibilities. Let's celebrate together!' "The servant who had received the two bags of silver came forward and said, 'Master, you gave me two bags of silver to invest, and I have earned two more.' "The master said, 'Well done, my good and faithful servant. You have been faithful in handling this small amount, so now I will give you many more responsibilities. Let's celebrate together!' "Then the servant with the one bag of silver came and said, 'Master, I knew you were a harsh man, harvesting crops you didn't plant and gathering crops you didn't cultivate. I was afraid I would lose your money, so I hid it in the earth. Look, here is your money back.' "But the master replied, 'You wicked and lazy servant! If you knew I harvested crops I didn't plant and gathered crops I didn't cultivate, why didn't you deposit my money in the bank? At least I could have gotten some interest on it.' "Then he ordered, 'Take the money from this servant, and give it to the one with the ten bags of silver. To those who use well what they are given, even more will be given, and they will have an abundance. But from those who do nothing, even what little they have will be taken away. Now throw this useless servant into outer darkness, where there will be weeping and gnashing of teeth" (Matt. 25:14-30).

WHY THIS LESSON IS IMPORTANT TO YOUR LIFE?

What we do with the cross determines where we will spend eternity, but the way we live as believers determines how we are going to spend eternity. "If the work survives, that builder will receive a reward. But if the work is burned up, the builder will suffer great loss. The builder will be saved, but like someone barely escaping through a wall of flames" (1 Cor. 3:14-15).

POWER TO LIVE ETERNALLY MINDED:
Now we must ask the question of how we walk this out. When you get serious in your life to be on purpose to do what you know is God's will for your life, then and only then will God's supernatural power enter your life to be different so you can make a difference! This is truly partnering with the "Great I am" to move into the greater things of God and live intimately with your Father God, Creator, Savior, Lord! "Yes, I am the vine; you are the branches. Those who remain in me, and I in them, will produce much fruit. For apart from me you can do nothing" (John15:5).
*(See Appendix, Teaching Note 1)

So, let's get started by first defining eternity. What do you first think of when you hear the word "eternity"? The dictionary defines it as infinite time, duration without beginning, or end. Name one thing that you know has no beginning or end. I know it is hard to even name one because that is a very hard concept to comprehend because everything, we know has a beginning and end, including ourselves and the life we know here on earth.

Understanding the concept of eternity:
Let's attempt to answer eight questions that might help to move you to a place of more understanding of the concept of eternity. Of course, the greatest source of all understanding grounded in truth is the Word of God. First, answer the following question and then look up each verse to get God's perspective. How did the two compare?

1. Do you live your life mostly by your five senses (name them) or eternally minded?

- "So, if you're serious about living this new resurrection life with Christ, act like it. Pursue the things over which Christ presides. Don't shuffle along, eyes to the ground, absorbed with the things right in front of you. Look up and be alert to what is going on around Christ—that's where the action is. See things from his perspective" (Col. 3:2 MSG).

2. What do you understand about what happens when you leave this life?

- "And just as each person is destined to die once and after that comes judgment" (Heb. 9:27).

3. Why do people fear things, people, etc.?

- "Fear of the Lord is the foundation of true knowledge, but fools despise wisdom and discipline" (Prov. 1:7).

4. Do you...should you fear God?

- "But I'll tell you whom to fear. Fear God, who has the power to kill you and then throw you into hell. Yes, he's the one to fear" (Luke 12:5).

- "It is a terrible thing to fall into the hands of the living God" (Heb. 10:31).

5. Do you...should you fear death?

- "Because God's children are human beings-made of flesh and blood-the Son also became flesh and blood. For only as a human being could he die, and only by dying could he break the power of the devil, who had the power of death. Only in this way could he set free all who have lived their lives as slaves to the fear of dying" (Heb. 2:14-15).

6. Do you...should you fear judgment? "There is only the terrible expectation of God's judgment and the raging fire that will consume his enemies" (Heb 10:27).

7. What do you understand about Biblical judgment? "God overlooks it as long as you don't know any better-but that time is past. The unknown is now known, and he's calling for a radical life-change. He has set a day when the entire human race will be judged, and everything set right. And he has already appointed the judge, confirming him before everyone by raising him from the dead" (Acts 17:30-31 MSG).

8. Is the judgment final? "Jesus said, "There was a certain rich man who was splendidly clothed in purple and fine linen and who lived each day in luxury. At his gate lay a poor man named Lazarus who was covered with sores. As Lazarus lay there longing for scraps from the rich man's table, the dogs would come and lick his open sores. "Finally, the poor man died and was carried by the angels to sit beside Abraham at the heavenly banquet. The rich man also died and was buried, and he went to the place of the dead. There, in torment, he saw Abraham in the far distance with Lazarus at his side. "The rich man shouted, 'Father Abraham, have some pity! Send Lazarus over here to dip the tip of his finger in water and cool my tongue. I am in anguish in these flames.' "But Abraham said to him, 'Son, remember that during your lifetime you had everything you wanted, and Lazarus had nothing. So now he is here being comforted, and you are in anguish. And besides, there is a great chasm separating us. No one can cross over to you from here, and no one can cross over to us from there.' "Then the rich man said, 'Please, Father Abraham, at least send him to my father's home. For I have five brothers, and I want him to warn them, so they don't end up in this place of torment.' "But Abraham said, 'Moses and the prophets have warned them. Your brothers can read what they wrote.' "The rich man replied, 'No, Father Abraham! But if someone is sent to them from the dead, then they will repent of their sins and turn to God.' "But Abraham said, 'If they won't listen to Moses and the prophets, they won't be persuaded even if someone rises from the dead" (Luke 16:19-31).

LESSON SUMMARY:

- "If the work survives, that builder will receive a reward. But if the work is burned up, the builder will suffer great loss. The builder will be saved, but like someone barely escaping through a wall of flames" (1 Cor. 3:14-15).

- "But the Holy Spirit produces this kind of fruit in our lives: love, joy, peace, patience, kindness, goodness, faithfulness, gentleness, and self-control. There is no law against these things" (Gal. 5:22-23)

- "Yes, I am the vine; you are the branches. Those who remain in me, and I in them, will produce much fruit. For apart from me you can do nothing" (John 15:5).

*Note: Lesson Slides end at this point.

OBEDIENCE PRECEDES BLESSING:

One again we have come to the place where we move from the abstract to the concrete. Where some say the rubber meets the road, and we move forward. Where we come to a definite fork in the road.

Are you going to acknowledge truth with your mind only and be a part of the majority or exercise the ninth fruit of the Holy Spirit and be part of the minority? Can you name it? "But the Holy Spirit produces this kind of fruit in our lives: love, joy, peace, patience, kindness, goodness, faithfulness, gentleness, and self-control. There is no law against these things" (Gal. 5:22-23)!

If you are a student of the Word of God for any length of time, you have come to know that Jesus is all about taking you from where you are to where He is. So, get ready to be challenged. Look up each verse and answer the question that will help to identify 3 basic steps that will lead you from living and experiencing this life with just your five senses to being eternally minded.

1. What is the first step you must take to be eternally minded so that you can learn from Adam and Eve's mindset that hindered them?

- "The man replied, "It was the woman you gave me who gave me the fruit, and I ate it." Then the Lord God asked the woman, "What have you done?" "The serpent deceived me," she replied. "That's why I ate it" (Gen. 3:12-13).

- "Afterward the Lord asked Cain, "Where is your brother? Where is Abel?" "I don't know," Cain responded. "Am I my brother's guardian" (Gen. 4:9)?

2. How do you pre- examine your actions of both what you do and what you don't do?

- "The one who plants and the one who waters work together with the same purpose. And both will be rewarded for their own hard work. For we are both God's workers. And you are God's field. You are God's building. Because of God's grace to me, I have laid the foundation like an expert builder. Now others are building on it. But whoever is building on this foundation must be very careful. For no one can lay any foundation other than the one we already have-Jesus Christ. Anyone who builds on that foundation may use a variety of materials—gold, silver, jewels, wood, hay, or straw. But on judgment day, fire will reveal what kind of work each builder has done. The fire will show if a person's work has any value. If the work survives, that builder will receive a reward. But if the work is burned up, the builder will suffer great loss. The builder will be saved, but like someone barely escaping through a wall of flames" (1 Cor. 3:8-15).

- "So, we are always confident, even though we know that as long as we live in these bodies we are not at home with the Lord. For we live by believing and not by seeing. Yes, we are fully confident, and we would rather be away from these earthly bodies, for then we will be at home with the Lord. So whether we are here in this body or away from this body, our goal is to please him. For we must all stand before Christ to be judged. We will each receive whatever we deserve for the good or evil we have done in this earthly body. Because we understand our fearful responsibility to the Lord, we work hard to persuade others. God knows we are sincere, and I hope you know this, too" (2 Cor. 5:6-11).

- "And I saw a great white throne and the one sitting on it. The earth and sky fled from his presence, but they found no place to hide. I saw the dead, both great and small, standing before God's throne. And the books were opened, including the Book of Life. And the dead were judged according to what they had done, as recorded in the books. The sea gave up its dead, and death and the grave gave up their dead. And all were judged according to their deeds. Then death and the grave were thrown into the lake of fire. This lake of fire is the second death. And anyone whose name was not found recorded in the Book of Life was thrown into the lake of fire" (Rev 20:11-15).

3. What would be a number one daily reminder before even getting out of bed to help you stay on the path of being eternally minded, which will bring great blessing here and in the next life?

- "Anyone with ears to hear must listen to the Spirit and understand what he is saying to the churches. To everyone who is victorious I will give fruit from the tree of life in the paradise of God. Don't be afraid of what you are about to suffer. The devil will throw some of you into prison to test you. You will suffer for ten days. But if you remain faithful even when facing death, I will give you the crown of life. "Anyone with ears to hear must listen to the Spirit and understand what he is saying to the churches. To everyone who is victorious I will give some of the manna that has been hidden away in heaven. And I will give to each one a white stone, and on the stone will be engraved a new name that no one understands except the one who receives it" (Rev. 2:7,10, 17).

- "To all who are victorious, who obey me to the very end, To them I will give authority over all the nations. They will rule the nations with an iron rod and smash them like clay pots. They will have the same authority I received from my Father, and I will also give them the morning star" (Rev. 2:26-28)!

- "Yet there are some in the church in Sardis who have not soiled their clothes with evil. They will walk with me in white, for they are worthy. All who are victorious will be clothed in white. I will never erase their names from the Book of Life, but I will announce before my Father and his angels that they are mine. All who are victorious will become pillars in the Temple of my God, and they will never have to leave it. And I will write on them the name of my God, and they will be citizens in the city of my God—the new Jerusalem that comes down from heaven from my God. And I will also write on them my new name. Those who are victorious will sit with me on my throne, just as I was victorious and sat with my Father on his throne" (Rev. 3:4-5, 12, 21).

*(See Appendix, Teaching Note 2)

MEMORY VERSE:
"I have been crucified with Christ; and it is no longer I who live, but Christ lives in me; and the life which I now live in the flesh I live by faith in the Son of God, who loved me and gave Himself up for me" (Gal. 2:20 NASB).

GROW DEEPER:
"Then Christ will make his home in your hearts as you trust in him. Your roots will grow down into God's love and keep you strong" (Eph. 3:17).

Wow, what an impactful lesson! Was this lesson an eye-opener for you? Are you a little fearful after seeing that we will be held accountable for every action we commit on this earth? Are you excited that we have the opportunity to live for Christ and store up treasures in Heaven? If you are looking for a more in-depth view of Eternity, we encourage you to read "Driven by Eternity: Making Your Life Count Today & Forever," by John Bevere.

DISCOVERING GOD'S HEARTBEAT:
FOR ETERNITY AND WINNING FOR TODAY AND BEYOND – Part 2

PURPOSE OF THIS LESSON:
To realize that salvation is a gift, but rewards both now and in heaven are earned.

- "And it is impossible to please God without faith. Anyone who wants to come to him must believe that God exists and that he rewards those who sincerely seek him" (Heb. 11:6).
- The commandments of the LORD are right, bringing joy to the heart. The commands of the LORD are clear, giving insight for living. (Ps.19:8)
- "They are a warning to your servant, a great reward for those who obey them" (Ps. 19:11).

INTRODUCTION:
We should live in such a way to receive a full reward. It is possible to be born again and not receive a full reward.

"Watch out that you do not lose what we have worked so hard to achieve. Be diligent so that you receive your full reward" (2 John 1:8). "All that you do must be done in love" (1 Cor. 16:14 NASB).

WHY THIS LESSON IS IMPORTANT TO YOUR LIFE?
What we do with the cross determines where we will spend eternity, but the way we live as believers determines how we are going to spend eternity.

"The one who plants and the one who waters work together with the same purpose. And both will be rewarded for their own hard work. For we are both God's workers. And you are God's field. You are God's building. Because of God's grace to me, I have laid the foundation like an expert builder. Now others are building on it. But whoever is building on this foundation must be very careful. For no one can lay any foundation other than the one we already have-Jesus Christ. Anyone who builds on that foundation may use a variety of materials-gold, silver, jewels, wood, hay, or straw. But on judgment day, fire will reveal what kind of work each builder has done. The fire will show if a person's work has any value. If the work survives, that builder will receive a reward. But if the work is burned up, the builder will suffer great loss. The builder will be saved, but like someone barely escaping through a wall of flames" (1 Cor. 3:8-15).

POWER TO LIVE ETERNALLY MINDED:
Life here on earth is filled with choices we must make every day; from what time we get up in the morning to what time we will lay our heads on our pillow at night and the thousands in between. Some of our choices have immediate results, and some we won't see the results for days, weeks, months, and even years to come. Some choices we make consciously, planning it out, and some we make subconsciously without even thinking about it. Even when we decide to not choose, we chose to not choose. The many life choices we face can be daunting for sure, but the freedom to choose is what makes life so wonderful!

Let's take this subject of choice to the next level. What about the choices we make here that affect the next life? Have you ever thought about what happens after you leave this earth…when you take your last breath? That can be daunting and often we push those thoughts to the back of our minds. What if our eternal destination came down to just two choices, we make here on earth?

"And I saw a great white throne and the one sitting on it. The earth and sky fled from his presence, but they found no place to hide. I saw the dead, both great and small, standing before God's throne. And the books were opened, including the Book of Life. And the dead were judged according to what they had done, as recorded in the books. The sea gave up its dead, and death and the grave gave up their dead. And all were judged according to their deeds. Then death and the grave were thrown into the lake of fire. This lake of fire is the second death. And anyone whose name was not found recorded in the Book of Life was thrown into the lake of fire" (Rev. 20:11-15)

"If you openly declare that Jesus is Lord and believe in your heart that God raised him from the dead, you will be saved. For it is by believing in your heart that you are made right with God, and it is by openly declaring your faith that you are saved" (Rom. 10:9-10).

What two choices and the results did you discover?

1. _____

2. _____

If you have spent any time in the reading and studying the Word of God, then you have come to understand that those apart from Christ in this life will face a judgment that will affect you eternally! Have you ever thought about whether Christians will ever face judgment? Discover what the Bible has to say about this. "For we must all stand before Christ to be judged. We will each receive whatever we deserve for the good or evil we have done in this earthly body" (2 Cor. 5:10). "And I tell you this, you must give an account on judgment day for every idle word you speak. The words you say will either acquit you or condemn you" (Matt. 12:36-37).

Are those verses scary? Who will be our Judge? Does that comfort you or cause uneasiness? It is certainly comforting that Jesus, who gave Himself to save us when we were still His enemies will be our judge as His friends! But this does not automatically mean that everything will be okay!

'For if you are trying to make yourselves right with God by keeping the law, you have been cut off from Christ! You have fallen away from God's grace" (Gal. 5:4).

Take a few minutes to read of Jesus' judgment of His churches.

"Write this letter to the angel of the church in Ephesus. This is the message from the one who holds the seven stars in his right hand, the one who walks among the seven gold lampstands: "I know all the things you do. I have seen your hard work and your patient endurance. I know you don't tolerate evil people. You have examined the claims of those who say they are apostles but are not. You have discovered they are liars. You have patiently suffered for me without quitting. "But I have this complaint against you. You don't love me or each other as you did at first! Look how far you have fallen! Turn back to me and do the work you did at first. If you don't repent, I will come and remove your lampstand from its place among the churches. But this is in your favor: You hate the evil deeds of the Nicolaitans, just as I do. "Anyone with ears to hear must listen to the Spirit and understand what he is saying to the churches. To everyone who is victorious I will give fruit from the tree of life in the paradise of God. "Write this letter to the angel of the church in Smyrna. This is the message from the one who is the First and the Last, who was dead but is now alive: "I know about your suffering and your poverty-but you are rich! I know the blasphemy of those opposing you. They say they are Jews, but they are not, because their synagogue belongs to Satan. Don't be afraid of what you are about to suffer. The devil will throw some of you into prison to test you. You will suffer for ten days. But if you remain faithful even when facing death, I will give you the crown of life. "Anyone with ears to hear must listen to the Spirit and understand what he is saying to the churches. Whoever is victorious will not be harmed by the second death. "Write this letter to the angel of the church in Pergamum. This is the message from the one with the sharp two-edged sword: "I know that you live in the city where Satan has his throne, yet you have remained loyal to me. You refused to deny me even when Antipas, my faithful witness, was martyred among you there in Satan's city. "But I have a few complaints against you. You tolerate some among you whose teaching is like that of Balaam, who showed Balak how to trip up the people of Israel. He taught them to sin by eating food offered to idols and by committing sexual sin. In a similar way, you have some Nicolaitans among you who follow the same teaching. Repent of your sin, or I will come to you suddenly and fight against them with the sword of my mouth. "Anyone with ears to hear must listen to the Spirit and understand what he is saying to the churches. To everyone who is victorious I will give some of the manna that has been hidden away in heaven. And I will give to each one a white stone, and on the stone will be engraved a new name that no one understands except the one who receives it. "Write this letter to the angel of the church in Thyatira. This is the message from the Son of God, whose eyes are like flames of fire, whose feet are like polished bronze: "I know all the things you do. I have seen your love, your faith, your service, and your patient endurance. And I can see your constant improvement in all these things. "But I have this complaint against you. You are permitting that woman—that Jezebel who calls herself a prophet-to lead my servants astray. She teaches them to commit sexual sin and to eat food offered to idols. I gave her time to repent, but she does not want to turn away from her immorality. "Therefore, I will throw her on a bed of suffering, and those who commit adultery with her will suffer greatly unless they repent and turn away from her evil deeds. I will strike her children dead. Then all the churches will know that I am the one who searches out the thoughts and intentions of every person. And I will give each of you whatever you deserve. "But I also have a message for the rest of you in Thyatira who have not followed this false teaching ('deeper truths,' as they call them-depths of Satan, actually). I will ask nothing more of you except that you hold tightly to what you have until I come. To all who are victorious, who obey me to the very end, To them I will give authority over all the nations. They will rule the nations with an iron rod and smash them like clay pots. They will have the same authority I received from my Father, and I will also give them the morning star! "Anyone with ears to hear must listen to the Spirit and understand what he is saying to the churches" (Rev. 2:1-29).

"Write this letter to the angel of the church in Sardis. This is the message from the one who has the sevenfold Spirit of God and the seven stars: "I know all the things you do, and that you have a reputation for being alive-but you are dead. Wake up! Strengthen what little remains, for even what is left is almost dead. I find that your actions do not meet the requirements of my God. Go back to what you heard and believed at first; hold to it firmly. Repent and turn to me again. If you don't wake up, I will come to you suddenly, as unexpected as a thief. "Yet there are some in the church in Sardis who have not soiled their clothes with evil. They will walk with me in white, for they are worthy. All who are victorious will be clothed in white. I will never erase their names from the Book of Life, but I will announce before my Father and his angels that they are mine. "Anyone with ears to hear must listen to the Spirit and understand what he is saying to the churches. "Write this letter to the angel of the church in Philadelphia. This is the message from the one who is holy and true, the one who has the key of David. What he opens, no one can close; and what he closes, no one can open: "I know all the things you do, and I have opened a door for you that no one can close. You have little strength, yet you obeyed my word and did not deny me. Look, I will force those who belong to Satan's synagogue-those liars who say they are Jews but are not-to come and bow down at your feet. They will acknowledge that you are the ones I love. "Because you have obeyed my command to persevere, I will protect you from the great time of testing that will come upon the whole world to test those who belong to this world. I am coming soon. Hold on to what you have, so that no one will take away your crown. All who are victorious will become pillars in the Temple of my God, and they will never have to leave it. And I will write on them the name of my God, and they will be citizens in the city of my God—the new Jerusalem that comes down from heaven from my God. And I will also write on them my new name. "Anyone with ears to hear must listen to the Spirit and understand what he is saying to the churches. "Write this letter to the angel of the church in Laodicea. This is the message from the one who is the Amen—the faithful and true witness, the beginning of God's new creation: "I know all the things you do, that you are neither hot nor cold. I wish that you were one or the other! But since you are like lukewarm water, neither hot nor cold, I will spit you out of my mouth! You say, 'I am rich. I have everything I want. I don't need a thing!' And you don't realize that you are wretched and miserable and poor and blind and naked. So, I advise you to buy gold from me-gold that has been purified by fire. Then you will be rich. Also buy white garments from me so you will not be ashamed by your nakedness, and ointment for your eyes so you will be able to see. I correct and discipline everyone I love. So be diligent and turn from your indifference. "Look! I stand at the door and knock. If you hear my voice and open the door, I will come in, and we will share a meal together as friends. Those who are victorious will sit with me on my throne, just as I was victorious and sat with my Father on his throne. "Anyone with ears to hear must listen to the Spirit and understand what he is saying to the churches" (Rev. 3:1-22).

What did you discover? You have been saved for a purpose, and when we aren't living in that purpose, it is a big deal to Jesus! So, even as Christians, we will have a judgment. God's hope for this judgment is not to condemn us, but to give us rewards. If we live obediently, we will inherit reward.

Read, "The one who plants and the one who waters work together with the same purpose. And both will be rewarded for their own hard work. For we are both God's workers. And you are God's field. You are God's building. Because of God's grace to me, I have laid the foundation like an expert builder. Now others are building on it. But whoever is building on this foundation must be very careful. For no one can lay any foundation other than the one we already have-Jesus Christ. Anyone who builds on that foundation may use a variety of materials-gold, silver, jewels, wood, hay, or straw. But on judgment day, fire will reveal what kind of work each builder has done. The fire will show if a person's work has any value. If the work survives, that builder will receive a reward. But if the work is burned up, the builder will suffer great loss.

The builder will be saved, but like someone barely escaping through a wall of flames" (1 Cor. 3:8-15). and write down two things you discovered.

1. _____

2. _____

When we think of judgment, we generally have very negative feelings, but your heavenly Father wants you to be able to think of this judgment with positive feelings as a time to receive rewards for the good done in this life! It is time we are serious about living obediently in His purposes!!

Let's take this abstract truth and move into concrete truth by answering the following two questions. What can we pursue with our lives that will last for all eternity?
What substitutes can we pursue with our lives that will be burned up in the end?
Every "yes" to one thing is a "no" to something else. When you say yes to the things of God, you say no to the things of this world. When you say yes to the things offered by this world, you are saying no to the things of God. In all things, there is a choice. There is a pressure from the world, and sometimes even from within us, to not act on, share, or display our faith, but to keep what we've received from Christ in a safe and hidden place. Don't bury what Jesus gives you but invest for Jesus' Kingdom. Now take a few moments to read the parable of the talents.

"Again, the Kingdom of Heaven can be illustrated by the story of a man going on a long trip. He called together his servants and entrusted his money to them while he was gone. He gave five bags of silver to one, two bags of silver to another, and one bag of silver to the last, dividing it in proportion to their abilities. He then left on his trip. "The servant who received the five bags of silver began to invest the money and earned five more. The servant with two bags of silver also went to work and earned two more. But the servant who received the one bag of silver dug a hole in the ground and hid the master's money. "After a long time, their master returned from his trip and called them to give an account of how they had used his money. The servant to whom he had entrusted the five bags of silver came forward with five more and said, 'Master, you gave me five bags of silver to invest, and I have earned five more.' "The master was full of praise. 'Well done, my good and faithful servant. You have been faithful in handling this small amount, so now I will give you many more responsibilities. Let's celebrate together! "The servant who had received the two bags of silver came forward and said, 'Master, you gave me two bags of silver to invest, and I have earned two more.' "The master said, 'Well done, my good and faithful servant. You have been faithful in handling this small amount, so now I will give you many more responsibilities. Let's celebrate together!' "Then the servant with the one bag of silver came and said, 'Master, I knew you were a harsh man, harvesting crops you didn't plant and gathering crops you didn't cultivate. I was afraid I would lose your money, so I hid it in the earth. Look, here is your money back.' "But the master replied, 'You wicked and lazy servant! If you knew I harvested crops I didn't plant and gathered crops I didn't cultivate, why didn't you deposit my money in the bank? At least I could have gotten some interest on it.' "Then he ordered, 'Take the money from this servant, and give it to the one with the ten bags of silver. To those who use well what they are given, even more will be given, and they will have an abundance. But from those who do nothing, even what little they have will be taken away" (Matt. 25:14-29).

Does everyone receive the same reward in Heaven?

Read the parable of money, "He said, "A nobleman was called away to a distant empire to be crowned king and then return. Before he left, he called together ten of his servants and divided among them ten pounds of silver, saying, 'Invest this for me while I am gone.' But his people hated him and sent a delegation after him to say, 'We do not want him to be our king.' "After he was crowned king, he returned and called in the servants to whom he had given the money. He wanted to find out what their profits were. The first servant reported, 'Master, I invested your money and made ten times the original amount!' "'Well done!' the king exclaimed. 'You are a good servant. You have been faithful with the little I entrusted to you, so you will be governor of ten cities as your reward.' "The next servant reported, 'Master, I invested your money and made five times the original amount.' "'Well done!' the king said. 'You will be governor over five cities.' "But the third servant brought back only the original amount of money and said, 'Master, I hid your money and kept it safe. I was afraid because you are a hard man to deal with, taking what isn't yours and harvesting crops you didn't plant.' "'You wicked servant!' the king roared. 'Your own words condemn you. If you knew that I'm a hard man who takes what isn't mine and harvests crops I didn't plant, why didn't you deposit my money in the bank? At least I could have gotten some interest on it.' "Then, turning to the others standing nearby, the king ordered, 'Take the money from this servant, and give it to the one who has ten pounds.' "'But, master,' they said, 'he already has ten pounds!' "'Yes,' the king replied, 'and to those who use well what they are given, even more will be given. But from those who do nothing, even what little they have will be taken away. And as for these enemies of mine who didn't want me to be their king—bring them in and execute them right here in front of me" (Luke 19:12-27).

Did the faithful servants receive the same reward? What was their reward based on? Now answer this question. Does God have a specific calling for EACH person or only a few?

"For we are God's masterpiece. He has created us anew in Christ Jesus, so we can do the good things he planned for us long ago" (Eph. 2:10). "Just as our bodies have many parts and each part has a special function, so it is with Christ's body. We are many parts of one body, and we all belong to each other. In his grace, God has given us different gifts for doing certain things well. So, if God has given you the ability to prophesy, speak out with as much faith as God has given you. If your gift is serving others, serve them well. If you are a teacher, teach well. If your gift is to encourage others, be encouraging. If it is giving, give generously. If God has given you leadership ability, take the responsibility seriously. And if you have a gift for showing kindness to others, do it gladly" (Rom. 12:4-8). "Now these are the gifts Christ gave to the church: the apostles, the prophets, the evangelists, and the pastors and teachers" (Eph. 4:11). "From one man he created all the nations throughout the whole earth. He decided beforehand when they should rise and fall, and he determined their boundaries" (Acts 17:26).

What did you discover?

*(See Appendix, Teaching Note 1)

Now let's go even deeper. Are the rewards we receive or don't receive based just on our actions or also based on the motives of the heart? "So don't make judgments about anyone ahead of time-before the Lord returns. For he will bring our darkest secrets to light and will reveal our private motives. Then God will give to each one whatever praise is due" (1 Cor. 4:5).

241

"Watch out! Don't do your good deeds publicly, to be admired by others, for you will lose the reward from your Father in heaven. When you give to someone in need, don't do as the hypocrites do—blowing trumpets in the synagogues and streets to call attention to their acts of charity! I tell you the truth, they have received all the rewards they will ever get. But when you give to someone in need, don't let your left hand know what your right hand is doing. Give your gifts in private, and your Father, who sees everything, will reward you. "When you pray, don't be like the hypocrites who love to pray publicly on street corners and in the synagogues where everyone can see them. I tell you the truth, that is all the reward they will ever get. But when you pray, go away by yourself, shut the door behind you, and pray to your Father in private. Then your Father, who sees everything, will reward you. "And when you fast, don't make it obvious, as the hypocrites do, for they try to look miserable and disheveled so people will admire them for their fasting. I tell you the truth, that is the only reward they will ever get. But when you fast, comb your hair and wash your face. Then no one will notice that you are fasting, except your Father, who knows what you do in private. And your Father, who sees everything, will reward you" (Matt. 6:1-6, 16-18). What did you discover, how does the Bible answer this question?

Let us check our motives for why we do what we do, even things that would seem like "right things." In the examples, you read about in Matt. 6, what reward will be given for charitable giving, praying, or fasting that is done with the motive of receiving praise from people? So, don't let your left hand know what your right hand is doing! Do your actions for God!!

We want to stop here for a moment to think about our whole mindset regarding these rewards we are talking about. Should these rewards be our focus and aim in life? What would happen if we placed our focus on these rewards? Bill Johnson said, "If we turn aside from seeking the Kingdom and instead seek the 'added' things, we will miss both."

"No one can serve two masters. For you will hate one and love the other; you will be devoted to one and despise the other. You cannot serve God and be enslaved to money. "That is why I tell you not to worry about everyday life—whether you have enough food and drink, or enough clothes to wear. Isn't life more than food, and your body more than clothing? Look at the birds. They don't plant or harvest or store food in barns, for your heavenly Father feeds them. And aren't you far more valuable to him than they are? Can all your worries add a single moment to your life? "And why worry about your clothing? Look at the lilies of the field and how they grow. They don't work or make their clothing, yet Solomon in all his glory was not dressed as beautifully as they are. And if God cares so wonderfully for wildflowers that are here today and thrown into the fire tomorrow, he will certainly care for you. Why do you have so little faith? "So, don't worry about these things, saying, 'What will we eat? What will we drink? What will we wear?' These things dominate the thoughts of unbelievers, but your heavenly Father already knows all your needs. Seek the Kingdom of God above all else, and live righteously, and he will give you everything you need. "So don't worry about tomorrow, for tomorrow will bring its own worries. Today's trouble is enough for today" (Matt. 6:24-34).

What did you discover your "why" should be? We are not acting just purely for rewards but acting because we love the Rewarder. This is not a teaching of works without a relationship. The people came to Jesus for teaching first, and He fed their bellies. After this, they ran around to catch Him so their bellies would again be filled, and they went away hungry without Jesus or the food. We need to seek Him first, and the added things will follow. Trust Him. He knows what He's doing.

LESSON SUMMARY:

- "And it is impossible to please God without faith. Anyone who wants to come to him must believe that God exists and that he rewards those who sincerely seek him" (Heb. 11:6).

- "All that you do must be done in love" (1 Cor. 16:14 NASB).

- "For no one can lay any foundation other than the one we already have—Jesus Christ. Anyone who builds on that foundation may use a variety of materials—gold, silver, jewels, wood, hay, or straw. But on judgment day, fire will reveal what kind of work each builder has done. The fire will show if a person's work has any value. If the work survives, that builder will receive a reward. But if the work is burned up, the builder will suffer great loss. The builder will be saved, but like someone barely escaping through a wall of flames" (1 Cor. 3:12-15).
  *Note: Lesson Slides end at this point.

OBEDIENCE PRECEDES BLESSING:

So once again, it is time to put all these eternal truths into action! Take a few minutes to read and meditate on, "Lord, remind me how brief my time on earth will be. Remind me that my days are numbered-how fleeting my life is" (Ps. 39:4). "How do you know what your life will be like tomorrow? Your life is like the morning fog—it's here a little while, then it's gone" (James 4:14). "Sensible people keep their eyes glued on wisdom, but a fool's eyes wander to the ends of the earth" (Prov. 17:24). Now meditate on the following sentence: Value time for it is a gift, a mirror, a season, a tool, it is short, and yet redeemable.

It is time to be responsible. "So be careful how you live. Don't live like fools, but like those who are wise. Make the most of every opportunity in these evil days. Don't act thoughtlessly but understand what the Lord wants you to do" (Eph. 5:15-17). "That's the whole story. Here now is my final conclusion: Fear God and obey his commands, for this is everyone's duty. God will judge us for everything we do, including every secret thing, whether good or bad" (Eccl. 12:13-14). "Remember, it is sin to know what you ought to do and then not do it" (James 4:17). What is your takeaway from these three verses? Take responsibility for your actions, for we will be accountable for what we do (or don't do). Remember, it is the outworking of our faith that produces rewardable fruit.

It is time to be free. "I will walk in freedom, for I have devoted myself to your commandments" (Ps. 119:45). How does this verse say we can be free? Now read, "Therefore, since we are surrounded by such a huge crowd of witnesses to the life of faith, let us strip off every weight that slows us down, especially the sin that so easily trips us up. And let us run with endurance the race God has set before us. We do this by keeping our eyes on Jesus, the champion who initiates and perfects our faith. Because of the joy awaiting him, he endured the cross, disregarding its shame. Now he is seated in the place of honor beside God's throne" (Heb. 12:1-2). What "hinders" freedom? Not everything that hinders us is sin; many "okay" things will have no fruit or reward. Even as born-again believers, we can pursue and become entangled in pleasures the world offers to distract us from the greater things the Kingdom offers.

It is time to be free and to be eternally minded. Remember, every "yes" to one thing is a "no" to something else. Some of us regularly say "Yes" to something that may be "okay," but are saying "No" to something far better.

243

It is time to take action. Now read, "Therefore, go and make disciples of all the nations, baptizing them in the name of the Father and the Son and the Holy Spirit. Teach these new disciples to obey all the commands I have given you. And be sure of this: I am with you always, even to the end of the age" (Matt 28:19-20). What is the action, and what is the reward? Remember the parable of the talents; doing nothing productive for the kingdom is an option... but not a good one when so much more has been offered to us!

Now it is time to **Evaluate Yourself**. Stop and sincerely answer the following two questions. What will you experience when you see God? Will what you've built endure, or will you be saved as one escaping through the flames? Let's live with a "YES, Holy Spirit" in our hearts. There is a great adventure awaiting each of us if we will just say yes. Above all, seek his presence. Let the Holy Spirit be your guide. Listen to him in all things.

Be ready with a "Yes" to the next step he gives you. The life surrendered to His leading is better than any you could plan for yourself. Be content in the calling, gifts, and talents that he has given you. When you discover and follow his unique purpose for your life, you'll no longer want to be anyone else but "you." You were uniquely created for "such a time as this" and given a purpose for your time. No one else can be you.

*(See Appendix, Teaching Note 2)

MEMORY VERSE:
"If the work survives, that builder will receive a reward" (1 Cor 3:14).

GROW DEEPER:
"Then Christ will make his home in your hearts as you trust in him. Your roots will grow down into God's love and keep you strong" (Eph. 3:17). So how do you have "roots that will grow down into God's love and keep you strong?"

"But don't just listen to God's word. You must do what it says. Otherwise, you are only fooling yourselves. For if you listen to the word and don't obey, it is like glancing at your face in a mirror" (James 1:22-23). What is the Holy Spirit telling you through this verse? Write it down right now.

_____
_____
_____

I want to take you back to the ten lessons we have had over the past ten weeks and let's "practice" being doers of God's Word and not hearers ONLY!!! Write down ONE thing from each lesson that you already have or will now apply to your life to make you an effectual "doer" of God's Word.

1. _____
2. _____
3. _____
4. _____
5. _____

6. _____

7. _____

8. _____

9. _____

10. _____

IMPORTANT TRUTH TO REMEMBER:

"Then he said to me, "This is what the Lord says to Zerubbabel: It is not by force nor by strength, but by my Spirit, says the Lord of Heaven's Armies" (Zech. 4:6).

My closing prayer for you!

Now may the grace of the Lord Jesus Christ be with you now and always to remain steadfast, unmovable, always abounding in the knowledge and love of your LORD and savior, Jesus Christ.

Appendix

- Discipleship Policy: Page 247

- Encounter Overview, Spiritual Profile, and Godly Beliefs: Page 250

- Grow I Create Interest and Teaching Notes: Page 263
  - No answer key required.

- Grow II Create Interest and Teaching Notes: Page 267
  - No answer key required.

- Grow III Create Interest and Teaching Notes: Page 269
  - Answer key provided.

- Make-up Lesson Sheet: Page 282

Discipleship

**Prerequisite
Attendance
Expectations
Participation**

Grow I

Prerequisite: Register with a desire to attend class and be a student of the Word.

Attendance, Expectations, Absences, and Participation Policy:

Attendance
- There will be eight (8) classes following the Encounter Weekend.
- For any class missed, the student will turn in a "Make-up Lesson Worksheet."

Expectations
- Must have and maintain and bring to class weekly a Grow workbook.
- Weekly class attendance
- Reading and studying of the lesson before class. Teachers will be asking students this on a random basis.
- **We strongly encourage students to connect and join a weekly Small Group**
- Absences
- We consider excusable absences to be unplanned events such as a death in the family, a family crisis with flu and other illness, unplanned work commitments, and military service.
- Excusable absences still require that a "Make-up Lesson Worksheet" be turned in to the teacher.

Participation
- Must have a Grow workbook.
- Reading assignments must be completed.
- Weekly class attendance
- We strongly encourage students to actively participate in class discussion, asking questions, and offering your insight into a biblical discussion.
- We strongly encourage students to actively and regularly participate in a weekly Small Group

Successful completion of the Grow I:
- The student will be encouraged to serve and help in ministries under the leadership of a Grow graduate.
- Students can continue in the Grow track by enrolling in the follow-on Grow II and III classes.

Grow II & III

Prerequisite: To participate in the Grow Track II and III Discipleship classes the student should complete the Encounter Weekend and Grow I.

Training, Attendance & Absences, and Participation Policy:

Training
- Grow II – Ten (10) weeks.
- Grow III – Ten (10) weeks.
- Typically, these classes should be completed serially, Grow II, and then Grow III.
- Lessons will be presented weekly.
- A training break may be taken. For example, you complete Grow I and, for some reason, are not able to attend Grow II. If you have completed Grow I, you may enroll in the next Grow II class offered.

Attendance & Absences
- Classes will be held weekly.
- Attendance is expected.
- Study the lesson before the class is expected.
- Attendance is required to complete each section:
- Grow II: Attend 7 of 10 classes.
- Grow III: Attend 7 of 10 classes.
- For any class missed, the student is required to complete and turn in a "Make-up Lesson Worksheet."
- We consider excusable absences to be unplanned events such as a death in the family, a family crisis with flu and other illness, unplanned work commitments, and military service.
- Ministry team serving commitments are allowable. However, the 70% class attendance mark must still be met. A "Make-up Lesson Worksheet" will be turned into the teacher. It will be the student's responsibility to inform the teacher of the dates that you will be serving.

Participation
- Must have Grow workbook.
- Reading assignments must be completed.
- Weekly class attendance
- We strongly encourage students to actively participate in class discussion, asking questions, and offering your insight into a biblical discussion.
- We strongly encourage students to participate in a weekly Small Group actively and regularly.

Graduation - successful completion of the Grow Track Discipleship Track:
- Complete Grow I, Grow II, and Grow III.
- The graduate student will have an opportunity to lead ministries under the leadership of our Senior Pastor.

Encounter Overview

**Introduction
Schedule
FAQ's
Spiritual Profile
Godly Beliefs**

Dear Friends in Christ,

We are glad you've decided to participate in the Encounter.

You might be wondering, "What is an Encounter weekend?" An Encounter weekend experiences God and, in turn, completely changes the course of our lives. All of us have experienced significant milestones or encounters in our lives. To name a few, such as falling in love, getting married, being accepted into a university, or obtaining a job, but of all the encounters we could have, the most important is an encounter with the living God! Matthew 16:26 says, "What good will it be for a man if he gains the whole world, yet loses his soul?"

The Encounter Weekend presents a series of personal teachings coupled with life experiences that result in a visible, manifest change in the lives of all who participate. It offers individuals an environment and opportunity to discover how to establish their relationship with God, fellowship with Him, and commit to His Lordship. Participants experience forgiveness of sin, deliverance from bondage, emotional and physical healing, and restoration of worth and value. They also learn how to walk in the blessings of a covenant relationship with God and His Family.

Being a Christian means having a real-life relationship with God that touches every area of life. The Bible gives many examples of people who experienced that and were radically transformed by their encounters with the Lord Jesus. Remember the stories of the Samaritan woman (John 4:5-29), Zacchaeus (Luke 19:1-10), the Gadarene demoniac (Matthew 8:28-34), and all the Disciples of Christ. After these people encountered the Lord Jesus Christ, they were never the same again. Consequently, we can be assured that we will never be the same when we encounter Him.

We pray that every person who attends the Encounter will seize the opportunity to experience God. The results will be manifested in transformed lives — lives that are saved, forgiven of sin, set free, and healed by the power of the living God, Jesus Christ, the Lord!

Our primary purpose and goal at the Encounters are to see you SET FREE and for you to walk in the FREEDOM of Christ living in your life for the rest of your life. Come expecting God to do great things in your life. Tell God what your desires are, things you want to be changed, and things you've tried before to change but never lasted.

When we are obedient and willing to submit to God and His will for our lives, the changes that will take place in us will be visible and evident to all who know us. Those changes come because of our obedience and submission to God.

We look forward to ministering to each of you this weekend. We challenge you to come expecting freedom. Make a list of your expectations and allow God to set you FREE.

Encounter Weekend

Typical Schedule

Friday
5:30 pm Sign-in
6:00 pm Dinner
6:45 pm Welcome
7:00 pm Fill Out Profiles
7:20 pm Worship
7:30 pm Ungodly Beliefs
8:00 pm Ministry Time
8:30 pm Break
8:45 pm Sexual Purity
9:15 pm Ministry Time
10:00 pm Break
10:15 pm Small Group
10:45 pm Dismiss

Saturday
8:00 am Breakfast
8:50 am Worship
9:00 am Generational Sin
9:30 am Ministry Time
10:15 am Break
10:30 am Worship
10:45 am Inner Healing
11:15 am Ministry Time
12:30 pm Lunch
1:45 pm Worship
2:00 pm Cross
2:30 pm Ministry Time
3:00 pm Small Group
3:30 pm Break
3:45 pm Deliverance
4:15 pm Ministry Time
5:15 pm Burn Profiles
5:45 pm Celebration
6:00 pm Dinner
7:00 pm Worship
7:15 pm Baptism of Holy Spirit
8:00 pm Ministry Time

ENCOUNTER FAQ's

As you prepare for the Encounter, you may find the following list of items helpful. Keep in mind that the purpose of the Encounter is spiritual, so prepare accordingly.

1. Bible, pen, or pencil.
2. Make sure to wear and pack comfortable shoes and modest, casual clothing.
3. If you are staying overnight on the campus the following applies:
   a. Sleeping night attire please bring modest pajamas or sleeping clothes.
   b. Bedding: Requirement for all bedding – sheets (bunk beds/twin size), covering of some type and pillow. We do not provide this, so be sure to bring personal sheets, blanket(s), and pillow.
   c. Showers: There are ample showers, ample lavatories, and AMPLE hot water – bring your personal washcloths, drying towels, and all personal toiletry items.
   d. Sleeping area: There will be separate sleeping areas for men and women. One side of our facilities accommodate the women, and the other side accommodates the men.
   e. We do not provide personal sheets, blanket(s), and pillow, washcloths, drying towels, or personal care toiletry items.
   f. You may also want to bring earplugs if you are a light sleeper and a flashlight in case you have to get up in the middle of the night.
4. During all classes we ask that you use your cell phones respectfully. If you need to keep your cell phone with you, please <u>TURN IT TO VIBRATE or KEEP IT ON SILENT and KEEP IT PUT AWAY DURING ALL SESSIONS!</u>
   a. If you must call and check on your children, then you may do so during break times.
   b. We would prefer that you not make any calls to anyone during the Encounter <u>SESSIONS OR SMALL GROUP MEETINGS</u>.
   c. This is asked of you so that you won't be distracted or distract someone else, and your mind will stay focused on what God wants to do in you. This weekend is about you and God and what God desires to do in you, so let's keep the distractions as minimal as possible.
5. **Above all, bring a willing heart to be ministered to by the Lord Himself!**
   Jesus was punished that you might be forgiven. Jesus was wounded that you might be healed. Jesus was made sin with your sinfulness that you might become righteous with His righteousness. Jesus died your death that you might share His life. Jesus became poor, without poverty, that you might become rich with His riches. Jesus bore your shame that you might share His glory. Jesus endured your rejection that you might have His acceptance as a child of God. Jesus became a curse that you might receive a blessing. **2 Chronicles 20:17 (NIV) "You will not have to fight this battle. Take up your positions; stand firm and see the deliverance the Lord will give you, O Judah and Jerusalem. Do not be afraid; do not be discouraged. Go out to face them tomorrow, and the Lord will be with you."** We're praying each of you will **stand firm** with your decision that nothing will stop you from your Encounter with God this weekend.

Objectives for the Encounter

1. To enable each participant to know and accept Jesus Christ as his own personal Lord and Savior and to receive assurance of that fact.
2. To make known the claims of the gospel and for each participant to experience personal forgiveness of sins, deliverance, healing, and prosperity.
3. To motivate the participant to develop a personal relationship with the Father, the Son, and the Holy Spirit and to help him grow in the knowledge of God's Word.
4. To encourage each participant to give witness to the work of God in his life at home, work, school, and the community to win souls.
5. To clarify the vision of the church – **Win Souls, Make Disciples & Destroy the Works of the devil. We want to Connect, Train,** and **Send** – by motivating each person to continue in the Journey and to begin leadership training in the Grow Classes.

Guidelines

1. Punctuality to each teaching session and activity is imperative.
2. Each group should submit to the authority and/or group leader who is assigned to them.
3. Moving from the assigned room or group is prohibited.
4. Respect the rule of "silent night." **Refrain from excessive talking**.
5. **Ministering, counseling, prophesying, or sharing dreams, visions, or counseling between participants on the retreat is strictly prohibited.** The only individuals who are authorized to do so are the pastors and guides leading the retreat.
6. During the ministering of the Word of God, leaving the area of ministry is not allowed, except for a valid emergency and after first speaking to a group leader.
7. The use of iPods, Phones, or anything that will distract you or others from God during the Encounter Sessions is prohibited.
8. We will not be held responsible for any loss to personal property.
9. Special diets: If you require any type of special food, drink or diet, please be sure to bring items with you. Mark them using your name written or labeled on the items. Notify the kitchen leaders if the items need to be stored in the cooler.

Spiritual Profile

Everyone to some degree has **Ungodly Beliefs** about God, themselves, or others. Read the following statements and put an **X** by each one that you relate to or agree with. Before you begin ask the Holy Spirit to show you the Ungodly Beliefs that you have and then mark accordingly.

Ungodly Beliefs About <u>MYSELF</u>

I. Theme: Rejection, Not Belonging

___ 1. I don't belong. I will always be on the outside [left out].
___ 2. My feelings don't count. No one cares what I feel.
___ 3. No one will love me or care about me just for myself.
___ 4. I will always be lonely. The special man [woman] in my life will not be there for me.
___ 5. I will isolate myself so that I won't be vulnerable to hurt, rejection, etc., anymore.

II. Theme: Unworthiness, Guilt, Shame

___ 6. I am not worthy to receive anything from God.
___ 7. I am the problem. When something is wrong, it is my fault.
___ 8. I am a bad person. If you knew the real me, you would reject me.
___ 9. I must wear a mask so that people won't find out how horrible I am and reject me.
___ 10. I have messed up so badly that I have missed God's best for me.

III. Theme: Doing to achieve Self-Worth, Value, Recognition

___ 11. I will never get credit for what I do.
___ 12. My value is in what I do. I am valuable because I do good to others, because I am "successful."
___ 13. Even when I do/give my best, it is not good enough. I can never meet the standard.
___ 14. I will choose to be passive in order to avoid conflict that would risk others' disapproval.
___ 15. God doesn't care if I have a "secret life", as long as I appear to be good.

IV. Theme: Control (To avoid hurt)

___ 16. I have to plan every day of my life. I have to continually plan/strategize. I can't relax.
___ 17. The perfect life is one in which no conflict is allowed, and so there is peace.

V. Theme: Physical

___ 18. I am unattractive. God shortchanged me.
___ 19. I am doomed to have certain physical disabilities. They are just part of what I have inherited.
___ 20. It is impossible to lose weight (or gain weight). I am just stuck.
___ 21. I am not competent/complete as a man (woman).

VI. Theme: Personality Traits / Identity

___ 22. I will always be _____ (angry, shy, jealous, insecure, fearful, etc.).
___ 23. I should have been a boy (girl). Then my parents would have valued/loved me more… etc.
___ 24. Men (women) have it better.
___ 25. I will never be known or appreciated for my real self.
___ 26. I will never really change and be as God wants me to be.

VII. Theme: Miscellaneous

___ 27. I have wasted a lot of time and energy, some of my best years.
___ 28. Turmoil is normal for me.
___ 29. I will always have financial problems.

Ungodly Beliefs about <u>OTHERS</u>

VIII.   Theme: Safety/Protection
___ 30. I must be very guarded about what I say, since anything I say may be used against me.
___ 31. I have to guard and hide my emotions and feelings. I cannot give anyone the satisfaction of knowing they have wounded or hurt me. I'll not be vulnerable, humiliated, or shamed.

IX.   Theme: Retaliation
___ 32. The correct way to respond if someone offends me is to punish them by withdrawing or cutting them off.
___ 33. I will make sure that _____ hurts as much as I hurt!

X.   Theme: Victim
___ 34. Authority figures will humiliate me and violate me.
___ 35. Others will just use and abuse me.
___ 36. My value is based totally on others' judgment/perception about me.
___ 37. I am completely under their authority. I have no will or choice of my own.
___ 38. I will not be known, understood, loved, or appreciated for who I am by those close to me.
___ 39. I am out there all alone; if I get into trouble or need help, there is no one to rescue me.

XI.   Theme: Defective in Relationships
___ 40. I will never be able to fully give or receive love. I don't know what it is.
___ 41. If I let anyone get close to me, I may get my heart broken again. I can't let myself risk it.
___ 42. If I fail to please you, I won't receive your pleasure and acceptance of me. Therefore, I must strive even more (perfectionism). I must do whatever is necessary to try to please you.

XII.   Theme: God
___ 43. God loves other people more than He loves me.
___ 44. God only values me for what I do. My life is just a means to an end.
___ 45. No matter how much I try; I'll never be able to do enough nor do it well enough to please God.
___ 46. God is judging me when I relax. I have to stay busy about His work or He will abandon me.
___ 47. God has let me down before. He may do it again. I can't trust Him or feel secure with Him.

Seven Root Spirits - Spiritual Profile

This profile assessment is between you and the Lord; NO ONE will see this unless you show it to him/her. Keep this with you during the entire Encounter so you can add to it if needed. After the Saturday evening session, this paper will be burned, and hopefully the issues you struggle with will be gone as well.

Please mark **all** that applies as truthfully as you can. Put an **X** by each one that applies to **yourself** – if you are currently struggling and/or have struggled with it in the past and **CIRCLE** each one that applies to **your family (parents, grandparents, great grandparents)** – if they struggled with any of the areas and/or you have observed any of these characteristics, events, or involvement in your family past or present.

Definitions for each word that has an*are on the next page following this list.

1. Fear & Rejection

Abandonment	Fear of future	Fear of the dark	Phobias*
Anxiety	Fear of men/women	Fright*	Rejection
Faithlessness	Fear of not being good enough	Inadequacy*	Self-Hatred
Fear of being wrong	Fear of not being pretty enough	Inferiority*	Self-Rejection
Fear of death	Fear of not being smart enough	Insanity	Timidity*
Fear of exposure	Fear of poverty	Isolation	Torment*
Fear of failure	Fear of success	Nightmares	

2. Sexual Immorality (whoredom & perverseness)

Abortion	Exhibitionism*	Multi-Partner Orgies	Sado Masochism*
Abduction	Fornication*	Polygamy*	Seduction/Alluring
Adultery	Homosexuality	Pornography	Sexual Abuse
Bestiality*	Lust/Fantasizing	Profanity	Unfaithfulness
Child Molestation	Masturbation	Rape	Voyeurism*
Evil Thoughts			

3. Heaviness (stupor/slumber & deaf /dumb)

Abnormal Grief & Mourning	Diseases of Eyes/Ears	Loneliness	Sleep Disorders/Insomnia
Accident Prone	Epilepsy*	Nerve Disease	Smothered/Bent over*
Condemned	Fatalistic*	Oppression*	Speech Impediments/Mute
Convulsions	Feeling Crushed	Passivity/Yielding/Ahab Spirit	Stressful
Daydreaming	Fixation with Death	Procrastination	Suicidal/Suicidal Thoughts
Daze/Mental Numbness	Grinding Teeth	Sadness	Suppressed Emotions
Deafness	Hopelessness	Seizures	Unable to Enjoy Life, Rejoice/Worship
Depression	Hypertension	Self-Mutilation	Unjustified Guilt
Despair	Inability to Discern	Self-Pity	Wounded Spirit/Victim Mentality
Discouragement	Laziness	Shame	Oversleeping

4. Infirmity

Allergies	Fungus/Chronic Rashes	Mental Disorders	Venereal Disease
Arthritis	Heart Disease	Nerve Disorders	Weakness/Feebleness
Cancer	High Blood Pressure	Organ Failure	Other
Diabetes	Lingering Disorders	Sinus	

5. Lying (error, anti-Christ & divination)

Anorexia/Bulimia	Domineering Control "Jezebel"	Intellectualism	Persecutes Christian
Astral Projection*	Doubt/Unbelief	Irresponsibility	Poor Self Image
Astrology/Horoscopes	Easily Mislead	Legalism*	Rationalizes the Word
Blasphemes Holy Spirit/Gifts	Exaggeration	Lies	Rebellion/Independent
Channeling*	False Doctrines/ Compromise	Manipulation	Satanism/Séance*
Compromise Convictions	Fortune Tellers/Palm Reading	New Age Articles	Self-Sabotage
Condemns the Church	Free Masonry	Opposes Christ Deity & Victory	Tarot Cards
Confusion	Habitual Wrong Decisions	Demonic Games/Role Playing	TM/Western Religion
Crystal/8 Balls	Humanism*	Opposes the Bible	Twists Scriptures
Cults/False Teachers	Hypnosis	Ouija Board	Witchcraft
Deception	Immaturity	False Responsibilities	

6. Bondage (Escapes)

- ___ Alcohol
- ___ Co-dependency
- ___ Drugs (Street & Rx)
- ___ Entertainment
- ___ Excessive Sleep
- ___ Food
- ___ Gambling
- ___ Insomnia
- ___ Internet
- ___ Sex
- ___ Soul Ties*
- ___ Tobacco (all tobacco products)
- ___ TV/Music
- ___ Video Games
- ___ Work
- ___ Other

7. Pride

- ___ Abortion
- ___ Accusative
- ___ Anger/Rage
- ___ Argumentative
- ___ Arrogant
- ___ Attention Seeking
- ___ Boastful
- ___ Can't Honor Others
- ___ Comparison
- ___ Complaining
- ___ Contentious*
- ___ Controlling
- ___ Covetousness/Greedy
- ___ Critical
- ___ Critical of Others Success
- ___ Cruelty
- ___ Cynicism*
- ___ Defensive
- ___ Dictatorial*
- ___ Distrustful
- ___ Divorce/Division
- ___ Domineering
- ___ Egotistical*
- ___ Excuses/Justifying
- ___ Gossip
- ___ Hatred/Murder
- ___ Highly Opinionated
- ___ Independent
- ___ Insecurity
- ___ Insulting
- ___ Jealousy
- ___ Judgmental
- ___ Love of Money
- ___ Love of Social Standing
- ___ Love of the World
- ___ Lust for Power/Control
- ___ Lust for Praise/Position
- ___ Mockery*
- ___ Oppressive*
- ___ Overly Sensitive
- ___ Perfectionism
- ___ Prejudice/Racist
- ___ Rebellious
- ___ Revenge
- ___ Rudeness
- ___ Seditious*
- ___ Self-Centered
- ___ Self-Justifying
- ___ Self-Righteousness
- ___ Strife
- ___ Stubborn
- ___ Superiority
- ___ Suspicion
- ___ Uncomfortable
- ___ Unnatural Competition
- ___ Vanity
- ___ Worship above God
- ___ Wrath/Vengeful

* Definitions

1. <u>**Fear & Rejection**</u>

   Fright = Sudden intense fear, as of something immediately threatening; alarm.

   Inadequacy = not capable or equipped.

   Inferiority = Feeling less important, valuable, or worthy; acting or performing in a way that is comparatively poor or mediocre.

   Phobias = a persistent, irrational fear of a specific object, activity, or situation that leads to a compelling desire to avoid it.

   Timidity = showing fear and lack of confidence

   Torment = extreme mental distress; intense feelings of suffering; acute mental or physical pain; an agony of doubt.

2. <u>**Sexual Immorality (whoredom & perverseness)**</u>

   Bestiality = sexual relations between a person and an animal; sodomy

   Exhibitionism = a perversion marked by a tendency to indecent exposure.

   Fornication = Sexual intercourse between partners who are not married to each other.

   Polygamy = having more than one spouse at a time

   Sado Masochism = the deriving of pleasure, especially sexual gratification, from inflicting or submitting to physical or emotional abuse.

   Voyeurism = perversion in which a person receives sexual gratification from seeing the genitalia of others or witnessing others' sexual behavior

3. <u>**Heaviness (stupor/slumber & deaf /dumb)**</u>

   Epilepsy = mild, episodic loss of attention or sleepiness; or severe convulsions with loss of consciousness

   Fatalistic = all events are predetermined by fate; unalterable.

   Oppression = feeling of being heavily weighed down in mind or body.

   Smothered/Bent Over = to feel suppressed, or the inability to stand up for oneself or those that you love.

4. <u>**Infirmity (Physical or mental weakness)**</u>

5. <u>**Lying (error, anti-Christ & divination)**</u>

   Astral Projection = intentional act of having the spirit leave the body, whereas an out-of-body experience happens involuntarily.

   Channeling = the practice of professedly entering a meditative or trancelike state in order to convey messages from a spiritual guide.

   Humanism = any system or mode of thought or action in which human interests, values, and dignity predominate.

   Legalism = strict adherence or to the letter rather than the Spirit; [Theology – the doctrine that salvation is gained through good works.]

   Satanism/Séance = a meeting in which a spiritualist attempts to communicate with the spirits of the dead.

6. <u>**Bondage**</u>

   Soul Tie = an emotional, sexual or spiritual tie that connects you to an ungodly relationship. Ungodly Soul Ties are open doors into your life for the enemy; whatever enters the person you have a soul tie with will have access into your life as well.

7. <u>**Pride**</u>

   Contentious = tending to argument or strife; quarrelsome

   Cynicism = cynical disposition, character, or belief. [Cynical = bitterly or sneeringly distrustful, contemptuous, or essimistic.]

   Dictatorial = inclined to dictate or command, overbearing, arrogant, bossy, domineering

   Egotistical = given to talking about oneself, vain, boastful, opinionated, selfish

   Mockery = ridicule, contempt; something absurdly or offensively inadequate or unfitting

   Oppressive = burdensome, unjustly harsh, distressing or grievous.

   Seditious = rebellious, disobedient, disorderly, disloyal, defiance.

Godly Beliefs

1. I am a child of God's; therefore, I have a special place in His family. (1 John 5:1; John 1:12)
2. My feelings do count, and with God's help, I can be open in expressing my feelings and emotions and trust Him as my healer; He will give me discernment to know what to say, who to say it to and how to speak so that others can receive. (Psalm 119:169)
3. God loves and cares about me; He has sent special people into my life who love and care about me, and I trust that He will send others. (John 16:27)
4. Jesus has promised never to leave me nor forsake me, and His love is never failing. (Deuteronomy 31:6, 8; Psalm 145:13)
5. God is bringing me to a place of healing so that I can be open and involved with those He brings into my life. (Proverbs 24:26; Proverbs 28:23)
6. The blood that Jesus shed on the cross for me has made me worthy to receive every good gift from my Heavenly Father, including complete healing. (1 Corinthians 11:25)
7. God has gifted me and has given me grace so that I can be part of the solution; I am a problem solver. (1 Peter 4:10)
8. God is pleased with me, and my choice is to please Him and leave the acceptance of others in His hands; I am an overcomer. (Psalm 41:11)
9. God is healing me. I was a sinner saved by grace, fully accepted in the beloved. As others get to know me, they will discover that I am becoming more and more like the wonderful God I worship. (Acts 15:11)
10. God is an awesome redeemer. I choose to believe that despite my shortcomings, THE BEST IS YET TO COME. (Isaiah 44:21-22)
11. God is my rewarder; I trust Him to promote me and bless me. (Psalm 31:19; 2 Samuel 22:21)
12. My value and worth are fully found in the unconditional love and approval of my heavenly Father. (Proverbs 12:2)
13. My best is good enough for God; therefore, I choose to do my best and rest in the Lord, knowing that is all He asks of me. God will promote me and exalt me in due time. With the Holy Spirit as my teacher, I will fulfill my God-given responsibilities and callings and will grow in them. I am willing! (1 Peter 5:6; Luke 14:11; James 4:10)
14. God has given me a will and a choice of my own so that I can discern, know, and believe what is right. With His help, I can set appropriate boundaries and say "no" when I need to. (Deuteronomy 30:19)
15. I choose to be open and honest and walk in the light as God is in the light. Integrity is important to me. (1 John 1:7)
16. I choose to give God control of my life and trust Him. I can rest/relax in His ability to take care of me. (Philippians 4:19)
17. The righteous are bold as a lion; therefore, I can and will deal with life and people as the Lord leads. (Proverbs 28:1)
18. I have been created in God's image; I am fearfully and wonderfully made. As He heals me, I will choose to see myself as He sees me. (Genesis 1:27)
19. A man may be pre-occupied with the outer appearance, but God is interested in what goes on in my heart. I am fully and complete in Christ. (Colossians 2:10)
20. I choose to believe that I have been given everything I need for life and godliness. I will continually ask Jesus to give me strength to overcome all my issues. I can do all things through Christ who strengthens me. (2 Peter 1:3)

21. I am made in the image of God; therefore, I am fully complete and competent in and through Christ. (Colossians 2:9-10)

22. I choose to walk in the fruits of the spirit... Love, joy, peace, patience, goodness, kindness, gentleness, faithfulness, and self-control. (Galatians 5:22-23)

23. I am a child of the King, precious in His sight; I am fearfully and wonderfully made. (Psalm 139:14)

24. God created both men and women; we are all equal in Christ. (Genesis 1:27, Galatians 3:28)

25. I am free to be who God created me to be; as I value myself, others will value me also. (Romans 6:22)

26. I am an overcomer and free to walk in victory over all my circumstances. God is changing me from glory to glory by His Spirit so that I will walk in the fullness of my destiny. (1 John 4:4)

27. The Lord is in the process of healing me and taking me from glory to glory so that I can have a deeper personal relationship with Him. The best is yet to come. (2 Corinthians 3:18)

28. Jesus has given me life and life more abundantly, and that includes His peace. Peace is normal for me. (John 14:27 "Peace, I leave you; my peace I give you. I do not give to you as the world gives. Do not let your hearts be troubled and do not be afraid.")

29. I trust the Lord to help me walk in self-control and be a good steward of the money He provides me. He is my provider, and I trust him to release financial blessings upon my family and me. (Galatians 5:22-23, Philippians 4:19)

30. As I grow in God's wisdom, I choose to believe that what He has to say through me is important. I can speak the truth to others with an attitude of love and leave them and their response to God. (Ephesians 4:15)

31. God is bringing godly people into my life who are trustworthy and who will treat me with respect and honor for the child of God that I am. (1 John 5:1)

32. The correct way to respond if someone offends me is to forgive and keep the communication open. I choose to walk in forgiveness daily. (Colossians 3:13)

33. When someone hurts or offends me, I can lovingly confront them with an attitude of forgiveness, reconciliation, and unconditional love. I choose to keep my heart open and allow God to be my shield and defender. (Psalm 18:2)

34. Because God is healing me, I can submit to authority with discernment and choose to believe that they will have my best interests at heart. (Hebrews 13:17; 1 Peter 2:13)

35. God is my protection and strength. He promises never to leave me or forsake me. I choose to embrace and rest in His loving, protective arms. (Psalm 18:2)

36. My value is based on my existence, not my performance; therefore, I choose to please the Lord because He values me. (Galatians 4:7)

37. God has given me a will and a choice of my own so that I can discern, know, and believe what is right. With His help, I can set appropriate boundaries and say "no" when I need to. (Deuteronomy 30:19)

38. God cares for me and Father's me as His child. I choose to believe that He will bring friends into my life that will love and appreciate me for who I am because they share the Father's heart. (John 15:14)

39. I am never alone – Jesus is my rescuer. (Psalm 91)

40. God is love, and I embrace His unconditional love; I can give and receive love because His love lives in me and flows through me. (1 John 4:16)

41. God is bringing me to a place of healing so that I can be open and involved with those He brings into my life. (Hebrews 13:20-21)

42. I choose to release the responsibility of others to the Lord and trust Him to give me discernment

to know those things He wants me to do or be responsible for. (Romans 14:10)

43. God is no respecter of persons; we are all favorites to Him; He loves me just as much as He loves others. (Acts 10:34)

44. God uniquely and fully loves me. He paid the highest price for my redemption. My heavenly Father loves me with the same love that he has for Jesus. (John 3:16)

45. Because my heavenly Father loves me unconditionally, I can serve Him with excellence and rest in His unwavering affirmation. His strength is perfected in my weakness. (2 Corinthians 12:9)

46. God is true to His promises. As he is healing me and restoring my perspective about His nature, I can trust Him with all my heart and not lean upon my understanding. (Proverbs 3:5)

47. God will never disappoint me; He is my Heavenly Father who wants to give me the desires of my heart. The promises of God are "yes" and "amen" in my life. He is the same yesterday, today, and forevermore. He will never leave me, forsake me nor let me down. (Hebrews 13:5 & 8, Deuteronomy 31:6 & 8)

Grow I

- Create Interest
- Teaching Notes
- No Answer Key Required.
- All questions are subjective to the student.

GROW I
CREATE INTEREST

Lesson 1

Congratulations! By choosing to take this class, you have begun a Journey to Freedom that can last a lifetime. From this point on, you can choose to enter a new way of living and a new way of looking at things. You can choose to leave the past behind and move toward a future filled with hope and promise.

Lesson 2 We are three-part beings: Spirit, Soul, and Body.

"Now may the God of peace make you holy in every way and may your whole spirit and soul and body be kept blameless until our Lord Jesus Christ comes again" (1 Thess. 5:23).

"For the word of God is alive and powerful. It is sharper than the sharpest two-edged sword, cutting between soul and spirit, between joint and marrow. It exposes our innermost thoughts and desires" (Heb 4:12).

Lesson 3 Winning the Battle

So, Christ has truly SET US FREE. Now make sure that you STAY FREE, and do not get tied up again in slavery to the law. Read, Gal. 5:1.

At the Encounter, Christ set you free. He has done His part. Now, your part is to STAY FREE! How do you do that? Over the next few lessons, we will be looking at ways that will help us STAY FREE and to walk out what we learned and experienced at the Encounter.

Do you like to win? In football, there is a Defense and an Offense. The defense is very important as they are trying to keep the other team from scoring, but they want to get the Offense on the field so points can be scored, and the game can be won.

It is the same in your spiritual walk with the Lord. We can choose to only defend ourselves from the attacks of the devil, or we can choose to go on the offense and win this battle. In Eph. 6:10-18, we see the plan for winning this battle.

Read Eph. 6:10-18. Name the pieces of armor that God has given you.

Each piece of the armor is Defensive and is designed to protect you from the attacks of the devil, except for one, the Sword of the Spirit.

What is the Sword of the Spirit?

The Sword of the Spirit is the only offensive weapon. It is the Word of God, the Bible. How does the Bible become a weapon that enables you to win? Eph. 6:17-18 tells us to take the Word and PRAY! That, my Brother and Sister in Christ, is how you win! We will explain later in this lesson what it means to "Take the Word and Pray," but first, let us establish the importance of the Word of God in our lives.

Lesson 4

Have you ever watched a Hallmark movie? Here is how the theme of each movie goes: Boy meets Girl. Boy falls in love with Girl. He talks texts, instant messages, or emails her every chance he gets, and he professes his love to her; then, life happens, and Boy loses Girl. Eventually, because it is the Hallmark Movie, Boy gets Girl back, they get married and live happily ever after because it is not real life. IF, Boy never talked to Girl in the beginning or professed his love to her later on, the rest of the Hallmark scenario would never have happened.

In any good relationship, talking to that person and expressing your love is of top priority! Having a relationship with Jesus is somewhat similar. He has written you a love letter (the Bible) that tells you everything you need to know. He showed His love to you (by going to the Cross) when you did not even love Him, and now He wants to have a great relationship with you. He wants to hear you talk and talk to you. He wants to hear that you love Him and to show you how much He loves you. Prayer and worship are how you build a great relationship with the Living God!

Lesson 5

Have you ever been ignored? It is not a pleasant experience, and in fact, it is quite painful, so why would you ignore the God of the Universe? The Holy Spirit is God, and He is a Person, with a mind, will, and emotions. He is with you in every life situation, so why would you ignore Him? How many times have you wondered what God has ahead for you? Read 1 Cor. 2:9-10. Through the Holy Spirit, what do you have access to, and what does this mean personally for you?

Lesson 6

In today's world of technology, people have many gadgets and devices. All of them require their batteries to be charged. Power strips are sometimes used so that many devices can be charged at the same time. But what would happen if the devices were plugged into the power strip, but the strip was never connected to a power source? Nothing would charge, and therefore nothing could perform the task they were created to do. The same thing happens to Christians who are not connected to other believers. They lose power and are unable to carry out the tasks God has created them to do. Staying connected to others helps people fulfill God's purpose in their lives.

What are some ways you can stay connected to other Christian believers?

Lesson 7

Refer to the Journey to Freedom Encounter Retreat Personal Spiritual Profile, on the last page of this lesson. Note the category of pride and remember the traits from which you were set free. As time has gone by, has pride begun to creep back in? Take yourself back through the pride category and identify the struggles you may be currently facing. The Bible warns against pride. all say, "God opposes the proud but gives grace to the humble" (1 Peter 5:5; James 4:6; Prov. 3:34). The only way to avoid a fall is to stay humble. As you look at the characteristics of pride on the spiritual profile, make a list of the characteristics of humility. What do you notice about the differences between pride and humility?

Lesson 8

Once Upon a Time...

Let play make-believe for a moment. Let's pretend that you are a homeowner, and a thief is stalking your home so that he can come in and not only steal all your good stuff, but he is planning on living there, too. Not only that, but the thief has invited seven other thieves, bigger, greedier, meaner, and viler than he is. Someone warns you that tomorrow morning, when you leave for work, the thief is planning on breaking into your home, with all his thief friends to steal your stuff and begin living in your home and destroying everything you own, including your family. So, when morning comes, you head out to work and even leave your door unlocked. That is unheard of, but that is exactly what you are doing when you do not follow what the Word of God teaches you AND the enemy of your soul is much more dangerous than any thief here on earth! The frightening part is this is not make-believe, and this enemy is not pretending!

Grow II

- Create Interest
- Teaching Notes
- No Answer Key Required.
- All questions are subjective to the student.

GROW II
CREATE INTEREST

Lesson 1
What is your title? (i.e., engineer, nurse, wife, etc.?) This could lead to a discussion on "What do you think God calls you?"

Lesson 2
What are your priorities in life?

Lesson 3
What prayer are you praying right now? Can someone share a prayer that has been answered?

Lesson 4
If you could ask Jesus to change one thing in the world right now, what would you ask for?

Lesson 5
Tell us a scripture verse or quote that has changed your life.

Lesson 6
In a few words, how would you describe the meaning of intimacy?

Lesson 7
There is probably a little dysfunction in every family. But, if you could have a perfect family, what would that perfect family look like?

Lesson 8
Husbands, who would your wife say leads your family, you or your wife? Who would you say leads your family?

Wives, would your husband say you submit to his authority in the home? Or would he say he has to fight you over decisions? What do you say?

Lesson 9
God did not give us children to bring us sorrow, but to bring us joy and pleasure. How do children bring us joy?

Lesson 10
Have you ever admired a family from afar? What was it about that family that caught your eye or touched your heart?

Grow III

- Create Interest
- Teaching Notes
- No Answer Key Required.
- All questions are subjective to the student.

GROW III
CREATE INTEREST

Lesson 1
Read: Prov.8:35-36

Leadership Quote: "There are two ways to fail; listen to everyone and listen to no one!" - Orrin Woodward

Ice-breaker question: If you could change one thing about yourself, what would it be?

Teaching notes:
1. Read: "Country Preacher."
A country preacher decided to skip services one Sunday and head to the hills to do some bear hunting. As he rounded the corner on a perilous twist in the trail, he and a bear collided, sending him and his rifle tumbling down the mountainside. Before he knew it, his rifle went one way, and he went the other, landing on a rock and breaking both legs. That was the good news. The bad news was the ferocious bear was charging at him from a distance, and he couldn't move. "Oh, Lord," the preacher prayed, "I'm so sorry for skipping services today to come out here and hunt. Please forgive me and grant me just one wish: Please make a Christian out of that bear that's coming at me. Please, Lord!" That very instant the bear skidded to a halt, fell to its knees, clasped its paws together and began to pray aloud right at the preacher's feet: "Dear God, bless this food I am about to receive . . .

- How often do we feel we cannot meet the expectations of being Holy, keeping pure, and living a righteous life? Not possible so why try. We exchange a spirit of excellence with a spirit of mediocracy and/or complancey?

- I have great news for you, God has given you everything you need to live a life of Holiness, and in this lesson, we are going to find out how!

2. In the current economy, the amount would be approximately equal to our US $6,400,000. Holiness is a changed life at any cost. Are you willing to pay it?

3. Recommend song: "What Do I Know of Holy" by Addison Road

4. Recommend song: "Unfinished" by Mandisa

Lesson 2
Read Prov. 15:1

Leadership Quote: An anonymous, but wise author once said, "There is no traffic jam on the extra mile!"

Icebreaker: Give a 3 point personal salvation testimony: When, Where, Who.

Teaching notes:

1. Read the following: "Praise Choruses."

An old farmer went to the city one weekend and attended the big city church. He came home, and his wife asked him how it was.

"Well," said the farmer, "It was good. They did something different, however. They sang praise choruses instead of hymns."

"Praise choruses," said his wife, "What are those?"

"Oh, they're okay. They're sort of like hymns, only different," said the farmer.

"Well, what's the difference?" asked the wife.

The farmer said, "Well, it's like this. If I were to say to you, 'Martha, the cows are in the corn,' well, that would be a hymn."

"If on the other hand, I were to say to you, 'Martha, Martha, Martha, Oh Martha, MARTHA, MARTHA, the cows, the big cows, the brown cows, the black cows, the white cows, the black and white cows, the COWS, COWS, COWS, are in the corn, are in the corn, are in the corn, are in the corn."

Well, that would be a praise chorus.

This is a funny story that is making a very strong and sad point that there is a scheme of the enemy to divide the body of believers over worshipping through hymns versus praise and worship. There are leaders within the body of Christ that are holding seminars for a prominent denomination to teach that churches that do not worship through hymns are an occult. Though the varying denominations can minister to the whole diverse body of believers with the truth of the Gospel of Jesus Christ, which is a good thing, Jesus is not behind the denomination division of the body of Christ that has become the result. He prayed for the opposite! (*John 17:20-23*)

2. SERVANT LEADER/UPENDED PYRAMID:

Fill in Pyramid From Bottom, Up:
Run to a Greater Purpose, Upend Pyramid, Raise the Bar, Blaze the Trail, Build on Strengths

Run to a greater purpose:
Beyond self-interest, strive for the impossible, bigger than you can do on your own, vision of excellence.

Read as you are closing the lesson:
*   Worship is more than a service.
*   Worship is more than a song.
*   It's an expression, an action.
*   An offering, a lifestyle.
*   Worship is how we connect with the God of the universe.
*   How we draw closer to Him. He even draws closer to us.
*   Quite dating God and marry Him!

3. Recommended song: "Place of Freedom" Church of the Highlands

Lesson 3
Read: Prov.28:1

Leadership Quote: If you tell the truth, it becomes part of your past; but if you tell a lie, it becomes part of your future. (Rick Pitino)

Ice-breaker question: Share a time when you had to submit to authority and its impact on you.

Teaching notes:

1. Read: "Standing at the Gates of Heaven"
At the end of the age, when all the believers were standing in line waiting to get into heaven, the angel Gabriel appeared and said, "I want all the men to form two lines. One line will be for the men who were the true heads of their households. The other will be for the men who were dominated by their wives."
Gabriel continued, "And now we need all of the women to report to Mary and Martha on the other side of the gate." The women left while the men hurriedly formed two lines.

The line of men who were dominated by their wives was seemingly unending. The line of men who were the true head of their household had just one man standing in it.

Gabriel said to the first line, "You men ought to be ashamed of yourselves. You were appointed to be the heads of your households, and you have not fulfilled your purpose. Of all of you, there is only one man who obeyed."

Then Gabriel turned to the lone man and asked, "How did you come to be in this line?"

The man sheepishly replied, "My wife told me to stand here."

2. To explain the "Serving Leader Pyramid" start at the bottom of the pyramid and fill in the lines:
- Run to a greater purpose: Beyond self-interest, strive for the impossible, bigger why?
- To upend the pyramid: you qualify to be first by putting others first, you're in charge principally to charge others up.
- Raise the Bar: a challenge to have a spirit of excellence.
- Blaze the trail: you are to show the way, get your hands dirty.
- Build on strength: put people in places of their strengths to overcome weaknesses.

3. Teaching thought: "Serving Leader Pyramid" the leaders support and empowers his people / team
"The World's Method Pyramid" the people support and empower the leader.

4. Song: "Difference" by Micah Tyler

Lesson 4
Read Prov. 12:18

Leadership Quote: "It is better to remain silent and be thought a fool, than to open your mouth remove all doubt." Abraham Lincoln

Ice Breaker: Share a time when someone shared an encouraging word to you, and how did that make a difference in you?

Teaching notes:

1. Read "The Touch of the Master's Hand."

Twas battered and scarred, and the auctioneer thought it scarcely worth his while to waste much time on the old violin, but held it up with a smile; "What am I bidden, good folks," he cried, "Who'll start the bidding for me?"

"A dollar, a dollar,"; then two!" "Only two? Two dollars, and who'll make it three? Three dollars, once; three dollars twice; Going for three..."

But no, from the room, far back, a gray-haired man came forward and picked up the bow; Then, wiping the dust from the old violin, and tightening the loose strings, He played a melody, pure and sweet as a caroling angel sings.

The music ceased, and the auctioneer, with a voice that was quiet and low, said, "What am I bid for the old violin?"

And he held it up with the bow.

A thousand dollars, and who'll make it two? Two thousand! And who'll make it three? Three thousand, once, three thousand, twice, and going and gone," said he.

The people cheered, but some of them cried, "We do not quite understand what changed its worth." Swift came to the reply: "The touch of a master's hand."

And many a man with life out of tune, and battered and scarred with sin, Is auctioned cheap to the thoughtless crowd, much like the old violin. "He is going once, going twice, He's going and almost gone." But the Master comes, and the foolish crowd never can quite understand the worth of a soul and the change that's wrought By the touch of the Master's hand.

Just like this old violin, we all have a melody inside us that is pure and sweet, but too often, we speak death instead of speaking life. We do not allow that pure and sweet melody to transform our lives and the lives of everyone around us. This melody is the very breath our Master gave us our spoken word. Let's find out just how powerful this melody can be in either building us up or tearing us down.

2. Baseball Diamond: Smile, Listener, Encourage, Mentor

273

3. Song: "Speak Life" by Toby Mac

Lesson 5
Read Prov. 11:30

Leadership Quote: We are born to win but conditioned to lose. Zig Ziglar

Icebreaker: If you had to go on a mission trip, would it excite or scare you, and what continent would you go to, USA, South America, Asia, Europe, Africa, or Antarctica?

Teaching notes:

1. Read "The Army of The Lord."

The story is told of a man coming out of the church one day, and the preacher was standing at the door as he always did to shake hands. He grabbed the man by the hand and pulled him aside.

Then the pastor said to him, "You need to join the Army of the Lord!"
The man replied, "I'm already in the Army of the Lord, Pastor."

Pastor questioned him, "How come I don't see you except at Christmas and Easter?"
He whispered back, "I'm in the secret service."

How many Christians, like this gentleman, are showings up at church every Sunday, but when it comes to Monday through Saturday, they are in the "secret service."
- Maybe this is describing you?
- Maybe you do not want to be in the "secret service," but you do not know how?
- Maybe when it comes to sharing the gospel with others, it intimidates you, scares you, and makes you sick to your stomach because you become so nervous?
- Maybe you do not realize how important sharing the gospel is? Well, I have great news; we are going to show you how and why!

2. Religion: A life of performance
   Christianity: A life of relationships

3. Not feeling qualified – Read, "Does My Life, Matter."

Does My Life Matter?

I cannot make a significant difference in this world.
And I refuse to believe.
My actions can impact the lives of those around me.
I know without a doubt that.
God has not given me anything to offer.
It is foolish to think that.
What I do with my time and resources matters
"I possess something the world needs."

Is a lie.
"My life is of little consequence."

All of this is true, unless I allow God to reverse my thinking!

Teaching note for the above: Read first time top to bottom.
Read second time bottom to top, beginning with, "My life…"

4. Not aware of unsaved and hurting people.
Recommended song: "Does Anyone Hear Her" Casting Crowns

5. Recommended Song: "Until the Whole World Hears" by Casting Crown

Lesson 6
Read Prov. 8:10-11

Leadership Quote: A person is anxious to change their circumstances, but are unwilling to change themselves, so they stay bound.
Icebreaker Question: Share one thing you have come to understand about the Holy Spirit

Teaching notes:

1. Read the story: "The Drowning Preacher."

There was a preacher who fell in the ocean, and he couldn't swim. When a boat came by, the captain yelled, "Do you need help, sir?" The preacher calmly said, "No, sir, God will save me." A little later, another boat came by, and a fisherman asked, "Hey, do you need help?" The preacher replied again, "No, sir, God will save me." Eventually, the preacher drowned & went to heaven. The preacher asked God, "Why didn't you save me?" God replied, "Fool, I sent you two boats!"

How many Christians are going to get to Heaven and ask God, "Why didn't you give me the power to live a fulfilled life and share your gospel?" and God is going to reply, "I did, I gave you the Holy Spirit!"

2. Read: "Communication in Question." This is a story where there is a conversation between a woman and a judge in a pending divorce proceeding.

Judge asks the following questions:
Q#1- What are the grounds for divorce?
    A: about 4 acres with a house in the middle by a stream

Q#2- What is the foundation for this case?
    A: Made of concrete, brick, and mortar

Q#3- What are your relations like?
    A: I have an aunt and uncle that lives in town, and my husband's parent do as well.

Q#4 Do you have a real grudge?

  A: No, a 2-car carport, but we never really use it.

Q#5: Is there any infidelity in your home?

  A: Well, our 2 daughters each have stereos; we don't like their music, but to answer
  Your question, yes!

Q#6: MAM! Does your husband ever beat you up?

  A: Oh Yes, about two days a week.

Q#7: LADY! Why do you want a divorce?

  A: Sir, I don't! I have never wanted one. My husband does, he says he can't
  communicate with me.

3. Read: "Two Great Stories" – Truthbook.com/Stories/Inspirational/Military

4. Recommended song: "My Life Song" by Casting Crowns

Lesson 7
Read Prov. 29:25

Leadership Quote: You are not here merely to make a living. You are here to enable the world to live more amply, with greater vision, with a finer spirit of hope and achievement. You are here to enrich the world, and you impoverish yourself if you forget the errand. -Woodrow Wilson

Icebreaker story: "Courage that Ripples"

The story is told of Chris Brady, who was vacationing with his family in Italy, and he met the senate leader of Italy. During their conversation, Chris learned he was a Christian and upon further discussion discovered he became born again at a Guy Sortila crusade. Chris is a lover of history and decided to find out about the history of how Guy Sortila became born again. Thus, the story began back in 1854.

Edward Kimball 1854 Volunteered to teach a Sunday school class of 16-17 yr. old boys. He didn't feel he was making much of an impact, so he decided to visit the boys throughout the week. One 17 yr. old boy worked at a store, and while this young boy was stocking shelves, Edward shared Jesus and that boy became born again. His name was…

Dwight L. Moody became a preacher in England and became a great evangelist sharing the Gospel with 100 million people. He founded the Moody Bible Institute and the Moody Church in Chicago. During one of his preaching, he shares his story of his S.S. Teacher. A man listening becomes so convicted and says, "I am going to be an evangelist!" His name was…

Frederick Brotherton Meyer became, a Baptist pastor, evangelist, wrote 70 books and had an inner-city ministry both in England and America. While in American preaching, a young man listening becomes a Christian. His name was…

J. Wilber Chapman becomes a pastor and evangelist and holds huge crusades. A young boy volunteers at one of his crusades becomes born again. His name was…

Billy Sundae was born into poverty, spent some years in an orphanage, and played eight years in the major league and was known for his running speed. He takes over Chapman's ministry, known as the most dynamic evangelist of that century, leading thousands to Christ. 1924 a group of inspired men at a Billy Sunday Crusade, keep it going every year. 1932, they invite evangelist…

Mordecai Ham- is known for keeping everyone spellbound while preaching. During one of his four-day crusades, a young, tall, lanky, 16 yrs. old sat and listened to this white hair man preach about Jesus. Finally, on the 4th day, he went forward and became born again. His name was…

Billy Graham-we all know Billy Graham as the greatest evangelist leading more people to Jesus than anyone else. During one of his crusades, a young man from Italy was on scholarship and he gave his life to Christ. His name was…

Guy Sortila-Guy marries an American woman who moves back to Italy and becomes known at the "Billy Graham of Italy." He leads the senate leader of Italy to the Lord.

It all started with a Sunday school teacher named Edward Kimball. Millions have been affected by his decision to go into a shoe store and share Christ with one 17yr boy while stocking shelves. Millions more will continue to feel his impact.

Teaching notes:

1. Read "Tag Changer"
During the Civil War, a nurse was working her night shift. The procedure for the night nurses at this makeshift hospital was to make the men as comfortable as possible. Before the hospital doctor would leave for the day, he would color code tag each patient. Three basic colors signified their condition and care. One meant "no hope," one meant "expedient care," and one meant "Not emergency." There was one rule that was stressed emphatically, and that was that the night nurses under any circumstances could NOT change the tags of the soldiers.

During Helen's shift, as she was going from one patient to the next performing her tasks, she notices that this one soldier who was tagged "no hope" was conscious, which was rare. They started talking and found out his name was John and was from her hometown. His condition was critical, and even with care, he probably wouldn't live. They continued to talk throughout the night. Then Helen did the unthinkable; she changed John's tag from "no hope" to "expedient care." That next morning, John received "expedient care," and though he lost his leg, he did live and left the hospital.
Jesus has called all His people to be "tag changers"!
Will you answer His call?

2. Recommended song: "Live Like That," by Sidewalk Prophet

Lesson 8
Read the story: "Father and Son."

Every Sunday afternoon, after the morning service at church, the pastor and his eleven-year-old son would go out into their town and hand out gospel tracts. This Sunday afternoon, as it came time for the pastor and his son to go to the streets with their tracts, it was very cold outside as well as pouring down rain. The boy bundled up in his warmest and driest clothes and said, "ok dad, I am ready!" The pastor asked, "ready for what?" Dad, it's time we gather our tracts together and go out." Pastor responded, son, it's very cold outside, and it's pouring down rain." The boy gives his dad a surprised look, asking, "but dad, aren't people still going to hell even though it's raining?" Dad answers, "Son, I am not going out in this weather." Despondently, the boy asks, "Dad, can I still go? Please?" His father hesitated for a moment then said, "Son, you can go. Here are the tracts. Be careful, son!" "Thanks, dad!" With that, he was off and out into the rain. This eleven-year-old boy walked the streets of the town going door to door and handing everybody he met in the street a gospel tract. After two hours of walking in the rain, he was soaking wet, chilled to the bone, and down to his very last tract. He stopped on a corner and looked for someone to hand a tract to, but the streets were deserted. He then turned toward the first home he saw and started up the sidewalk to the front door and rang the bell, but nobody answered! He rang it again, and still, no one answered. Finally, this eleven-year-old trooper turned to leave, but something stopped him. Again, he turned to the door and rang the bell and knocked loudly on the door with his fist. He waited, something holding him there on the front porch. Then the door slowly opened, and standing there in the doorway was a very sad-looking elderly lady. She softly asked, "what can I do for you, son?" With radiant eyes and a smile that lit up her world, this little boy said, "mam I am sorry if I disturbed you, but I just wanted to tell you that Jesus really does love you, and I came by to give you my very last tract which will tell you all about Jesus and his great love!" With that, he handed her his last tract and turned to leave. She called to him as he departed, "thank you, son, and God bless you!" Well, the following Sunday morning in church, the pastor asked at the beginning of the service if anyone had a testimony or wanted to say anything? Slowly in the back row of the church an elderly lady stood to her feet. As she began to speak, a glorious radiance came from her face, "no one in this church knows me. I've never been here before. You see, before last Sunday, I was not a Christian. My husband passed on some time ago, leaving me alone in this world. Last Sunday, being a particularly cold and rainy day, it was even more so in my heart that I came to the end of the line where I no longer had any hope or will to live. So, I took a rope and a chair and ascended the stairway into the attic of my home. I fastened the rope securely to a rafter in the roof, then stood on the chair and fastened the other end of the rope around my neck. Standing there on the chair, so lonely and broken-hearted, I was about to leap off when suddenly the loud ringing of my doorbell downstairs startled me. I thought I'll wait a minute, and whoever it is will go away. I waited and waited, but the ringing doorbell seemed to get louder and more insistent, and then the person ringing also started knocking loudly. I thought to myself again, who on earth could this be? Nobody ever rings my bell or comes to see me. I loosened the rope from my neck and started for the front door, all the while, the doorbell rang louder and louder. When I opened the door and looked, I could hardly believe my eyes for there on my front porch was the most radiant and angelic little boy I had ever seen in my life. His smile, oh, I could never describe it to you! The words that came from his mouth caused my heart that had long been dead to leap to life as he exclaimed with the sweetest voice, "mam, I just came by to tell you that Jesus really does love you!" Then he gave me this gospel tract that I now hold in my hand. As the little angel disappeared back into the cold and rain, I closed my door and read slowly every word of this gospel tract. Then I went up to my attic to get my rope and chair. I wouldn't be needing them anymore. You see, I am now a happy child of the king. Since the address of your church was on the back of this gospel tract, I have come here to personally say thank you to God's little angel who came just in the nick of time and by so doing, spared my soul from an eternity in hell. There was not a dry eye in the church, and as shouts of praise and honor to the king resounded off the very rafters of the building, the pastor descended from the pulpit to the front pew where the little angel was seated. He took his son in his arms and sobbed uncontrollably! Probably no church has had a more glorious moment, and probably this universe has never seen a Papa that was more filled with love and honor for his son, well… except for one! Our father also sent his son into a cold and dark world. He received his son back with joy unspeakable, and as all heaven shouted praises and honor to the King, the Father sat His beloved Son on a throne far above all principalities and powers and every name that is named!

Teaching note:

Recommended song: "God Is on The Move" by 7th Time Down

Lesson 9
Proverb: Prov. 24:14

Leadership Quote: Average leaders raise the bar on themselves; good leaders raise the bar for others; great leaders inspire others to raise their own bar. Orrin Woodward

Icebreaker: What would you change if Jesus came to you and said that the way you spend the next 24 hours will determine how you will spend all eternity?
Teaching notes:

1. Recommended song: "Different" by Micah Tyler

2. Recommended song: "Soul on Fire" by Third Day

Lesson 10
Read: Prov.11:18

Leadership Quote: The greatest leader is not necessarily the one who does the greatest things. He is the one that gets the people to do the greatest things. Ronald Reagan

Icebreaker: How would you react at the end of the year to hear that only those employees that met certain requirements received full bonuses and you weren't one of them?
Note: When you asked why you didn't, you were told that when you were hired, you received a manual and were told to read it.

Teaching notes:

1. Recommended video: "Called" by John Bevere on YouTube

2. Recommended song: "Write Your Story" by Francesca Battistelli

Additional teaching resources:
1. "Experinceing God Through Prayer" by Keith Hodges avaible via Amazon
2. Door knocker designed by your church to be left on a door.
3. Church info flyer – designed by your church.
4. Holiness – a seven-day devotional on holiness (a devotion of your choice)
5. Prayer Circles - The Circle Maker: Praying Circles Around Your Biggest Dreams and Greatest Fears by Mark Batterson
6. F.A.I.T.H. The Ticket to Heaven by Gary Ledbetter (YouTube)
7. "Circles of Commitment" by Rick Warren
8. Write "My Story": Use the following format on a blank sheet of paper:

9. I, the undersigned, give my life and future to you God, Creator, Father. I forever name you Lord and give you the right to add anything you desire to this covenant. Students can sign the bottom and keep as a reminder of their covenant.

GROW III
Answer Key
<u>Lesson 1</u>
N/A
<u>Lesson 2</u>
<u>Page 182</u>
Substitution
Pride
Hedonism
Spectator
Tradition
Sin
<u>Page 182</u>
Play music
satan would depart
<u>Page 185</u>
Worship
Thank
Offer
Include
Worship
Love
Lesson 3
<u>Page 198</u>
Yield before walk
Possess before give
<u>Page 199</u>
Know God
Find freedom
Discover your
purpose
Make a difference
<u>Page 200</u>
1. Souls of men
2. Sickness
3. Demonic
oppression
4. Evil spirits
5. devil

6. Your own
thoughts
7. Your actions
Lesson 4
<u>Page 203</u>
1. Death
2. Judgment
3. True to God
4. Have hope
5. God's Word
<u>Page 205/206</u>
Negativity
Prepare
Eternity
Guard
Build
Hope
Throne
Faith
Good
Bad
Lesson 5
<u>Page 210</u>
Broadcast
Relational
Conversational
Communion
Confidence
Commitment
<u>Page 211/212</u>
Testimony
Word
Authenticity
Pray
<u>Page 212/213</u>
Loves
Wants
Involved
Go
Send

Have
Lesson 6
<u>Page 217</u>
Personal relationship
with Jesus
Depenedency on the
Holy Spirit
<u>Page 218</u>
Hopeless
Acvtivated
Act
Draw
Lift
<u>3 Hindrance</u>
Darkness
Unbelief
Approval
God
<u>Page 219/220</u>
Receive
Filled
Empowered
Sent
Discern
Open
Expecting
<u>Page 22</u>
Prayer
Devotion
Action
Lesson 10
<u>Page 236</u>
Reject and be judged
Receive and be
saved
<u>Page238</u>
Gospel of Christ is
the foundation.
Word of God will
never pass away.

Grow Class <u>I</u>   <u>II</u>   <u>III</u>
Please circle class #

Make-up Lesson Worksheet
(Return written make-up lesson the Sunday after the week missed or as the teacher has directed)

Lesson Title _____

Student Name _____

Read the entire lesson and associated bible verses and write a summary statement defining your understanding of the lesson.

Write a short narrative, using a bible verse that spoke to you, related to how you will apply this lesson to your life.

List any questions that you want to ask.

Grow Class I   II   III
Please circle class #

Make-up Lesson Worksheet
(Return written make-up lesson the Sunday after the week missed or as the teacher has directed)

Lesson Title _____

Student Name _____

Read the entire lesson and associated bible verses and write a summary statement defining your understanding of the lesson.

Write a short narrative, using a bible verse that spoke to you, related to how you will apply this lesson to your life.

List any questions that you want to ask.

Grow Class <u>I</u>   <u>II</u>   <u>III</u>
Please circle class #

Make-up Lesson Worksheet
(Return written make-up lesson the Sunday after the week missed or as the teacher has directed)

Lesson Title _____

Student Name _____

Read the entire lesson and associated bible verses and write a summary statement defining your understanding of the lesson.

Write a short narrative, using a bible verse that spoke to you, related to how you will apply this lesson to your life.

List any questions that you want to ask.

Grow Class <u>I</u>   <u>II</u>   <u>III</u>
Please circle class #

Make-up Lesson Worksheet
(Return written make-up lesson the Sunday after the week missed or as the teacher has directed)

Lesson Title _____

Student Name _____

Read the entire lesson and associated bible verses and write a summary statement defining your understanding of the lesson.

Write a short narrative, using a bible verse that spoke to you, related to how you will apply this lesson to your life.

List any questions that you want to ask.

Made in the USA
Middletown, DE
24 August 2024

59198986R00159